DISCOURSES ON

AṢṬĀVAKRA GĪTĀ

DISCOURSES ON

AṢṬĀVAKRA GĪTĀ

Original Upaniṣad Text in Devanāgrī
with Transliteration in Roman letters,
Word-for-Word meaning in Text order with Translation

and

c o m m e n t a r y

by

Swāmī Chinmayānanda

CENTRAL CHINMAYA MISSION TRUST

Printed up to	June	2001	14,000	copies
Reprint	Feb. 2003 to Dec.	2010	8,000	copies
Reprint	July	2012	1,000	copies
Reprint	April	2013	2,000	copies

Published by :
CENTRAL CHINMAYA MISSION TRUST
Sandeepany Sadhanalaya,
Saki Vihar Road,
Mumbai 400 072, India
Tel. : (91-22) 2857 2367 / 2857 5806
Fax : (91-22) 2857 3065
E-mail : ccmtpublications@chinmayamission.com
Website : www.chinmayamission.com

Distribution Centre in USA :
CHINMAYA MISSION WEST
Publications Division,
560 Bridgetown Pike,
Langhorne, PA 19053, USA.
Phone : (215) 396-0390 • Fax : (215) 396-9710
Email : publications@chinmayamission.org
Website : www.chinmayapublications.org

Printed by :
PRIYA GRAPHICS
Unit No. J - 120, Ansa Industrial Estate,
Saki Vihar Road, Sakinaka, (Andheri)
Mumbai - 400 072. (India)
Tel. No. 6695 9935 / 4005 9936
Email: chinmayapriya@hotmail.com

Price : Rs : 165.00

ISBN: 978-81-7597-062-5

About *Aṣṭāvakra Gītā*

In communicating to the seekers the unsurpassing beauty and indefinable perfections of the Absolute, the *Upaniṣad*-s stammer; the *Brahma-sūtrā-s* exhaust itself, and the *Bhagavad-Gītā* hesitates with an excusable shyness. A theme, in dealing with which, even these mighty books of *Hindūism* are thus, at best, unsatisfactory; we must, in sheer gratitude, admire *Aṣṭāvakra Saṁhitā* for the brilliant success it has achieved in communicating, through words, perhaps, more clearly the nature and glory of the Supreme Reality, than by the *Prasthāna Traya.*

The student of this *Saṁhitā* is himself giving the autobio-data of the liberated-in-life. We have here in this book a revealing autobiography of the Saint, the Liberated-in-life in King *Janaka.*

Beyond all assertions and denial, beyond the concepts of bondage and liberation, lies this Realm of the Self, wherein there is neither the individual-ego (*jīva*), nor is there even the Supreme-Reality (*Brahman*)!

Svāmī Chinmayānanda

Contents

Preface to the Revised Edition

Aṣṭāvakra Gītā also known as *Aṣṭāvakra Saṁhitā* is a short treatise on *Advaita Vedānta* in the *Upaniṣadik* style i.e. in the form of a dialogue between *Aṣṭāvakra*, the *guru* and his disciple, the king-seer *Janaka*. This fascinating legend is vividly described in Chapters 132 to 134 in the *Vana Parva* portion of the epic, *Mahābhārata* where *Maharṣi Lomaśa* narrates it to *Dharmaputra Yudhiṣṭhira*—the eldest of *Pāṇḍava* princes.

In General Introduction and later in the commentary, it is repeatedly emphasised that *Aṣṭāvakra Gītā* is meant only for those advanced *sādhakā*-s who have purified their minds through *sādhanā* and are engaged in meditation. To such committed students alone would this book show light and be a true guide. To the unprepared, unmature students, the subtle thoughts contained in this *Gītā* can be explosively dangerous and result in erasing their faith entirely from the higher Reality.

Aṣṭāvakra in *Saṁskṛta* means—*aṣṭa* i.e. eight and *vakra* is crooked or curbed—with eight crooked (limbs). How he was cursed by his father while still in his mother's womb has already been explained in the General Introduction. As a result of the curse, he developed eight deformities like hunch-backed, hump, knock-knees, bow-legs, flat-footed etc., and was, therefore, named *Aṣṭāvakra*.

How *Aṣṭāvakra* reached the court of the king of *Videha—Rājā Janaka* in search of his father has been explained in the Introduction. There is a slightly different version, believed by traditionals about the chance meeting of *Aṣṭāvakra*—the young sage with King *Janaka* in search of his father.

Janaka was a benevolent king and to have first hand knowledge of his subjects, was on his rounds when he saw the young sage limping steadily. After alighting from his horse, he prostrated before the teenager sage, who was hardly twelve then. The deformities of the young ascetic became more vivid when he moved, and viewed from close the king felt aversion to the curvatures of his anotomy. The young sage who was expert in *Yoga-vidyā* as well as established in Self-knowledge (*Ātma-jñāna*) read the king's mind and addressed him as follows:—

> "O King, just as the shape of a temple does not affect the *ākāśa* (sky), the crookedness of the physical body has no effect on *Ātmā* (Soul). A wise man has *Ātma-dṛṣṭi* i.e. he looks at the Reality behind this manifested world, whereas an ignorant one has *Carma-dṛṣṭi* i.e. he gets lost in names and forms."

The king was taken aback by such an incise wisdom of the young sage and requested him to grace his palace to which he acceded. *Aṣṭāvakra* was, thus, given a place of honour in king's palace; he removed all doubts from *Janaka*'s mind. By defeating *Bandī*, the royal scholar, he got his father released from his captivity.

In *Mahābhārata,* there is a slightly different version. *Aṣṭāvakra* accompanied by his maternal uncle (of his own age) *Śvetaketu* reached *Janaka*'s kingdom to observe *Mahāyajña* being conducted there, as also to search his father. The king was proceeding to *Yajñaśālā* and attendants accompaning him were diverting traffic to clear passage for the king.

By his precise knowledge of *Śāstrā*-s, *Aṣṭāvakra* pointed out that a *brāhmaṇa* had priority in the right of passsage over even the king. On hearing, the king was impressed with the knowledge of the young medicant, and acceded the point and requested him to proceed ahead of him.

Although the *Mahāyajña* was open only to established scholars, the king took him along to the *Mahāyajña*. On learning about his motive of defeating *Bandī*—the royal scholar, the king tested his knowledge of the *Śāstrā*-s by questioning. With appropriate and precise answers he impressed the king who invited *Bandī* to engage the young sage in arguments. *Aṣṭāvakra* defeated *Bandī* and thus got his father released.

In the earlier edition, readability was poor in small print. This aspect is taken care of in the revised layout, the credit for which is due to Shri Vishwamitra Puri who diligently scrutinised the entire book very minutely to identify misprints, missing words and lines; added diacritical marks; and pursued steadfastly the suggested changes/ improvements with the *Ācārya* of *Sāndīpany Mumbai* for approval.

Keeping in view the high standing of this book in *Vedāntik* thought, to help readers not knowing *Saṁskṛta*, transliteration has been added even to references which have been lifted from foot-notes to the body of the text.

In this revised edition, diacritical marks are used for Transliteration of *Saṁskṛta* words in the verses as well as commentary. Non-English words have been italicised. In the 'free translation' section where the entire text is italicised, to distinguish *Saṁskṛta* words 'normal' fonts are used.

Another important feature of this edition is the addition of transliteration in 'word-for-word meaning' section for the benefit of readers not knowing *Devanāgarī*. This will help readers to identify and pronounce the words correctly.

The English plural sign 's' has been added to untranslated *Saṁskṛta* words after a hyphen (-) to show that it is not elemental to the words e.g., *mantrā-s, Vedā-s Ṛṣī-s* etc. Macrons are used on the last letter e.g., '*ā, ī*' of such words to lengthen the quantity of sound in consonance with the prolonged sound in pronunciation.

To facilitate easy location of a particular verse and/or Chapter distinctive markings are given on the top of each page in the header. On even pages after Page No. appears Name of the book in centre, followed by Chapter No. in Roman letters succeeded by Verse No. after a hyphen (-). Similarly on odd pages, Chapter No. in Roman letter is followed by Verse No. after a hyphen (-); then the name of Chapter in centre, followed by Page No. at the extreme right.

To be true to the *Saṁskṛta* text in transliteration, we have used "*brāhmaṇa*" for the first *Varṇa* instead of the commonly used word "*brahmin.*" It need not be confused with the term "*Brahman*" of the *Vedāntin*-s.

A key to the transliteration and pronunciation has been added in the beginning, while Alphabetical Index at the end of the book.

Śrī Rāma Navamī: the 16th April, 1997. **Publishers**

TRANSLITERATION AND PRONUNCIATION GUIDE					
ॐ	oṁ	home	ॐ	oṁ	Rome
अ	a	fun	ट	ṭa	touch
आ	ā	car	ठ	ṭha	ant-hill
इ	i	pin	ड	ḍa	duck
ई	ī	feet	ढ	ḍha	godhood
उ	u	put	ण	ṇa	thunder
ऊ	ū	pool	त	ta	(close to) think
ऋ	ṛ	rig	थ	tha	(close to)pathetic
ॠ	ṝ	(long ṛ)	द	da	(close to) father
लृ	ḷ	(long ṛ)	ध	dha	(close to)breathe hard
ए	e	play	न	na	numb
ऐ	ai	high	प	pa	purse
ओ	o	over	फ	pha	sapphire
औ	au	cow	ब	ba	but
अं	aṁ	**	भ	bha	abhor
अः	aḥ	***	म	ma	mother
क	ka	kind	य	ya	young
ख	kha	blockhead	र	ra	run
ग	ga	gate	ल	la	luck
घ	gha	log-hut	व	va	virtue
ङ	ṅa	sing	श	śa	shove
च	ca	chunk	ष	ṣa	bushel
छ	cha	match	स	sa	sir
ज	ja	jug	ह	ha	house
झ	jha	hedgehog	ळ	(Note 1)	(close to) world
ञ	ña	bunch	क्ष	kṣa	worksheet
त्र	tra	three	ज्ञ	jña	*
ऽ	'	unpronounced अ (a)	ऽऽ	"	unpronounced आ (ā)

Note 1 : "I" itself is sometime used. * No English Equivalent

** Nasalisation of the preceding vowel. *** Aspiration of preceding vowel

General Introduction

Among the world's classical works on contemplative experience *Aṣṭāvakra Gītā,* which is sometimes called as *Aṣṭāvakra Saṁhitā,* is a unique text-book. It systematically deals with the mystical experiences of an individual in his flight to the transcendental peace and bliss. It has been said that the thoughts of this *Gītā* are compatible with the "Dialogues of Plato" and the *Bhagavad-Gītā,* as all of them truthfully record the universal insight and spiritual experiences which a seeker gathers during moments of his intense meditation.

As in *Bhagvad-Gītā,* here in *Aṣṭāvakra Gītā* also, we find the subtle philosophical truths expounded in the form of a lucid dialogue between the king-seer (*Rāja-Ṛṣi*) *Janaka,* the disciple, and *Aṣṭāvakra,* the teacher.

In *Mahābhārata** the legend of *Aṣṭāvakra* is fascinating and vivid. When *Aṣṭāvakra* was in the womb of *Sujātā,* his mother, his father, *Kahor,* a mighty student of the *Vedā-s,* used to read aloud the sacred *Maṇḍalā-s,* each day late into the nights. The unborn genius, even from the womb, suddenly cried out : "Tut, Tut! Father, through your grace I have already learned all the *Vedā-s,* even while I am in my mother's womb. But I am sorry to say that you often make mistakes in your recitation." Enraged by this grave insult the father cursed his son, and the boy was therefore born deformed with eight curvetures in his anatomy.

The learned *Kahor,* pressed by his poverty, made a pilgrimage to king *Janaka*'s courts to beg for some royal

* Vana Parva, 132-134.

patronage. There, he got defeated in an intellectual dual with *Śrī Vandin*, the court-philosopher of *Janaka*. The victorious *Paṇḍita Vandin*, employed the defeated *brāhmaṇa* in the service of his father, *Varuṇa*. Years rolled by, and the family had no news of the whereabouts of the reverend *brāhmaṇa Kahor*.

Though a splendid student, *Aṣṭāvakra* in the school was teased by his fellow-students saying "you have no father." The worried boy returned home, and enquired of his mother. The boy came to know from his mother that his father had once gone to *Janaka*'s palace and had not ever returned from there. *Aṣṭāvakra*, at that time, was only a mere boy of 12 years. He decided to make enquires and started on his pilgrimage to *Videha*.

He was stopped at the gate of the palace; but he, however, got finally his admission into the court, where he proved that though physically a boy, he had the wisdom of the ancients. There, in the court, the handicapped boy defeated the revered philosopher, *Vandin*, and won the freedom of his father. The father let his son bathe in the river *Samangā*; and blessed by the father the deformed child walked out of the waters cured completely—a handsome boy of brilliant charms.

Aṣṭāvakra Gītā, both in its style and structure of composition closely resembles the epics. It belongs to an age prior to the systemization of philosophical thoughts in India. Like the *Bhagavad Gītā* it has a simplicity of diction and clarity of expression, 'without losing the forcefulness of language and the pregnancy of its thoughts. Like the *Bhagavad Gītā* here also we find that the teacher refuses to indulge in any involved philosophical discussion, but the teacher constantly directs the entire attention of the student, on to the Spiritual Reality behind life and its expressions.'

Erudite scholars after laborious study and research have assigned *Aṣṭāvakra Gītā* to a period immediately after the *Bhagavad Gītā*, and just before the rise of the great philosophical schools. *Aṣṭāvakra Gītā* must have appeared at a time close to the latter *Upaniṣad*-s : *Śvetāśvatara*,

Muṇḍaka, Māṇḍūkya Kārikā and others. There is a suspicion of a reference to the *Budhistik* concept of Non-Existence (*Śūnya-vāda*).

Aṣṭāvakra Gītā does not show any inclination to accept a personal God, as we find in the *Bhagavad Gītā*. In this sense, thoughts of *Aṣṭāvakra* are more faithful to the major *Upaniṣad*-s and their monistic idealism. To all advanced students of meditation *Aṣṭāvakra Gītā* directly points out the way and the goal. Those who have not had the early groundings in meditation and have not experienced the inner silence of meditation, to them this *Gītā* is a mute instrument. To the unprepared, the subtle thoughts of this *Gītā* can become explosively dangerous. These can blast the student's faith and can even shake his entire hold of the Higher Reality. To those who have purified their minds and are engaged really in meditation, to such committed students alone, this text-book can show light and can serve as a true guide.

As an unrelenting Non-dualist, rooted in the vivid experience of the transcendental spiritual Oneness, Saint *Aṣṭāvakra* never compromises. He rejects completely the worlds of objects, emotions and thoughts perceived through the delusory body, mind and intellect. As such he refutes and totally rejects the principle of '*Māyā*.' To him there is neither an individual ego (*Jīva*), nor a Creator (*Īśvara*), nor any delusion (*Māyā*), nor a universe (*Jagat*) other than the One-Infinite-Consciousness, the Self. This clearly gives us an idea of the platform of *Aṣṭāvakra*, and the types of students whom he is addressing. To *Aṣṭāvakra* there is only one goal to be aspired for and reached, and that is Self-knowledge through direct mystical intuition : he calls it *Vijñāna*.

The final spiritual experience in *Aṣṭāvakra Gītā* arises to profound ruptures of vision and insight, and culminates in the sovereign unity of the Self that dissolves all duality, such as the knower, knowledge and knowing. In fact, the deeper essence of this *Aṣṭāvakra*-Song cannot be explained in words, but is to be experienced in the dynamic silence of one's own deepest meditations. It is addressed to all the royal-saints of the calibre of *Janaka*, to whom is attributed the oft-quoted observation in *Mahābhārata* (*Śānti Parva*, VII-1).:

अनन्तमिव मे वित्तं यस्य मे नास्ति किंचन ।
मिथिलायां प्रदीप्तायां न मे किंचन दह्यते ॥

Anantam-iva me vittaṁ yasya me nāsti kiñcan,
mithilāyāṁ pradīptāyāṁ na me kiñcan dahyate.

"Infinite is indeed my wealth, of which nothing is mine. If *Mithilā* is burnt, nothing that is mine is burnt."

In *Aṣṭāvakra Gītā* also *Janaka* declares :

मे नास्ति किंचन अथवा मे सर्वं ।
Me nāsti kiñcan athavā me sarvaṁ.

"In fact, one way, nothing belongs to me; or in another way, everything is mine only."

Chapter—I

Self—Witness in All

Introduction

In this opening stanza of the *Aṣṭāvakra Gītā*, the brilliant disciple, the royal-seer, *Janaka*, expresses his problems and the teacher, totally established as he is in the experience of the Transcendental Truth, answers questions raised by the student. The Pure Effulgent Self is ever the Unattached, and the Peaceful, the all-knowing Seer and the Witness of everything that is happening in all creatures. It is the One Supreme and Eternal God, the *Brahman* or the Ultimate Reality. The perceived world of forms and names outside, and the experienced worlds of emotions and thougths within, all exist in and sport only the All-pervading Immutable Self.

This One Universal Consciousness Supreme, which is the substratum for the changing world of phenomena should be realised through practice of meditation till we rise above the misconception that we are the limited-ego—the Self, reflected-in-our-thoughts.

When I, the Supreme Self, become conscious of and get utterly identified with my body, mind and intellect, I become the limited ego: the perceiver-feeler-thinker-entity. This ego through its own illusions misconceives the Infinite Self as the sorrow-ridden calamitous world of birth and death. This individualized ego gets itself completely bound to the wheel of happenings, and appears to get crushed by the world that it has imagined itself through its own delusions. When true knowledge dawns, the misconceptions end and the little ego in the meditator rediscovers itself to be the Infinite *Brahman*.

जनक उवाच ।

कथं ज्ञानमवाप्नोति कथं मुक्तिर्भविष्यति ।
वैराग्यं च कथं प्राप्तमेतद् ब्रूहि मम प्रभो ॥ १ ॥

Janaka Uvāca :

Kathaṁ jñānam-avāpnoti kathaṁ muktir bhaviṣyati,
vairāgyaṁ ca kathaṁ prāptam-etad brūhi mama prabho.

कथम् *katham* = how (man); ज्ञानम् *jñānam* = knowledge; अवाप्नोति *avāpnoti* = acquires; कथम् *katham* = how; मुक्तिः *muktiḥ* = liberation; भविष्यति *bhaviṣyati* = comes; वैराग्यम् *vairāgyam* = renunciation; च *ca* = and; कथम् *katham* = how; प्राप्तम् *prāptam* = is achieved; एतत् *etat* = this; ब्रूहि *brūhi* = teach; मम *mama* = me; प्रभो *prabho* = O Lord.

Janaka Said :

1. *Teach me this, O Lord, how can knowledge be acquired? How can liberation come? How is renunciation achieved?*

When a patient approaches a doctor, it is the duty of the suffering one to explain, as best as he can, of his difficulties, and the doctor will them diagnose and prescribe remedies to cure the disease. If the patient goes to the doctor and remains mum, the doctor will not be able to immediately detect what exactly is the trouble in the patient. Similarly, when a student reaches a spiritual Master, it is the duty of the seeker to express his difficulties and from the doubts so expressed by the student, the teacher can evaluate the psychological and spiritual problems in the student. Here we find the *Aṣṭāvakra Gītā* opens with the questions raised by *Janaka*, the disciple. The royal-seer asks three pertinent questions.

The ignorance of the *post*, in the dim-light of the dusk, can produce the illusion of a *ghost*. This illusory *mis-apprehension* of the *ghost*, sprung from the *non-apprehension* of the *post*, frightens the deluded observer and brings to him all his sorrows. From the 'ignorance' of the *post* is born the *ghost.* This 'ignorance' is constituted of both these factors : the *non-apprehension* of Reality, and the *mis-apprehension* of the Self. This 'ignorance' can be removed only by 'knowledge': with the apprehension of the *post,* the *non-apprehension* ends— and when the *non-apprehension* of the *post* had ended, the *mis-apprehensions* of the *ghost* cannot remain. This 'knowledge' alone is the antidote for 'ignorance.'

The 'ignorance' of the spiritual-Essence, as the blissful immutable Self, gives us the 'mis-apprehensions' of a world-of-plurality around us, and of a suffering miserable perceiver, the ego. These 'misapprehensions' of a *subject-object*-world can be ended only when the 'non-apprehension' of the Self is ended. To apprehend the Self is to have the 'knowledge' of it. Hence, the student very aptly asks the question : "How can 'knowledge' be acquired."

A seeker, so long as he is recognising a world of objects, emotions and thoughts, through his body, mind and intellect, he cannot escape his sense of limitations and his experiences of suffocating sorrows. The world of joys and sorrows will buffet him mercilessly amidst the roaring waves of the world's tumultuous happenings. A sensitive student cannot but feel himself bound and gagged everywhere, at all times. Naturally, *Janaka* asks here in his second questions : "How can liberation come?" To liberate ourselves from our identification with our own body, mind and intellect equipments is to liberate ourselves from the thraldom of our ego and make us realise our Infinite Stature Divine.

In order to attain this sense of complete liberation, we must learn to detach from our own equipments of perceptions, feelings and thoughts. Naturally, the subtle thinker in the disciple asks the third question: "How is renunciation achieved?" Each one will have to discover in himself the capacity to renounce. Renunciation is not a mere giving up of possession, or a sudden cutting away from all relationships of the world.

Without mental detachment outer renunciation amounts to only an unproductive calamitous escapism. To "run-away" from life and its duties is not to run into the spiritual dimensions.

Sense of attachment springs in us when the ego feels incomplete, and when, in its illusion, it hopes to become full and complete by the acquisition, possession and enjoyment of objects which it perceives outside itself. Thus, where plurality is experienced, there is a *subject*-ego perceiving world of *objects*. In this sense of duality the perceiving-*subject* cannot avoid labelling and classifying things perceived, and developing a sense of likes and dislikes for them. The ego, thereafter, gets itself attached to the things it likes, and comes to feel extremely disturbed and therefore, impatient with the things that it dislikes.

As long as individual lives in this sense of duality, he cannot avoid his sense of attachment. The ego is that aspect of our personality that perceives the plurality; and the ego arises in our identifications with our body, mind and intellect. Therefore, true renunciation or detachment is in withdrawing ourselves from our equipments. How are we to withdraw our consciousness from our equipments through meditation and come to experience the infinitude of the Self as our own Real Nature is the deep significance of this small looking question: "How is renunciation achieved?" Attachment gurgles forth from 'ignorance,' and renunciation or unattachment flows out from 'Knowledge.'

When the student has expressed himself exhaustively, the teacher elaborately answers each one of the questions raised by *Janaka*. And that constitutes this entire chapter.

अष्टावक्र उवाच ।

मुक्तिमिच्छसि चेत्तात् विषयान् विषवत्त्यज ।
क्षमार्जवदयातोषसत्यं पीयूषवद्भज ॥ २ ॥

Aṣṭāvakra Uvāca

Muktim-icchasi cet-tāt viṣayān viṣavat-tyaja,
kṣamā-ārjava-dayā-toṣa-satyam pīyūṣa-vad-bhaja.

मुक्तिम् *muktim* = liberation; इच्छसि *icchasi* = wish (you); चेत् *cet* = if; तात् *tāt* = O child; विषयान् *viṣayān* = the objects of the senses; विषवत् *viṣavat* = like poison; त्यज *tyaja* = reject; क्षमा *kṣamā* = forgiveness, आर्जव *ārjava* = straight-forwardness; दया *dayā* = kindness, तोष *toṣa* = cheerfulness; सत्यम् *satyam* = truth; पीयूषवत् *pīyūṣa-vat* = like nectar; भज *bhaja* = seek.

Aṣṭāvakra replied :

2. *If you aspire for liberation, my child, reject the objects of the senses as poison, and seek forgiveness, straight-forwardness, kindness, cheerfulness and truth as nectar.*

In this pithy statement, the teacher of the Transcendental Reality, *Aṣṭāvakra*, provides us with two unfailing schemes by which our spiritual pilgrimage can always be smooth, and ever assured of success. Negatively we are shown what all we must give up and positively we are told what are the values of life that we must cultivate.

Mind is "thought-flow." The more the flood of the thoughts gushes through us, the more uncontrolable becomes the mind. So all factors that contribute to the quietening of the mind are to be cultivated, and all sources from which mind gets disturbed are to be rejected and eliminated.

The teacher advises that we must reject the objects of the senses as poison. The sense-objects attract the sense-organs and bring stormy agitations into the mind. It is an incontrovertible fact that around us, sense-objects are constantly present. There is no space in the universe that we can escape into where the sense-objects are not present. Hence the beauty of the simile implied here. There are many poisonous weeds, and various kinds of poisons all around us in life—we cannot run away from them; but we have the liberty to reject them with our better understanding and to handle them, whenever necessary, with all careful precautions. Similarly, the sense-objects are to be considered as dangerous poison to the mental tranquillity, and accordingly handle them with great caution.

This process of rejecting the sense-objects and not allowing them to enter us and disturb our mind is technically called in *Vedānta* as *Dama*—sense-control. This by itself is not sufficient, Mind, even from a solitary-cave in the *Himālayā-s*, can, by its own imagination, get agitated, all by itself! Mind is to be constantly guarded and carefully protected from its own inherent sensuality, by inculcating into it the healthier values of life and thus re-educating the wayward mind.

These noble disciplines within are enumerated as the healthy values of life here: "forgiveness, straight-forwardness, kindness, cheerfulness and truth." These are to be regularly lived and enjoyed as 'nectar.'

A little thought can convince us how these values can bring calm and serenity in any boisterous mind. The sense of angry revengefulness can bring endless disturbances into us, but the moment we forgive those who have done harm to us, mental calm prevails, so too, crookedness in our relationship with others can bring unending tensions to the mind; therefore, *straight-forwardness* is recommended here as a healthier value of life. So, too, *kindness*, and a sense of *cheerfulness* can always bring the mind to poise and grandeur. *Truthfulness* meaning intellectual honesty, is an un-avoidable requisite in every spiritual seeker. To think one way and to feel differently, and ultimately to act belying one's own convictions, is to live a dishonest life which brings disintegration of ones inner personality.

Spiritual development and higher meditation are possible only for a totally integrated inner personality. These five values of life are the essential nurture and nourishment for the inner spiritual seeker on his hazardous path to the peaks of his realisation of the Infinite Self.

This, however, is the only occasion, when *Aṣṭāvakra*, throughout his song, talks of moral values. From a transcendental standpoint, this Master is pointing out to the student a State of Perfection, experienced beyond the mind. All values of life and moral injunctions regulate the mental reactions and physical relationships in the world-of-plurality. When the mind is transcended, these values, valid in the relative plains, can have no more any meaning in the realm of the universal Oneness. It is the Master's Infinite kindness that he condescends to climb down, from his unapproachable heights of realization, to the relative fields, where his disciple now stands, eagerly questioning the goal and the way.

न पृथ्वी न जलं नाग्निर्न वायुर्द्यौर्न वा भवान् ।
एषां साक्षिणमात्मानं चिद्रूपं विद्धि मुक्तये ॥ ३ ॥

Na pṛthvī na jalaṁ nāgnirna vāyur-dyaurna vā bhavān
eṣāṁ sākṣiṇam-ātmānaṁ cid-rūpaṁ viddhi muktaye.

न *na* = not; पृथ्वी *pṛthvī* = earth; न *na* = not; जलम् *jalam* = water; न *na* = not; अग्निः *agniḥ* = fire; न *na* = not; वायुः *vāyuḥ* = air; द्यौः *dyauḥ* = space; न *na* = not; वा *vā* = or; भवान् *bhavān* = you; एषाम् *eṣām* = of these; साक्षिणम् *sākṣiṇam* = witness; आत्मानम् *ātmānam* = Self; चिद्रूपम् *cidrūpam* = embodiment of Pure Consciousness; विद्धि *viddhi* = know; मुक्तये *muktaye* = for the sake of freedom.

3. *You are neither earth, nor water, nor fire, nor air, nor space. In order to attain freedom know the Self as the 'witness' of all these—the embodiment of Pure Consciousness itself.*

The five great-elements are the "material-cause" with which the gross physical structure is constructed : The *subtle* aspects of these five great-elements constitute the mind-intellect equipment in man, considered in *Vedānta* as the *subtle*-body. The Gross-body is the vehicle through which the Subtle-body functions in expressing itself and discovering its whimsical gratifications. The residual *Vāsanā-s* in each one of us swell up to express and exhaust themselves. A *vāsanā* sprouts first as a desire-disturbance in the intellect, which in the mental-zone produces thought-disturbances, and they, in their turn, precipitate, at the body level, as the exhausting activities of the individual in society. The gross and the subtle equipments precisely needed by an individual, for the expression of his existing *vāsanā-s*, are fabricated by nature out of these five great-elements. Here the teacher declares the ultimate truth that at the exhaustion of the *Vāsanā-s*, the subtle and gross bodies have no more any function, and the individualised-ego-sense awakes itself to rediscover its nature as the Pure-Infinite-Consciousness, the Self.

Aṣṭāvakra thus points to the student what is to be negated in the first line of the verse : "You are not the five elements." A mere negation by itself can take us only into an empty dark pit of 'Non-Existence' (*śūnya*). And yet, the negation process is unavoidable as the individual-ego in the seeker had lived through millenniums, and had repeated the misconceptions that he was the body and the mind. To complete the process, a positive assertion of our spiritual nature, as the Self, is necessary. This is being accomplished with the second line of this verse.

The teacher advises the student that in order to liberate himself from the delusory sorrows of the body and the mind, he should come to experience the Self within. The principle of Consciousness in everyone of us is the illumining factor that brings into our awareness all our physical and mental experiences. We are constantly conscious of our experiences without and within us. In the light of Consciousness all happenings are brought into our knowledge, or our awareness.

Just as in the light of the sun, the objects of the room become illuminated for us, so in the light of Consciousness our experiences become vivid to us. Just as the sun-light does not ever get involved in, or conditioned by, the objects that it illumines, the Consciousness in us also is ever apart from and unattached to the illusory dance of the objects, outside and to the delusory sport of the rollicking thought-disturbances inside.

This relationless-relationship of the light of Consciousness with the world of objects and thoughts is particularly emphasised here to help the students of meditation. When the teacher says that we must 'realize' the Self as the 'witness' of all the play of the elements, it provides a technique of meditation for the sincere seekers. Objectless-Consciousness is the nature of the Self; when objects are not there for the Consciousness to illumine, it cannot be even indicated by the term "Consciousness." The Ultimate Reality is indeed ever beyond the powers of finite words to express!

At this moment, identifying with the five-elements and their fabrications, we suffer in a world of delusions and imperfections. Through meditation when we withdraw our identifications with our gross and subtle-bodies, in the inward stillness, the existing *vāsanā*-s get all burnt up, uplifting the meditator into the plain of the Pure Consciousness itself.

A 'witness' is one who stands on the foot-path, uninvolved in the happenings on the road—say an accident. The Consciousness is a 'witness' in all the life's experiences, in every individual-living-creature. In our ignorance we become so totally involved with the happenings, and get wholly committed to the joys and sorrows of our body and mind. The moment a seeker rediscovers the realm of the Self in him, he understands that, as the Self, he is ever as far removed from the pluralistic world-of-change-and-sorrow as the sun-light is from the daily drama of the world. The illuminator is always different from the illumined : "I am the Self, the Illuminator, and not the illumined."

To stand as a 'witness,' detached from all that is happening within and without us, is one of the most effective early exercises in meditation. This verse reminds us of the songful declaration in the *Kaivalyopaniṣad* (23-24) :

न भूमिरापो न च वह्निरस्ति न चानिलो मेऽस्ति न चाम्बरं च ।
एवं विदित्वा परमात्मरूपं गुहाशयं निष्कलमद्वितीयम् ॥ २३ ॥

Na bhūmir-āpo na ca vahnir-asti
na cānilo me'sti na cāmbaraṁ ca,
evaṁ viditvā parmātma-rūpaṁ
guhāśayaṁ niṣkalam-advitīyam

समस्तसाक्षिं सदसद्विहीनं
प्रयाति शुद्धं परमात्मरूपम् ॥ २४ ॥

Samasta-sākṣiṁ sad-asad-vihīnaṁ,
prayāti śuddhaṁ paramātma-rūpam.

"To me there is neither earth, nor water, nor fire, nor air, nor ether. Thus realising the nature of the *Parmātman*—the One who is in the cavity-of-the-heart, who is without-parts, without-a-second, the 'witness'-of-all, beyond both existence and non-existence—the seeker attains the very nature of the Supreme *Ātman*."

यदि देहं पृथक्कृत्य चिति विश्राम्य तिष्ठसि ।
अधुनैव सुखी शान्तः बन्धमुक्तो भविष्यसि ॥ ४ ॥

Yadi dehaṁ pṛthak-kṛtya citi viśrāmya tiṣṭhasi,
adhunaiva sukhī śāntaḥ bandha-mukto bhaviṣyasi.

यदि *yadi* = if; देहम् *deham* = body; पृथक्-कृत्य *pṛthak-kṛtya* = separating (detaching); चिति *citi* = in consciousness; विश्राम्य *viśrāmya* = resting; तिष्ठसि *tiṣṭhasi* = remains (you); अधुना *adhunā* = now itself; एव *eva* = even; सुखी *sukhī* = happy; शान्तः *śāntaḥ* = peaceful; बन्ध-मुक्तः *bandha-muktaḥ* = free from bondage; भविष्यसि *bhaviṣyasi* = will be (you).

4. *If you detach yourself from the body and abide in Consciousness, you will at once become happy, peaceful and free from bondage.*

Here the student is assured of the final result of utter fulfilment, if he pursues and accomplishes the path of negation and assertion prescribed in the previous stanza. Merely withdrawing the body-consciousness is not sufficient. In deep-sleep, none of us have consciousness of our body; yet we have no spiritual experience therein. Meditation is an attempt to consciously withdraw our identification with the body, and "abide ourselves in Consciousness."

In *Vedānta* there are two schools : one believes that freedom from bondages is possible only after death, when the body falls off. They believe in *Videha-Mukti*. The other school, headed by *Aṣṭāvakra, Śaṅkara* and others, declares that the realisation of the Self is possible even while the saint lives in his body and functions apparently as any other mortal. This is called *jīvan-mukti*—liberation right now and here, even while living in this body. This *jīvan-mukti*-state is being indicated in this verse. The essential import of this stanza goes through a verse in *Yoga-Vāsiṣṭha* :

यदि सर्वं परित्यज्य तिष्ठस्युत्क्रान्तवासनः ।
अमुनैव निमेषेण तन्मुक्तोऽसि न संशयः ॥

Yadi sarvaṁ parityajya tiṣṭhasy-utkrānta-vāsanaḥ,
amunaiva nimeṣeṇa tan-mukto'si na saṁśayaḥ.

"In case renouncing all, without *vāsanā-s*, you can stay, then right now, this very moment, you are liberated—no doubt about it."

In fact, *Aṣṭāvakra Gītā* has laid the foundations and indicated the path for *Māṇḍūkya-Kārikā, Yoga-Vāsiṣṭha* and such other brilliant books, that expound the Infinite Oneness and the "theory of Non-creation" of the universe (*Ajāt-vāda*).

There is no harm if we possess things of the world, but it would be a tragedy if the things of the world possess us. For example, if we possess wealth, we are free to be rich, but when the wealth possesses us, we become a slave to our own wealth! It is indeed perfectly natural that we eat food, but should never allow the food to eat us!!

If the above is crystal clear to us, let us apply the same logic to our spiritual life. There is no harm if we possess, handle, drive and function through our equipments of body, mind and intellect. These will be the expressions of the freedom of the wise. But in our ignorance we allow the equipments-of-experiences to entrap us, and then we are employed to serve them as their slaves—lo we are caught up thus to become the miserable "ego" in each one of us!!

The *Vedānta Sādhanā* consists in the ego in each seeker, revolting against its own thraldom. To assert the clear understanding that one is not one's own body, mind and intellect, and to come to experience the nature of the Pure Self, is the entire programme to be accomplished through *Vedānta* Meditation. This entire scheme is very precisely indicated in this verse.

न त्वं विप्रादिको वर्णो नाश्रमी नाक्षगोचरः ।
असङ्गोऽसि निराकारो विश्वसाक्षी सुखी भव ॥ ५ ॥

Na tvaṁ viprādiko varṇo nāśramī nākṣa gocaraḥ,
asaṅgo- 'si nirākāro viśva-sākṣī sukhī bhava.

न *na* = not; त्वम् *tvam* = you; विप्रादिकः *viprādikaḥ* = *brāhmaṇa* or any other; वर्णः *varṇaḥ* = caste; न *na* = not; आश्रमी *āśramī* = belonging to any station-in-life; न *na* = not; अक्षगोचरः *akṣa-gocaraḥ* = perceivable through the senses; असङ्गः *asaṅgaḥ* = unattached (non-dual); असि *asi* = are (you); निराकारः *nirākāraḥ* = formless; विश्वसाक्षी *viśva-sākṣī* = witness of all; सुखी *sukhī* = happy; भव *bhava* = be.

5. *You do not belong to the* brāhmaṇa *or any such other caste. Nor do you belong to any station-in-life* (Āśrama). *You are not perceivable by the senses. Unattached, formless and 'witness'-of-all you are, be happy.*

In *Hindūism,* human personalities are divided into four categories called "castes." These divisions are essentially based upon the inherent qualities of the predominent *vāsanā-s* in each individual. Since the Pure Self is beyond the *vāsanā-s,* it is not conditioned by any of these categories. Similarly in *Hindūism,* men living in the society are considered as belonging to and functioning in different stations-in-life. These are called *Āśramā-s*; student-life (*Brahmacarya*), house-holders' life (*Gṛhasta*), life-of-retirement (*vāna-prasta*) and life-of-renunciation (*Saṁnyāsa*). It is vividly clear that these *Āśramā-s* are classifications of the different attitudes of the growing mind, and depend upon mind's different relationships with the world around it. In the Infinite Self, which is One-whithout-a-second, there cannot be any attitudes and relationships and, therefore, the obligations of the different stations-in-life cannot bind the Self.

Neither caste and its duties, nor the different status of social life and their obligations can ever be predicated of the Self. These are extremely helpful in the early stages of self-discipline for spiritual growth, as long as a seeker is still identifying with his mind and body. As Pure Consciousness you are not even perceivable by either the sense-organs or conceivable by the mind or the intellecct.[1]

Thus Pure Consciousness, as the illuminator, is completely detached from the entire world-of-objects, as the sun-light is unattached with the world of things and beings, which it daily illumines. Self is without any form (*Nirākāra*), as It is unconditioned by any thing other than itself; the Consciousness in us is "the 'witness' of the universe" (*Viśva-sākṣī*). The idea that the Self is a 'witness' is repeated some four times in this very chapter. The concept of *Sarva-Sākṣī* and *Viśva-sākṣī* is found in the *Śvetāśvatara Upaniṣad* (VI-11) also, where the Lord is described as the All-Encompassing-Witness indicating that the Self is a disinterested onlooker upon all the pranks of the mind and the intellect. The idiom used here reminds us of the *Kaivalya Upaniṣad* (M-18) declaration :

त्रिषु धामसु यद्भोग्यं भोक्ता भोगश्च यद्भवेत् ।
तेभ्यो विलक्षणः साक्षी चिन्मात्रोऽहं सदाशिवः ॥

1. In short the Self is not an *object*, but it is ever the Existence-Knowledge (*Sat-Cit*). In *Saṁskṛta Akṣi* means "the Eyes," but the term *Akṣa* is used as a common-noun to indicate the entire set of our instruments-of-experience—the sense-organs, the mind and the intellect.

Triṣu dhāmasu yad-bhogyaṁ bhoktā bhogaś-ca yadbhavet,
tebyo vilakṣaṇaḥ sākṣī cinmātro-'haṁ sadāśivaḥ.

"All that constitutes the *enjoyable*, the *enjoyer* and the *enjoyment*, in the three states of Consciousness.... different from them all am I, the *Witness*, the Ever-Auspicious, Pure Consciousness."

Contemplating thus that your are the Self, the Formless 'Witness'-of-the-universe, "be happy." The sorrows, the tensions, and the stresses of the world and its problems, our passions and our lusts, all end at once, and naturally, there is a growing sense of peace and happiness flooding the bosom of the seeker as he moves towards the sanctum of the Self.

धर्माधर्मौ सुखं दुःखं मानसानि न ते विभो ।
न कर्ताऽसि न भोक्ताऽसि मुक्त एवासि सर्वदा ॥ ६ ॥

Dharma'dharmau sukhaṁ duḥkhaṁ mānasāni na te vibho,
na kartā-'si na bhoktā-'si mukta evāsi sarvadā.

धर्म-अधर्मौ *dharma-adharmau* = virtue and vice; सुखम् *sukham* = happiness; दुःखम् *duḥkham* = sorrow; मानसानि *mānasāni* = mental and intellectual; न *na* = not; ते *te* = yours; विभो *vibho* = O All-Pervading-One; न *na* = not; कर्ता *kartā* = doer; असि *asi* = are (you); न *na* = not; भोक्ता *bhoktā* = enjoyer; असि *asi* = are (you); मुक्तः *muktaḥ* = free; एव *eva* = surely; असि *asi* = are (you); सर्वदा *sarvadā* = ever.

6. *Virtue and vice, happiness and sorrow are all attributes of the mind, not of Yourself, O All-Pervading-One! You are neither the 'doer' nor the 'enjoyer.' Indeed, You are ever-free.*

So long as the ego exists, it asserts in two ways : in the sense of "*doership*," and in the sense of "*enjoyership*." The ego in its relationship with the outer-world maintains a vanity: "*I am the doer*." The same ego functioning within-the-bosom constantly maintains a vanity : "*I am the enjoyer.*" Both these assertions, together constitute, the illusory sense-of-ego.

Now, this ego, while functioning in the world-of-objects, pursues virtues and indulges in vices. As a *doer*, one cannot but get oneself involved in actions, both good and bad. Again, the same ego, as an *enjoyer*, must necessarily get tossed about in its experiences of "happiness and sorrow." In short, the ego cannot escape the conflicts created by the pairs-of-objects.

Here, the teacher advises that the conflicts of good and bad, and the struggles for pleasure and against pain, are all in fact evaluation of the mind, and therefore, they belong to the mind only, never are they yours... You are nothing but the All-Pervading-Consciousness. As the Pure Self you are ever-free from the conflicts and confusions of your own ego.

Virtue and vice are the evaluations of the intellect, identifying with which the sense of '*doership*' is maintained. Happiness and sorrow are the values of the mind, identifying with which the sense of '*enjoyership*' is sustained. Thus, identifying with the intellect and the mind, the sense of '*doership*' and '*enjoyership*' gush forth from us, and they, in their confluence, become the ego in us. When once all its identifications with the intellect and the mind are ended, the ego disappears to become the Blissful Self.

एको द्रष्टाऽसि सर्वस्य मुक्तप्रायोऽसि सर्वदा ।
अयमेव हि ते बन्धो द्रष्टारं पश्यसीतरम् ॥ ७ ॥

Eko draṣṭā-'si sarvasya mukta-prāyo'si sarvadā,
ayam-eva hi te bandho draṣṭāraṁ paśyasītaram.

एक: *ekaḥ* = one; द्रष्टा *draṣṭā* = seer; असि *asi* = are (you); सर्वस्य *sarvasya* = of all; मुक्त-प्राय: *mukta-prāyaḥ* = surely free; असि *asi* = are (you); सर्वदा *sarvadā* = ever; अयम् *ayam* = this; एव *eva* = alone; हि *hi* = indeed; ते *te* = your; बन्ध: *bandhaḥ* = bondage; द्रष्टारम् *draṣṭāram* = the Seer; पश्यसि *paśyasi* = see (you); इतरम् *itaram* = as another.

7. *You are the One-Seer-of-All, and are surely ever-free. Indeed, this alone is your bondage that you see yourself not as the Seer; but as something different.*

The Consciousness in me is the light in which my sense-organs, mind and intellect are able to function. These are equipments through which the *Seer*, the Consciousness, perceives the world of objects, emotions, and thoughts. Thus the Self is the Sole-*Seer* in me, experiencing the world through my life. This Self is the One consciousness in all bosoms and, therefore, through all sense-organs, mind and intellect in the universe, this One Consciousness is the Sole-*Seer* of all perceptions, all emotions and all thoughts in the universe. This Consciousness you are : "That Thou Art" (*Tat-Tvam-Asi*). Therefore, you are necessarily ever-free.

The only apparent illusion of a bondage under which you are now suffering is that you recognise yourself not as this Universal-*Seer*, but as something different—as the limited ego, conditioned by your given equipments-of-experiences.

Self is the only one *Subject*—everything else belongs to the world-of-objects. You are the *Subject*; the world-of-objects are illusory, superimposed upon the Infinite Self, the *Subject*. Here I am reminded of the thunderous assertions of the *Kaivalyopaniṣad* (M-21):

अपाणिपादोऽहमचिन्त्यशक्तिः पश्याम्यचक्षुः स शृणोम्यकर्णः ।
अहं विजानामि विविक्तरूपो न चास्ति वेत्ता मम चित्सदाऽहम् ॥

Apāṇi-pādo-'ham-acintya-śaktiḥ
paśyāmy-acakṣuḥ sa sṛṇomy-akarṇaḥ,
ahaṁ vijānāmi vivikta-rūpo
na cāsti vettā mama cit-sadā-'ham.

"I am without hands and legs, of incomprehensible power. I, who see without eyes, hear without ears, am devoid of all forms. I am knowing (everything), and there is none that knows Me. I am the Ever-Pure-Knowledge."

अहं कर्तेत्यहंमानमहाकृष्णाहिदंशितः ।
नाहं कर्तेति विश्वासामृतं पीत्वा सुखी भव ॥ ८ ॥

Ahaṁ kartety-ahaṁ-māna-mahā-kṛṣṇāhi-daṁśitaḥ,
nāhaṁ karteti viśvās-āmṛtaṁ pītvā sukhī bhava.

अहम् *aham* = I; कर्ता *kartā* = doer; इति *iti* = this; अहंमान-महा-कृष्णाहि दंशितः *ahaṁmāna-mahā-kṛṣṇāhi-daṁśitaḥ* = bitten by the great black-serpent of egoism; न *na* = not; अहम् *aham* = I; कर्ता *kartā* = doer; इति *iti* = such; विश्वास अमृतम् *viśvāsa amṛtam* = nectar of faith; पीत्वा *pītvā* = drinking (you); सुखी *sukhī* = happy; भव *bhava* = be.

8. *You, who have been bitten by the great black-serpent of egoism "I am the doer," please drink the nectar of faith, "I am not the doer,"—and be happy.*

The sense of 'doership' is the arrogant ego expressing in all our perceptions, feelings and thoughts as "I see," "I hear," "I feel," "I think," etc. These false attitudes arise out of our identifications with our eyes, ears, mind and intellect. Seeing, hearing, feeling and thinking are really the functions of the eyes, ears, mind or intellect. As the Self, you are but the illuminator of these functions, which really belong to the different equipments. To arrogate "*I am the doer*" is the essence of the ego.

Once this ego starts functioning, we become smitten by the sense-objects, and become polluted by the poison of sensuality. We become agitated with our passionate urgency to acquire, possess and enjoy the sense-objects. These would bring about our spiritual annihilation. Hence *Aṣṭāvakra* compares the ego here with the black-serpent and its poisonous bite.

The only remedy is to de-hypnotise ourselves by consciously maintaining the wisdom "*I am not the doer.*" This is to be constantly maintained with ardent faith. This mental assertion is a specific cure for the poison-of-ego, and, therefore, it is compared here with nectar, the life-giving ambrosia.

एको विशुद्धबोधोऽहमिति निश्चयवह्निनाँ ।
प्रज्वाल्याज्ञानगहनं वीतशोकः सुखी भव ॥ ९ ॥

Eko viśuddha-bodho-'ham-iti niścaya-vihninā
prajvālyā-jñāna-gahanaṁ vīta-śokaḥ sukhī bhava.

एकः *ekaḥ* = one; विशुद्धबोधः *viśuddha-bodhaḥ* = Pure Consciousness; अहम् *aham* = I; इति *iti* = thus; निश्चयवह्निना *niścaya-vihninā* = by the fire of certitude; प्रज्वाल्य *prajvālya* = having burnt down; अज्ञान-गहनम् *ajñāna-gahanam* = the forest of ignorance; वीत-शोकः *vīta-śokaḥ* = discarding all grief (you); सुखी *sukhī* = happy; भव *bhava* = be.

9. *Having thus burnt down the forest of ignorance with the fire of certitude "I am the One, Pure Consciousness," and discarding all grief—be happy.*

The non-apprehension of our spiritual nature, indicated in *Vedānta* as "ignorance" (*Ajñāna*), is considered here as a "forest" in as much as having gone into a dense forest one is sure to lose one's way therein and keep wandering within it, until hunger and thirst, exhaustion and fatigue, reach to destroy him. Just as in the forest, there are merciless wild beasts of prey, in the dense forest of ignorance, ego and its passions can pounce upon the way-farer. This is an efficient and vivid metaphorical phrase often used in our *śāstrā-s*.

At this moment the knowledge we gather, through our restless intellect, is of the world of time-and-space, and of the various modifications happening in a web of the cause-effect-relationship. When through *Sādhanā*, the intellect becomes calmer and quieter, it automatically turns inward to experience therein the dynamic silence of a spiritual peace.

Such a serene intellect, contemplating subjectively, upon the Self within, is considered by the *Vedānta Śāstra* as the purified intellect. A clean intellect alone can come to apprehend in meditation, the Infinite Self.

The 'knowledge' of the world outside is gathered, for each one of us, by our sense-organs, mind and intellect, only when the Consciousness in us comes to illumine them. Where *Consciousness is not*, as in a block of stone, or a piece of wood, *there is no 'knowledge'*; where Consciousness *is*, 'knowledge' also is. Therefore, Consciousness *is* often equated with 'knowledge.' At this moment our Consciousness is always sullied by the presence of the objects of our experiences. Consciousness-of-objects is the 'knowledge'-of-objects.

Consciousness-of-objects devoid of all objects would be Pure Consciousness—Pure knowledge (*Viśuddha-Bodhaḥ*).

On transcending the body-mind-equipment, the seeker in meditation comes to experience "I am the One, Pure Consciousness." When a seekers gets himself established in this experience of Pure Consciousness, the "fire of the certitude," declares *Aṣṭāvakra*, "shall burn down the forest of ignorance" within the meditator.

Grief is the mental condition when a dear object possessed by it comes to decay. Joy and grief, happiness and sorrow are all emotions and sentiments, experienced by the mind. In Pure Consciousness we have transcended the mind and, therefore, we automatically go beyond all grief. Attaining to this State of the Self, "be happy."

यत्र विश्वमिदं भाति कल्पितं रज्जुसर्पवत् ।
आनन्दपरमानन्दः स बोधस्त्वं सुखं चर ॥ १० ॥

Yatra viśvam-idaṁ bhāti kalpitaṁ rajju-sarpavat,
ānanda-paramānandaḥ sa bodhastvaṁ sukhaṁ cara.

यत्र *yatra* = that in which; विश्वम् *viśvam* = universe; इदम् *idam* = this; भाति *bhāti* = appears; कल्पितम् *kalpitam* = imagined; रज्जु-सर्पवत् *rajju-sarpavat* = like snake in a rope; आनन्द-परमानन्दः *ānanda-param-ānandaḥ* = bliss-supreme-bliss; सः *saḥ* = that; बोधः *bodhaḥ* = consciousness; त्वम् *tvam* = you; सुखम् *sukham* = happily; चर *cara* = live.

10. *You are that Consciousness, Bliss—Supreme Bliss—upon which this universe appears superimposed, like a snake on a rope. Live happily as that Blissful Consciousness.*

In the previous verse, the teacher has asserted that the student, in the final essence, is nothing but Pure Consciousness. In our empirical experience, we live every moment of our life, perceiving a world-of-objects outside. Subjectively, what about our mind and its feelings, and our intellect and its thoughts? Where did all these come from? If the Pure Consciousness alone is the One Reality, these vehicles-of-experiences and their perceptions should be unreal. From where did the unreal spring from? Can the Real create the unreal?

In order to explain this illusory world-of-plurality, the *Seers* of *Vedānta* have been giving us an eloquent analogy. In the dim-light of the dusk a rope may be misunderstood as a serpent. The moment we have the 'knowledge' of the rope, the illusion of the serpent disappears totally. The non-apprehension of the rope gives us the mis-apprehension of the serpent; and subsequent fears and sorrows are all provided by the mis-apprehensions. Similarly, the non-apprehensions of our spiritual nature as the Pure Self, occasions the mis-apprehensions of a subjective and objective world-of-experiences. On "apprehending" the Self, the illusory super-impositions, shall immediately disappear, as the delusion of the snake ends in the 'knowledge' of the rope.

You are this Consciousness of the Nature of "Supreme Bliss," confirms *Aṣṭāvakra* : "upon which the world is super-imposed, like a snake on a rope." Abiding in this Blissful Consciousness, "be Happy."

All these verses are extremely helpful to a student who has started crawling upon the path-of-meditation. To remember verses and chant them slowly to ourselves, in some quiet place, with eyes open, and our attention turned into ourselves, shall lift us into profound heights in subjective reflections (*Manana*). Practice of *Manana* puts a tiger in the tank of the vehicle of meditation.

मुक्ताभिमानी मुक्तो हि बद्धो बद्धाभिमान्यपि ।
किंवदन्तीह सत्येयं या मतिः सा गतिर्भवेत् ॥ ११ ॥

Muktābhimānī mukto hi badddho baddhābhimānyapi,
kiṁ-vadantīḥ satyeyaṁ yā matiḥ sā gatir-bhavet.

मुक्त-अभिमानी *mukta-abhimānī* = one who considers himself free; मुक्तः *muktaḥ* = is free; हि *hi* = indeed; बद्धः *baddhaḥ* = becomes bound; बद्ध-अभिमानी *baddha-abhimānī* = one who considers himself bound; अपि *api* = also; किं-वदन्ती *kiṁ-vadantī* = proverbial saying; इह *iha* = in this world; सत्या *satyā* = true; इयम् *iyam* = this; या *yā* = as; मतिः *matiḥ* = the thought; सा *sā* = so; गतिः *gatiḥ* = attainment, the goal; भवेत् *bhavet* = is.

11. *He who considers himself free becomes free indeed, and he who considers himself bound remains bound.. "As one thinks, so one becomes," is a proverbial saying in this world and it is indeed quite true.*

Yā matiḥ sā gatiḥ (या मतिः सा गतिः) – "As we think, so we become" is a famous saying. If you assert yourself that you are a helpless, weak and desperate creature of passions and impluses, you cannot grow into the higher heights of beauty and strength of your personality. On the other hand to assert our own Divine Nature constantly, and to try to live without compromising this godly status, is to a seeker the royal path for gaining Self-unfoldment. The *Upaniṣad-s* also uphold this thought :

मन एव मनुष्याणां कारणं बन्धमोक्षयोः ।

Mana eva manuṣyāṇām,
kāraṇaṁ bandha-mokṣayoḥ.

"Mind alone is the cause for the state of bondage or liberation in man."

In the *Yoga-Vāsiṣṭha* also we find a very similar statement most emphatically put:

यत् चित्तं तन्मयो भवति पुरुषः ।

Yat cittaṁ tanmayo bhavati puruṣaḥ.

"Whatever springs in mind, man expresses it."

This is equally true in the spiritual life also, because our apparent illusion of snake has not brought about any change in the rope, which is the only reality therein. Similarly, the Pure, Infinite Consciousness has never modified itself, ever into the experiencing-ego, nor into the experienced world-of-plurality. From the delusion-created *vāsanā-s* in us, desires gurgle forth, which express as thoughts, and the thoughts in the mind project the world of experiences—just as in a dream. Awaker never becomes the dreamer, but during the delusion apparently he suffers the tragedies of his dream. At the *non-apprehension* of the Self, the *mis-apprehensions* of the world and its sorrows rise. By asserting our nature as the Pure, Infinite Consciousness, we can come to awake to this new dimension of Experience-Divine.

आत्मा साक्षी विभुः पूर्ण एको मुक्तश्चिदक्रियः ।
असङ्गो निस्पृहः शान्तो भ्रमात् संसारवानिव ॥ १२ ॥

Ātmā sākṣī vibhuḥ pūrṇa eko muktaś-cid-akriyaḥ,
Asaṅgo nispṛhaḥ śānto bhramāt saṁsāra-vān-iva.

आत्मा *ātmā* = Self; साक्षी *sākṣī* = witness; विभुः *vibhuḥ* = all pervasive; पूर्णः *pūrṇaḥ* = perfect; एकः *ekaḥ* = one (non-dual); मुक्तः *muktaḥ* = free; चित् *cit* = Consciousness; अक्रियः *akriyaḥ* = actionless; असङ्गः *asaṅgaḥ* = unattached; निस्पृहः *nispṛhaḥ* = desireless; शान्तः *śāntaḥ* = quiet; भ्रमात् *bhramāt* = through illusion; संसारवान् *saṁsāravān* = absorbed in the world; इव *iva* = as if (is).

12. *The Self is Witness, All-pervading, Perfect, Non-dual, Free, Consciousness, Actionless, Unattached, Desireless and Quiet. Through illusion, It appears as if It is absorbed in the world.*

This verse is a peroration as it were of what have been so far declared by the transcendental sage, *Aṣṭāvakra*. You are not the body, nor the mind; in your spiritual essence you are the Pure Infinite Consciousness.

The Ultimate Reality, being infinite and eternal, cannot be defined directly by the finite words. However, the *Hindū* Masters had evolved a secret technique of expressing this inexpressible Truth. They succeeded in defining the Truth by indicating the Supreme through rich suggestive terms deftly employed. The words, as such, with their direct meaning do not define the Truth, but they can lift a reflective-mind to the realms of direct experiences. Such illuminating terms are employed here summarising the great dictum : "That Thou Art" (*Tat-tvam-asi*), which have been so elaborately discussed in all the pervious eleven verses.

The Self is the "Witness" (*Sākṣī*) : indicating that the Consciousness, which is the illuminator, is not in any way involved in what it illumines. This 'witness' is 'All-pervasive' (*vibhuḥ*). Just as the rope is all-pervasive in the illusion of the snake, so too the world-of-plurality is pervaded by its substratum, the Reality. The immanence of the Self in all beings is declared here. It is "Perfect" (*Pūrṇaḥ*) : nothing can be added to It, nor can we substract anything from It; it is ever just as It is. Nothing is added to the *post* when the '*ghost*' is seen; nor do we take anything away from the *post* when the *ghost*-vision disappears. The Self is the substratum for all the illusory names and forms.

This Self is "Non-dual" (*Ekaḥ*) and, therefore, "Ever-Free" (*muktaḥ*). As "Consciousness" (*Cit*) it is by itself "Actionless" (*Akriyaḥ*) although all actions in the cosmos are taking place in It. All movements in the world can take place only in space—but space by itself has no movement.

Like space, which allows everything to remain in it, but itself is not involved with any one of the objects, so too the Self, as Consciousness, is "Unattached" (*Asaṅgaḥ*). In its Infinite Perfection, It has "no desires" (*Nispṛhaḥ*). Desires are the expressions of *vāsanā-s*; the Self is the Consciousness that illumines the very *vāsanā-s*. In its Supreme Perfection It has nothing to desire for, other than Itself. Since there are no desires, there cannot be any thought-agitations, nor any restless activities of the body. Therefore, this great Reality is indicated by the suggestive term 'ever quiet' (*Śāntaḥ*).

A mind that is capable of reflecting upon each one of these ten suggestive terms, indicating the Self, can, in its totality, get itself spontaneously pushed into the experience of a voiceless dynamic void, wherein the Self is directly experienced. This Immutable Self "through our illusion appears as if" suffering as an ego (*Jīva*) in the world.

As the perceiver-feeler-thinker-entity, the individualised ego, in everyone of us, gets entraped in the world of enchantments, within and without. Thereafter bound to the wheel-of-*karma* in order to exhaust the gathered debris of *vāsanā-s*, the ego is driven from body to body, in an unending circle of birth and death. This is the involvement in the world (*Saṁsāravān*).

In fact, the Self does not become the ego (*Jīva*). The *rope* is not becoming the serpent, the *post* cannot change itself to be the *ghost*. It *only appears* (*Iva*) as though the Infinite Consciousness, I, have become the limited-ego, a victim of circumstances, and a helpless floatsome upon the waves of the daily happenings around me.

कूटस्थं बोधमद्वैतमात्मानं परिभावय ।
आभासोऽहं भ्रमं मुक्त्वा भावं बाह्यमथान्तरम् ॥ १३ ॥

Kūṭasthaṁ bodhaṃ-advaitam
ātmānaṁ paribhāvaya,
ābhāso'haṁ bhramaṁ muktvā
bhāvaṁ bāhyam-atha-antaram.

कूटस्थम् *kūṭastham* = immutable; बोधम् *bodham* = Consciousness; अद्वैतम् *advaitam* = non-dual; आत्मानम् *ātmānam* = Self; परिभावय *paribhāvaya* = meditate upon; आभास: *ābhāsaḥ* = reflection of Self (ego); अहम् *aham* = I; भ्रमम् *bhramam* = illusion; मुक्त्वा *muktvā* = having given up; भावम् *bhāvam* = identifications, fluctuations; बाह्यम् *bāhyam* = external; अथ *atha* = so also; अन्तरम् *antaram* = internal.

13. *Having given up all external and internal fluctuations, and the illusion : "I am the reflected-Self (ego)," meditate upon the Self, as Immutable Non-dual Consciousness.*

Having given ten suggestive arrow-marks to indicate the nature of the Self in the meditator, here, in this verse, *Aṣṭāvakra* insists, that the student, with an undisturbed calm mind, should try to given up his ego-centric sense of limitations, and meditate upon the already indicated spiritual "centre" in him as the Immutable, Non-dual Consciousness.

This is the only verse in the entire song of *Aṣṭāvakra*, where the *Ācārya* prescribes meditation for the student. Later on, the teacher transcends even this position and thunders that the very idea of meditation is a declaration of one's own sense of imperfection—an unforgivable sin against the Perfect Self.

A mechanical mental repetition of the qualities of the Self is not meditation. An intellect that has been soaked with its reflections upon these suggestive terms, must come to a point where it has no more any doubts to disturb it... And so it halts. When the intellect has thus reached a state of supreme serenity, if the seeker can hold his mind in a sense of breathless expectation, alert and vigilant, ready to experience a spontaneous 'awakening'..... then the individual is at the highest state of meditative equipoise. This state of utter balance within, and total oblivion of the outer happenings, is indicated here by the term "meditate" (*Paribhāvaya*).

The term "*Kūṭastha*" employed in the verse is a very suggestive term, rich in its meanings. The *Saṁskṛta* term '*kūṭa*' has three distinct meanings : (a) mountain top, (b) mystery, (c) anvil; all these three meanings are suggested in this term. The *Brahman*, the Self, (a) is the *highest Reality*; (b) is the *mystery* behind all the play-of-*Māyā*; (c) is the *One that changes not* while everything in the universe gets changed in contact with It, and thus serves like an anvil.

The Self, viewed as the substratum for the whole universe, is termed in *Vedānta-śāstrā-s* as the '*Brahman*'; and as expressed through an individual mind and intellect, It is called as 'reflection' (*Ābhāsaḥ*), meaning the ego (*Jīva*).

देहाभिमानपाशेन चिरं बद्धोऽसि पुत्रक ।
बोधोऽहं ज्ञानखड्गेन तन्निष्कृत्य सुखी भव ॥ १४ ॥

Dehābhimāna-pāśena ciraṁ baddho'si putraka,
bodho'haṁ jñāna-khaṅgena tanniṣkṛtya sukhī-bhava.

देहाभिमान पाशेन *dehābhimāna pāśena* = by the rope of body-consciousness; चिरम् *ciram* = long; बद्धः *baddhaḥ* = bound; असि *asi* = are (you); पुत्रक *putraka* = dear son; बोधः *bodhaḥ* = intelligence; अहम् *aham* = I; ज्ञान खड्गेन *jñāna khaṅgena* = with the sword of knowledge; तत् *tat* = that; निष्कृत्य *niṣkṛtya* = rending asunder; सुखी *sukhī* = happy; भव *bhava* = be.

14. *My dear son, you have been bound with the rope of your body-consciousness. Rend it asunder with the sword of the knowledge "I am Consciousness," and be happy.*

Recently a christian priest Rev. George was re-converted into *Hindūism* and he was given the new name *Śrī Janārdan*. That very afternoon when he was hailed by his name, he ignored and continued along his way. Even when the person ran to him, tapped on his shoulders, and said : "Excuse me,. I hope you are *Janārdan*?" The new-convert smiled and apologetically exclaimed : "Sorry, you are mistaken." Having lived as George for a long number of years, even though he has gone through the elaborate ceremonies of convertion and has been told that his new name is *Janārdan*, it will yet take time for him to forget his George-identity and get established in his new *Janārdan*-identity.

You have been for trillions of years moving along the path of your biological evolution, from the unicellular existence, steadily progressing on to gain this noble human-birth and to learn to assert the human intelligence. In all these long periods of evolution you have been living the delusion of your body-consciousness. Naturally, the idea "I am the body" is very strong in you. The deep paternal anxiety and concern of the teacher for the student is indicated here when he addresses the student as 'dear son' (*putraka*).

Having explained to the student the nature of the Reality, and having indicated the path of realising It, now the teacher can do nothing more. The delusion is in the student's mind, and none can help him, save himself. He must awake himself to his own Real Nature. Therefore, the teacher with anxious urgency insists : "Rend asunder" the noose of your body-consciousness, in which you are at this moment caught unawares, by your own spiritual "ignorance." This can be done only with the sharp sword of one's own direct realization "I am Consciousness."

Thus redeem yourself, from your own delusion of body and mind. Get away from the illusory sorrows of life, and "be happy." Intuitive illumination occurs the very instance when "ignorance" is dispelled. Realising "I am the Consciousness," abide in the Self, and "be happy."

निःसङ्गो निष्क्रियोऽसि त्वं स्वप्रकाशो निरञ्जनः ।
अयमेव हि ते बन्धः समाधिमनुतिष्ठसि ॥ १५ ॥

Niḥsaṅgo niṣkriyo-'si tvaṁ svaprakāśo nirañjanaḥ,
Ayam-eva hi te bandhaḥ samādhim-anutiṣṭhasi.

निःसङ्गः *niḥsaṅgaḥ* = unattached; निष्क्रियः *niṣkriyaḥ* = actionless; असि *asi* = are; त्वम् *tvam* = you; स्वप्रकाशः *sva-prakāśaḥ* = Self-effulgent; निरञ्जनः *nirañjanaḥ* = without taints (stainless); अयम्

ayam = this; एव *eva* = indeed; हि *hi* = surely; ते *te* = your; बन्धः *bandhaḥ* = bondage; समाधिम् *samādhim* = meditation; अनुतिष्ठसि *anutiṣṭhasi* = practice.

15. *You are unattached, actionless, self-effulgent, and without-any-taints. 'You practise meditation,'—this indeed is your bondage.*

As the Self, you are unattached with your body-mind-equipments, and with their perceived-objects or entertained thoughts. The *post* is unattached with every part of the *ghost.* It is the limited, the finite alone that can act; the Self, being All-Pervading and Infinite, is ever 'Actionless' (*Niṣkriyaḥ*). Where will the All-Pervading act, as It has no field other than Itself to act. In Its Supreme Perfection it can desire nothing, and without a desire how can action ever spring forth? As Consciousness, the Self is 'Self-Effulgent' (*Sva-prakāśaḥ*), and this Light-of-Consciousness is never dimmed as It is 'without any taints' (*Nirañjanaḥ*). Beyond *vāsanā-s*, illumining them, revels the Pure Seat of Consciousness, the Self, and as such It is stainless. The Consciousness in us illumines for us our gross, subtle and causal bodies.

The Self is Ever-free; therefore, It needs no meditation. So long as we are meditating, there are still traces of the ego in us, which alone can *aspire* for the Selfhood and *practise* meditation. One who is trying to sleep, so long as he is trying, he is not asleep. Once having reached sleep, the sleeper is no more *trying to sleep.* It is only the waker who can try to gain his sleep-state. In the same way, so long as an individual is meditating, he has not apprehended the State of Pure Consciousness.

Rare indeed are the Seers of the calibre of *Aṣṭāvakra*, who has the audacity to declare, so openly, that to meditate upon the Ever-Free and the Ever-Liberated Supreme Reality is itself a symptom of the meditator's state of bondage. The limited alone will strive to reach the Unlimited; the bound and the shackled alone need struggle to attain liberation.

To a sincere student of meditation this verse has a precious secret suggestion. When all other thoughts have subsided, the mind and therefore, the ego survives itself with the subtle vanity: "I am meditating." Even this idea must be finally given up. So long as one maintains the awareness that 'I am trying to sleep,' he cannot enter the state of sleep. 'I meditate' is perhaps the *last lingering thought* in almost all the seekers in higher-meditation. The moment even this vanity is given up, "the ego completely disappears into the vision of the Reality." In short, in the Supreme Silence of meditation, a seeker should give up even the idea of "doership" experienced within him, as "I am meditating"—this seems to be the mystic import of this direct advise.

In *Yoga Vāsiṣṭha* (Ch. 62-9) also we read verses indicating the same import :

साधो ! समाधिशब्देन परा प्रज्ञोच्यते बुधैः ।
अजस्रमंबुवहनाद् यथा नद्या न रुध्यते ॥

Sādho! samādhi-śabdena parā prajñocyate budhaiḥ,
ajastra-mambu-vahanād yathā nadyā na rudhyate.

"O saint! the term 'Samādhi' means the awareness of the Supreme Consciousness as one's own Self. A river, being a continuous flow of water, is never halted in its flow."

So too the awareness 'I-am-the-Self' is never broken in the man-of-*Samādhi*. How can then he meditate? Upon what? And why should he?

तथात्मज्ञानहीनात्मा कालो ज्ञस्य न लभ्यते ।

(Ch. 62-19).

Tathātma-jñāna-hīnātmā kālo jñasya na labhyate.

"Thus to the man-of-wisdom there is no time when he is not aware of the Self-in-Him."

Vāsiṣṭha concludes by wondering :

सर्वगः सर्वदैवात्मा सर्वमेव च सर्वथा ।
असमाधिर्हि कोऽसौ स्यात् समाधिरपि कः स्मृतः ॥

(Chapter 62-24)

"When the Self is All-Pervading, expressing as Consciousness in everything, and in every being, at all times, then where is *non-Samādhi*; and what is *Samādhi.*"

त्वया व्याप्तमिदं विश्वं त्वयि प्रोतं यथार्थतः ।
शुद्धबुद्धस्वरूपस्त्वं मा गमः क्षुद्रचित्तताम् ॥ १६ ॥

Tvayā vyāptam-idaṁ viśvaṁ tvayi protaṁ yathārthataḥ
śuddha-buddha-svarūpas-tvaṁ mā gamaḥ kṣudra-citta-tām.

त्वया *tvayā* = by you; व्याप्तम् *vyāptam* = pervaded; इदम् *idam* = this; विश्वम् *viśvam* = universe; त्वयि *tvayi* = in you; प्रोतम् *protam* = strung or woven (and); यथार्थतः *yathārthataḥ* = really; शुद्ध बुद्ध स्वरूपः *śuddha-buddha-svarūpaḥ* = by nature Pure Consciousness; त्वम् *tvam* = you; मा *mā* = not; गमः *gamaḥ* = attain; क्षुद्र-चित्ततम् *kṣudra-cittatām* = petty-mindedness.

16. *You pervade this universe and this universe is strung or woven only in You. Really, by nature, You are Pure Consciousness. Do not give way to petty-mindedness.*

The material cause of a thing must pervade the thing made out of it. Mud, the cause, pervades the entire pot made out of mud. The Self, the Consciousness, from which the world gets projected, must necessarily pervade the entire universe. Out of the human mind when a dream gets projected, the mind should pervade the entire world, dreamt by the dreamer. You are this Self; therefore, "you pervade this universe."

Not only the mind pervades the dream-world of the dreamer, but the entire dream is woven into or strung upon the mind. In the mud is the pot supported and the pot-form exists only in the substance of the pot—the mud. Thus, You, as the Self, carry "this universe strung, or woven, only in Yourself."

Though, the universe thus exists in You, and though it has no existence apart from You, yet, You are not involved in, or in any way conditioned by the universe; for, as the Infinite Self, "really, by nature, You are Pure Consciousness." In Consciousness the "subject" and "object" get woven as the warp and woof of this magnificient tapestry of the universe.

When you are thus the very substratum of the universe, upon whom the universe of names-and-forms is but a delusory projection, you should not get identified with these *mis-apprehensions* and come to suffer the limitations and sorrows of the little-ego. To do so is mean. Cautions *Aṣṭāvakra* : "Do not give way to petty-mindedness." To live, feeling and acting as the limited-ego, is unbecoming to Your Divine and Infinite True Nature. There is nothing greater than Your essential spiritual being.

निरपेक्षो निर्विकारो निर्भरः शीतलाशयः ।
अगाधबुद्धिरक्षुब्धो भव चिन्मात्रवासनः ॥ १७ ॥

Nirapekṣo nirvikāro nirbharaḥ śītalāśayaḥ,
agādha-buddhir-kṣubdho bhava cinmātra-vāsanaḥ.

निरपेक्षः *nirapekṣaḥ* = unconditioned; निर्विकारः *nirvikāraḥ* = changeless; निर्भरः *nirbharaḥ* = dense; शीतलाशयः *śītalāśayaḥ* = of cool disposition (serene); अगाध-बुद्धिः *agādha-buddhiḥ* = of profound intelligence; अक्षुब्धः *akṣubdhaḥ* = unperturbed (you); भव *bhava* = be; चिन्मात्र-वासनः *cinmātra-vāsanaḥ* = desiring of Consciousness alone.

17. *You are unconditioned, changeless, dense, of profound intelligence, serene and unperturbed. Desire Consciousness alone.*

As Pure Consciousness You depend upon nothing (*Nirapekṣaḥ*) : You are unconditioned. Everywhere, at all times, You are full and so the term is used here "dense" (*nirbharaḥ*). As a contrast to the burning passions that constantly agitate the ego-centric-life, the Infinite Self in Its Supreme Peace and Perfection is ever-serene—"of cool disposition" (*Śītala-āśayaḥ*).

This great spiritual centre, Consciousness, is indicated by some Masters by explaining the conditions under which the Self can be experienced. Very often this technique is employed in the *Upaniṣad-s*, wherein an adjectival-noun, indicating the Self, can in itself be a discourse upon an exercise in realising the Self. Here the Self is declared as "profound Intelligence—serene and unperturbed" (*Agādha-budhiḥ akṣubdhaḥ*): meaning when the intellect is devoid of all its thought-disturbances, the Self, as Pure Consciousness, comes to manifest in a clear and direct experience.

The common advice of all Masters to the seekers is one and the same : "Desire this Consciousness alone." (*Bhava Cinmātra Vāsanaḥ*). As our desires, so our thoughts; as our thoughts so our experiences. Desires of world-of-objects, shall create sensuous thoughts and we shall come to experience the world-of-plurality. Ardently desire for a direct apprehension of the Pure Consciousness alone; our thoughts shall be of the Divine Self only—and we shall come to experience the Great Grand Reality of the universe and the life therein.

साकारमनृतं विद्धि निराकारं तु निश्चलम् ।
एतत्तत्त्वोपदेशेन न पुनर्भवसम्भवः ॥ १८ ॥

Sākāra-manṛtaṁ viddhi nirākāraṁ tu niścalam,
etat-tattvo-padeśena na punar-bhava-sambhavaḥ.

साकारम् *sākāram* = that which has form; अनृतम् *anṛtam* = false; विद्धि *viddhi* = know; निराकारम् *nirākāram* = the formless; तु *tu* = but; निश्चलम् *niścalam* = changeless; एतत्-तत्त्व-उपदेशेन *etat-tattva-upadeśena* = by this instruction regarding the truth; न *na* = not; पुनर्भव-सम्भवः *punar-bhava-sambhavaḥ* = possibility of rebirth (is).

18. *Know, that which has form to be false and the formless to be changeless. Through this spiritual instruction you shall escape the possibility of rebirth.*

When a sincere seeker tries to practise what has been suggested in the previous verse, the meditator may meet with a persistent obstacle at almost every moment of his meditation. He has been advised in the previous verse that the Self is "profound intelligence—serene and unperturbed." Yet, in the meditator, thought-waves do rise up continuously to disturb and distract his attention. How is he to dry up this continuous eruption of mental pictures, drawn from the past-memories, or fancied by his faculty of imagination? Here *Aṣṭāvakra* very subtly suggests, to the seekers, a technique on how to hush up the mind and silence the intellect.

The student must have a clear idea of what he is seeking. In meditation, the student is seeking the *Real*, in and through his own mental-web, woven by the erratic play of the illusory names and forms that constitute the *unreal*. In the mystic literature, "that which remains changeless in the past, present and future" is the *Real*, and "that which was not and will not be, but apparently seems to exist in the present" is the *unreal*. Thus, the *post* is 'real'; the *ghost* is '*unreal*.' The *waking* is 'real'; the *dream* is '*unreal*.' The *ocean* is '*real*,' the *waves* are '*unreal*.' The changing world-of-plurality is the *unreal*; the permanent substratum is the *Real*.

The body, the mind, the intellect and their perceptions, emotions and thoughts are all constantly changing and therefore, they are *unreal*. The Consciousness that illumines their rise, their existence and their dis-appearance is permanent, and, therefore, is the *Real*. Having thus a clear notion of what is *Real* and what is *unreal*, the meditator can very easily reject the *false*, the unreal and aspire to apprehend the *true*, the Real. "Know that which has form," meaning every object-of-experience, "*to be false*" and "the formless to be the changeless," meaning the *true*.

Naturally, therefore, the attention of the meditator is directed, away from his equipments-of-experiences, into the Pure seat of All-Consciousness. When the knowledge of this True Nature of the Self reaches the meditator, his illusory ego and its *mis-apprehensions* of the universe shall roll away.

यथैवादर्शमध्यस्थे रूपेऽन्तः परितस्तु सः ।
तथैवास्मिन् शरीरेऽन्तः परितः परमेश्वरः ॥ १९ ॥

Yathaiv-ādarśa-madhya-sthe rūpe'ntaḥ paritastu saḥ,
tathaiv-āsmin śarīre'ntaḥ paritaḥ parameśvaraḥ.

यथा *yathā* = as; एव *eva* = just; आदर्शमध्यस्थे *ādarśa-madhyasthe* = existing in a mirror; रूपे *rūpe* = in an image; अन्तः *antaḥ* = within; परितः *paritaḥ* = without; तु *tu* = and; सः *saḥ* = that (mirror exists); तथा *tathā* = so too; एव *eva* = just; अस्मिन् शरीरे *asmin śarīre* = in this body; अन्तः *antaḥ* = inside; परितः *paritaḥ* = outside; परमेश्वरः *parameśvaraḥ* = the Supreme Lord (exists).

19. Just as a mirror exists inside and outside the image reflected in it, so the Supreme Self exists inside and outside this body.

Although during meditation one meditates upon the spiritual-centre as a point *within* himself, when he withdraws himself from all the agitations created by his matter-vestures and apprehends this Seat-of-Consciousness within, he awakes to realise the Boundless State of the Infinite Self. The Eternal Self, Infinite and Unconditioned, is ever-present everywhere, both within and without. In fact, the very idea of inside and outside is only with reference to the meditator's body-awareness. As a matter of fact when you are asleep, what is your dimension? Where is your location? When the body is not perceived, the concepts of within and without are no longer valid.

With reference to a room, or a pot, we can qualify space as space-within and space-without. But when the pot is broken or the walls are pulled down, there can be only one all-pervading space. Similarly, the seeker, so long as he is within his conditionings, he meditates upon his Self, as the Pure-Subject *within* himself. But on apprehending the Self, he experiences Its All-Pervading-Infinite-Nature.

In order to communicate this idea, *Aṣṭāvakra* uses here a very original example. The reflection is in the mirror and the mirror pervades within and without the reflection caught in it. The reflection has no existence apart from the mirror. Even when the reflection is not there, the mirror continues to be. Similarly, reflected in the three bodies—the gross, the subtle and the causal—the Consciousness appears to dance to the rhythm of the bodies and this reflection (*ābhāsaḥ*), caught in our bosom, is the ego (*Jīva*).

The very existence of the three-bodies is brought about by one's own illusions. They are superimposed upon the Self by "ignorance." As the *post* is *within* the *ghost*-vision, the Self is *within* the body.

But the Infinite Self, the Consciousness, is within and without the individualised-ego and its matter-wrappings. Just as the reflection cannot in any way disturb the reflecting medium, so too the Self is not affected by the superimposition of the equipments, or the reflection of the ego.

In this eloquent and striking metaphor employed here, the teacher in *Aṣṭāvakra* deliberately employs the word '*Parmeśvara*' (God) in the place of Supreme Consciousness. In fact, the individual (*Jīva*), the universe (*Jagat*) and Lord, the Creator (*Īśvara*) are all different manifestations of the same Infinite Consciousness.

एकं सर्वगतं व्योम बहिरन्तर्यथा घटे ।
नित्यं निरन्तरं ब्रह्म सर्वभूतगणे तथा ॥ २० ॥

Ekaṁ sarva-gataṁ vyoma bahir-antar-yathā ghaṭe,
nityaṁ nirantaraṁ brahma sarva-bhūta-gaṇe tathā.

एकम् *ekam* = the one and the same; सर्वगतम् *sarvagatam* = all pervading; व्योम *vyoma* = space; बहिः *bahiḥ* = outside; अन्तः *antaḥ* = inside (exists); यथा *yathā* = as; घटे *ghaṭe* = in a jar; नित्यम् *nityam* = immutable; निरन्तरम् *nirantaram* = all pervasive; ब्रह्म *brahma* = *Brahman*; सर्व-भूत-गणे *sarva-bhūta-gaṇe* = in all things and beings (exists); तथा *tathā* = so.

20. *Just as the same all-pervading space is inside and outside the jar, so the Immutable and All-Pervading* Brahman *exists in all beings and things.*

In the previous verse, with his enchanting metaphor of a reflection and the mirror, the All-Pervasiveness of the Self was indicated, and the *transcendance* of the Self was established. While, in the present verse with which the chapter concludes, the *immanence* of the Self is being emphasised. In order to communicate this idea *Aṣṭāvakra* again employs a very suggestive analogy borrowed from the *Upaniṣad-s*. The all-pervading space exists both within and without every pot. Similarly, the Infinite Consciousness is present in the bosom of every existence—in all beings and things (*Sarva-Bhūta-Gaṇe*).

The pot-space may apparently look as though conditioned by the pot—there can be, less space or more space according to the volume of the pot; there can also be, clean-space or dirty-space according to the condition of the pot. But in fact space, as such, can never be conditioned by the pot that exists only in space. Similarly, the Infinite Consciousness in which all equipments exist and play about, apparently seems to get conditioned by the individual equipments.

The presence of the Self in all beings and things is emphasized in this famous and oft-repeated *Vedāntik* illustration.

Chapter—II

The Marvellous Self

Introduction

All mystic saints when trying to verbalise their experiences of the Transcendental, become mute with wonderment, at the ecstatic marvel of the very experience divine. Even the unusually eloquent mystics of the *Upaniṣad-s*, who have evolved to themselves a sane vocabulary and an intelligent technique of communication—even they are often compelled to employ a stammering diction, punctuated with endless exclamations!! In this chapter, in many verses, *Janaka* tumbles himself through jungles of exclamations!!!

As a student *Janaka* approaches his teacher *Aṣṭāvakra* in the previous chapter, and words springing from Master's bosom of lived subjective-experience of the Self, have rocketed the student into an immediate subjective experience of the Reality. The staggering uniqueness of the experience, and the breathless vividness of his direct enlightenment, chokes the student and deprives him of his eloquence.

When a human intellect can understand and comprehend a happening, it is no more a wonder. The intellect is then satisfied by its description or explanation. But when we experience something for which our intellect cannot immediately provide with a logical explanation, the incomprehensibility of it all makes it a wonder. In moments of wonderment the intellect is stunned into a bewildering silence. Hence the Supreme is often indicated by the term "Wonder of Wonders" : *(Atyāścarya-mayam-devam)*. We read this 'term' *(āścarya)* employed both in the *Gītā* and in the *Upaniṣad-s*.

In this chapter the "joy-of-realisation" is expressed in a language at-once fluid and soul-stirring. The graphic diction employed here can stimulate the contemplative faculty in the students of meditation. The description of the universe, sustained and illumined by the Self, is so impressive that a sincere reflective mind can readily feel the extensive cosmos around him as nothing but an insignificant limb of his own Infinite Self! To the little-ego, familiar with its meagre selfish-world, such an expansion of its experience within, should be a staggering wonder!

King *Janaka*, the disciple, in this chapter demonstrates that the words of the Master have brought into the royal bosom an immediate enlightenment. All his illusions have been suddenly lifted. The *knowledge-knower-knowable*-triad has fused to disappear, along with the ego, into the vision of the Infinite Tranquillity—the Self. The description of this merger is made unforgettably vivid, by the striking examples so dexterously employed by *Janaka*.

जनक उवाच ।

अहो निरञ्जनः शान्तो बोधोऽहं प्रकृतेः परः ।
एतावन्तमहं कालं मोहेनैव विडम्बितः ॥ १ ॥

Janaka Uvāca :

Aho nirañjanaḥ śānto bodho'haṁ prakṛteḥ paraḥ,
etāvantam-ahaṁ kālaṁ mohe-naiva viḍambitaḥ.

अहो *aho* = O!; निरञ्जनः *nirañjanaḥ* = taintless; शान्तः *śāntaḥ* = serene; बोधः *bodhaḥ* = consciousness (am); अहम् *aham* = I; प्रकृतेः *prakṛteḥ* = of nature; परः *paraḥ* = beyond; एतावन्तम् *etāvantam* = so long; अहम् *aham* = I; कालम् *kālam* = time, days; मोहेन *mohena* = by delusion; एव *eva* = only; विडम्बितः *viḍambitaḥ* = bewildered.

Janaka said :

1. *O! I am taintless, serene, Pure Consciousness, and beyond Nature. So long I have spent My days bewildered by delusion.*

The student-of-Realisation is here regretting the pitiable sorrows through which he had lived for aeons, due to his own delusions that he is his body and mind. Now he has realised that he is the Pure Consciousness, at once 'taintless'—because he is beyond the *Vāsanā-s*; and 'serene'—because he has transcended the agitation-breeding-mind. In fact, he experiences that he is "beyond-matter" (*Prakṛteḥ paraḥ*), and is of the nature of Pure Consciousness.

The regret is that, for a span of time, rolling back to trillions of years, in various embodiments, he had, as an individualised-ego continued his dream-play of sense-pursuits, seeking in them his satisfaction and happiness, and had thus lived in sorrow and pain because of his own delusions.

We have already described that this "delusion" streams forth from one's identifications with one's body, mind and intellect.

According to the *Sānkhyan* philosophy, the cause for the entire universe of names-and-forms is Nature (*Prakṛti*); and the Spirit (*Puruṣa*) enlivens the inert Nature. In his Song, *Aṣṭāvakra* seems to have no patience with such rational explanations which are all *views* of the intellect, not the *visions* of the Spirit. *Aṣṭāvakra* recognises the Self alone as the One Ultimate Cause for everything, and the Self as Consciousness is the illuminator of both Matter (*Prakṛti*) and Spirit (*Puruṣa*).

यथा प्रकाशयाम्येको देहमेनं तथा जगत् ।
अतो मम जगत्सर्वमथवा न च किञ्चन ॥ २ ॥

Yathā prakāśa-yāmyeko deha-menaṁ tathā Jagat,
ato mama jagat-sarvam-athavā na ca kiñcana.

यथा *yathā* = as; प्रकाशयामि *prakāśayāmi* = illumine (I); एकः *ekaḥ* = the one; देहम् *deham* = body; एनम् *enam* = this; तथा *tathā* = so (also); जगत् *jagat* = the universe (I reveal); अतः *ataḥ* = therefore; मम *mama* = mine; जगत् *jagat* = the universe; सर्वम् *sarvam* = all; अथवा *athavā* = or; न *na* = not; च *ca* = indeed; किञ्चन *kiñcana* = anything (mine).

2. *I, the One, illumine this body and also reveal this universe. Therefore, mine is all this universe, or indeed nothing is Mine.*

Established as he is at this moment in Consciousness, *Janaka* declares, "I am the sole One, who illumines the body and reveals the universe." Matter by itself has no light of its own. Matter is to be illumined by some other 'source' of light. My body, mind and intellect are equipments, made up of matter. The sense-stimuli received by the mind are again inert matter. If the Consciousness were not in me, who else would have illumined this panorama of the subject-object-world?

It is in the Light of the Consciousness that all *perceptions* of the sense-organs, all the *emotions* of the mind, and all the *thoughts* of the intellect become our experiences. If this Principle of Consciousness were not in the universe, there would have been no 'knowledge'—everything would have been an empty void, a barren stretch of non-existence.

With his new-found-wisdom, the royal saint *Janaka* looks around, and concludes that everything of the subjective and the objective worlds are illumined by Himself, the Consciousness. Thus, from the relative stand-point meaning, accepting the delusion of pluralistic phenomenal world—*Janaka* thunders that He, the Self, is the One that illumines the entire plurality.

Immediately, he gets himself uplifted into the Sanctum of the Self, and from this Absolute-stand-point, He roars : "Or, Indeed, nothing is Mine"—viewed from the non-dual Self there are no worlds of multiplicity, and therefore, "nothing is mine."

The Self as Consciousness (*Cit*) illumines the plurality; and as existence (*Sat*) is the very substratum for the entire universe.

सशरीरमहो विश्वं परित्यज्य मयाऽधुना ।
कुतश्चित् कौशलादेव परमात्मा विलोक्यते ॥ ३ ॥

Saśarīram-aho viśvaṁ parityajya mayā'dhunā,
kutaścit kauśalā-deva paramātmā vilokyate.

सशरीरम् *saśarīram* = with the body; अहो *aho* = O!; विश्वम् *viśvam* = universe; परित्यज्य *parityajya* = abandon; मया *mayā* = by me; अधुना *adhunā* = now; कुतश्चित् *kutaścit* = through some; कौशलात् *kauśalāt* = skill (dexterity); एव *eva* = only; परमात्मा *paramātmā* = Supreme Self; विलोक्यते *vilokyate* = is apprehended.

3. *O! Having abandoned the universe together with the body, I now perceive the Supreme Self through the dexterity of some teacher.*

If, in the above two verses, the spirit of wonderment was only whispered between the lines, from here onwards we hear clear open exclamations of amazement directly spelt out (*Aho*).

As an ego we are constantly aware of our equipments, the body, and their perceptions, together called as the universe. On transcending the equipments, the fields of experiences are also transcended. Thus "having abandoned the universe together with the body" the student reaches not an empty void, but comes to live the dynamics of the Whole—the Self. *Janaka* confesses in this verse : "I now perceive the Supreme Self."

Here the term "perceive" should not be understood as experience of something different from himself. There is no duality as experiencer and the experienced, when one awakes into the Non-dual *Brahman*. Yet, the term 'vision' (*Darśana*) is often employed to emphasize the idea that afterwards there cannot be, to the individualised ego, any traces of doubts regarding the Self. "To see" is to believe; the direct apprehension is an unquestionable authority in itself.

How then in this 'vision' accomplished by the student? Is it because of the teacher? Is it because of the study? Is it the result of his devotion? Is it accomplished through service?... How did he manage to gain this unique experience?

According to the *Vedāntik* thinkers, the Self cannot be the 'effect' of anything, the 'result' of any special endeavour undertaken. It is not produced because of *Sādhanā*. The Self is;

it ever exists, same as ever-before. It is not caused by anything, in as much as whatever is caused, that necessarily undergoes a change, and that which is changeable is ever perishable. The Imperishable Infinite is ever-present.

Then, does it mean that all spiritual practices are of no avail? Is religion a belief? Are the different *Yogā*-s mere deceptions?... No. All of them are necessary in order to de-hypnotise our agitated mind and riotous intellect. When the thought-process slows down and stops, the mind-intellect is transcended. Then the ego ceases. Where the illusion of ego is lifted, the Reality is revealed. When the illusion of the *serpent* has ended, the *rope* is seen remaining the same as ever before.

In this verse, therefore, *Janaka* in supreme honesty tries to explain that he has arrived at this marvellous Self-Realisation by the mysterious power, so far unknown, risen out of the cumulative effect of all his studies and all his practices, and he owes his gratitude to all the Masters of the *Upaniṣad*-s and all the teachers he had served in his life. Hence, the student here declares : "through the dexterity of some teacher," he has attained to the Self.

The student cannot point out who his teacher is; nor can he honestly pin-point by what exact practice has he arrived at the gates of Truth and exploded himself into Its presence. The entire universe with all its happenings, together is a university educating the ego to grow and evolve to the ultimate realisation of its essential Reality. How then can any man of wisdom claim any particular teacher as his sole guide, or any particular path as his only way? Lost in wonderment, the student can only declare that he has come to his Realisation, in himself, by the dexterity of *some* Master.

यथा न तोयतो भिन्नास्तरङ्गाः फेनबुद्बुदाः ।
आत्मनो न तथा भिन्नं विश्वमात्मविनिर्गतम् ॥ ४ ॥

Yathā na toyato bhinnās-taraṅgāḥ fena-bud-budāḥ,
ātmano na tathā bhinnaṁ viśva-mātma-vinir-gatam.

यथा *yathā* = as; न *na* = not; तोयत: *toyataḥ* = from water; भिन्ना: *bhinnāḥ* = different; तरङ्गा: *taraṅgāḥ* = waves; फेन-बुद्‌बुदा: *fena-bud-budāḥ* = foam and bubbles; आत्मन: *ātmanaḥ* = from the Self; न *na* = not; तथा *tathā* = similarly; भिन्नम् *bhinnam* = different; विश्वम् *viśvam* = universe; आत्म विनिर्गतम् *ātma-vinirgatam* = streaming out from the Self.

4. *As waves, foam and bubbles are not different from the waters, so the universe, streaming forth from the Self, is not different from the Self.*

In this stupendous experience of the Infinite Consciousness where does the world-of-matter and energy stand? *Janaka* explains here that they have all become one-with-the-Infinite Consciousness. But how?....Is this rational to say so? How are we to understand this declarations? *Janaka* employs an analogy, to help us intellectually to evaluate the spiritual experience, which is always trans-intellect. The material-cause is that from which the effects arise, and the effects so risen can never be anything different from the cause. The waves, foam, bubbles etc., risen from the waters, can never be anything other than water itself.

An effect is nothing other than its own cause in another form. The universe that has stemmed out from the Self, is also nothing different from It. At the moment of wisdom, when the Self is realised, on gaining the Vision of the Self, the disturbing plurality of the universe ceases to be. In the understanding that the ocean is an immeasurable mass of water, the crowd of waves, foams and bubbles no longer disturb and distract, although they may exist and play about on the surface of the ocean. The universe is nothing but the Self, and is never in any way different from It.

तन्तुमात्रो भवेदेव पटो यद्वद्विचारितः ।
आत्मतन्मात्रमेवेदं तद्वद्विश्वं विचारितम् ॥ ५ ॥

Tantu-mātro bhave-deva paṭo yadvad-vicāritaḥ,
ātma-tanmātra-mevedaṁ tadvad-viśvaṁ vicāritam.

तन्तु-मात्रः *tantu-mātraḥ* = thread only; भवेत् *bhavet* = is; एव *eva* = certainly; पटः *paṭaḥ* = cloth; यद्वत् *yadvat* = as; विचारितः *vicāritaḥ* = analysed; आत्म-तन्मात्रम् *ātma-tanmātram* = nothing but the Self; एव *eva* = certainly; इदम् *idam* = this; तद्वत् *tadvat* = even so; विश्वम् *viśvam* = universe; विचारितम् *vicāritam* = examined carefully.

5. *Just as cloth, when analysed, becomes nothing but thread, even so this universe, when examined carefully is found to be nothing but the Self.*

The unique visions of the mystic sages are not readily comprehensible to the seekers in their early stages of study and practice. And this is as it should be. The vision of the Masters is the intuitive apprehension of the Reality, when they transcend their intellects. But the student is rooted in his body-consciousness and is trying to comprehend the Reality with his intellect. Necessarily the intellectual faculties of logic and reason must stand aghast at the daring words of the mystic apprehension.

Yet, the function of the scriptures is to help the student to conceive and understand the Reality as clearly as it is possible for the rational comprehension of man. This communication is accomplished by the scriptural Masters of the world all over, through the use of effective examples and eloquent analogies, boistrous mataphors, and expressive similies.

Aṣṭāvakra here employs a familiar example of the *Upaniṣad-s*.

Ordinarily, in our day-to-day transactions, we use cloth and view it from its utility stand-point. But a little thoughtful examination can easily reveal that what we consider as cloth is nothing but threads woven together. Yet, if you go to a trader in textile goods, and demand a pound of thread, how few of them would really cut a piece of cloth to the weight of one pound! Every shopkeeper would declare that he has no thread for sale! In the vision of the cloth, the existence of the thread is not generally recognised. To see the thread, a little discriminative thinking is necessary.

In our day-to-day life, we are jostled about by the moment to moment happenings around us, and in the laughter and tears of living through them, we take the world-of-plurality (*Viśvam*) for its face-value. Here the *Ācārya* reminds the student that with a little discrimination, world can be discovered as nothing but the Consciousness, the Self. "A stress in Consciousness" is a thought. "A continuous stream of thoughts maintained in our bosom" provides us with a delusory expression of the mighty and the powerful *mind.* Through the mind we see the world of names and forms projected upon the consciousness. Thus the perceived objects and the perceiving equipments are all 'stresses' in Consciousness. When this illusion-creating, delusion-breeding 'stresses' are relinquished, through deep meditation, the thoughts cease; the mind is lifted; and the hallucination of the universe rolls-away.

With a little scientific thought the essential Reality of the Universe can be detected as the Pure Consciousness only.

यथैवेक्षुरसे क्लृप्ता तेन व्याप्तैव शर्करा ।
तथा विश्वं मयि क्लृप्तं मया व्याप्तं निरन्तरम् ॥ ६ ॥

Yathai-vekṣur-ase klṛptā tena vyāptaiva śarkarā,
tathā viśvaṁ mayi klṛptaṁ mayā vyāptaṁ nirantaram.

यथा *yathā* = as; एव *eva* = just; इक्षुरसे *ikṣurase* = in the juice of the sugar-cane; क्लृप्ता *klṛptā* = produced; तेन *tena* = with that (juice); व्याप्ता *vyāptā* = pervaded; एव *eva* = entirely; शर्करा *śarkarā* = sugar; तथा *tathā* = so; विश्वम् *viśvam* = the universe; मयि *mayi* = in Me; क्लृप्तम् *klṛptam* = produced; मया *mayā* = by me; व्याप्तम् *vyāptam* = permeated; निरन्तरम् *nirantaram* = within and without.

6. *Just as sugar made from the sugar-cane-juice is entirely pervaded by that juice, so the universe, produced in Me, is permeated by Me, both within and without.*

When an example is used as an analogy, teachers are compelled to draw a picture from the finite world which is familiar to the student; and the Infinite can never be fully explained by the finite! Thus, an analogy can help to explain to us only some one aspect of truth; very often the same analogy may give us a false impression of Truth, in some other aspects.

In the example of the cloth, no doubt, it is made up of the thread; apart from the thread there is no existence for the cloth. But in a woven cloth there should be microscopic spaces interlacing the woven threads that form its warp and woof. The example given in the above verse, may thus lead the student into a misconception that the Consciousness exists in the things and beings of the universe, with lots of inter-spaces! This would contradict the All-Pervasiveness of the Self. Hence to re-inforce the previous example, the teacher doles out yet another analogy, in this verse, supplementing the understanding derived from the previous.

Sugar is made out of the sugar-can-juice, and the juice pervades every part of the sugar so crystallised. A sugar-crystal is homogeneous with the sweetness of the juice. "Similarly," indicates *Janaka* : "I, as the Self, pervade, inside and outside the universe, that has crystallised in Me."

All the above three verses, through different analogies lift the student's understanding to comprehend that the world-of-plurality is nothing but Consciousness Infinite in an apparent state of disturbance. In reality the world is nothing but the Self alone.

Then, why this experience of the universe? What makes the world appear? Who creates it? Thus many similar questions are natural in the bosom of a seeker in the early stages of his study. They are answered in the following verse :

आत्माऽज्ञानाज्जगद्भाति आत्मज्ञानान्न भासते ।
रज्ज्वज्ञानादहिर्भाति तज्ज्ञानाद्भासते न हि ॥ ७ ॥

Ātmā'jñānāt-jagat-bhāti ātma-jñānāt-na bhāsate,
rajjva-jñānāt-ahir-bhāti taj-jñānād-bhāsate na hi.

आत्मा अज्ञानात् *ātmā-ajñānāt* = from the 'ignorance' of the Self; जगत् *jagat* = the universe; भाति *bhāti* = appears; आत्मज्ञानात् *ātma-jñānāt* = from the 'knowledge' of the Self; न *na* = not; भासते *bhāsate* = appears; रज्जु अज्ञानात् *rajju-ajñānāt* = from the non-apprehension of the rope; अहिः *ahiḥ* = serpent; भाति *bhāti* = appears; तत्-ज्ञानात् *tat-jñānāt* = from the apprehension of that; भासते *bhāsate* = appears; न *na* = not; हि *hi* = indeed.

7. *The universe appears from the 'ignorance' of the Self, and disappears with a 'knowledge' of the Self, just as the serpent, indeed, appears from the 'non-apprehension' of the rope and disappears with its 'apprehension.'*

Supplying the student with an explanation on, why the creation of an illusory world-of-plurality, and how this creation is maintained, we have here the oft-quoted *Vedāntik* example of the rope and the serpent. When the substratum, the rope, is not cognised, in this 'non-apprehension' (*ignorance*) of the rope, the restless mind imagines various 'misapprehensions.' When the intellect is veiled, the mind projects. Then the illusion is sustained by the fanciful imagination of the mind. Thereafter follows all the confusions and sorrows. When the substratum, the rope, is 'apprehended', the 'non-apprehension' of the rope is ended; naturally, therefore, all 'mis-apprehensions' also end.

In our 'ignorance' of the Self, the experiencer-experienced-universe (*Jagat*) manifests to supply the confusions and sorrows in the experiencing-ego. When the miserable ego rediscovers itself to be nothing other than the Pure Self, the plurality merges to disappear into the One, Non-dual Reality.

That *Janaka* here is employing the *Upaniṣadik* example, need not necessarily be a mere slavish repetition. The royal saint in the king *Janaka*, on realising the Self, has now the same experience as the saints of the *Upaniṣad*-s had in their mysic moments of their Spiritual Realisation. Therefore, there can certainly be a similarity of expression.

In that case what exactly is My nature as Self? At this moment I have an identity—a location in space, an expression in time. But once this ego in me has ended, it would be the total destruction of my individuality. And, thereafter, how do I survive? What would be My nature?.... These questions are answered by *Janaka*, in the following verse, by defining his own spiritual Nature as he directly experiences.

प्रकाशो मे निजं रूपं नातिरिक्तोऽस्म्यहं ततः ।
यदा प्रकाशते विश्वं तदाऽहंभास एव हि ॥ ८ ॥

Prakāśo me nijaṁ rūpaṁ nātirikto'smyahaṁ tataḥ,
yadā prakāśate viśvaṁ tadā-'haṁ-bhāsa eva hi.

प्रकाश: *prakāśaḥ* = light; मे *me* = my; निजम् *nijam* = own; रूपम् *rūpam* = nature; न *na* = not; अतिरिक्त: *atiriktaḥ* = different; अस्मि *asmi* = am; अहम् *aham* = I; तत: *tataḥ* = from that; यदा *yadā* = when; प्रकाशते *prakāśate* = manifests; विश्वम् *viśvam* = universe; तदा *tadā* = then; अहम् *aham* = I; भास *bhāsa* = shine; एव *eva* = alone; हि *hi* = indeed.

8. *Light is my very nature; I am nothing other than that Light. When the universe manifests, indeed, it is I alone who shine.*

The life, as Consciousness, brings to our awareness all our experiences, physical, mental and intellectual. In this sense of the term, the *Upaniṣad-s* very often indicate the Self as 'Light' (*Caitanya*). This example is very often taken by the student too literally and in their over zealous enthusiasm they start imagining in their meditation that they had *seen* the Truth as a dazzling "mass-of-light." *Hindū* teachers, while teaching us the *Upaniṣad*-s, take special pains to remind us that the term 'Light' as used here is not "light" as we experience in the world outside. What we experience can only be an "*object*," not the "*subject*." *Śrī Rāmakṛṣṇa Paramahaṁsa* had once defined the Reality as "Light without its properties." In *Vedānta* the Self is considered as Light because of its essential expression, in all living beings, as Consciousness.

When the ego is ended, the seeker rediscovers himself to be the Light of Consciousness that illuminates both the *subject,* and its world-of-*objects*—the experiencing-ego, and the entire field of its experiences.

Janaka from his own inward experience of this transcendental Self identifies himself with the Infinite Consciousness and declares : "Light is my very nature; I am nothing other than that light." This 'light'-nature is inexpressible for the human intellect, and when this Consciousness is viewed through our disturbing equipments of the body, mind and intellect, it is visualised as the world of objects, emotions and thoughts.

In a Cinema-theatre, inside the machine-room, is the white arc-light which is spread on the entire area of the screen, facing the audience. But when the film passes in front of the arc-light within the machine-room, the audience observes the world of names and forms, and their movements, revealing the theme of the story. In the same way, the Consciousness within is viewing the Consciousness which is the substratum of the whole universe, through our equipments, and, therefore, the world-picture is perceived.

In short, the universe is nothing but a projection of the Effulgent Self. We are irresistibly reminded of a similar assertion in the *Bhagavad-Gītā* (XIII-33):

> यथा प्रकाशयत्येकः कृत्स्नं लोकमिमं रविः ।
> क्षेत्रं क्षेत्री तथा कृत्स्नं प्रकाशयति भारत ॥

> *Yathā prakāśayaty-ekaḥ kṛtsnaṁ lokam-imaṁ raviḥ,*
> *kṣetraṁ kṣetrī tathā kṛtsnaṁ prakāśayati bhārata.*

> "Just as the one Sun illumines the whole world, so also the Lord of the Field (*Paramātmā*) illumines the whole field, O *Bhārata.*"

Upaniṣadik Ṛṣī-s also are insisting that all that exists, shines, and rejoices are all variegated expressions of the One, Existence-

Knowledge-Bliss: *Saccidānanda*-Reality. The awareness of the universe is itself a play of the Awareness.

अहो विकल्पितं विश्वमज्ञानान्मयि भासते ।
रूप्यं शुक्तौ फणी रज्जौ वारि सूर्यकरे यथा ॥ ९ ॥

Aho vikalpitaṁ viśvam-ajñānān-mayi bhāsate,
rūpyaṁ śuktau phaṇī rajjau vāri sūryakare yathā.

अहो *Aho* = O! Marvellous! विकल्पितम् *vikalpitam* = misapprehended; विश्वम् *viśvam* = the universe; अज्ञानात् *ajñānāt* = through ignorance; मयि *mayi* = in Me; भासते *bhāsate* = appears; रूप्यम् *rūpyam* = silver; शुक्तौ *śuktau* = in the mother-of-pearl; फणी *phaṇī* = snake; रज्जौ *rajjau* = in the rope; वारि *vāri* = water (so); सूर्यकरे *sūryakare* = in the sun-light; यथा *yathā* = as.

9. *O! Marvellous! The universe appears in Me, misapprehended through 'ignorance'—just as silver in the mother-of-pearl, snake in the rope, and water in the sun-light.*

In all the immediately preceeding five verses we have been provided with as many as five different examples to prove, or to indicate, that the Self is the cause for the universe and as such it pervades every thing and being. If a pot is made out of mud, certainly the mud pervades the pot. But this is possible only because the mud can undergo modifications.

The Changeless Infinite knows no modifications, and therefore, even to assume that the world-of-plurality is an effect of the Supreme—the Cause, is to accept the idea that in the Supreme a change had occured. That which is changeable, is perishable. Thus, if we accept this assumption, the entire philosophy would crash into a jumble of twisted contradictions and logical absurdities!!!

Janaka, here supplies us, in this verse, with another three famous examples of *Vedānta*, to indicate that the universe of names-and-forms is itself only an apparent illusion projected by the mind of the observer. Illusion cannot affect the substratum. They appear to exist only when the substratum is not directly perceived. With the *apprehension* of the Reality, the *mis-apprehensions* cease to be.

As the silvery shine in a sea-shell, or the vision of the snake on a rope, or as mirage-waters, so too the universe is apparently perceived upon Me, the Self. In my ignorance of the nature of the Self, I imagine and project the universe, and with the discovery of the Self—with the Realisation that I am the Self—all illusions end.

मत्तो विनिर्गतं विश्वं मय्येव लयमेष्यति ।
मृदि कुम्भो जले वीचिः कनके कटकं यथा ॥ १० ॥

Matto vinirgataṁ viśvaṁ mayyeva layam-eṣyati
mṛdi kumbho jale vīciḥ kanake kaṭakaṁ yathā.

मत्तः *mattaḥ* = from Me; विनिर्गतम् *vinirgatam* = had streamed forth; विश्वम् *viśvam* = the universe; मयि *mayi* = in Me; एव *eva* = surely; लयम् *layam* = dissolution; एष्यति *eṣyati* = will attain; मृदि *mṛdi* = clay; कुम्भः *kumbhaḥ* = pot; जले *jale* = in water; वीचिः *vīciḥ* = wave; कनके *kanake* = in gold (dissolves); कटकम् *kaṭakam* = bangles; यथा *yathā* = just as.

10. Just as the pot dissolves into clay, the wave into water, or the bangle into gold, so the universe which has streamed forth from Me will attain dissolution in Me.

When the *ghost* appears, or when the *ghost* disappears, it cannot be said that the illusory *ghost* had reached the *post* from any distant definite point in space, nor that the *ghost* has gone to any destination in space. It is a delusion, and as such it exists only in the imagination of the observer. In fact, the *ghost*-vision that apparently rose in the *post* must be considered as having dissolved back again into the very same *post*.

Janaka, numbed with his own sense of wonderment, continues to verbalise what has happened to him, and how his vision of the universe has ended. Just as the effect merges back into its cause, similarly the illusion of the subject-object-world has, in him, re-entered to become one with the Self.

अहो अहं नमो मह्यं विनाशो यस्य नास्ति मे ।
ब्रह्मादिस्तम्बपर्यन्तं जगन्नाशेऽपि तिष्ठतः ॥ ११ ॥

Aho ahaṁ namo mahyaṁ vināśo yasya nāsti me,
brahmādi-stamba-paryantaṁ jagan-nāśe-'pi tiṣṭhataḥ.

अहो *aho* = O! Marvellous! अहम् *aham* = I; नमः *namaḥ* = adoration; मह्यम् *mahyam* = to Me; विनाशः *vināśaḥ* = destruction; यस्य *yasya* = whose; न *na* = not; अस्ति *asti* = is; मे *me* = My; ब्रह्मादि-स्तम्ब-पर्यन्तम् *brahmādi-stamba-paryantam* = from the Creator down to a grass-blade; जगत्-नाशे *jagat-nāśe* = when there is destruction of the universe; अपि *api* = even; तिष्ठतः *tiṣṭhataḥ* = existing.

11. *Marvellous am I! Adoration to Myself who know no decay and survive even the destruction of the universe, from the Creator (*Brahmā*) down to a blade of grass.*

From this point starts a set of four verses each an explosive exclamation over the-new-found glory and divinity of the Essential Self, which is the One-Universal-Reality that supports the entire flux of matter in the medium of time and space.

Wonder of wonders! "Marvellous am I! To me all adorations! (अहो अहं नमो मह्यम् । *Aho ahaṁ namo mahyam*). This seems to be the chorus running all through the set of four verses here. With the Realisation of the Self, It is recognised as something not merely fantastic, but also as something divine and beautiful that demands one's own reverence and adoration.

The Absolute Self knows no decay. It serves as the substratum, upon which the Creator and the created come, play and disappear. The Supreme ever remains just as It is—unaffected by the illusory play of the cosmos upon Its serene tranquillity.

"This Infinite Self am I," is the realisation. Therefore, in these verses when *Janaka* uses the first-person singular pronoun, he is identifying himself with the Supreme *Brahman*; the *Upaniṣad-s* are never tired of asserting :

ब्रह्मवेद ब्रह्मैव भवति । (*Muṇḍaka Up.* (III-ii-9)

Brahmaveda brahmaiva bhavati.

"The knower of the *Brahman* becomes *Brahman.*"

Same idea has been couched in a more beautiful style in *Varāha Upaniṣad* (II-33):

सर्वभूतान्तरस्थाय नित्यमुक्तचिदात्मने ।
प्रत्यक् चैतन्यरूपाय मह्यमेव नमोनमः ॥

Sarva-bhūtāntara-sthāya nitya-mukta-cidātmane,
pratyak caitanya-rūpāya mahyam-eva namo-namaḥ.

"I salute Me Myself who am the indweller in all beings, ever-free, intelligent Consciousness, who is the light-within, the Self."

We find this very same verse repeated in *Yoga Vāsiṣṭha.* The *Upaniṣad mantra* also says:

"Adoration for you and for me, who is Infinite; for me and for you who is Pure Intelligence."*

अहो अहं नमो मह्यमेकोऽहं देहवानपि ।
क्वचिन्न गन्ता नागन्ता व्याप्य विश्वमवस्थितः ॥ १२ ॥

* Plural subject and singular verb used here is not a grammatical mistake, but it is used with a deliberate philosophical intention. It pointedly asserts that the Adorable, Infinite, Pure Intelligence in me and in you is one and the same.

Aho ahaṁ namo mahyameko'haṁ dehavānapi,
kvacinna gantā nāgantā vyāpya viśvam-avasthitaḥ.

अहो *aho* = Marvellous; अहम् *aham* = I; नमः *namaḥ* = adoration; मह्यम् *mahyam* = to Myself; एकः *ekaḥ* = one; अहम् *aham* = I; देहवान् *dehavān*= having a body; अपि *api* = even; क्वचित् *kvacit* = anywhere; न *na* = not; गन्ता *gantā* = going; न *na* = not; आगन्ता *āgantā* = coming; व्याप्य *vyāpya* = pervading; विश्वम् *viśvam* = the universe; अवस्थितः *avasthitaḥ* = existing.

12. *Marvellous am I! Adoration to Myself, who, though with a body, am One, who neither go anywhere, nor come from anywhere but ever abide pervading the universe.*

The voiceless wonderment at the revelation of the beauty and glory of the Self continues to express itself in stammering words from *Janaka*, who is pressed down under the weight of his own direct experience.

My sense-organs, mind and intellect can go and come to different points in space and time, and this phenomena of movement was very familiar to me all through my existence as a limited-Self. On regaining the Divine State of Selfhood in Me, I have realised that all movements were in Me, and that "I neither go to nor come from anywhere." I am ever-abiding in my own Infinite Nature, pervading and penetrating the entire universe of disturbances—which take place in one insignificant part of Me!!!

अहो अहं नमो मह्यं दक्षो नास्तीह मत्समः ।
असंस्पृश्य शरीरेण येन विश्वं चिरं धृतम् ॥ १३ ॥

aho ahaṁ namo mahyaṁ dakṣo nāstīha matsamaḥ,
asaṁspṛśya śarīreṇa yena viśvaṁ ciraṁ dhṛtam.

अहो *aho* = O! Marvellous; अहम् *aham* = I; नमः *namaḥ* = salutations; मह्यम् *mahyam* = to Myself; दक्षः *dakṣaḥ* = capable, competent; न *na*

= not; अस्ति *asti* = is; इह *iha* = in this world; मत्समः *matsamaḥ* = like Me; असंस्पृश्य *asaṁspṛśya* = without touching; शरीरेण *śarīreṇa* = with the body; येन *yena* = by whom; विश्वम् *viśvam* = universe; चिरम् *ciraṁ* = ever; धृतम् *dṛtam* = is held.

13. *O! Marvellous am I! Salutations to Myself ! There is none so competent in this world as Me, who am holding the universe eternally without touching it with My body.*

The efficiency and competency that we see among the living creatures are all expressions of Life that enlivens the creatures; and this is the expression of the Self through the equipment, and as such the Supreme, conceived as God, is generally indicated as the Omnipotent. Here *Janaka* points out the marvellous competency in the Infinite Self to uphold this illusory universe of such dynamic possibilities, and yet, there is no actual contact between the unreal world and the real Self.

This "relationless-relationship" is the only relation between the real and unreal, between the true and the false. The *post* supports the *ghost*; yet, the *post* never touches the *ghost*! The dreamer suffers, struggles, endures, and weeps in his sorrows and tragedies; yet I, the waker, is not affected by the tragedies of the dreamer in me.

When we reflect upon this unique relationship, our reverence for the Self increases. The equipments of experience project their fields of experiences and create for themselves a world of joy and sorrow, success and failure, birth and death; and in the midst of it all, unaffected by them, stands the Self. This Self am I; the world-play derives its existence from Me, the Self. Indeed, I am the most worshipful, the eminently adorable factor in existence.

अहो अहं नमो मह्यं यस्य मे नास्ति किञ्चन ।
अथवा यस्य मे सर्वं यद्वाङ्मनसगोचरम् ॥ १४ ॥

Aho ahaṁ namo mahyaṁ yasya me nāsti kiñcana,
athavā yasya me sarvaṁ yadvāṅ-manasa-gocaram.

अहो *aho* = O! Marvellous, अहम् *aham* = I; नमः *namaḥ* = salutations; मह्यम् *mahyam* = to Myself; यस्य *yasya* = whose; मे *me* = My; न *na* = not; अस्ति *asti* = is; किञ्चन *kiñcana* = anything; अथवा *athavā* = or; यस्य *yasya* = whose; मे *me* = My (to that); सर्वम् *sarvam* = all; यत् *yat* = which; वाङ् मनस-गोचरम् *vāṅ manasa-gocaram* = is accessible to speech and mind (that).

14. *O! Marvellous am I! Prostrations to Myself who have nothing—or all, that which is accessible to speech and mind, belongs to Me only.*

This is the concluding verse of "Hymn to the Self," the spontaneous offering of Self-prostrations. The Self is the substratum and as such it can claim that everything in the universe belongs to It. Or, it can, in Its perfect understanding of the illusoriness of the world-of-plurality realise that nothing belongs to It. Identifying with this Self, the man-of-realisation in the Royal-saint, declares in the language of a pleasant paradox: "All belongs to Me, or I have nothing."

The same idea was expressed by *Janaka* earlier in this chapter when he said, "Mine is all this universe; or, indeed nothing is mine." When *Janaka* says "all that is accessible to speech and mind" (*Vaṅ-manasa-gocaram*), it includes all that can be defined or felt. That means everything. For wealth of suggestiveness, no language can stand equal to the *Saṁskṛta* idioms.

ज्ञानं ज्ञेयं तथा ज्ञाता त्रितयं नास्ति वास्तवम् ।
अज्ञानाद्भाति यत्रेदं सोऽहमस्मि निरञ्जनः ॥ १५ ॥

Jñānaṁ jñeyaṁ tathā jñātā tritayaṁ nāsti vāstavam,
ajñānād-bhāti yatredaṁ so'ham asmi nirañjanaḥ.

ज्ञानम् *jñānam* = knowledge; ज्ञेयम् *jñeyam* = knowable; तथा *tathā* = as well as; ज्ञाता *jñātā* = knower; त्रितयम् *tritayam* = the triad; न *na* = not;

अस्ति *asti* = is; वास्तवम् *vāstavam* = in fact; अज्ञानात् *ajñānāt* = through 'ignorance'; भाति *bhāti* = appears to exist; यत्र *yatra* = where; इदम् *idam* = this (triad); सः *saḥ* = that; अहम् *aham* = I; अस्मि *asmi* = am; निरञ्जनः *nirañjanaḥ* = taintless.

15. *The 'knowledge,' the 'knowable' and the 'knower'— these triple categories do not in fact exist. I am that taintless Self, in which, through 'ignorance,' this triad appears to exist.*

In the relative field of multiplicity, every experience rises up, due to the play of three factors— the *experiencer*, the *experienced*, and the *experiencing*. Without these three entities "I, the knower," the "thing known," and the "knowledge of the thing"—no perception is possible at any of the equipments of experience.

When the ego, the "experiencer" is transcended to become the Pure Self, in the Infinite expanse of the Pure Consciousness, there is no more the play of this traid. In the Taintless Self these triple categories appear to exist due to the 'ignorance' of the nature of the Self. They are the illusions of the mind when the true-knowledge does not illumine it. When the seeker realises "I am the Stainless Self", the misconceptions roll away.

When we are dreaming, the dream is sustained by the play of the dreamer, the dream world-of-objects and the dream-experiences. When the dreamer wakes up, the triple-factors that maintained the dream, all merge back to become the one mind of the waker. The waking-mind projects itself as the dreamer, as his world-of-objects, and as the knowledge of his own experiences, joyful or sad, pleasant or terrible, horrible or peaceful. So long as these triple-factors were maintained, the illusion of the dream was sustained. On waking up, the dream merges into the waking-mind, from which it had apparently got projected. From the plane-of-ego-Consciousness, when the seeker wakes up to the plane-of-God-Consciousness, in the vivid and direct realisation that "I am the Self," the ego, its world and its sorrows merge back to become the One, Pure, Infinite Consciousness.

In *Yoga-Vāsiṣṭha* (81-9) we read :

मृतं चित्तं गता तृष्णा प्रक्षीणो मोहपंजरः ।
निरहंकारता जाता जाग्रत्यस्मिन् प्रबुद्धवान् ॥

Mṛtaṁ cittaṁ gatā tṛṣṇā prakṣīṇo moha-paṁjaraḥ,
nir-ahaṁkāratā jātā jāgraty-asmin prabuddhavān.

"Mind dead, desires gone, freed from the cage of delusion, released from all ego-sense, the Enlightened One wakes up into It."

This supreme state of Oneness, where the vision is not clouded by any disturbing factor is thundered by *Śrī Avadhūta Dattātreya* in his *Avadhūta Gītā (III-41)*.:

ध्याता न ते हि हृदये न च ते समाधिः
ध्यानं न ते हि हृदये न बहिः प्रदेशः ।
ध्येयं न चेति हृदये न हि वस्तुकालो
ज्ञानामृतं समरसं गगनोपमोऽहम् ॥

Dhyātā na te hi hṛdaye na ca te samādhiḥ
dhyānaṁ na te hi hṛdaye na bahiḥ pradeśaḥ,
dhyeyaṁ na ceti hṛdaye na hi vastukālo
jñānā-mṛtaṁ sama-rasaṁ gagan-opamo'ham.

"In the Supreme Infinitude of the Self,
No meditator—
Indeed, in your heart, there is no *Samādhi*,
No meditation—
In your heart no space outside;
No point of meditation—
In your heart no time or object.
That I am—
The Blissful Immortal Self,
Evenness of feeling—ever,

Like unto the sky—
Untouched, Unbound!!"

Such mystic realms of experiences are beyond the comprehension of finite intellect. Hence the best commentary upon them is to be discovered through one's own deep meditation.

द्वैतमूलमहो दुःखं नान्यत्तस्यास्ति भेषजम् ।
दृश्यमेतन्मृषा सर्वं एकोऽहं चिद्रसोऽमलः ॥ १६ ॥

Dvaita-mūlam-aho duḥkham nānyat-tasyāsti bheṣajam,
dṛśyam-etan-mṛṣā sarvaṁ eko-'haṁcidraso-'malaḥ.

द्वैत-मूलम् *dvaita-mūlam* = having duality as root; अहो *aho* = O! दुःखम् *duḥkham* = misery; न *na* = not; अन्यत् *anyat* = other; तस्य *tasya* = of that (misery); अस्ति *asti* = is; भेषजम् *bheṣajam* = remedy; दृश्यम् *dṛśyam* = visible objects; एतत् *etat* = this; मृषा *mṛṣā* = unreal; सर्वम् *sarvam* = all; एकः *ekaḥ* = non-dual; अहम् *aham* = I; चित् *cit* = Consciousness; रसः *rasaḥ* = Bliss; अमलः *amalaḥ* = Pure, Undefiled (am I).

16. *O! The root of all misery is the sense of duality. There is no other remedy for this (misery) except the realisation that all visible objects-of-experiences are unreal, and that I am the Non-dual, Pure, Consciousness and Bliss.*

Misery, pain or sorrow, are all subjectively nothing but mental states of disturbances. The more the mental agitations, the more the sorrow. Quieter the mind, happier the man. These disturbances are caused by the mind's perceptions of the pluralistic world, both within itself and outside. All miseries stem forth from the perception of duality. With the realisation of one's own nature to be Pure Non-dual Consciousness, the world-of-plurality will be re-cognised as unreal, and therefore, it can no longer contribute any miseries to the Man-of-realisation. In fact, *Na-anyat-tasya-asti bheṣajam* : there is no other remedy for this continuous sense of sorrow and misery at the ego-plane-of-Consciousness.

बोधमात्रोऽहमज्ञानादुपाधिः कल्पितो मया ।
एवं विमृशतो नित्यं निर्विकल्पे स्थितिर्मम ॥ १७ ॥

Bodha-mātro-'ham-ajñānād-upādhiḥ kalpito mayā,
evaṁ vimṛśato nityaṁ nirvikalpe sthitir-mama.

बोध-मात्रः *bodha-mātraḥ* = Pure Consciousness (am I); अहम् *aham* = I; अज्ञानत् *ajñānāt* = through ignorance; उपाधिः *upādhiḥ* = equipments such as body; कल्पितः *kalpitaḥ* = projected (imagined); मया *mayā* = by me; एवम् *evam* = in this way; विमृशतः *vimṛśataḥ* = reflecting; नित्यम् *nityam* = constantly; निर्विकल्पे *nirvikalpe* = purged of all mental disturbances; स्थितिः *sthitiḥ* = abiding; मम *mama* = my.

17. *I am Pure Consciousness. Through 'Ignorance' I have projected my equipments, such as the body, upon the Self. Constantly reflecting thus I abide in the Self, purged of all mental activities.*

Here for the first time, we meet with the significant term '*Nir-vikalapa*' meaning "devoid of all imaginations," suggesting "the spiritual state of thoughtless-ness." This seems to be an original phrase minted in the inspired bosom of Saint *Aṣṭāvakra*. Later on, however, *Patañjali* popularised it, and *Śaṅkara* and other Masters had freely employed it. But it is significant that we meet this phrase neither in major *Upaniṣad*-s, nor even in the *Bhagavad-Gītā*.

It is only when we come to forget our waking-state-personality that the dream is ever possible. To reflect constantly that "I am the Consciousness," and to play with the equipments of experiences in the constant understanding that "they are mere illusory projections upon Me, the Self, is the secret of abiding Myself ever in the Supreme State—without any mental disturbances" (*Nir-vikalpa*). The body, mind, and intellect may be allowed to mingle with and sport among their objects, emotions and thoughts. As long as the spiritual understanding is steady, the outer world can never penetrate into the sanctum of our personality to create even a ripple of disturbance in our mind.

This state of thoughtless-ness is indicated by employing the very same 'term' (*Nir-Viklapa*) some six times in this very text-book. *Guaḍapāda's Kārikā* on *Māṇḍūkya Upaniṣad*, a later work, which apparently has drawn much of its inspiration from the Song of *Aṣṭāvakra*, has also liberally employed the term '*Nir-vikalpa*' to indicate the final Experience Divine wherein the *Subject-object*-distinction has completely ended.

न मे बन्धोऽस्ति मोक्षो वा भ्रान्तिः शान्ता निराश्रया ।
अहो मयि स्थितं विश्वं वस्तुतो न मयि स्थितम् ॥ १८ ॥

Na me bandho-'sti mokṣo vā brāntiḥ śāntā nirāśrayā,
aho mayi sthitaṁ viśvaṁ vastuto na mayi sthitam.

न *na* = not; मे *me* = My; बन्धः *bandhaḥ* = bondage; अस्ति *asti* = is; मोक्षः *mokṣaḥ* = liberation; वा *vā* = or; भ्रान्तिः *bhrāntiḥ* = illusion; शान्ता *śāntā* = has ended; निराश्रया *nirāśrayā* = without any support; अहो *aho* = O!; मयि *mayi* = in Me; स्थितम् *sthitam* = abides; विश्वम् *viśvam* = universe; वस्तुतः *vastutaḥ* = in fact; न *na* = not; मयि *mayi* = in Me; स्थितम् *sthitam* = exists.

18. *I have neither bondage nor freedom. The 'illusion,' having lost its support, has ended. O! The universe, though it abides in Me, does not in fact exist in Me.*

Early students of *Vedānta*, who live in poignant awareness of their imperfections, and are acutely sensitive to their slavishness to the incessant demands of their equipments, are told of how they can realise their freedom from all their bondage. When the student, through meditation, awakes to the Reality, in the State of Pure Consciousness, there is no meaning to the term 'freedom'; for the Self is eternally free. In a dream

I may experience that I was suffering confinement in a prison. On waking up, can I congratulate myself that I have been released? In the same way, having realised the Self, *Janaka* declares : "I have neither bondages nor freedom."

The illusory-ego has ceased to function in his bosom, because the sense of ego stems forth from the *ignorance* of the Self. How can the "ignorance" continue when the 'wisdom' of the Self has dawned?

Last night's dream, no doubt, played out itself in me, but I, the waker, is untouched by the experiences of my dreams. In the same way, *Janaka* here declares that the universe "though it abides in Me, does not in fact exist in Me." From the *relative stand-point*, when the man-of-wisdom chooses to look out through his body, mind and intellect, the world of objects, emotions and thoughts are there for his experiences; but he ever abides in the Self. When the Man-of-wisdom s in his own Pure Self, in the *absolute view-point*, there are neither the equipments of experiences nor has the fields of experiences.

सशरीरमिदं विश्वं न किञ्चिदिति निश्चितम् ।
शुद्धचिन्मात्र आत्मा च तत्कस्मिन् कल्पनाऽधुना ॥१९॥

Sa-śarīram-idaṁ viśvaṁ na kiñcid-iti niścitam,
śudha-cin-mātra ātmā ca tat-kasmin kalpanā-'dhunā.

सशरीरम् *sa-śarīram* = with the body; इदम् *idam* = this; विश्वम् *viśvam* = universe; न *na* = not; किञ्चत् *kiñcit* = anything; इति *iti* = thus; निश्चितम् *niścitam* = known for certain; शुद्धचिन् मात्रः *śudha-cin-mātraḥ* = Pure Consciousness alone; आत्मा *ātmā* = Self; च *ca* = and; तत् *tat* = so; कस्मिन् *kasmin* = upon what; कल्पना *kalpanā* = imagination (can stand); अधुना *adhunā* = now.

19. *I have known, for certain, that the body and the universe are unsubstantial, and that the Self is Pure Consciousness alone. So, now, upon what can imaginations stand?*

Having awakened to the higher plane-of-Consciousness *Janaka* realises his Oneness with the Infinite Self (*Śuddha-cinmātraḥ*). A man when he wakes up, he not only understands that he is the 'waker,' but this knowledge in him includes the total rejection of his illusory dream. Similarly, in the realisation "I am the Self," the destruction of the illusory ego and its world are inherent and included. When, thus, one has realised, in his knowledge of the rope, the total non-existence of the illusory serpent, how can he, thereafter, imagine the vicious fangs of the murderous serpent pursuing him? All imaginations are possible only when the illusory snake is consistently perceived. Similarly, when we perceive the world, an endless dream of imagination can continuously maintain the experience of a sorrow-ridden world of stormy lusts and surging passions. *Janaka* here exclaims, in his new-found wisdom and his spiritual awakening : "Upon what can imaginations stand?" The Man-of-realisation can only act—he will not be ever found to react.

शरीरं स्वर्गनरकौ बन्धमोक्षौ भयं तथा ।
कल्पनामात्रमेवैतत् किं मे कार्यं चिदात्मनः ॥ २० ॥

Sarīraṁ svarga-narakau bandha-mokṣau bhayaṁ tathā
kalpanā-mātram-eva-etat kim me kāryaṁ cidātmanaḥ.

शरीरम् *sarīram* = body; स्वर्ग-नरकौ *svarga-narakau* = heaven and hell; बन्ध-मोक्षौ *bandha-mokṣau* = bondage and freedom; भयम् *bhayam* = fear (anxiety); तथा *tathā* = as also; कल्पना-मात्रम् *kalpanā-mātram* = mere imagination; एव *eva* = surely; एतत् *etat* = all this; किम् *kim* = what; मे *me* = my (with these); कार्यम् *kāryam* = purpose; चिदात्मनः *cidātmanaḥ* = whose nature is Consciousness.

20. *Body, the notions of heaven and hell, bondage and freedom, as also anxiety—all these are mere imaginations. What purpose have I with all these—I whose nature is Pure Consciousness.*

In the previous verse, *Janaka* despaired that he finds no basis to build up a fanciful world-of-imaginations. Here in this verse he enumerates some of the common imaginations of the spiritual seekers in religion and philosophy.

The gross, the subtle and the causal bodies are all examples of our imaginations. They in their turn, feed the imaginations of their individual world of experiences and objects—the sum total of them all crystallised, is the fanciful scepture of the miserable 'ego.' None of them can survive in one, who has become the Pure Self.

In the relative field, the human mind-and-intellect, in terms of joys and sorrows, imagines states of perfect joys existing in heavens, or of impossible sorrows of a hell; he imagines that he is bound by the equipments and he strives to free himself by continuous effort; in the midst of it all he gets strangled with the anxiety for the future, smothered by fears and crushed by other emotions born out of his sense of fear.

For all these imaginations, there is no occasion in the bosom of one who is revelling in the Infinite Bliss of the Supreme Self. Therefore, the realised Saint in *Janaka* exclaims: What purpose have I with all these whiffs of imagination? None of these fanciful factors can pursue and disturb him, who has attained to the State of the Self. He is ever at rest abiding in His own Real Nature.

अहो जनसमूहेऽपि न द्वैतं पश्यतो मम ।
अरण्यमिव संवृत्तं क्व रतिं करवाण्यहम् ॥ २१ ॥

Aho jana-samūhe'pi na dvaitaṁ paśyato mama
araṇyam-iva saṁvṛttam kva ratiṁ karvāṇy-aham.

अहो *aho* = O! जन-समूहे *jana-samūhe* = in the crowds of human beings; अपि *api* = even; न *na* = not; द्वैतम् *dvaitam* = duality; पश्यत: *paśyataḥ* = seen; मम *mama* = my; अरण्यम् *araṇyam* = like a forest; इव *iva* = as if; संवृत्तम् *saṁvṛttam* = become; क्व *kva* = where; रतिम् *ratim* = spirit of attachment; करवाणि *karavāṇi* = should feel; अहम् *aham* = I.

21. *O! Marvellous! I do not find any duality even in the midst of human crowds. I feel like I am in a forest. Towards what then should I feel attachment?*

In the previous verses *Janaka* had explained how the universe of names-and-forms had rolled away from his perception and he was established in the experience of the Infinite Self. All concepts of the body, feelings of the mind and judgements of the intellect have now no place in "I, who am the Pure Consciousness."

Naturally, one may wonder what would be the reaction of the Man-of-wisdom in the social living, while he is moving amidst the jostling crowd of other members of his community? Here is the question answered by *Janaka* himself. The plurality is perceived only through the mind and intellect. When they are transcended, there is no perceiver to experience the plurality. *Janaka* living his own Real Nature, exclaims here : "O! Marvellous! I find no duality anywhere."

Even in the midst of the crowds of other human beings, viewed from the seat of Pure Consciousness, he recognises but the One Self that revels every-where. The majestic aloneness felt by a wanderer in a forest is the example *Janaka* is forced to employ here. Even in a crowd, at some busy market-place, he feels undisturbed as though he is in a deep forest, all alone.

Since he is thus experiencing only the Vision of the Self every-where, how can attachments to the worldly things ever spring forth in the bosom of such a Man-of-realisation? How can he come to sport with sense-objects? He is ever-identified with the Divine Self, and all his movements and relationships are his spontaneous play.

नाहं देहो न मे देहो जीवो नाहमहं हि चित् ।
अयमेव हि मे बन्ध आसीद् या जीविते स्पृहा ॥ २२ ॥

Nāhaṁ deho na me deho jīvo nāham-ahaṁ hi cit,
ayameva hi me bandha āsīd yā jīvite spṛhā.

न *na* = not; अहम् *aham* = I; देहः *dehaḥ* = body; न *na* = not; मे *me* = my; देहः *dehaḥ* = body; जीवः *jīvaḥ* = finite Self; न *na* = not; अहम् *aham* = I; अहम् *aham* = I; हि *hi* = indeed; चित् *cit* = intelligence; अयम् *ayam* = this; एव *eva* = alone; हि *hi* = indeed; मे *me* = my; बन्धः *bandhaḥ* = bondage; आसीत् *āsīt* = was; या *yā* = that; जीविते *jīvite* = to live; स्पृहा *spṛhā* = desire;

22. *I am not the body. Nor have I a body. I am not a being (ego). I am Pure Consciousness. That I had desired to live—this indeed was my bondage.*

Once having reached the State of God-Consciousness, the daring Man-of-Wisdom in *Janaka* is, as it were, in this verse, examining himself as he is, and comparing himself with what he was.

As he is, in the state of his Selfhood, he realises, "I am not this body." The term 'body' stands for all the three equipments-of-experiences. As All-Pervading, Infinite,Unlimited Consciousness, there cannot be any material adjuncts in the Self.

"Nor have I a body." As the Self, *Janaka* cannot now feel any sense of attachment with anything. All bodies are in Him, but no bodies are His. A similar idea has been beautifully expressed in the eloquent idiom of the *Bhagavad-Gītā* (VII-12):

न त्वहं तेषु ते मयि ।

Na tvahaṁ teṣu te mayi.

"I am not in them; they are in Me."

Bhagavān Kṛṣṇa repeats the same idea in *Bhagavad-Gītā* (IX-4):

मया ततमिदं सर्वं जगदव्यक्तमूर्तिना ।
मत्स्थानि सर्वभूतानि न चाहं तेष्ववस्थितः ॥

Mayā tata-midaṁ sarvaṁ jagad-vyakta-mūrtinā,
mat-sthāni sarva-bhūtāni na cāhaṁ teṣva-vasthitaḥ.

> "This entire world is pervaded by Me, in My unmanifested form; all beings exist in Me, but I do not dwell in them."

Since, *Janaka* feels that he is not the body, nor has he a body—meaning he is not aware of his equipments of experiences and, therefore, he cannot identify with them and develop any sense of ego (*Jīva*) in himself: "I am Pure Consciousness" (*Aham hi cit*).

If thus, I was the Pure Infinite Consciousness and I have now rediscovered my Real Nature, what was then my sense of bondage that I suffered in between?—thus enquires the royal-Saint. And he himself answers that his only bondage was that while living in his delusion, as an ego, he had a thirst for life; as an ego he desired to live the joys of the sense-gratifications. This alone was the bondage. When thus, the misconception ended, the ego has dissolved and disappeared into the vision of the Self.

अहो भुवनकल्लोलैर्विचित्रैर्द्राक् समुत्थितम् ।
मय्यनन्तमहाम्भोधौ चित्तवाते समुद्यते ॥ २३ ॥

Aho bhuvana-kallolair-vicitrair-drāk samutthitam,
mayya-nanta-mahām-bhodhau cittavāte samudyate.

अहो *aho* = O! Marvellous!; भुवन-कल्लोलैः *bhuvana-kallolaiḥ* = waves of worlds; विचित्रैः *vicitraiḥ* = diverse; द्राक् *drāk* = instantly; समुत्थितम् *samutthitam* = are produced; मयि *mayi* = in me; अनन्त-महाम्भोधौ *ananta-mahāmbhodhau* = in the limitless ocean; चित्तवाते *cittavāte* = the mental-storm; समुद्यते *samudyate* = when rises.

23. *O! Marvellous! In the limitless ocean of Me, when mental-storms rise, diverse waves of worlds are instantly produced.*

Here we have an enthralling set of three extremely lyrical verses with which the chapter ends. *Aṣṭāvakra* dandles his favourite metaphor of the ocean in these three verses. Waves rise in the ocean due to the wild winds in the atmosphere, and those waves calm themselves down to become the ocean when the whistling winds become quiet and peaceful.

Whenever the mind is quiet, as in deep sleep, there are no perceptions; the moment we wake up, the mind gets active and with the agitations of the mind, the pluralistic world rises up into our awareness.

"In the limitless ocean of Pure Consciousness which is my Real Nature," confesses *Janaka* "when mental storms stir up tumultuous agitations, mountaineous waves are created and they represent the endless variety of experiences." In short, when the mind is calm, the world-of-plurality rolls away. In reality there is nothing but the Self. The world of things-and-beings in an illusory super-imposition maintained by our mind-in-agitation.

मय्यनन्तमहाम्भोधौ चित्तवाते प्रशाम्यति ।
अभाग्याज्जीववणिजो जगत्पोतो विनश्वरः ॥ २४ ॥

Mayya-nanta-mahām-bhodhau cittavāte praśāmyati,
abhāgyāj-jīva-vaṇijo jagat-poto vinaśvaraḥ.

मयि *mayi* = in Me; अनन्त-महाम्भोधौ *ananta-mahāmbhodhau* = in the limitless ocean; चित्तवाते *cittavāte* = the storms of the mind; प्रशाम्यति *praśāmyati* = ceases; अभाग्यात् *abhāgyāt* = unfortunately; जीव-वणिजः *jīva-vaṇijaḥ* = of the *Jīva*, the trader; जगत्-पोतः *jagat-potaḥ* = the ship of the universe; विनश्वरः *vinśvaraḥ* = (gets) wrecked and sunk.

24. *With the calming of the storms of the mind, in the limitless-ocean of Myself, unfortunately for the* Jīva, *the trader, the ship of the universe gets wrecked and sunk!!*

The graceful picture of the previous verse is carried on and *Janaka* explains that when the "storms of the mind are abated, the world-of-plurality gets sunk and disappears into the ocean of the Self." Here the poetic fancy suffers a sudden hyjacking. The individualised-ego (*Jīva*) is pictured here as a trader who is crossing the seas with all his merchandise. The ego moves from port to port, transacting business in the field of worldly-experiences, gathering more and more, and growing ever more rich in his *vāsanā*-s.

When the mind is at rest, the ego, his ship, along with his collected merchandise all get sunk! What is left over is but the Shore-less Glory of the Infinite Self!!

मय्यनन्तमहाम्भोधावाश्चर्यं जीववीचयः ।
उद्यन्ति घ्नन्ति खेलन्ति प्रविशन्ति स्वभावतः ॥ २५ ॥

Mayya-nanta-mahām-bhodhāv-āścaryaṁ jīva-vīcayaḥ,
udyanti ghnanti khelanti praviśanti svabhāvataḥ.

मयि *mayi* = in Me; अनन्त-महाम्भोधौ *ananta-mahāmbhodhau* = in the limitless ocean; आश्चर्यम् *āścaryam* = Wonderful! Marvellous! जीव-वीचयः *jivā-vīcayaḥ* = the waves of individual Self; उद्यन्ति *udyanti* = rise; घ्नन्ति *ghnanti* = strike each other, jostle about; खेलन्ति *khelanti* = play; प्रविशन्ति *praviśanti* = enter (to disappear therein); स्वभावतः *svabhāvataḥ* = according to their nature.

25. *Wonderful! Marvellous! In Me, the limitless ocean, the waves of individual selves, according to their nature rise, jostle about, play for a time and disappear.*

The beauty of this lyrical verse, with which the chapter is concluding, can ring an echo for a long time in the bosom of the student even when he has shut the book and finished his studies.

It is not only the worlds that are rising in Me, the Consciousness but all other living creatures are also born from the same Self in Me. In our dreams we all experience the same; and on waking up, all the creations of the dreaming-mind get merged with our waking mind.

Just as in a dream, the individuals rise, fight their competitive existence, play their sensuous games and in the end each die away in the world—only to be born again, as another wave! When my mind is at rest, all names-and-forms must necessarily disappear into the Pure Consciousness, the Self.

Chapter—III

Self in All—All in Self

Introduction

The *Upaniṣadik* declaration '*Brahman* am I' is the ultimate Truth. Established in this Non-dual Self, man comes to experience that the phenomenal world around him is a meaningless empty illusion. The fear of death, the pangs of attachment, the fatigue of greed and the tantrum of passions—all these end with Self-realisation. The Self glows through him in his life flooding all around Its glory and beauty.

In this chapter *Aṣṭāvakra*, in a teasing tone, redicules the royal king *Janaka*'s apparent involvement in the functions of his throne, inspite of his Self-realisation. On transcending the mind, if the Self is realised, and the universe of names-and-forms has rolled away, where is the occasion for such a realised-saint to continue the outer duties of the world? The pomp and show of life, the passions and excitements of the court, the worries of conducting the state's administration and responsibilities of maintaining law and order—these are unavoidable for a king. From the Self when viewed, the world is merely an illusion. Therefore, to involve oneself in them should be considered as a sign of one's own spiritual 'ignorance.'

In this line of argument, *Aṣṭāvakra* tests the depth of realisation in his student. In the following chapter, we shall hear *Janaka*'s spirited answers to all the points raised by his teacher in his impeachment of the royal saint of *Videha*. These two chapters together read an exciting dialogue, extremely enlightening to the students of *Advaita*.

The taunting words of the Master are tipped with sharp ridicule, and they should really wound the student's vanity, if he is not already fully established in the Pure Immutable Self!

अष्टावक्र उवाच ।

अविनाशिनमात्मानमेकं विज्ञाय तत्त्वतः ।
तवात्मज्ञस्य धीरस्य कथमर्थार्जने रतिः ॥ १ ॥

Aṣṭāvakra Uvāca :

Avināśinam-ātmānam-ekaṁ vijñāya tattvataḥ
tavātma-jñasya dhīrasya katham-arthārjane ratiḥ.

अविनाशिनम् *avināśinam* = indestructible; आत्मानम् *ātmānam* = Self; एकम् *ekam* = one; विज्ञाय *vijñāya* = having known; तत्त्वतः *tattvataḥ* = in its true nature; तव *tava* = your; आत्मज्ञस्य *ātmajñasya* = knower of the Self; धीरस्य *dhīrasya* = poised-in-wisdom; कथम् *katham* = how; अर्थार्जने *arthārjane* = in the accumulation of wealth; रतिः *ratiḥ* = attachment.

Aṣṭāvakra Said :

1. *Having known the Self in its true nature as Indestructible and One, how is it that you, a knower of the Self and One poised-in-wisdom, feel passion for the accumulation of wealth?*

The Self-realised Saint *Janaka* continued to administer his Kingdom all through his life. *Aṣṭāvakra* is, in these taunting verses, ridiculing the apparent contradiction in *Janaka*'s claimed inner-vision and demonstrated outer-actions. Having realised the Self, as the One Indestructible Supreme Truth, how can he still continue the vigorous activity of the world outside, acquiring and spending wealth, and living the political and social responsibilities of a righteous ruler?

आत्माज्ञानादहो प्रीतिर्विषयभ्रमगोचरे ।
शुक्तेरज्ञानतो लोभो यथा रजतविभ्रमे ॥ २ ॥

Ātmā-jñānā-daho-prītir-viśaya-bhrama-gocare,
śukter-ajñānato lobho yathā rajata-vibhrame.

आत्म-अज्ञानात् *ātma-ajñānāt* = from 'ignorance' of the Self; अहो *aho* = alas; प्रीतिः *prītiḥ* = attachment; विषय-भ्रम-गोचरे *viśaya-bhrama-gocare* = in the illusory world of the senses; शुक्तेः *śukteḥ* = of the mother-of-pearl; अज्ञानतः *ajñānataḥ* = from ignorance; लोभः *lobhaḥ* = greed; यथा *yathā* = as; रजत-विभ्रमे *rajata-vibhrame* = due to illusion of silver.

2. *Alas! Just as, due to ignorance, a sea-shell is sought, mistaking it for silver, even so, due to the 'ignorance' of the Self, there is attachment to the illusory world-of the-senses.*

Amplifying the previous verse *Aṣṭāvakra* here explains that only in the 'ignorance' of the Self can the deluded-ego get fascinated by the enchanting world of illusory sense-objects. If *Janaka* is a Man-of-realisation, there should not have been in him any fascination for the world-of-sense-objects. He claims that he is man-of-Self-realisation. Yet, as a king, he pursues wealth. Is not wordly activities and service of the society contradictory to the State of Self-realisation? Only in the *non-apprehension* of the sea-shell can one *apprehend* a silvery-shine, and stoop to pick it up!

To taunt *Janaka*, *Aṣṭāvakra* is pointing out that the king's attachment to the throne and its power are all eloquent symptoms of his spiritual 'ignorance'!

विश्वं स्फुरति यत्रेदं तरङ्गा इव सागरे ।
सोऽहमस्मीति विज्ञाय किं दीन इव धावसि ॥ ३ ॥

Viśvaṁ sphurati yatredaṁ taraṅgā iva sāgare,
so-'ham-asmīti vijñāya kiṁ dīna iva dhāvasi.

विश्वम् *viśvam* = universe; स्फुरति *sphurati* = arises; यत्र *yatra* = where; इदम् *idam* = this; तरङ्गाः *taraṅgāḥ* = waves; इव *iva* = like; सागरे

sāgare = in the ocean; सः *saḥ* = that; अहम् *aham* = I; अस्मि *asmi* = am; इति *iti* = thus; विज्ञाय *vijñāya* = realising; किम् *kim* = why; दीनः *dīnaḥ* = a wretched creature; इव *iva* = like; धावसि *dhāvasi* = you run about.

3. *Having realised, "I am that," from which the universe arises, like waves from the sea; why do you run about like a wretched creature?*

An Individualised-ego in its own sense of imperfection generally desires for the acquisition, possession and enjoyment of other objects that it perceives in a world-of-multiplicity that lies spread out in all directions around it. But having realised that you are essentially nothing but the Pure Source of all Consciousness, the Self in You—the Infinite Self from which the universes rise, play about and die away like waves in the ocean—why do you sweat and toil, work and exert, plan and execute programmes for the service of the world? Like any other wretched creatures drowned in their ignorance, if *Janaka* also is driven to feel committed to the activities of the world-of-plurality, is there, then, any true "wisdom" in him?

Remember, *Aṣṭāvakra* is deliberately teasing his disciple to get out of the student a confirmation of his deepest realisation.

श्रुत्वाऽपि शुद्धचैतन्यमात्मानमतिसुन्दरम् ।
उपस्थेऽत्यन्तसंसक्तो मालिन्यमधिगच्छति ॥ ४ ॥

Śrutvā'pi śuddha-caitanyam-ātmānam-ati-sundaram,
upasthe'tyanta-saṁsakto mālinyam-adhigacchati.

श्रुत्वा *śrutvā* = having heard (having experienced); अपि *api* = even; शुद्ध-चैतन्यम् *śuddha-caitanyam* = Pure Consciousness; आत्मानम् *ātmānam* = Self; अतिसुन्दरम् *ati-sundaram* = supremely beautiful; उपस्थे *upasthe* = in sensuous objects; अत्यन्त-संसक्तः *atyanta-saṁsaktaḥ* = deeply attached (entangled); मालिन्यम् *mālinyam* = impurity; अधिगच्छति *adhi-gacchati* = attains.

4. *Even after hearing that the Self is Pure Consciousness, supremely beautiful, how can one yet be deeply entangled in sensuous objects and thus become impure?*

Even to hear and intellectually comprehend the nature of the Self as the Beauty of Beauties, the only Reality behind the universe, is to drop all our meaningless fascination for the sense-objects of the illusory world. Having woken up, who will pine over his beautiful beloved of his own dream? As a king, *Janaka* is seen in his royal chambers, surrounded by sense-objects, music and dance, wealth and splendour. *Aṣṭāvakara* wonders how can a Man-of-wisdom ever get deeply entangled in sense-objects? They should generate disturbing agitations in the mind and make him impure. Lust creates an extreme body-consciousness in the lusty. This must necessarily bring storms of agitations into the mind. Agitated mind veils the Vision of the Self; thus a sincere seeker must become 'impure' in contact with sense-objects.

सर्वभूतेषु चात्मानं सर्वभूतानि चात्मानि ।
मुनेर्जानत आश्चर्यं ममत्वमनुवर्तते ॥ ५ ॥

Sarva-būteṣu cātmānaṁ sarva-bhūtāni cātmāni,
muner-jānata āścaryaṁ mamatvam-anuvartate.

सर्वभूतेषु *sarva-būteṣu* = in all things; च *ca* = and; आत्मानम् *ātmānam* = Self; सर्वभूतानि *sarva-bhūtāni* = all things; च *ca* = and; अत्मानि *ātmāni* = in the Self; मुनेः *muneḥ* = of the sage; जानतः *jānataḥ* = knowing; आश्चर्यम् *āścaryam* = amazing; ममत्वम् *mamatvam* = mine-ness; अनुवर्तते *anuvartate* = continues (this).

5. *This is amazing that the sense-of-ownership (mine-ness) should still continue in the wise-men who has realised "the Self in all beings and all beings in the Self."*

The sense-of-ownership, experienced in the attitude of 'mine-ness' in an ordinary worldly man's mind, is an expression of his 'ego.' The sense-of-individuality (ego) is experienced, within one's own bosom, as the I-ness and the very same 'ego' experienced, in terms of the objects around it, is the mine-ness. The combination of this 'I' and 'mine' is the individuality, which is a product of the 'ignorance' of the Nature of the Self.

Sage *Aṣṭāvakra*, with his tongue in his cheeks, audibly wonders how a Man-of-realisation can still maintain his sense of 'mine-ness' to the objects of the world. The suggestion is that *Janaka* is continuing to rule over the kingdom of *Videha* because of his continued sense of possession to his throne : "This kingdom is mine."

In the following chapter we shall listen to the eloquent self-defence of the humble disciple, who is being nailed to 'ignorance' by these sharp and sturdy verses.

The vision of Man-of-realisation described here, by *Aṣṭāvakra* in the first line, is a faithful echo of the *Bhagavad-Gītā* (VI-29):

सर्वभूतस्थमात्मानं सर्वभूतानि चात्मनि ।
ईक्षते योगयुक्तात्मा सर्वत्र समदर्शनः ॥

Sarva-bhūta-stham-ātmānaṁ sarva-bhūtāni cātmani,
īkṣate yoga-yuktātmā sarvatra sama-darśanaḥ.

"With the mind harmonised by *Yoga*, he sees the Self abiding in all beings and all beings abinding in the Self, he sees the same everywhere."

आस्थितः परमाद्वैतं मोक्षार्थेऽपि व्यवस्थितः ।
आश्चर्यं कामवशगो विकलः केलिशिक्षया ॥ ६ ॥

Āsthitaḥ paramā-dvaitaṁ mokṣārthe'pi vyavas-thitaḥ,
āścaryaṁ kāma-vaśago vikalaḥ keli-śikṣayā.

आस्थित: *āsthitaḥ* = abiding; परम-अद्वैतम् *parama-advaitam* = in the transcendent non-duality; मोक्ष-अर्थे *mokṣa-arthe* = for the goal of liberation; अपि *api* = even; व्यवस्थित: *vyavasthitaḥ* = fixed; आश्चर्यम् *āścaryam* = strange indeed; काम-वशग: *kāma-vaśagaḥ* = come under the sway of lust; विकल: *vikalaḥ* = weakened, distraught; केलि-शिक्षया *keli-śikṣayā* = by the sexual-habit.

6. *It is strange indeed, that one abiding in the Transcedent Non-duality, and set for the goal of liberation should yet come under the sway of lust and distraught by his sexual habits.*

The smothering hammer of ridicule is mercilessly laid upon the student, blow after blow, delivered by his teacher. The humble student, in utter silence, maintains his inner balance, as he discovers a deeper assurance in his heart, provided by his own Wisdom.

As a king living his normal house-holder's life, fulfilling his duties towards his queens, how can *Janaka* continue living in the palace when he is abiding within himself in the Trancendental Non-dual Self? How can he indulge in sex and derive out of it the normal pleasure of a man of body-Consciousness, when he claims that he is in a different plane of spiritual experience in himself?

Inspite of the hammerings, the spiritual material in the student survives with its unique temper!

उद्भूतं ज्ञानदुर्मित्रमवधार्यातिदुर्बलः ।
आश्चर्यं काममाकाङ्क्षेत् कालमन्तमनुश्रितः ॥ ७ ॥

Udbhūtaṁ jñāna-durmitram-avadhāryati-durbalaḥ,
āścaryaṁ kāmam-ākāṅkṣet kālam-antam-anuśritaḥ.

उद्भूतम् *udbhūtam* = the upsurging of (sex); ज्ञान-दुर्मित्रम् *jñāna-durmitram* = enemy of knowledge; अवधार्य *avadhārya* = knowing for certain; अति-दुर्बल: *ati-durbalaḥ* = extremely weak; आश्चर्यम् *āścaryam* = strange and wonderful; कामम् *kāmam* = sex-gratification;

आकाङ्क्षेत् *ākāṅkṣet* = should desire (this); अन्तम्-कालम् *antam-kālam* = last days; अनुश्रितः *anuśritaḥ* = approaching.

7. *Strange it is, that knowing sex to be an enemy of Knowledge, even a man who has grown extremely weak and has reached his last days should yet desire for sex-gratifications!*

Evidently *Janaka* was not a young man when he approached *Aṣṭāvakra.* All hungers of the flesh produce storms of restlessness and agitations in the mind. A restless mind is never available for the pursuits of the spiritual life. And every spiritual student knows that sex is an enemy to knowledge.

If the student is young, at least his youthfulness itself can plead for him an excuse. But *Janaka* has grown extremely feeble and has approached his last days. Yet, his life apparently shows that he is still anxious for his gratifications—as he is continuing his life, as a king, admidst lavish sensuous objects of pleasure. Is this Self-realisation? Or does it betray an utter spiritual 'ignorance' and base worldly delusions?

इहामुत्र विरक्तस्य नित्यानित्यविवेकिनः ।
आश्चर्यं मोक्षकामस्य मोक्षादेव विभीषिका ॥ ८ ॥

Ihāmutra viraktasya nityānitya-vivekinaḥ,
āścaryaṁ mokṣa-kāmasya mokṣā-deva vibhīṣikā.

इह-अमुत्र *iha-amutra* = in this world and the next; विरक्तस्य *viraktasya* = who is unattached; नित्य-अनित्य विवेकिनः *nitya-anitya-vivekinaḥ* = who discriminates the eternal from the ephemeral; आश्चर्यम् *āścaryam* = strange and wonderful; मोक्ष-कामस्य *mokṣa-kāmasya* = of one who aspires for liberation; मोक्षात् *mokṣāt* = from the dissolution of the body; एव *eva* = even; विभीषिका *vibhīṣikā* = fear.

8. *It is strange that one who is unattached to the pleasures of this world and the next, who discriminates the eternal from the ephemeral, and*

who aspires for liberation, should yet fear the dissolution of the body!

The power of 'ignorance' is so strong that even in a true seeker the attachment to his body is strong. We may cultivate complete detachment from all the pleasures and objects of this world, or of the worlds we might visit after our death. We may develop a high discriminating intellect to distiguish the Real from the unreal, the Changeless from the Changeful. We may maintain in us a burning aspiration to liberate us from our own clinging entanglements with our body, mind and intellect.

Yet, in the higher climbs of meditation, the student is jerked out of his inner equipoise, merely because of his fear to lose his last lingering hold of attachment with his sense of individuality! This inherent psychological fear-complex is one of the most difficult obstacles to cross over, on the way to Self-realisation. The love for the body is natural for every individual, and it is out of this love that the 'ego' gathers all its anxieties to supply the body with endless varieties of sensual pleasures. These cravings and desires strengthen the body-consciousness. The 'ego' gets fattened!

Upto this verse, *Aṣṭāvakra* has teased and taunted his disciple for the apparent contradictions in *Janaka*'s superficial habits of living and in his deep spiritual understanding.

धीरस्तु भोज्यमानोऽपि पीड्यमानोऽपि सर्वदा ।
आत्मानं केवलं पश्यन् न तुष्यति न कुप्यति ॥ ९ ॥

Dhīrastu bhojyamāno-'pi pīḍyamāno-'pi sarvadā,
ātmānaṁ kevalaṁ paśyan na tuṣyati na kupyati.

धीरः *dhīraḥ* = wise person; तु *tu* = indeed; भोज्यमानः *bhojyamānaḥ* = feted and feasted; अपि *api* = even; पीड्यमानः *pīḍyamānaḥ* = tormented; अपि *api* = even; सर्वदा *sarvadā* = ever; आत्मानम् *ātmānam* = Self; केवलम् *kevalam* = absolute; पश्यन् *paśyan* =

seeing; न *na* = not; तुष्यति *tuṣyati* = is pleased; न *na* = not; कुप्यति *kupyati* = is angry.

9. *The wise person ever sees the Absolute Self, and is neither pleased nor angry, indeed, even when feted and feasted or tormented.*

The Man-of-wisdom is established in the Infinite Self, and as such he is not agitated by the happenings around him, be he feted and feasted, or be he hunted down and tormented by the world—he meets his experiences, moment-to-moment, in spontaniety of his quiet awareness. A Man-of-wisdom *acts*; he never *reacts*. This ability to maintain his inner equipoise is gained because of his continuous experience of the Higher-plane of Consciousness.

This is considered as a sure test for a Man-of-realisation. Life-stories of all the saints and sages of the world bring out this common salient feature in all of them: their ability to keep an undisturbed mental tranquillity in them inspite of the most disturbing environments around them. Their identity is with the Self 'alone' (*Kevalam*), in its Absolute All-pervading nature. Hence their steady inner peace, always, under all conditions-—let them be vociferously congratulated or viciously condemned.

चेष्टमानं शरीरं स्वं पश्यत्यन्यशरीरवत् ।
संस्तवे चापि निन्दायां कथं क्षुभ्येत् महाशयः ॥ १० ॥

Ceṣṭamānaṁ śarīraṁ svaṁ paśyaty-anya śarīravat,
saṁstave cāpi nindāyāṁ kathaṁ kṣubhyet mahāśayaḥ.

चेष्टमानम् *ceṣṭamānam* = acting; शरीरम् *śarīram* = body; स्वम् *svam* = his own; पश्यति *paśyati* = sees (so); अन्य-शरीरवत् *anya-śarīravat* = like another's body; संस्तवे *saṁstave* = in praise; च *ca* = and; अपि *api* = even; निन्दायाम् *nindāyām* = in blame; कथम् *katham* = how; क्षुभ्येत् *kṣubhyet* = should be perturbed; महाशयः *mahāśayaḥ* = a great-souled person.

10. *A Great-Souled-Person watches his own body acting as if it were another's. As such, how should he be perturbed by praise or blame.*

As the Pure Self, he is the Awareness, not only behind perceptions, emotions and thoughts, but also of the very equipments of the body, mind and intellect. He stands ever as a "witness" of himself, the subject and its world of experiences. This attitude can be only demonstrated, if the student can imagine a unique condition wherein while his dream is continuing, he happens to maintain his waking-consciousness! As a waker he knows that he is dreaming, and from this higher state of Consciousness he could "witness" the dreamer in him dreaming his own dream-world, projected by his own imaginations!!

If the above unique condition could even be intellectually comprehended, students of *Vedānta* can gain at least a dim concept of the vision of the world as perceived by a Man-of-Spiritual-Wisdom from his fully-awakened inner State of Absolute Bliss. To such a Wise-man how can the worldly praise or the clamorous criticism of the blabbering crowd ever bring any restlessness to disturb his serene bosom?

In these verses *Aṣṭāvakra* is enumerating the attitudes and behaviours of a Man-of-perfection. In fact, the theme in the Song of *Aṣṭāvakra* is the glory of the Man-of-perfection,—a Hymn to the God-man, playing in the finite world, amidst its crowds of miserable mortal entities.

मायामात्रमिदं विश्वं पश्यन् विगतकौतुकः ।
अपि सन्निहितं मृत्यौ कथं त्रस्यति धीरधीः ॥ ११ ॥

Māyā-mātram-idaṁ viśvaṁ paśyan vigata-kautukaḥ,
api sannihitaṁ mṛtyau kathaṁ trasyati dhīradhīḥ.

माया-मात्रम् *māyā-mātram* = mere illusion; इदम् *idam* = this; विश्वम् *viśvam* = universe; पश्यन् *paśyan* = seeing; विगत-कौतुकः *vigata-kautukaḥ* = all zest gone; अपि *api* = even; सन्निहितम् *sannihitam* =

approaching; मृत्यौ *mṛtyau* = in the death; कथम् *katham* = how; त्रस्यति *trasyati* = fears; धीर-धीः *dhīra-dhīḥ* = a man of poised intellect.

11. *Realising this universe as a mere illusion and having lost all zest in life, how can even such a man of poised-intellect fear the approach of death.*

"The zest to live," here means the continuous hunger to seek one's a happiness and fulfilment in sense-gratifications, which is the continuous motive-force which propels the individual entities to continue the race. From the womb to the tomb, individuals are goaded to move through the ups and downs of life's paths, tantalised by the empty hope that they would ultimately find complete happiness, in the immediately following set-of-experiences—although they realise that they have been completely cheated by the world till their present moment! A Man-of-wisdom in his newly awakened inner Consciousness realises the universe as a mere illusion projected by his own mind and, naturally, this self-defeating "zest in life" is totally lost for him.

The fascinating objects-outside alone bring all the storms that disturb the mental tranquillity and the intellectual equipoise in man. A man re-inforced with this great Wisdom of the Self, becomes impervious to all such worldly agitations. Even the approaching death can have no fear for him! Death is only the end of the body, the destruction of the perishable; the saint has realised that he is the Deathless, Imperishable Self. Hence, he is not threatened even by the approaching challenge of death.

निःस्पृहं मानसं यस्य नैराश्येऽपि महात्मनः ।
तस्यात्मज्ञानतृप्तस्य तुलना केन जायते ॥ १२ ॥

Niḥspṛhaṁ mānasaṁ yasya nairāśye'pi mahātmanaḥ,
tasyātma-jñāna-tṛptasya tulanā kena jāyate.

निःस्पृहम् *niḥspṛham* = free from desires; मानसम् *mānasam* = mind; यस्य *yasya* = whose; नैराश्ये *nairāśye* = in frustration; अपि *api* = even;

महात्मनः *mahātmanaḥ* = great sage; तस्य *tasya* = that; आत्मज्ञान-तृप्तस्य *ātmajñāna-tṛptasya* = contented in Self-knowledge; तुलना *tulanā* = comparison; केन *kena* = with whom; जायते *jāyate* = can be.

12. *With whom can we compare that great Sage, whose mind is free from desires; who, even in his frustration experiences contentment in his Self-knowledge.*

Human mind works under a uniform pattern of behaviours everywhere. It perceives an object, and discovers for itself a great sense of fulfilment in possessing that object and in enjoying it. Thus a desire is born. This desire goads him on to struggle hard to gain the object of the desire. The desirable-objects are few in number, and the desiring-minds are always many. Naturally, that vast majority must necessarily get disappointed, because all cannot possess the same object. When the desire is not fulfilled, the sorrows of dis-appointment rise in the mind; sometimes the desire is fulfilled, but the object possessed, after very great struggle, may not provide the expected happiness and, therefore, the mind suffers a sense of dis-illusionment. The emotions of dis-appointment and dis-illusionment together constitute the "sense of frustration." Repeated waves of frustrating experiences together build up the sad and sorrowful worldly-life (*Saṁsāra*). This is the dissection of an average individualised-mind.

The Man-of-realisation, whose mind is calm and serene even in the midst of great disappointment in life, is a unique phenomenon and, therefore, *Aṣṭāvakra* exclaims : "With whom can we compare a Great-souled One?" Such exclamations we find sprinkled all over in the text books that expound the goal and the way of *Vedāntik* realisation. In *Yoga-Vāsiṣṭha* (XVII-50) we read :

वितातता हृदयस्य महामतेः हरिहराब्जज लक्षशतैरपि ।
तुलनामेति न............

Vitatatā hṛdyasya mahāmateḥ hariharābjaja lakṣaśatairapi,
tulanāmeti na...........

"The great-sage, who has snapped asunder all the bonds of his heart cannot be compared even with hundreds of lakhs of trinities."

The term "*Nairāśye*" translated here as 'frustration' is employed, though rarely, in our scriptures in the sense of the "state-of-desireless-ness," and so it implies "liberation." In this sense, the stanza would mean "He whose mind has lost even its desire-for-liberation."

स्वभावादेव जानानो दृश्यमेतन्न किञ्चन ।
इदं ग्राह्यमिदं त्याज्यं स किं पश्यति धीरधीः ॥ १३ ॥

Svabhāvād-eva jānāno dṛśyam-etan-na kiñcana,
idaṁ grāhyamidaṁ tyājyaṁ sa kiṁ paśyati dhīradhīḥ.

स्वभावात् *svabhāvāt* = in its own nature; एव *eva* = indeed; जानानः *jānānaḥ* = knowing (this); दृश्यम् *dṛśyam* = perceived world; एतत् *etat* = this; न *na* = not; किञ्चन *kiñcana* = anything; इदम् *idam* = this; ग्राह्यम् *grāhyam* = acceptable; इदम् *idam* = this; त्याज्यम् *tyājyam* = rejectable; सः *saḥ* = that; किम् *kim* = why; पश्यति *paśyati* = sees; धीर-धीः *dhīra-dīḥ* = man-of-poised-intelligence, steady minded.

13. *Why should that wise-minded man, who knows that the perceived-world, in its own nature, has no substance, consider one thing acceptable and another unacceptable?*

He who has awakened to the Higher-plane of Consciousness, to him, from his eminence, the illusory world-of-objects is already lifted. It is only the individualised-ego perceiving the world-of-plurality, through its intellect, evaluates each object as pleasant; and unpleasant; and on the basis of it, rejects or accepts the available field in front of it. All these processes are possible only under an assumption that the perceived-world is *real*.

Man-of-wisdom also sees the world-of-objects, but this viewing the objects is distinctly different from the ways of the wordly-man. We view the scenes around us through the web of our own *Vāsanā-s* and, therefore, we cannot hold ourselves back from our utilitarian point-of-view! The Man-of-perfection perceives the world without rejecting or accepting it and, in fact, he sees things as they are and not as interpreted by his own *Vāsanā-s.*

Having recognised a sea-shell, as it is, who will stoop down to pick it up, even though, it may continue shining as a piece of silver?

In *Mahopaniṣad* (VI-13,14) we find a similar sentiment expressed in a lyrical verse :

ततेे ब्रह्मघने नित्ये संभवन्ति न कल्पिताः ।........................ ॥

Tate brahmaghane nitye saṁbhavanti na kalpitāḥ,

यदस्तीह तदेवास्ति विज्वरो भव सर्वदा ।...................................... ॥

yadastīha tadevāsti vijvaro bhava sarvadā, ...

"In the Eternal Homogeneous *Brahman*, which is the substratum, the illusion created by imagination can have no existence. It remains the same as ever before—here and there the same. May you be, therefore, ever calm and serene."

अन्तस्त्यक्तकषायस्य निर्द्वन्द्वस्य निराशिषः ।
यदृच्छयाऽऽगतो भोगो न दुःखाय न तुष्टये ॥ १४ ॥

Antas-tyakta-kaṣāyasya nir-dvandvasya nirāśiṣaḥ,
yadṛcchayā-''gato bhogo na duḥkhāya na tuṣṭaye.

अन्तः त्यक्त कषायस्य *antaḥ-tyakta-kasāyasya* = one who has given up all worldly passions from the mind; निर्द्वन्द्वस्य *nir-dvandvasya* = who is beyond the pairs-of-opposites; निराशिषः *nirāśiṣaḥ* = of one who is free from desires; यदृच्छया *yadṛcchayā* = unexpectedly; आगतः *āgataḥ* = which has reached; भोगः *bhogaḥ* = objects of enjoyment; न *na* = not; दुःखाय *duḥkhāya* = for pain; न *na* = not; तुष्टये *tuṣṭaye* = for pleasure.

14. *He who has given up all wordly passions from his mind, who is beyond the pairs-of-opposites, and who is free from desires—to him objects of enjoyment, unexpectedly reaching him, can cause neither pleasure nor pain.*

The subtle impulses and urgencies, dwelling in the depth of a man's personality, that ultimately determine the emotional and the intellectual profile of that individual, are called *vāsanā-s*. These subtle impressions colour our vision of the world-around and compel us to divide the perceived realm into two categories, the conducive and the non-conducive. Thereafter, the individual starts his flight away from the non-conducive, in search of and pursuing the conducive objects.

In the bargain the mind is molested, tossed about and shattered by the pairs-of-opposites; joy and sorrow, success and failure, heat and cold and a thousand such other varieties. The Man-of-Perfection is one who has conquered all his *Vāsanā-s* and, therefore, he no more comes under the tyranny of his mind and its inherent mischiefs. De-hypnotising thus from the enchantments of the sense-objects, he lives, deriving his satisfaction and fulfilment from the Self, and, therefore, any object-of-experience that reaches him accidentally, be it good or bad, can cause in him neither a great pleasure nor a terrible pain. No object of the world gained can add to his Absolute Bliss, nor can the loss of any objects reduce his Infinite Bliss.

A Man-of-wisdom is ever-rooted in the Infinite Bliss, which is the nature of his own Self. He lives *in* the world, but he is never *of* the world.

Chapter—IV

Glory of Realisation

Introduction

This chapter is the eloquent defence, pleading "not guilty," by king *Janaka*. All the taunting criticisms of the king's behaviour made by his teacher *Aṣṭāvakra* are satisfactorily explained and vividly clarified.

One who has realised the Self-in-him to be the Self every-where understands the universe as Himself, and Himself as the Lord-of-the-universe. He lives thereafter in perfection freedom, fearless and ever-blissful. Such a magnificient soul can never be compared with the ignorant individuals, who live upon the surface of the world, dragging themselves through life like miserable beasts-of-burden—each a sad victim of his lusts and inhibitions, mercilessly weighed down by the loads of his fears and miseries!

The entire universe is but one's own essential form; one is not separate from it. An individual is not built as a sewing-machine or a tape-recorder! An individual cannot come into being by assembling his parts : by welding a head to the trunk, by connecting the brain to the heart, by screwing in a liver, etc. The head, the brain, the heart, the liver are different names, but not separate "events." Similarly, an individual is separate from the universe *only* in name. In fact you are not only an essential part of the universe, but you are the very being of the universe—just as the heart, or the liver, is not a part of you, but an essential aspect of the whole.

When this oneness with the universe is not realised, you are fooled by your own name! Hence, the *Ṛṣī*-s had described this hallucination, called the *Jagat*, as a mere bundle of names and forms. All fears arise from the dreadful sense of alienation from the world; on realising that you are the Infinite Self, there is no more any sense of alienation. To realise that "I am the Self" is to recognise at once that the society and the world are but extensions of my own mind and body.

Space is not contaminated by the things existing in it, nor by the movements and activities that are taking place therein. The objects-of-pleasure around and the activities of the body among them, cannot in any way affect the Pure Self with which the Man-of-realisation has discovered his complete identity. The subtler is not conditioned by the grosser.

जनक उवाच ।

हन्तात्मज्ञस्य धीरस्य खेलतो भोगलीलया ।
न हि संसारवाहीकैर्मूढैः सह समानता ॥ १ ॥

Janaka Uvāca :

Hant-ātmajñasya dhīrasya khelato bhoga-līlayā,
na hi saṁsāra-vāhīkair-mūḍhaiḥ saha samānatā.

हन्त *hanta* = O! Marvel!; आत्मज्ञस्य *ātmajñasya* = of the knower of the Self; धीरस्य *dhīrasya* = the Man-of-understanding; खेलतः *khelataḥ* = playing; भोग-लीलया *bhoga-līlayā* = with the sport of life, the game of enjoyment; न *na* = not; हि *hi* = indeed; संसार-वाहीकैः *saṁsāra-vāhīkaiḥ* = a beast-of-burden of the world; मूढैः *mūḍhaiḥ* = deluded; सह *saha* = with; समानता *samānatā* = similarity.

Janaka said :

1. *O! Marvel! The Man-of-understanding, the knower-of-the-Self, who plays the sport of life, has no comparison with the deluded beasts-of-burden of the world.*

In the very opening verse *Janaka* crystallises all his defences into this pithy statement. The behaviour of Man-of-perfection in the world outside at his body level should not be compared with those of the ordinary people, who drag themselves through life as beasts-of-burden, carrying the loads of their *vāsanā-s*, panting in exhaustion, desiring to graze on sense-gratifications, here and there, along its bridle-path.

One whose identity has been firmly established in the Higher-Consciousness, he, thereafter, with his body, mind and intellect only "plays the sport of life." To play is natural for a child, and if you ask children at play why they are playing, they are at a loss how to answer such a ridiculous question? Play (*līlā*) cannot be any longer a play if it is played for a purpose—to achieve a profit. Sport is a natural explosion of one's inherent energy—free and spontaneous. Play itself is its own fulfilment. It is in this spirit that a Man-of-perfection exists in all fields of his endeavour, apparently functioning as any other man in the world.

The difference between a worldly-man of passions and a God-man of inner peace, is not in the type of actions they perform but in the Conscious understanding with which they enter their fields-of-actions. The idle crowds of unintelligent onlookers are not generally subtle enough in their perceptions to recognise this significant distinction between the selfish man-of-ignorance and selfless Man-of-Wisdom.

In short, *Janaka* defends himself with the plea that his actions should not be measured with the same yard-stick that is applied in measuring the size of worldly-beings.

The same idea is found thundred in the *Annapūrṇopaniṣad* (I-57) :

अन्तः संसिक्तनिर्मुक्तो जीवो मधुरवृत्तिमान् ।
बहिः कुर्वन्नकुर्वन् वा कर्ता भोक्ता नहि क्वचित् ॥

Antaḥ saṁsikta-nirmukto jīvo madhura-vṛttimān,
bahiḥ kurvan-nakurvan vā kartā bhoktā nahi kvacita.

"A màn who has liberated himself completely from his inner attachments, whose thoughts are ever pure and sweet, such a man, whether he undertakes an action or not, there can never be in his bosom, at any time, under any circumstances, the sense of doership or enjoyership."

यत्पदं प्रेप्सवो दीनाः शक्राद्याः सर्वदेवताः ।
अहो तत्र स्थितो योगी न हर्षमुपगच्छति ॥ २ ॥

Yat-padaṁ prepsavo dīnāḥ śakrādyāḥ sarva-devatāḥ,
aho tatra sthito yogī na harṣa-mupa-gacchati.

यत्-पदम् *yat-padam* = which state; प्रेप्सवः *prepsavaḥ* = hankering after; दीनाः *dīnāḥ* = unhappy; शक्राद्याः *śakrādyāḥ* = beginning with *Indra*; सर्व-देवताः *sarva-devatāḥ* = all gods; अहो *aho* = O! Marvel!; तत्र *tatra* = there; स्थितः *sthitaḥ* = abiding; योगी *yogī* = *Yogin*; न *na* = not; हर्षम् *harṣam* = elation; उपगच्छति *upagacchati* = attains.

2. *O! Marvel! The* Yogin *does not feel elated abiding in that State which* Indra *and others hanker after and become unhappy (because they cannot attain it).*

The happiness and bliss experienced by a Man-of-perfection is from the Blissful Self. It is this State of Perfect Happiness that the gods and their king, *Indra*, are seeking in the subtle sensuous fields of the heavens! They feel disappointed and cheated, because of the inherent imperfections in the incompleteness of even the heavenly sense-objects.

In this state of Absolute Bliss also, the Man-of-Wisdom cannot be considered as fully elated, because it is his own nature, and there is no subject to experience this Source of All-Bliss. In deep sleep, the sleeper is not separate from the sleep.

Janaka here points out from his own deep inner sense of fulfilment and bliss in the experience of the Self. In view of this complete satisfaction, ever lived within, why should he get himself involved in the apparent sensuous fields of pleasures available in his palace? How then can the responsibilities of the throne ever distract him?

तज्ज्ञस्य पुण्यपापाभ्यां स्पर्शो ह्यन्तर्न जायते ।
न ह्याकाशस्य धूमेन दृश्यमानाऽपि सङ्गतिः ॥ ३ ॥

Tajjñasya puṇya-pāpābhāṁ sparśo hyantarna jāyate,
na hyākāśasya dhūmena dṛśyamānā-'pi saṅgatiḥ.

तज्ज्ञस्य *tajjñasya* = of one who has comprehended that; पुण्य-पापाभ्याम् *puṇya-pāpābhām* = with virtue and vice; स्पर्शः *sparśaḥ* = touch; हि *hi* = indeed; अन्तः *antaḥ* = of inside; न *na* = not; जायते *jāyate* = exists; न *na* = not; हि *hi* = just as; आकाशस्य *ākāśasya* = of the space; धूमेन *dhūmena* = with smoke; दृश्यमाना *dṛśyamānā* = apparently; अपि *api* = though; सङ्गतिः *saṅgatiḥ* = contact.

3. *Indeed, the heart (inside) of one who has comprehended the Self is not touched by virtue and vice—just as the space is uncontaminated by smoke even though apparently it exists in space.*

Dust, smoke, clouds, etc., remain hung up in space and, yet, because of its greater subtlety, it is not contaminated by the existence of these. In the same way, virtue and vice cannot affect one who has comprehended the Self, and has come to identify himself with this All-Pervading Consciousness. Virtue and vice are the negative and positive *vāsanā-s*, which create healthy and unhealthy thought-currents—which again become the very propelling force behind all good and bad actions. A man-of-wisdom is one who has withdrawn himself from all material equipments, and as such he is ever beyond even the *vāsanā-s*.

The royal activities and their anxieties, the court and its pleasures, the throne and its responsibilities, all are apparently around the saintly king, but none of them can affect his deep Spiritual-wisdom, just as space is not contaminated by the dust, or smoke, that is held suspended in it.

आत्मैवेदं जगत्सर्वं ज्ञातं येन महात्मना ।
यदृच्छया वर्तमानं तं निषेद्धुं क्षमेत कः ॥ ४ ॥

Ātmai-vedaṁ jagat-sarvaṁ jñātaṁ yena mahātmanā
yadṛcchayā vartamānaṁ taṁ niṣeddhuṁ kṣameta kaḥ.

आत्मा *ātmā* = Self; एव *eva* = alone; इदम् *idam* = this; जगत् *jagat* = universe; सर्वम् *sarvam* = all; ज्ञातम् *jñātam* = is known; येन *yena* = by whom; महात्मना *mahātmanā* = the wise-man; यदृच्छया *yadṛcchayā* = as he likes (spontaneously); वर्तमानम् *vartamānam* = remaining; तम् *tam* = him; निषेद्धुम् *niṣeddhum* = to prohibit; क्षमेत *kṣameta* = can; कः *kaḥ* = who.

4. *The wise-man, who has known this entire universe to be the Self Alone, acts spontaneously. Who can forbid him?*

Even the *Vedā-s* dare not prescribe do's and don'ts to such a Man-of-realisation. In fact, the *Vedik* injuctions are records of the observed behaviours and attitudes of such Men-of-realisation.

The freedom has been allowed to a Man-of-perfection by scriptures only because, in his transcendance, his ego has completely ended, and, therefore, he has been rendered incapacitated to act wrongly, or to think ever viciously! Just as a great musician cannot go wrong in his time and tune—just as a great dancer can never go wrong in her steps—so too, a Man-of-perfection cannot step out from the righteous path. His actions might be misunderstood by his generation; how can the beasts-of-burden, panting with their instinctive activities, understand the harmony and rhythm in the bosom of the Perfect?

In *Mahābhārata (Śukāṣṭakam) Śukadeva* himself says :

भेदाभदौ सपदि गलितौं पुण्यपापे विशीर्णे ।
मायामोहौ क्षयमुपगतौ नष्टसन्देहवृत्ते: ॥
शब्दातीतं त्रिगुणरहितं प्राप्य तत्वावबोधं ।
निस्त्रैगुण्ये पथि विचरतां को विधि: को निषेध: ॥

Bhedā-bhedau sapadi galitau puṇya-pāpe viśīrṇe,
māyā-mohau kṣayam-upagatau naṣṭa-sandeha-vṛtteḥ.
śabdā-tītaṁ triguṇa-rahitaṁ prāpya tatvāv-bodhaṁ,
nis-traiguṇye pathi vicaratāṁ ko vidhiḥ ko niṣedhaḥ.

"One in whom all sense of distinctions has ended; concepts of virtue and vice have rotted away; *Māyā* and its delusions have lifted; all doubts have ceased; One who dwells beyond words; without the three-qualities, awakened to the Reality—ever after, moving on the Path of Ego-less-ness, to him who can prescribe what he must do and what he should not do?"

आब्रह्मस्तम्बपर्यन्ते भूतग्रामे चतुर्विधे ।
विज्ञस्यैव हि सामर्थ्यमिच्छाऽनिच्छाविवर्जने ॥५॥

Ābrahma-stamba-paryante bhūta-grāme catur-vidhe,
vijñasyaiva hi sāmarthyam-icchā-'nicchā-vivarjane.

आब्रह्म-स्तम्ब-पर्यन्ते *ābrahma-stamba-paryante* = from *Brahmā* down to a grass-blade; भूत-ग्राने *bhūta-grāme* = in all beings; चतुर्विधे *catur-vidhe* = of the four categories of existence; विज्ञस्य *vijñasya*

= the wise-one; एव *eva* = alone; हि *hi* = indeed; सामर्थ्यम् *sāmarthyam* = capacity; इच्छा-अनिच्छा-विवर्जने *icchā-anicchā vivarjane* = in renouncing desires and aversion.

5. *Of the four-categories of existence, from* Brahmā *down to a grass-blade, it is the Wise-one alone who has the capacity to renounce desires and aversions.*

According to the *Upaniṣad-s,* the total world-of-beings dwelling in the surface of this globe, fall under four types :

1. *Jarāyuja or Garbhaja :* those that are born from the womb;
2. *Aṇḍaja :* those that are born from eggs;
3. *Svedaja :* those that are born from warm vapour or sweat; and
4. *Udbhijja :* those that are born of seeds or sprouting up.

All these together indicate the entire world of beings that exist here amidst us. In order to indicate the entire cosmos, *Janaka* amplifies his statement and says : "From the Creator down to a grass-blade."

In short, in the entire cosmos of created-beings, the Man of Self-realisation alone is the sole-being who has in him the unique capacity to renounce all his desire and aversions. These two feelings represent the entire activities of the mind. The Man-of-perfection alone is the one who has gone beyond his mind, and hence this uniqueness in him. There is no ego in him, and therefore, he does not react to the external world, in terms of likes and dislikes or in terms of desires and aversions.

Our minds are coloured by our perceptions and therefore, loaded down with its own *vāsanā-s,* it lives its days in self-created bondages. The liberated-one is he who has renounced the world of perceptions—meaning who has risen above his mind and has apprehended the Self. This is the burden of a *mantra* in *Mahopaniṣad* (VI-35):

दृश्यमाश्रयसीदं चेत् तत् सचित्तोऽसि बन्धवान् ।
दृश्यं संत्यजसीदं चेत् तदाऽचित्तोऽसि मोक्षवान् ॥

Dṛśyam-āśraya-sīdaṁ cet tat-sacitto'si bandhavān,
dṛśyaṁ saṁtya-jasīdaṁ cet tadā'citto'si mokṣavān.

In case you depend upon the world-of-perceptions then your mind is "bound," in case your mind has fully renounced the world-of-perceptions, then your mind is "liberated."

आत्मानमद्वयं कश्चिज्जानाति जगदीश्वरम् ।
यद्वेत्ति तत् स कुरुते न भयं तस्य कुत्रचित् ॥ ६ ॥

Ātmānam-advayaṁ kaścij-jānāti jagadīśvaram,
yadvetti tat sa kurute na bhayaṁ tasya kutracit.

आत्मानम् *ātmānam* = Self; अद्वयम् *advayam* = One without-a-second, non-dual; कश्चित् *kaścit* = rarely one; जानाति *jānāti* = knows; जगदीश्वरम् *jagadīśvaram* = Lord of the Universe; यत् *yat* = which; वेत्ति *vetti* = knows; तत् *tat* = that; सः *saḥ* = he; कुरुते *kurute* = does; न *na* = not; भयम् *bhayam* = fear; तस्य *tasya* = his; कुत्रचित् *kutracit* = anywhere.

6. *Rare indeed is the one who knows the Self, as One, without-a-second, and as the Lord of the Universe. He does what comes to his mind, and has no fears from any quarters.*

In this concluding stanza, the disciple discovers a daring courage, in the depth of his own experienced sense of divinity as the Self. He has realised himself not only as the One Infinite Self, but also as the Governor, the Ruler, the Controller, the Lord of Universe of names-and-forms. Such an individual "does whatever comes to his mind"—meaning he fearlessly undertakes to do whatever he considers worth doing. Nothing, low and base, can ever come to molest his thoughts. Ever-identified with the Infinite, his inspired bosom overflows ever with his divinely brilliant and sweet thoughts for the benefit and glory of the world. He is always confident that his actions are expressions of the divine blessings conveyed to the community, through his equipments. He has no fear of criticism from any quarters. Evidently, the teacher *Aṣṭāvakra* is satisfied with the student's confidence in his own Wisdom and therefore, he continues his discourse in the following chapter.

Chapter—V

Four Methods:—Dissolution of Ego

Introduction

In the direct experience of the Transcendental Self, to dissolve the *perceiving* equipments and the *perceived* world-of-experiences, is to *Aṣṭāvakra* the significance of the term *Laya*, dissolution. This is to be attained in different stages, as it is impossible for any one to achieve it in one sudden leap. The four different stages through which a sincere seeker can accomplish this total dissolution of his ego-Consciousness is the theme of this chapter.

This technique of '*Laya*' starts with the ending of the body-consciousness, and then stage-by-stage it ultimately takes the seeker to the experience of the Absolute Aloneness of the Self-Divine (*Kaivalya*). To contemplate upon the Supreme Self with such intensity and consistency that the mind has no accommodation to entertain thoughts of the body, or the sense-objects, is the state of "total-dissolution." Unbroken and continuous God-rememberance is one of the simplest practices in ultimately achieving this state of "total-dissolution" (*Laya*).

अष्टावक्र उवाच ।

न ते सङ्गोऽस्ति केनापि किं शुद्धस्त्यक्तुमिच्छसि ।
सङ्गातविलयं कुर्वन्नेवमेव लयं व्रज ॥ १ ॥

Aṣṭāvakra Uvāca :

Na te saṅgo-'asti kenāpi kiṁ śuddhas-tyaktum-icchasi,
saṅghāta-vilayaṁ kurvan-nevam-eva layaṁ vraja.

न *na* = not; ते *te* = your; सङ्गः *saṅgaḥ* = contact; अस्ति *asti* = is; केन *kena* = with anything; अपि *api* = verily; किम् *kim* = what; शुद्धः *śuddhaḥ* = pure; त्यक्तुम् *tyaktum* = to renounce; इच्छसि *icchasi* = wish; संघात-विलयम् *saṁghāta-vilayam* = dissolution of the body-complex; कुर्वन् *kurvan* = effecting; एवम् *evam* = thus; एव *eva* = indeed; लयम् *layam* = the state of dissolution; व्रज *vraja* = attain.

Aṣṭāvakra said :

1. You have no contact with anything whatsoever. Pure as you are, what do You want to renounce? Having dissolved the body-complex, enter into Laya—the state of dissolution.

As the Infinite Self, the very 'Substratum' for the entire illusory-world superimposed upon You, what is there in You, the Pure Self, to renounce? You have no contract with anything. The *post* is untouched by the *ghost*; what can the *post* renounce?

The body-complex, generally indicated in the *Vedānta-Śāstra* by the term '*Saṅghāta*', is constituted of the sense-organs, mind, intellect and ego. Even though in the Pure Self there is nothing other than Itself, we have found how, when there is *non-apprehension* of the Self, such *mis-apprehensions* do powerfully surge up. At this moment we live identified with these and act and live as though we are nothing but the body complex in us. In the continuous confident self-assertion, "I am the Infinite Self," to dissolve away the matter-aggregate about us, is to end the ego. "In this way enter *Laya*—the state of dissolution," advises *Aṣṭāvakra*.

We are reminded of a similar assertion in *Annapūrṇopaniṣad* (IV-68,69) :

पदमाद्यमनाद्यन्तं तस्य बीजं न विद्यते ॥
तत्र संलीयते संवित् निर्विकल्पं च तिष्ठति ।
भूयो न वर्तते दुःखै .... ॥

Padamā-dyamanā-dyantaṁ tasya bījaṁ na vidyate.
tatra saṁlīyate saṁvit-nir-vikalpaṁ ca tiṣṭhati,
bhūyo na vartate duḥkhai ....

"That which has neither a beginning nor an end, can have no cause for itself. Therein dissolve (*Laya*) your mind-intellect equipment and remain ever undisturbed. Such an individual shall never have to ever return into misery and pain."

उदेति भवतो विश्वं वारिधेरिव बुद्बुदः ।
इति ज्ञात्वैकमात्मानमेवमेव लयं व्रज ॥ २ ॥

Udeti bhavato viśvaṁ vāridhe-riva budbudaḥ,
iti jñātvaikam-ātmānam-evameva layaṁ vraja.

उदेति *udeti* = rises; भवतः *bhavataḥ* = from You; विश्वम् *viśvam* = universe; वारिधेः *vāridheḥ* = from the sea; इव *iva* = like; बुद्बुदः *budbudaḥ* = bubble; इति *iti* = thus; ज्ञात्वा *jñātvā* = having apprehended; एकम् *ekam* = one; आत्मानम् *ātmānam* = Self; एवम् *evam* = in this way; एव *eva* = verily; लयम् *layam* = a state of dissolution; व्रज *vraja* = enter.

2. *The universe rises from You, like a bubble from the sea, thus comprehend the Non-dual Self. In this way, enter into* Laya*—the state of dissolution.*

"The sea and the waves or bubbles" is a very fascinating metaphor that *Aṣṭāvakra* employs very often all through his Song. Here is an exercise in contemplation. Just as the bubbles rising from the sea are all nothing but the waters of the sea, and they rise in different forms, they exist and play about for a time and then disappear to become, in the end, nothing but the waters of the sea; so too, universes spring up from the Self.

Consistently thus contemplating, quieten the demands and the agitations, passions and restlessness of the equipments. In the hushed silence of such a deep meditation, the undisturbed Consciousness in Its Great Grand Infinitude can then be apprehended. "In this way enter into *Laya*—the state of dissolution."

Here in the second stage of the dissolution. *Aṣṭāvakra* indicates that the seeker must dissolve his mind and its desire-prompted storms within.

The assertion "I am the Infinite Self" is a daring one, and the heroic in heart, protected by his deep understanding of the scriptural texts alone can undertake to walk this majestic path of *Vedāntik*-meditation. The implication to the assertion: "I am the Self," is declared in a verse in *Yoga-Vāsiṣṭha* (Ch. 121-8) :

ब्रह्मेन्द्रविष्णुवरुणाः यद्यत्कर्तुं समुद्यताः ।
तदहं चिद्वपुः सर्वं करोमीत्येव भावयेत् ॥

Brahmendra-viṣṇu-varuṇāḥ
yadyat-kartuṁ samudyatāḥ
tad-ahaṁ cid-vapuḥ sarvaṁ
karomī-tyeva bhāvayet.

"Maintain the attitude that whatever the Creator, *Indra*, *Viṣṇu* and *Varuṇa* can achieve and accomplish, that I, the Pure Consciousness, can indeed achieve."

This is not a blasphemy; this is Pure Spiritual Might! This state cannot be reached all of a sudden; this is to be achieved in slow and steady stages as indicated in the *Bhagavad-Gītā* (VI-25) :

> शनैः शनैरुपरमेद्बुद्ध्या धृतिगृहीतया ।
> आत्मसंस्थं मनः कृत्वा न किंचिदपि चिन्तयेत् ॥
>
> *Śanaiḥ śanair-uparamed-buddhyā dhṛti-gṛhītayā,*
> *ātma-saṁsthaṁ manaḥ kṛtvā na kiñcid-api cintayet.*
>
> "Little by little, let him attain quietude by the intellect held in firmness; having established the mind in the Self, let him not think of anything."

प्रत्यक्षमप्यवस्तुत्वाद्विश्वं नास्त्यमले त्वयि ।
रज्जुसर्प इव व्यक्तमेवमेव लयं व्रज ॥ ३ ॥

Pratyakṣam-apy-avastutvād-viśvaṁ nāstyamale tvayi,
rajju-sarpa iva vyaktam-evam-eva layaṁ vraja.

प्रत्यक्षम् *pratyakṣam* = visible; अपि *api* = though; अवस्तुत्वात् *avastutvāt* = on account of being unreal; विश्वम् *viśvam* = universe; न *na* = not; अस्ति *asti* = is; अमले *amale* = Pure; त्वयि *tvayi* = in you; रज्जुसर्पः *rajju-sarpaḥ* = the snake in the rope; इव *iva* = like; व्यक्तम् *vyaktam* = manifested; एवम् *evam* = thus; एव *eva* = verily; लयम् *layam* = the state of dissolution; व्रज *vraja* = attain.

3. *The universe even though visible, because it is unreal, like the snake-in-the-rope does not exist in You, who are Pure. Thus, in this way, enter into* Laya, *the state of dissolution.*

Ordinarily, when we perceive a thing, we take it for granted that the thing exists, but there are examples wherein perception is not a sure guarantee for the actual existence of the thing perceived. The "snake in the rope," the "silver in the sea-shell," the "ghost in the post" are all illusions. Employing this very familiar analogy of the *Upaniṣads*

Aṣṭāvakra points out that even though the universe is manifested, and is available for our direct perception in moments of Self-unfoldment, in the Higher-plane of Consciousness, it has no existence at all. Thus having known the universe to be a mere illusion, superimposed upon the Self, negate the universe of names and forms, and thus, "in this way enter into *Laya*—the state of dissolution."

This is the third stage in *Laya*, where the universe is negated and dissolved into the Consciousness of the meditator. *Annapūrṇopaniṣad* (I-33) applauds this technique and says that :

यथा विपणगा लोका विहरन्तोऽप्यसत्समाः ।
असम्बन्धात् तथा ज्ञस्य ग्रामोऽपि विपिनोपमः ॥

Yathā vipaṇagā lokā viharanto'py-asat-samāḥ,
asambandhāt tathā jñasya grāmo'pi vipinopamaḥ.

"One who has accomplished this dissolution is ever in the aloneness of the Infinitude; even in a croweded city, his aloneness is not disturbed."

Guaḍapāda in his *Kārikā* also recommends the practice of *Laya* by completely withdrawing the mind from all sense-objects through-single-pointed contemplation upon the Self. In *Aparokṣānubhūti, Ācārya Śaṅkara* indicates three stages of *Laya* through contemplation :

1. dis-association from the body and the world;
2. identification with the Self, and
3. forgetting to remember even the knowledge of the Self.

The process of *Laya* should not be misunderstood as a path of mere negation. Neither *Aṣṭāvakra*, nor the *Bhagavad-Gītā* recommends this technique of mere negation; this is a negative path and can get the student only into a dark pit of "non-existence" (*śūnya*). The process recommended by the *Upaniṣadik Ṛṣī-s* is to flush out the ego-centric-mind of all its thoughts of the pluralistic world with a continuous flood of contemplation upon the non-dual Self.

समदुःखसुखः पूर्ण आशानैराश्ययोः समः ।
समजीवितमृत्युः सन्नेवमेव लयं व्रज ॥ ४ ॥

Sama-duḥkha-sukhaḥ pūrṇa āśā-nairāśyayoḥ samaḥ,
sama-jīvita-mṛtyuḥ sanneva-meva layaṁ vraja.

सम-दुःख-सुखः *sama-duḥkha-sukhaḥ* = to whom pain and pleasure are the same; पूर्णः *pūrṇaḥ* = perfect; आशा-नैराश्ययोः *āśā-nairāśyayoḥ* = in hope and disappointment; समः *samaḥ* = same; सम-जीवितः मृत्युः *sama-jīvitaḥ mṛtyuḥ* = to whom life and death are the same; सन् *san* = being; एवम् *evam* = thus; एव *eva* = verily; लयम् *layam* = the state of dissolution; व्रज *vraja* = attain.

4. *You are perfect and the same in pain and pleasure, in hope and disappointment, and in life and death. Thus, in this way, enter into* Laya—*the state of dissolution.*

In this fourth and the last stage of *Laya*, *Aṣṭāvakra* prescribes for the seeker a process by which all his intellectual estimates and responses are dissolved in the steady contemplation upon the nature of the Self.

Pain and pleasure, hope and disappointment, life and death, are all intellectual evaluations and its habitual concepts. To dissolve the intellect is to end its functions. In the Self there are none of these intellectual evaluations—they are all objects of Consciousness. Above the intellect, and therefore, beyond its estimates, shines the Self that illumines the very intellect. "In this way enter into *Laya*—the state of dissolution."

To contemplate upon the Self as the one constant Witness of all agitations of the mind and intellect and all functions of the body, is to bring about complete dissolution of the ego and the world interpreted by the ego.

These are the four stages prescribed by *Aṣṭāvakra* for accomplishing the total dissolution of the individualised Consciousness, and for merging it into the Infinite Self.

Chapter—VI

The Self Supreme

Introduction

The entire song of *Aṣṭāvakra* is conceived in the form of a dialogue between himself and his royal-disciple, *Janaka*. We, as students, aspiring to comprehend the *Vedāntik* vision of the non-dual Self, are staggered at the vision *Aṣṭāvakra* points out. We get dumb-founded at the giddy heights to which the uncompromising Pure Vision of *Janak* lifts us.

In the previous chapter, saint *Aṣṭāvakra* prescribes the path of *Laya-Yoga*, but here his disciple, the royal-*Seer*, *Janaka* complains that in his vision of the Supreme Self, he finds nothing to dissolve! What can there be in the One Non-dual Self other than Itself for us to dissolve? It is beyond everything—'Beyond the beyond' (*Prakṛteḥ-paraḥ*; *Parāt-paraḥ*). Even the very effort at *Laya-Yoga* declares the existence of 'ignorance.'

The Self in this Absolute sense is the theme of discussion in this chapter. The Self is indicated here as the Cosmic-space and the universe a pot in it; once the Self is realised, the universe cannot ever condition the Infinite Self.

In *Aṣṭāvakra-Gītā* the transcendence and the immanence of the Self are equally emphasised; this is the Grand Style of the *Gītā* philosophy: "All in the One Self, and the One Self in All." In such a state no *Laya* can be practised. To pursue *Laya-Yoga* a residual amount of ignorance is necessary to maintain in the seeker—the witnessing-ego, to strive for the dissolution of itself in the Supreme Self.

जनक उवाच ।

आकाशवदनन्तोऽहं घटवत्प्राकृतं जगत् ।
इति ज्ञानं तथैतस्य न त्यागो न ग्रहो लयः ॥ १ ॥

Janaka Uvāca :

Ākāśa-vad-ananto-'haṁ ghaṭavat-prākṛtaṁ jagat,
iti jñānaṁ tathai-tasya na tyāgo na graho layaḥ.

आकाशवत् *ākāśa-vat* = like space; अनन्तः *anantaḥ* = limitless; अहम् *aham* = I; घटवत् *ghaṭavat* = like a jar; प्राकृतम् *prākṛtam* = phenomenal; जगत् *jagat* = world; इति *iti* = this; ज्ञानम् *jñānam* = true knowledge; तथा *tathā* = then; एतस्य *etasya* = of this; न *na* = not; त्यागः *tyāgaḥ* = relinquishment; न *na* = not; ग्रहः *grahaḥ* = acceptance; लयः *layaḥ* = dissolution.

Janaka Said :

1. *Infinite as space am I, and the phenomenal world is like a limited-jar; this is "true knowledge." There is nothing then to be renounced, nor to be accepted, nor to be destroyed.*

In the previous chapter the teacher, *Aṣṭāvakra*, out of his Infinite kindness, came down a little from the peak of the Absolute and recommended to his student the path-of-dissolution (*Laya*). *Janaka*, the disciple, however, from a still higher stand-point ridicules the very idea of merging the ego into the Supreme Consciousness which is Ever-Infinite and One-without-a-second.

In the very opening verse *Janaka* takes the thunder away from *Aṣṭāvakra*'s discourse on the technique of the merger (*Laya*).

The Supreme Self is often compared with the cosmic-space in which the universes move; and individualised ego-Consciousness as a limited, insignificant mud-pot and its pot-space. Space (*Ākāśa*) is a very familiar comparison oft-repeated by various *Ṛṣī-s* in different *Upaniṣad*-s.[1]

Māṇḍūkya Kārikā is considered as a text in *Vedānta* that has come to be written after *Aṣṭāvakra Gītā*, and the *Kārikā* is generally considered to have drawn its inspiration from this *Gītā*. The *Kārikā* elaborates this analogy of the space and the pot-space, illustrating the Infinite Consciousness and the limited ego-Consciousness. The elaboration by the author of the *Kārikā* is very illuminating for the students to reflect upon.[2]

From the Absolute stand-point of the One Homogeneous Supreme Consciousness, there is neither an ego, nor and ego-perceived illusory world-of-plurality. No doubt, this is the goal—the highest State of Realisation. *Janaka* abiding in this Reality complains that he cannot practise *Laya*, as in the Pure Self "there is nothing to be renounced, or to be accepted, or to be destroyed." The *Kārikā* sings the same idea as a chorus to the Song of *Aṣṭāvakra* :

ग्रहो न तत्र नोत्सर्गः चिन्ता यत्र न विद्यते ।
आत्मसंस्थं तदा ज्ञानं अजाति समतां गतम् ॥

(*Māṇḍūkya Kārikā, Advaita Prakaraṇa*...III-38).

Graho na tatra notsargaḥ cintā yatra na vidyate,
ātma-saṁsthaṁ tadā jñānaṁ ajāti samatāṁ gatam.

"There, in the Self, which is the final fulfilment of the actions of the mind, there is neither any perception, nor any Self-projection into ideas. Established in the Self, the Self revelling in Knowledge, the *Jñāna* reaches the state of immutability and homogeneity."

---

1. "आकाशं आत्मा" *Ākāśaṁ ātmā (Bṛhadāraṇyakopaniṣad).*
"आकाश आत्मा" *Ākāśa ātmā (Taittirīyopaniṣad*...II-2*)*
"आकाशं ब्रह्म" *Ākāśaṁ brahma (Chāndogyopaniṣad)*
2. *Māṇḍūkya Kārikā, Advaita Prakaraṇa*....III-7

One who is the Self already, he has nothing to bring into *Laya. Mahopaniṣad* (VI-63) sings :

सर्वातीतपदालम्बी परिपूर्णैकचिन्मयः
नोद्वेगी न च तुष्टात्मा संसारे नावसीदति ॥

Sarvā-tīta-padā-lambī pari-pūrṇaika cinmayaḥ,
nodvegī na ca tuṣṭātmā saṁsāre nāva-sīdati.

"One who dwells in the Transcendental State, as Full and Perfect Mass-of-Consciousness, neither perturbed nor fulfilled, he no more lives in the world-of-change."

महोदधिरिवाहं स प्रपञ्चो वीचिसन्निभः ।
इति ज्ञानं तथैतस्य न त्यागो न ग्रहो लयः ॥ २ ॥

Mahodadhir-ivāhaṁ sa prapañco vīci-sannibhaḥ,
iti jñānaṁ tathai-tasya na tyāgo na graho layaḥ.

महोदधिः *mahodadhiḥ* = ocean; इव *iva* = like; अहम् *aham* = I am; सः *saḥ* = that; प्रपञ्चः *prapañcaḥ* = phenomenal universe; वीचिसन्निभः *vīci-sannibhaḥ*= like the wave; इति *iti* = this; ज्ञानम् *jñānam* = true knowledge; तथा *tathā* = then; एतस्य *etasya* = of this; न *na* = not; त्यागः *tyāgaḥ* = relinquishment; न *na* = not; ग्रहः *grahaḥ* = acceptance; लयः *layaḥ* = dissolution.

2. *I am like the ocean and the universe is like a wave: this is "true knowledge." There is nothing then to be renounced, nor to be accepted, nor to be destroyed.*

All scriptures are forced to talk of the Supreme through myth—through special metaphors, analogies and images, which express what *It is like*, and not what *It is*. The Supreme is an experience that is inexpressible in language. It is beyond our thoughts and our speech. It is

That because of which we are conscious of our thoughts and by which we are able to verbalise our thoughts.

Such myths are extremely useful for communicating the Spiritual-knowledge to the prepared students. Don't we employ them often in interpreting science to the average man? Do we not explain electric forces by comparing them with the behaviour of water-waves, or air-movements? Here electricity is neither water nor air; to confuse the image for the fact is as ridiculous as climbing up the sign-post instead of pursuing the road!

Such a warning is necessary, lest we are carried away by the impressive images, rather than the Truth that the images indicate. Here *Janaka* explains how from the State of Pure Self, he is like a shoreless-ocean, and the universes rising in himare like its waves. A wave, we can say, is a limited and conditioned ocean; yet the wave once merged back into the ocean is nothing but the ocean. The limitations and the conditionings in the wave are all apparent, temporary and of no great significance. What is the sense in asking the ocean to merge the waves to realise its own peaceful vastness and majesty?

With this striking example, the idea that the Infinite gets conditioned is totally removed from the reflective mind of the contemplative student. Yet, the idea that the Infinite undergoes modifications, in expressing as the pluralistic phenomenal world, is not excluded from the picture of the ocean-and-the waves. Hence, the justification for the examples repeated in the following verse.

अहं स शुक्तिसङ्काशो रूप्यवद्विश्वकल्पना ।
इति ज्ञानं तथैतस्य न त्यागो न ग्रहो लयः ॥ ३ ॥

Ahaṁ sa śuktisaṅkāśo rūpyavad-viśva-kalpanā,
iti jñānaṁ tathai-tasya na tyāgo na graho layaḥ.

अहम् *aham* = I; सः *saḥ* = that; शुक्ति-सङ्काशः *śukti-saṅkāśaḥ* = like sea-shell, mother of pearl; रूप्यवत् *rūpyavat* = like the silvery shine; विश्व-कल्पना *viśva-kalpanā* = the illusion of the universe; इति *iti* = this; ज्ञानम् *jñānam* = true knowledge; तथा *tathā* = then; एतस्य *etasya* = of this; न *na* = not; त्यागः *tyāgaḥ* = relinquishment; न *na* = not; ग्रहः *grahaḥ* = acceptance; लयः *layaḥ* = dissolution.

3. *I am like the sea-shell, and the illusion of the universe is like the silveriness, this is "true knowledge." There is nothing then to be renounced, nor to be accepted, nor to be destroyed.*

This famous example hinted at here is only to disabuse the mind of the student who suspects that the Infinite Self has undergone a temporary modification in Itself to play as the finite world of names-and-forms. The silveriness is not a modification of the shell; the shell remains as it is. The substratum is not affected by the illusory projections that are apprehended upon it. True knowledge is when I realise that I am the Pure Consciousness, and the ego and its fields of experiences are all illusory imaginations of the ego. From such a perfect State of Universal Oneness, no doubt, the *Laya-Yoga* cannot be practised.

अहं वा सर्वभूतेषु सर्वभूतान्यथो मयि ।
इति ज्ञानं तथैतस्य न त्यागो न ग्रहो लयः ॥ ४ ॥

Ahaṁ va sarva-bhūteṣu sarva-bhūtāny-atho mayi,
iti jñānaṁ tathai-tasya na tyāgo na graho layaḥ.

अहम् *aham* = I; वा *vā* = indeed; सर्व-भूतेषु *sarva-bhūteṣu* = in all beings (am); सर्व-भूतानि *sarva-bhūtāni* = all beings; अथो *atho* = and; मयि *mayi* = in Me; इति *iti* = this; ज्ञानम् *jñānam* = true knowledge; तथा *tathā* = then; एतस्य *etasya* = of this; न *na* = not; त्यागः *tyāgaḥ* = relinquishment; न *nâ* = not; ग्रहः *grahaḥ* = acceptance; लयः *layaḥ* = dissolution.

4. *I am, indeed, in all beings and all beings are in Me : this is "true knowledge." There is nothing then to be renounced, nor to be accepted, nor to be destroyed.*

According to the *Upaniṣad*-s, Self-Realisation does not mean the discovery of the seeker's divinity, and the recognition of the un-divinity of all other things in the Universe! To awake to the Higher-Consciousness is to recognise, thereafter, nothing but the splash of the blinding Beauty Divine in all Its glory, spread all around for all times. When awakened from the dream, the entire dream should get drowned in the waking-Consciousness.

This total transmutation of the vision of the Man-of-perfection, is indicated in the *Iśāvāsya Upaniṣad* and repeated in the *Bhagavad-Gītā* :

यस्तु सर्वाणि भूतान्यात्मन्येवानुपश्यति ।
सर्वभूतेषु चात्मानं ततो न बिजुगुप्सते ॥

(Īśā-6)

Yastu sarvāṇi bhūtāny-ātmanyevā-nupaśyati,
sarva-bhūteṣu cātmānaṁ tato na biju-guptase.

"He who recognises all names and forms as his own Self and recognises his own Self in every name and form, to such an individual there is no revulsion in life".

सर्वभूतस्थमात्मानं सर्वभूतानि चात्मनि ।
ईक्षते योगयुक्तात्मा सर्वत्र समदर्शनः ॥

(*B.G.* VI-29)

Sarva-bhūta-stham-ātmānaṁ sarva-bhūtāni cātmāni
īkṣate yoga-yuktātmā sarvatra sama-darśanaḥ.

"with the mind harmonised by *Yoga* he sees the Self, abiding in all beings, and all beings in the Self; he sees the same everywhere."

Janaka faithfully follows the scriptures, both in language and thought-content, when he declares "I am indeed in all beings and all beings are in Me." The entire *ghost* is in the *post*, and the *post* pervades the *ghost.*

From this stand-point, what is there, other than the Self to dissolve in the Self, through the process of *Laya*?

Chapter—VII

That Tranquil Self

Introduction

Even intelligent educated men readily accept the idea that we come into the world, and this implies that the world is something alien to us—something totally different from us. If we pause for a moment to think, it is evidently clear that this idea that we come into the world is against all our day's scientific knowledge. Science insists upon and proves that we do not come into the world; in fact we come out of the world.

In this chapter *Aṣṭāvakra* goes yet one step further, ahead of the knowledge of the scientists, and declares that the universe itself comes out of the Self!

As ocean 'waves,' the Self 'universes,' and the universe peoples'—if we are permitted to coin and use such strange-looking but eloquent terms. In short, just as the waves are the ocean, we are not isolated 'egoes' functioning inside separate bodies, nor is the world populated by masses of such separate entities. They all rise from the Ocean-of-Self, when the storms of the mind howl through Consciousness.

Even without bringing this surging mind, through contemplation, into its dissolution (*Laya*), the Infinite Self, ever peaceful, from which the very mind has risen, is ever beyond all agitations. Except for its waves on the surface, the ocean is calm and serene in its immeasurable depths.

Abide in the Self, wherein due to the desires of the mind, worlds of names-and forms heave forth, as though produced at the raising of a magician's wand. The creation and the dissolution of the universe are both illusions of the unsteady mind. To the Self there is neither the enxiety to accept, nor the labour to reject the mind and its imaginary worlds. The Ocean of Consciousness ever remains the same, and apparently waves up to play the illusion of names-and-forms.

Having hinted that *Laya-Yoga*, itself is only for those who have in themselves lingering shadows of 'ignorance' (ego), *Janaka* seems to feel yet unsatisfied, and so he bursts forth into a lyrical song upon the glory of the Tranquil Self in this Chapter.

जनक उवाच ।

मय्यनन्तमहाम्भोधौ विश्वपोत इतस्ततः ।
भ्रमति स्वान्तवातेन न ममास्त्यसहिष्णुता ॥ १ ॥

Janaka Uvāca:

Mayya-nanta-mahām-bhodhau viśva-pota itas-tataḥ,
bhramati svānta-vātena na mamāsty-asahiṣṇutā.

मयि *mayi* = in Me; अनन्त-महाम्भोधौ *ananta-mahāmbhodhau* = in the shoreless ocean; विश्वपोत: *viśva-potaḥ* = the ark of the universe; इतस्तत: *itas-tataḥ* = here and there; भ्रमति *bhramati* = moves; स्वान्तवातेन *svānta-vātena* = by the wind of its own mind (Universal Mind); न *na* = not; मम *mama* = My; अस्ति *asti* = is; असहिष्णुता *asahiṣṇutā* = impatience.

Janaka Said :

1. *In Me, the shoreless ocean, the ark of the universe, moves here and there, driven by the wind of its own mind (Universal-Mind). I am not impatient.*

In a man-of-realisation it is absurd to say that he recognises no world of plurality around him, nor that his mind and intellect have no thought-flow in them. But unlike us he is never disturbed by the confusions within and without him, because he is ever-abiding in his deep experience : "I am the Infinite Self."

In this shoreless Ocean-of-Consciousness, like the waves, the universe rises up, plays about and merges back. The peaceful surface of the clear Consciousness is whipped up into waves of names-and-forms by our own mental storms.

An individual mind creates individual worlds of its own likes and dislikes, of its joys and sorrows. Thus, my world is created by my mind; and your world is created by your mind. Though, we both are living in one and the same universe—perhaps, at the one and the same time and space—yet, each one of us lives in an individual, self-interpreted, private world of one's own.

The universe is the common field where all the existing minds can experience freely their own individual worlds of joys and sorrows. Therefore, the total universe is the projection of not an individual-mind but it is the play of the Total-Mind, or we may call it as the Universal-Mind. "By the mind of its own mind" (*svānta-vātena*), the universe of names-and-forms moves along its path of history, bumping along, now through brilliant eras of creative beauty and now through dark ages of miseries and sorrows.

Janaka realises that the disturbances in the individual-life and in the universal-life around are all illusory confusions projected by the individual-mind and the Universal-mind. The royal-Saint, naturally, confesses, "I am not impatient." No wise man is impatient either with the disturbances around him, or at the daily stories of achievements and failures of the world of his era. This ever-changing phenomenal world and its ceaseless modifications do not affect the Self in the least.

मय्यनन्तमहाम्भोधौ जगद्वीचिः स्वभावतः ।
उदेतु वास्तमायातु न मे वृद्धिर्न च क्षतिः ॥ २ ॥

Mayyananta-mahāmbhodhau jagad-vīciḥ svabhāvataḥ.
udetu vāsta-māyātu na mẹ vṛddhir-na ca kṣatiḥ.

मयि *mayi* = in me; अनन्त-महाम्भोधौ *ananta-mahāmbhodhau* = in the limitless ocean; जगद्वीचिः *jagad-vīciḥ* = the waves of the world; स्वभावतः *svabhāvataḥ* = spontaneously; उदेतु *udetu* = may rise; वा *vā* = or; अस्तम् *astam* = dissolution; आयातु *āyātu* = may attain; न *na* = not; मे *me* = my; वृद्धिः *vṛddhiḥ* = increase; न *na* = not; च *ca* = and; क्षतिः *kṣatiḥ* = decrease.

2. *In Me, the limitless ocean, let the waves of the world rise and vanish spontaneously. I experience neither increase nor decrease (of Me) thereby.*

Janaka amplifies the significance of the metaphor that he has used in the previous verse. When the waves heave up in the ocean, each wave has a different form and an apparent identity of its own, sufficient to distinguish it from all other waves. Yet, in a sense, they are all nothing else but ocean-water. If more waves settle down, because it has swallowed up all the waves, the ocean does not thereby get swelled up! The world of names-and-forms are nothing but a ripple upon the Infinite Self. "I am the Self," is the spiritual experience, the final Wisdom. Naturally, in Me the spontaneous rise of the worlds, or their dissolution, cannot bring any disturbance at all—I know, I am the Changeless, Immutable Self.

To *Aṣṭāvakra, Māyā* is not, it seems, a very attractive philosophic principle. He recognises and deals with only the concept of 'ignorance' (*Avidyā* or *Ajñāna*). Due to the non-apprehension of the Self, there are the *mis-apprehensions* of the worlds, and this 'ignorance' manifests as the mind. *Śaṅkara* in *Vivekacūḍāmaṇi*—Verse-171 clarifies it :

न ह्यस्त्यविद्या मनसोऽतिरिक्ता मनो ह्यविद्या भवबन्धहेतुः ।
तस्मिन्विनष्टे सकलं विनष्टं विजृम्भितेऽस्मिन्सकलं विजृम्भते ॥

Nahyastya-vidyā manaso-'tiriktā
mano hya-vidyā bhava-bandha-hetuḥ,
tasmin-vinaṣṭe sakalaṁ vinaṣṭaṁ
vijṛmbhite-'smin-sakalaṁ vijṛmbhate.

There is no "ignorance" beyond the mind; the mind alone is "ignorance"—the cause for all the sorrows-of-change. When it is destroyed, all are destroyed; when it projects, everything gets projected.

मय्यनन्तमहाम्भोधौ विश्वं नाम विकल्पना ।
अतिशान्तो निराकार एतदेवाहमास्थितः ॥ ३ ॥

Mayyananta-mahāmbhodhau viśvaṁ nāma vikalpanā,
ati-śānto nirākāra etad-eva-aham-āsthitaḥ.

मयि *mayi* = in Me; अनन्त-महाम्भोधौ *ananta-mahāmbhodhau* = in the shoreless ocean; विश्वम् *viśvam* = universe; नाम *nāma* = called; विकल्पना *vikalpanā* = imagination; अति-शान्तः *ati-śāntaḥ* = profoundly Tranquil; निराकारः *nirākāraḥ* = formless; एतत् *etat* = this; एव *eva* = alone; अहम् *aham* = I; आस्थितः *āsthitaḥ* = abiding.

3. *In Me, the shoreless-ocean, is the imagined illusion of the universe. I am the Profoundly Tranquil and Formless. In this Knowledge alone, I abide.*

In the previous verse we have the metaphor of the ocean and the waves, which might probably give a hasty student a suspicion that the world of names-and-forms is a modification, temporary though it be, of the Infinite Self. To contradict this false notion this verse is employed.

The world of names-and-forms is only the imagination (*Vikalpanā*) of the Total-Mind. It has no existence whatsoever. The Self is Undisturbed, Profoundly Peaceful and ever-Formless. Earlier in the opening chapter (Ch. I-18) it was said:

साकारमनृतं विद्धि निराकारं तु निश्चलम् ।

Sākāram-anṛtaṁ viddhi nirākāraṁ tu niścalam.

"All which have form are false, the formless is the changeless."

नात्मा भावेषु नो भावस्तत्रानन्ते निरञ्जने ।
इत्यसक्तोऽस्पृहः शान्त एतदेवाहमास्थितः ॥ ४ ॥

Nātmā bhāveṣu no bhāvas-tatrā-nante nirañjane,
itya-sakto-'spṛhaḥ śānta eta-devāham-āsthitaḥ.

न *na* = not; आत्मा *ātmā* = Self; भावेषु *bhāveṣu* = in the objects; न *na* = not; भावः *bhāvaḥ* = object; तत्र *tatra* = in That (Self); अनन्ते *anante* = limitless; निरञ्जने *nirañjane* = taintless; इति *iti* = hence; असक्तः *asaktaḥ* = unattached; अस्पृहः *aspṛhaḥ* = desireless; शान्तः *śāntaḥ* = Tranquil; एतत् *etat* = this; एव *eva* = alone; अहम् *aham* = I; आस्थितः *āsthitaḥ* = abide in.

4. *The Self is not in the object, nor is the object in this Self, which is Infinite and Taintless. Hence, it is free from attachment and desire; it is Tranquil. In this knowledge alone I abide.*

The *post* is not in the *ghost*; the *ghost* is illusory; nor is the *ghost* at any time in the *post*. Similarly, the objects of the world, being imaginations of the mind, are not in the Self, which is the substratum of the world perceived; nor can the Self be in the illusory objects! Naturally, the Infinite and the Taintless, the Self is free from any attachment to anything; nor can It entertain any desire for anything—nothing can ever remain as other than the Self : आत्मा एकमेव इदं सर्वं । *Ātmā ekameva idaṁ sarvaṁ*: "The One Self alone is all these," says the *Upaniṣad*. Attachment and desires are delusions of the mind. When these two are transcended the mind is also transcended. Where the mind is not, there is nothing to disturb the Consciousness, and therefore, it is ever-Tranquil. In this firm-Knowledge, born out of his direct experience, *Janaka* confesses, "I abide."

अहो चिन्मात्रमेवाहमिन्द्रजालोपमं जगत् ।
अतो मम कथं कुत्र हेयोपादेयकल्पना ॥ ५ ॥

Aho cin-mātram-eva-aham-indra-jālopamaṁ jagat,
ato mama kathaṁ kutra heyo-pādeya-kalpanā.

अहो *aho* = O! Marvellous!; चिन्मात्रम् *cin-mātra* = Pure Consciousness; एव *eva* = really; अहम् *aham* = I; इन्द्रजाल-उपमम् *indrajāla-upamam* = like a magic show; जगत् *jagat* = world; अतः *ataḥ* = therefore; मम *mama* = My; कथम् *katham* = how; कुत्र *kutra* = where; हेय-उपदेय-कल्पना *heya-upadeya-kalpanā* = notions of rejection or acceptance (can be).

5. *O! Marvellous! I am really Pure Consciousness. The world is like a magic-show. Hence, how and where can there be any notion of rejection or acceptance in Me?*

Nothing in this world can either attract or repel a Man-of-wisdom. He, in perfect detachment, continuously enjoys this free show of the seeing universe of multiplicity around him. To him the world-show is a fantasy created by his mind with its imagination. There is no reality in it, though it apparently is available, for the time being, for his perception. Naturally, therefore, there is nothing for him to accept or to reject in this vast illusory show of his own mind-in-agitation!

This attitude of the Wise helps him even while he is functioning in the world, for the guidance of the community. *Mahopaniṣad* (VI-68) advises:

बहिः कृत्रिमसंरम्भो हृदि संरम्भवर्जितः ।
कर्ता बहिरकर्ताऽन्तर्लोके विहर शुद्धधीः ॥

Bahiḥ kṛtrima-saṁrambho hṛdi saṁrambha-varjitaḥ,
kartā bahira-kartā-'ntar-loke vihara śuddha-dhīḥ.

> "O Man of pure intelligence! With mind at rest, though restlessly working outside—as an apparent 'doer' outside, but really as a 'non-doer' within—play about in the world of activities and achievements."

Abiding in the Self, Men-of-wisdom apparently function in the world outside, though in their depths they are ever-Actionless, ever-Tranquil.

Chapter—VIII

Bondage and Freedom

Introduction

If what has been so beautifully described by *Janaka* in the previous chapter be the true knowledge of the Tranquil Self, why is it that this blissful experience is denied to the majority of the suffering humanity? *Aṣṭāvakra* takes up this logical doubt for discussion and explains in this chapter how the 'bondage,' and why the 'freedom.' The extrovertedness of the mind and, therefore, the outgoing tendencies of the ego, characterise the state of bondage. The mind and the ego-sense turning towards the Self, and the state of mind's dissolution and ego's rediscovery of its permanent identity with Self, constitute the state of 'freedom.'

When the mind rushes out, recognising a world-of-objects, it runs wild among them, rejecting things that are not conducive and pursuing things that are imagined to be conducive to its happiness. Desiring and hating, accepting and rejecting; hunting after some things and being hunted after by other things: constructing and destroying; loving and fighting—from womb to the tomb, the ego strives and struggles, pants and suffers; this is bondage. *Mahopaniṣad* (IV-72) defines 'bondage' with one word i.e. "*Mameti*"—'mineness,' and with another single word "*Nir-mameti*" i.e. not-'mineness'—the "freedom' as follows:

द्वे पदे बन्धमोक्षाय निर्ममेति ममेति च ।
ममेति बध्यते जन्तुर्निर्ममेति विमुच्यते ॥

Dve pade bandha-mokṣāya nirmameti mameti ca,
mameti bandhyate jantur-nirmameti vimucyate.

"For 'bondage' and 'freedom,' there are two words '*nirmameti*' and '*mameti*'; while '*mameti*' binds, '*nirmameti*' releases living beings."

अष्टावक्र उवाच ।

तदा बन्धो यदा चित्तं किञ्चिद्वाञ्छति शोचति ।
किञ्चिन्मुञ्चति गृह्णाति किञ्चिद्धृष्यति कुप्यति ॥ १ ॥

Aṣṭāvakra Uvāca:

Tadā bandho yadā cittaṁ kiñcid-vāñchati śocati
kiñcin-muñcati gṛhṇāti kiñcid-dhṛṣyati kupyati.

तदा *tadā* = then; बन्धः *bandhaḥ* = bondage; यदा *yadā* = when; चित्तम् *cittam* = mind; किञ्चित् *kiñcit* = anything; वाञ्छति *vāñchati* = desires; शोचति *śocati* = grieves; किञ्चत् *kiñcit* = anything; मुञ्चति *muñcati* = rejects; गृह्णाति *gṛhṇāti* = accepts; किञ्चित् *kiñcit* = anything; हृष्यति *hṛṣyati* = feels joy; कुप्यति *kupyati* = feels angry.

Aṣṭāvakra Said :

1. *It is bondage when the mind desires or grieve at anything; does reject or accept anything; does feel happy or angry at anything.*

First of all *Aṣṭāvakra* defines the state-of-bondage, since this is the condition which is very familiar to we students in general. If they were not already in bondage, they would not study *Aṣṭāvakra-Gītā*, but would keep on singing *their own Gītā*!! Having brought the condition of bondage acutely to the awareness of a student, it should be relatively easy for that student to at least vaguely grasp what exactly is the state-of-freedom.

Desire is an emotion that rises up to disturb the mind when it recognises an object outside itself, and passionately hopes that the object of its fascination can give it a covetable satisfaction. When, having procured an object-of-desire, if it decays in the embrace of the mind, the sorrow suffered by the mind is called *grief.*

Things that the mind feels are not for itself conducive, it rejects, and things that are conducive, it accepts. Again, when the worldly objects assembled around a mind in a pattern that is in line with its present idea of joy, the mind feels happy; and when the things get arranged in a pattern contrary to the mind's present ideas of happiness, the mind revolts against them—and this is expressed as *anger.*

To live thus a slave to the mind and its death-dance is to live in 'bondage.' Slavish obedience of the individual to the endless demands of the body, mind and intellect for sense-gratifications, among the objects of the world outside, is the state-of-bondage.

तदा मुक्तिर्यदा चित्तं न वाञ्छति न शोचति ।
न मुञ्चति न गृह्णाति न हृष्यति न कुप्यति ॥ २ ॥

Tadā muktir-yadā cittaṁ na vāñchati na śocati,
na muñcati na gṛhṇāti na hṛṣyati na kupyati.

तदा *tadā* = then; मुक्तिः *muktiḥ* = freedom; यदा *yadā* = when; चित्तम् *cittam* = mind; न *na* = not; वाञ्छति *vāñchati* = desires; न *na* = not; शोचति *śocati* = grieves; न *na* = not; मुञ्चति *muñcati* = rejects; न *na* = not; गृह्णाति *gṛhṇāti* = accepts; न *na* = not; हृष्यति *hṛṣyati* = feels joy; न *na* = not; कुप्यति *kupyati* = is angry.

2. *Freedom is attained when the mind* does not *desire or grieve,* does not *reject or accept,* does not *feel happy or angry at anything.*

In one line, that is the state-of-freedom, which is opposite to what has been described earlier as the state-of-bondage of the mind. This state-of-freedom cannot be attained unless the mind discovers the source of a greater bliss in itself, so that in its utter satisfaction, the mind gets no more tempted to gush out to embrace the sense objects. Thunders *Annapūrṇopaniṣad* (II-23):

न मोक्षो नभसः पृष्ठे न पाताले न भूतले ।
सर्वाशासंक्षये चेतःक्षयो मोक्ष इतीष्यते ॥

Na mokṣo nabhasaḥ pṛṣṭhe na pātāle na bhūtale,
sarva-aśāsaṁ-kṣaye cetaḥ-kṣayo mokṣa itīṣyate.

"There is no freedom found either in the outer space, or in the nether kingdom, or on the sürface of the earth. It is found only in the mind, in which all desires have dried up. When desires are conquered, the march of thoughts cease, and the mind ends; this is the state-of-freedom."

The same idea is supported by the crisp statement in *Yoga-Vāsiṣṭha* (Ch. 85-119):

भावनातानवं मोक्षो बन्धो हि दृढ़भावना ।

Bhāvanā-tānavaṁ mokṣo bandho hi dṛḍha-bhāvanā.

"Thought-reduction is 'freedom'; thought-assertion is 'bondage.'

There is no other escape. The seeker must learn to rise above his desire-promptings. Elsewhere it is said:

इच्छामात्रमविद्येयं तन्नाशो मोक्ष उच्यते ।
स चासंकल्पमात्रेण सिद्धो भवति वै मुने ॥

Icchā-mātram-avidyeyaṁ tannāśo mokṣa ucyate,
sa cāsaṁkalpa-mātreṇa siddho bhavati vai mune.

"This 'ignorance' is nothing but desires; when desires have ended, that state is called the state of freedom. The moment you become desireless, instantaneously that man of reflection has established himself in 'freedom'.

तदा बन्धो यदा चित्तं सक्तं कास्वपि दृष्टिषु ।
तदा मोक्षो यदा चित्तमसक्तं सर्वदृष्टिषु ॥ ३ ॥

Tadā bandho yadā cittaṁ saktaṁ kāsvapi dṛṣṭiṣu,
tadā mokṣo yadā cittam-asaktaṁ sarva-dṛṣṭiṣu.

तदा *tadā* = then; बन्धः *bandhaḥ* = bondage; यदा *yadā* = when; चित्तम् *cittam* = mind; सक्तम् *saktam* = attached; कासु अपि *kāsu-api* = to any; दृष्टिषु *dṛṣṭiṣu* = sensory perceptions; तदा *tadā* = then; मोक्षः *mokṣaḥ* = freedom; यदा *yadā* = when; चित्तम् *cittam* = mind; असक्तम् *asaktam* = unattached; सर्व-दृष्टिषु *sarva-dṛṣṭiṣu* = in all sensory perceptions.

3. *It is bondage, when the mind is attached to any of the sensory perception. It is freedom when the mind is detached from all perceptions.*

In the opening stanza, through its songful words, the teacher had indicated that the *sensuousness in the mind is bondage*, and in the last verse it was indicated that *detachment from them is freedom*. In both these verses, mind's relationship with the world of its own thoughts was indicated. A mere detachment from the sensuous thoughts in the inner mind by itself can have no valid effect upon the spiritual seekers.

Here in the verse *Aṣṭāvakra* completes his thought by suggesting that a seeker should carefully cultivate a sense of detachment from his outer world-of-perceptions. The world-of-objects have a terrific enchantment over the human mind. Even if an individual is capable of ignoring the demands of his inner mind, the outer perceptions can generate devastating sensuous storms in the mind. To live susceptible to the various perceptions is *ignorance* and it will bring about *bondage*. To learn to live in detachment of the perceived-world is *freedom*.

यदा नाहं तदा मोक्षो यदाहं बन्धनं तदा ।
मत्वेति हेलया किञ्चित् मा गृहाण विमुञ्च मा ॥ ४ ॥

Yadā nāhaṁ tadā mokṣo yadāhaṁ bandhanaṁ tadā,
matveti helayā kiñcit mā gṛhāṇa vimuñca mā.

यदा *yadā* = when; न *na* = not; अहम् *aham* = I; तदा *tadā* = then; मोक्षः *mokṣaḥ* = freedom; यदा *yadā* = when; अहम् *aham* = I; बन्धनम्

bandhanam = bondage; तदा *tadā* = then; मत्वा *matvā* = knowing; इति *iti* = thus; हेलया *helayā* = playfully; किञ्चित् *kiñcit* = anything; मा *mā* = not. गृहाण *gṛhāṇa* = accept; विमुञ्च *vimuñca* = reject; मा *mā* = not.

4. *When there is no ego—'I,' there is 'freedom,' when there is ego—'I,' there is 'bondage.' Knowing thus, stop from accepting or rejecting anything playfully.*

In this closing verse of this chapter, *Aṣṭāvakra* warns the student that he should not even playfully—even as a joke—accept any perception. Even to reject a perception is to crystallise the ego and recognise the illusory 'perceiver' within! Be a detached witness of the things and happenings around, and look at them with the eyes of steady-wisdom; where there is no 'I,' the perceiver, that is the *state-of-freedom*; and wherever there is the perceiver—'I' expressing, that is the *state-of-bondage*.

Chapter—IX

Indifference

Introduction

Aṣṭāvakra recommends a three-forked effort in the realisation of the seeker's Real Nature (*Svarūpa*). This triple means for Self-realisation is constituted of 'Indifference' (*Nirveda*), 'equanimity' (*Samatā*) and 'logical-reasoning' (*Yukti*). Each one of these is reinforced by the other two. Without indifference and equanimity, logical reasoning is impossible, and indifference will not be dynamic without mental equanimity and intellectual reasoning. In fact, all the three are to be integrally followed at the body, mind and intellect levels.

Indifference to the enchanting objects of the outer world is a discipline for the body. Equanimity, maintained by not allowing the mind to dance to the rhythm of its likes and dislikes, is an exercise for the mind. And to learn to logically reason out the illusory nature of the world around, and to come to detect the Eternal Self is a training for the intellect.

Clinging attachment to the body, and through the body to the sense-objects strengthens the ego and deepens one's spiritual 'ignorance.' Indifference is the remedy; the seeker then becomes free from his bonds to the world of sense-pleasures. This world of sense-objects is really made up of the five great elements[1] and their modifications. They in themselves are utterly valueless. Yet our false notions, born of our passions, cloak them with an imaginary beauty and a facied value. Having thus super-imposed unreasonable values upon the material objects, man runs after

1. They are Sparce, Air, Fire, Water and Earth... their modifications are the objects-of-the-world.

them, and thus creates for himself the painful *Saṁsāra* and its tragic destinies. Cultivate '*Nirveda*' towards them all. Desire cannot grow where indifference has arrived.

Desire indeed is *Saṁsāra*. Indifference is only way to reach the state-of-freedom.

अष्टावक्र उवाच ।

कृताकृते च द्वन्द्वानि कदा शान्तानि कस्य वा ।
एवं ज्ञात्वेह निर्वेदाद्भव त्यागपरोऽव्रती ॥ १ ॥

Aṣṭāvakra uvāca:

Kṛtā-kṛte ca dvandvāni kadā śāntāni kasya vā,
evaṁ jñātveha nirvedād-bhava tyāga-paro-'vratī.

कृताकृते *kṛtākṛte* = duties performed and not performed; च *ca* = and; द्वन्द्वानि *dvandvāni* = pairs-of-opposites; कदा *kadā* = when; शान्तानि *śāntāni* = ended; कस्य *kasya* = whose; वा *vā* = or; एवम् *evam* = thus; ज्ञात्वा *jñātvā* = having fully enquired; इह *iha* = in this world; निर्वेदात् *nirvedāt* = indifference; भव *bhava* = become; त्यागपरः *tyāga-paraḥ* = devoted to renunciation; अव्रती *avratī* = passionless.

Aṣṭāvakra Said:

1. *To whom does the conflicts of duties performed and not performed, and of the pairs-of-opposites belong? When do they cease? End for whom? Having thus fully enquired, through complete indifference to the world, become passionless and be devoted to renunciation.*

The line of enquiry is exhaustively indicated here. The duties performed and not performed can bring disturbances only to the ego in us that arrogates to itself the "doership."

It is the ego's sense "enjoyership" that experiences the tyranny of the pairs-of-opposites. They can cease only when the ego is no more; and these illusory concepts belongs to the equally illusory and unreal ego.

The *ghost* and its sorrows should not affect the *post*, the *ghost* itself being an illusion. The ego is itself a projection upon the Self, and so its conflicts and anxieties, sorrows, etc., cannot affect Me, the Self, who is the Substratum for all the super-impositions.

What should then be my attitude towards the world-of-objects? If you see a pair of horns and a tail in me, what should be my relationship with my non-existent horns and tail? Will it not be an expression of my sympathy to you and your illusions if I keep an attitude of indifference to my horns and tail? And, supposing, you in your friendship, would like to oil and massage my horns! Certainly, I should allow you to do so, because the oil cannot soil me, and you, my friend, shall gain a great satisfaction!!

If this attitude can be understood, then you have understood the attitude of all Men-of-Perfection towards the world of objects and beings. He is passionless, and lives ever-devoted to the spirit of renunciation and negation of all illusory imaginations in the Self.

Here the term '*Avratī*' is translated as 'passionless'. Literally the word means 'one who is no more observing the religious vows' (*vrataḥ*). These observances are generally undertaken for the fulfilment of some or other worldly desire. Hence the term in the mouth of *Aṣṭāvakra* gathers a significant meaning, as "completely passionless."

Declares *Mahopaniṣad* (IV-41) :

नाकृतेन कृतेनार्थो न श्रुतिस्मृतिविभ्रमैः ।
निर्मन्धर इवाम्भोधिः स तिष्ठति यथास्थितः ॥

Nākṛtena kṛtenārtho na śruti-smṛti-vibhramaiḥ,
nirmandhara ivām-bhodhiḥ sa tiṣṭhati yathā-sthitaḥ.

"Indifferent to duties performed and not performed, as laid out in the sacred texts, he remains in His Pure Self, as an ocean stilled!"

कस्यापि तात धन्यस्य लोकचेष्टावलोकनात् ।
जीवितेच्छा बुभुक्षा च बुभुत्सोपशमं गताः ॥ २ ॥

Kasyāpi tāta dhanyasya loka-ceṣṭāva-lokanāt,
jīvitecchā bubhukṣā ca bubhutso-paśamaṁ gatāḥ.

कस्य *kasya* = whose; अपि *api* = even; तात *tāt* = My son; धन्यस्य *dhanyasya* = of the blessed one; लोक-चेष्टावलोकनात् *loka-ceṣṭāva-lokanāt* = by observing the ways of men; जीवितेच्छा *jīvitecchā* = passion for living; बुभुक्षा *bubhukṣā* = desire to enjoy; च *ca* = and; बुभुत्सा *bubhutsā* = hunger to learn and know; उपशमम् *upaśamam* = has extinguished; गताः *gatāḥ* = attained.

2. *Rare indeed, my son, is that blessed person whose passions for living, desire to enjoy, and hunger to learn and know have been extinguished by observing the ways of men.*

Aṣṭāvakra addresses *Janaka*, with infinite love as "my son," and sympathetically exclaims how man though he lives in this world, all the times amidst the clamorous sorrows of others, he fails to understand the calamitous life lived by people in selfish passions, in fruitless tragedies, and in barren sorrows. This is happening everywhere around everyone, all the time, openly, for anyone to see!! Yet, the deluded individual-egos refuse to read these words of warning, written so clearly on the walls of life.

In our identification with the body, mind and intellect, we pant to gain, to enjoy and to know. The physical-personality in us is excited with its passion for living (*jīvita-ecchā*); the psychological-entity in us is drowned in the desire to enjoy (*Bubhūkṣā*); and the intellectual-man in us is ever hungry to learn and to know (*Bubhutsā*).

Rare indeed is that intelligent man who looks around, recognises the hollowness of life, and cultivates his indifference to the world and its destinies. The majority of us will have to get into the scorching embrace of *Māyā* and experience its suffocating agonies, repeatedly many times, in order to realise that the world of sense-objects and a life of sense-gratifications cannot satisfy the deeper yearning for a permanent bliss in us.

In short, a purified mind alone can, in its, subtle perception, discover a smartness in itself to cultivate indifference to the world of sense-pleasures, by intelligently observing the world of tears and sobs that is screaming at all times, all around him. But, alas, the majority are intellectually blind and deaf. They see, but do not comprehend—they hear, but do not listen to what they hear.

अनित्यं सर्वमेवेदं तापत्रितयदूषितम् ।
असारं निन्दितं हेयमिति निश्चित्य शाम्यति ॥ ३ ॥

Anityaṁ sarvam-evedaṁ tāpa-tritaya-dūṣitam,
asāraṁ ninditaṁ heyam-iti niścitya śāmyati.

अनित्यम् *anityam* = transient; इदम् सर्वमेव *idam sarvam-eva* = all this world indeed; ताप त्रितय-दूषितम् *tāpa tritaya-dūṣitam* = filthy (vitiated) with the triple misery; असारम् *asāram* = worthless; निन्दितम् *ninditam* = contemptible; हेयम् *heyam* = rejectable; इति *iti* = thus; निश्चित्य *niścitya* = knowing for certain; शाम्यति *śāmyati* = becomes serene (Man-of-wisdom).

3. *The Man-of-wisdom becomes serene by realising that this world indeed, is transient, filthy with the triple misery, worthless, contemptible, and as something to be rejected.*

In the previous verse *Aṣṭāvakra* mourned at the tragedy of man's intellectual blindness and deafness. There is sufficient evidence all around him in life to help him realise that the life of sense-pursuits is doomed for disappointment. Here in this verse, *Aṣṭāvakra* states what would be the logical conclusion of an intelligent man, when he evaluates, without prejudices, the world-drama as it is played everywhere.

The Man-of-wisdom becomes serene in this very world, where the ignorant man suffers from conflicts, contradictions and confusion in himself. The serenity of the Wise-man is based upon his understanding that the world is transient and never permanent—it is worthless and contemptible, and therefore, something to be discarded. It is full of sorrows, streaming in gushing haste towards him from three permanent sources.

These triple sources of sorrow are: (a) from the organism—the body, mind and intellect (*ādhyātmik*); (b) from the sentient beings and insentient objects that constitute the world around him (*Ādhi-bhautik*); and (c) from the cosmic accidents like floods, earthquakes etc., which we generally indicate by the expression "the hand of God" (*Ādhi-daivik*).

काऽसौ कालो वयः किं वा यत्र द्वन्द्वानि नो नृणाम् ।
तान्युपेक्ष्य यथाप्राप्तवर्ती सिद्धिमवाप्नुयात् ॥ ४ ॥

Ko'sau kālo vayaḥ kiṁ vā yatra dvandvāni no nṛṇām,
tānyu-pekṣya yathā-prāpta-vartī siddhim-avāpnuyāt.

कः *kaḥ* = what; असौ *asau* = that; कालः *kālaḥ* = time; वयः *vayaḥ* = age; किम् *kim* = what; वा *vā* = or; यत्र *yatra* = where; द्वन्द्वानि *dvandvāni* = pairs-of-opposites; नो *no* = not; नृणाम् *nṛṇām* = of men; तानि *tāni* = those; उपेक्ष्य *upekṣya* = abjuring; यथा-प्राप्तवर्ती *yathā-prāptavartī* = one who rests contented with what comes unasked; सिद्धिम् *siddhim* = perfection; अवाप्नुयात् *avāpnuyāt* = reaches.

4. *What is that time, or that age, in which the pairs-of-opposites do not exists for man? He who, adjuring these, rests contented with what comes to him unasked, reaches Perfection.*

The more we revel in the relative-plane of joy and sorrow, the more we will be tossed about between the pairs-of-opposites. We cannot say that these will not affect us when we grow old. Age cannot dullen, nor time soften the harsh brutalities and sharp sorrows of the pairs-of-opposites. So long as we are living identified with the mind, the ego will have to suffer the buffeting storms of joy and sorrow, of success and failure, of likes and dislikes, and thousand other such pairs-of-opposites. The question of *Aṣṭāvakra* implies in itself the answer that never is a time, or an age when the pairs-of-opposites will not affect an ego-entity.

Detachment from the mind is the only way to detach from the merciless brutalities of the pairs-of-opposites. He alone can realise the Supreme Peace and Perfection who has transcended the mind and therefore, has abandoned these pairs-of-opposites. He, thereafter, lives contented and happy with whatever comes to him unasked (*Yathā-prāpta-vartī*). In such a peaceful man, the ego is dead; he "reaches perfection." This reminds us of a similar statement expressed in *Mahopaniṣad* (IV-35):

सन्तोषामृतापानेन ये शान्तास्तृप्तिमागताः ।
आत्मारामा महात्मानस्ते महापदमागताः ॥

Santoṣāmṛtā-pānena ye śāntās-tṛptim-āgatāḥ,
ātmārāmā mahātmā-naste mahā-padam-āgatāḥ.

"Drunk in the nectar of cheerfulness, those peaceful men, who have reached the sense of contentment, ever-revelling in the Self, are the saintly ones who have already reached the Great State."

There cannot be any cessation in the alternate play of joy and sorrow. The pairs-of-opposites represent the two poles of the same factor. As there cannot be a piece of magnet with only one south-pole, so too there cannot be joy without sorrow. This, too, is beautifully expressed in an eloquent verse :

सुखस्यानन्तरं दुःखं दुःखस्यानन्तरं सुखं ।
द्वे एतत् हि जन्तूनां अलध्यम् दिनरात्रिवत् ॥

Sukhasyā-nantaraṁ duḥkaṁ duḥkhasyā-nantaraṁ sukhaṁ
dve etat hi jantūnāṁ aladhyam dina-rātri-vat.

"End of joy is sorrow; end of sorrow is joy; these two are for the living creatures as inescapable as day and night."

In fact, we cannot run away from sorrow without stepping into joy; nor can we retreat from joy without stepping into sorrow. There cannot be the crux of a wave without its hollows. Thus, by moving horizontally, we cannot escape the pairs-of-opposites. However far we may go, we cannot escape the waves of the ocean, can we? Yet, vertically, by rising into a Higher-plane of Consciousness we can definitely end the restlessness and exhaustions provided by the pairs-of-opposites.

नाना मतं महर्षीणां साधूनां योगिनां यथा ।
दृष्ट्वा निर्वेदमापन्नः को न शाम्यति मानवः ॥ ५ ॥

Nānā mataṁ maharṣīṇāṁ sādhūnāṁ yogināṁ yathā,
dṛṣṭvā nirveda-māpannaḥ ko na śāmyati mānavaḥ.

नाना *nānā* = diverse; मतम् *matam* = opinions; महर्षीणाम् *maharṣīṇām* = great seers; साधूनाम् *sādhūnām* = of sages; योगिनाम् *yoginām* = of *Yogin-s*; यथा *yathā* = as well as; दृष्ट्वा *dṛṣtvā* = seeing; निर्वेदम् *nirvedam* = indifference; आपन्नः *āpannaḥ* = attained; कः *kaḥ* = what; न *na* = not; शाम्यति *śāmyati* = attains tranquillity; मानवः *mānavaḥ* = man.

5. *Where is that man, who having observed the diversities of opinions among the great seers, sages and* Yogin-s, *and thus becoming completely indifferent, does not attain tranquillity.*

Though the Infinite experience is one and the same, when, based upon their direct experience, different intellectual Masters try to explain the Truth and expound the methods of achieving It, it is natural that there should be as many different points of view as there are Masters. Thereafter, mere erudite scholars try to distill the philosophy of each Master; through these mere intellectual interpretations, different schools are born. Amidst the logical arguments arrayed by each school, in support of itself, and for the condenmation of all other schools, an ordinary student must necessarily get utterly confused. This is unavoidable. Even *Śaṅkara* in *Vivekacūḍāmaṇi*-62 warns us :

शब्दजालं महारण्यं चित्तभ्रमणकारणम् ।
अतः प्रयत्नाज्ज्ञातव्यं तत्त्वज्ञात्तत्त्वमात्मनः ॥

Śabda-jālaṁ mahāraṇyaṁ citta-bhramaṇa-kāraṇam,
ataḥ prayatnāj-jñātavyaṁ tattvajñāt-tattvam-ātmanaḥ.

"The wordy-arguments are a dense-forest which makes the mind lose its way and wander about. Hence, intelligent seekers should earnestly set about to realise the illumining Principle of Consciousness—the Essential Self."

When an intelligent student carefully reads the various view-points, he must necessarily come to the same conclusion that by words and arguments Truth can never be finally ascertained. A true student, therefore, becomes indifferent to mere intellectual learning and logical argumentation. They discuss the nature of the Truth with their teachers and among themselves. There is a lot of difference between arguments and discussions. Exchange of ignorance is arguments (*vāda*); and exchange of intelligence is discussion (*vicāra*). True seekers, after some amount of study and discussion must turn indifferent to mere learning and should strive their best to cultivate and experience the Tranquillity of the Self in themselves.

If these *Ācāryā-s* are contradicting among themselves, and each is championing one school or the other, whom should a seeker follow as his preceptor, guide, or *Guru*. *Aṣṭāvakra* explains the qualifications of a *Guru* in the following verse :

कृत्वा मूर्तिपरिज्ञानं चैतन्यस्य न किं गुरुः ।
निर्वेदसमतायुक्त्या यस्तारयति संसृतेः ॥ ६ ॥

Kṛtvā mūrti-parijñānaṁ caitanyasya na kiṁ guruḥ,
nirveda-samatā-yuktyā yas-tārayati saṁsṛteḥ.

कृत्वा *kṛtvā* = gaining; मूर्ति-परिज्ञानम् *mūrti-parijñānam* = realisation of the true Nature; चैतन्यस्य *caitanyasya* = of Pure Consciousness; न *na* = not; किम् *kim* = is he not? (interrogative); गुरुः *guruḥ* = spiritual guide; निर्वेद-समता-युक्त्या *nirveda-samatā-yuktyā* = by indifference, equanimity and logical reasoning; यः *yaḥ* = who; (सः *saḥ* = he) तारयति *tārayati* = saves himself; संसृतेः *saṁsṛteḥ* = from *Saṁsāra.*

6. *He who apprehends the true nature of Pure Consciousness, by complete indifference to the world, by equanimity and by logical reasoning, and thus saves himself from the round of birth and death—is he not really the spiritual guide?*

The qualification of a teacher is not his great knowledge of the *Vedik*-content. Knowledge of the scriptures (*śrotriyatvam*) is, no doubt, an added beauty in a spiritual teacher. But the essential qualification for a teacher is his own inner awakening, accomplished by the three means—of indifference, of equanimity and of logical reasoning. According to *Aṣṭāvakra* the *Brahma-niṣṭhatvam*, the direct experience of the Self, is the most valid qualification for a teacher.

In the *Guru-Gītā*, we are advised :-

ज्ञानहीनो गुरुस्त्याज्यो।

Jñāna-hīno gurus-tyājyo

Reject an incompetent and an ignorant *Guru.*

स्वविश्रानित्यं न जानाति परशान्तिं करोति किम्।

Sva-viśrānityaṁ na jānāti para-śāntiṁ karoti kim?

"He who knows no peace in himself, how can he bring peace into the bosom of others."

पश्य भूतविकारांस्त्वं भूतमात्रान् यथार्थतः ।
तत्क्षणाद्बन्धनिर्मुक्तः स्वरूपस्थो भविष्यसि ॥ ७ ॥

Paśya bhūta-vikārāṁ-stvaṁ bhūta-mātrān yathārthataḥ,
tat-kṣaṇāt-bandha-nirmuktaḥ svarūpa-stho bhaviṣyasi.

पश्य *paśya* = see; भूत-विकारान् *bhūta-vikārān* = the modifications of the great elements; त्वम् *tvam* = you; भूत-मात्रान् *bhūta-mātrān* =

nothing but the great elements; यथार्थत: *yathārthataḥ* = in reality; तत्-क्षणात् *tat-kṣaṇāt* = at once; बन्ध-निर्मुक्त: *bandha-nirmuktaḥ* = free from bondage; स्वरूपस्थ: *svarūpa-sthaḥ* = abiding in your own nature; भविष्यसि *bhaviṣyasi* = will be.

7. *Recognising the modificaions of the elements as nothing in reality, but the five elements themselves, you will at once be free from their bondage, and thus abide in your True Nature.*

The elements are the fundamental material with which the entire world of forms is built up. That which is made out of gold cannot be anything other than gold; similarly, all that is made out of the five-elements cannot be anything other than the inert and insentient five-elements, expressing in a particular given combination. Taking the objects of the world as something real our mind comes to entertain a desire to acquire, to possess and to enjoy. Thus we create a world of struggles, riddled with stresses and strains. Once we realise that the entire perceived world is a play of inert and insentient elements, there is an immediate sense-of-disenchantment, as all our likes and dislikes shall, then, instantaneously disappear from our hearts. When the mind is thus quiet, in that tranquil bosom, the Pure Consciousness, undisturbed by thoughts, can be apprehended.

वासना एव संसार इति सर्वा विमुञ्च ताः ।
तत्त्यागो वासनात्यागात् स्थितिरद्य यथा तथा ॥ ८ ॥

Vāsanā eva saṁsāra iti sarvā vimuñca tāḥ,
tattyāgo vāsanā-tyāgāt sthitiradya yathā tathā.

वासना: *vāsanāḥ* = desire; एव *eva* = surely; संसार: *saṁsāraḥ* = world; इति *iti* = so; सर्वा *sarvā* = all; विमुञ्च *vimuñca* = renounce; ता: *tāḥ* = those; तत्-त्याग: *tat-tyāgaḥ* = renunciation of that; वासना-त्यागात् *vāsanā-tyāgāt* = by the giving up of desires; स्थिति: *sthitiḥ* = you may live; अद्य *adya* = now; यथा तथा *yathā tathā* = wherever you may be.

8. *Desires alone constitute the world; therefore, you please renounce them all. The giving up of desires is*

the renunciation of the world. Now you may live anywhere you like.

Vāsanā-s are the subtle impulses and tendencies deep in our personality that determine the emotional and the intellectual profile in us. Its subtle expression is our 'desire' in our intellect. Therefore, *Vāsanā* is often found translated as 'desire,' although *Vāsanā* is essentially the very seed from which a 'desire' springs forth. All the *Vāsanā-s* put together in an individual, constitute his 'Causal-body'[1]—that which determines the nature and quality of that individual's subtle and gross bodies.

These *Vāsanā-s* experienced as desires, thoughts and actions at the intellectual, mental and body levels, shackle the ego in a cage of selfishness, and chain him to the wheel of birth-and-death. These *Vāsanā-s* alone constitute the world (*Vāsanā* eva *Saṁsāraḥ*). Therefore, give up all 'desires.' Giving up of 'desires' is giving up of *Saṁsāra.*

Now (*Adya*) meaning "having renounced all desires; having sublimated all your *Vāsanā-s*"—the individual is free to live anywhere he likes. The outer world can no longer bind him. He is free. Says *Yoga Vāsiṣṭha*:

बन्धो हि वासनाबन्धो मोक्षः स्याद्वासनाक्षयः ।
वासनास्त्वं परित्यज्य मोक्षार्थित्वमपि त्यज ॥

Bandho hi vāsanā-bandho mokṣaḥ syād-vāsanā-kṣayaḥ,
vāsanās-tvaṁ pari-tyajya mokṣārthi-tvam-api tyaja.

"The bondage is, the bondage of *Vāsanā-s*; freedom is, the freedom from *Vāsanā-s*; you renounce completely the *Vāsanā-s* and then renounce the very *vāsanā* for freedom. You have reached the goal."

---

1. कारणशरीर-सर्वाः शरीराभिमानी (नि.) समष्टिकारणशरीराभिमानि परमात्मा-ईश्वरः॥
The "Total-*Vāsanā-s*" of all living creatures together becomes *Māyā*, and Supreme Self expressed through *Māyā* is God (*Īśvara*) — who is the very power behind Creation, Sustenance and Destruction in the Cosmos.

Chapter—X

Dispassion

Introduction

Without leaving none can reach; all progress is leaving the present state and moving to reach a greater goal, to attain a greater purpose. If ignorance is not left behind, into knowledge we cannot enter. Where the emotion of anger has left, there alone calmness can reach. In short, without renunciation of the false we cannot attain the Real. Therefore, in *Vedānta*, from the *Vedik* texts onward, we find the teachers emphasising the need for the spirit of renunciation (*vairāgya*). It is the desires and passions that propel a mind towards the world around it, and make that mind a slave to its own environments. Therefore, the principle of renunciation is indicated by a significant term '*vairāgya*,' literally meaning, 'dispassion.' Where our attachments to body, mind and intellect have ended through *vairāgya*, there we are in the Self.

The previous chapter discussed an emotional attitude of 'indifference' to fields of experiences of our limited ego. There the emphasis was upon the world-of-*objects*. In this section defining and exploring the significance and spirit of dispassion, *Aṣṭāvakra* is placing all emphasis upon the seeker's intellect and its attitude towards the world around him.

The joys or the destinies of the world are impermanent. A consummate sense of contentment can reach only a bosom emptied of all its desires and passions. Ultimately, we must give up even our anxiety to fulfil the traditionally accepted and recommended great "ends of human-life" such as Piety

(*Dharma*), Wealth (*Artha*), Desires (*Kāma*) and anxiety for liberation (*Mokṣa*).

The Self alone is Real; the universe is false—as false as a magician's show. All activities in the pursuit of Piety, Wealth and Desires are also unreal. The very anxiety for Liberation is an illusion; therefore, all these are to be renounced. This is the state of Supreme Dispassion (*Param Vairāgya*).

The awareness in us that illumines the very 'ignorance' in us, and makes us conscious of it, is the Supreme Self. Therefore, earlier it was also indicated that even 'ignorance' is unreal, an illusion.

अष्टावक्र उवाच ।

विहाय वैरिणं काममर्थं चानर्थसङ्कुलम् ।
धर्ममप्येतयोर्हेतुं सर्वत्रानादरं कुरु ॥ १ ॥

Aṣṭāvakra Uvāca:

Vihāya vairiṇaṁ kāmam-arthaṁ cānartha-saṅkulam,
dharmam-apy-etayor-hetuṁ sarvatrā-nādaraṁ kuru.

विहाय *vihāya* = forsaking; वैरिणम् *vairiṇam* = enemy; कामम् *kāmam* = desire; अर्थम् *artham* = wealth; च *ca* = and; अनर्थ-सङ्कुलम् *anartha-saṅkulam* = full of mischief; धर्मम् *dharmam* = piety; अपि *api* = also; एतयोः *etayoḥ* = of these two; हेतुम् *hetum* = cause; सर्वत्र *sarvatra* = everywhere; अनादरम् *anādaram* = disregard; कुरु *kuru* = do.

Aṣṭāvakra said :

1. *Having given up 'desire' (*Kāma*) which is the enemy, 'wealth' (*Artha*—i.e. wordly prosperity) which is attended with mischief, and 'piety' (*Dharma*—performance of good* deeds*) which is the cause of these two, cultivate indifference to everything.*

In the traditional Indian scheme-of-life, the *Ṛṣī-s* found out four distinct destinations enroute to the final achievement of life, one's total spiritual emancipation. These four way-side stations are Piety, wealth, desires and liberation[1]; the interpretation of these four goals at the level of a new initiate in a *Hindū* family is that he must be rooted in righteousness and 'piety', and without contradicting this *Dharma* he must seek, serve and procure the necessary 'wealth' (*Artha*)—with which he must learn to fulfil his honest and just 'desires' (*kāma*). By thus living a steady life of spiritual discipline he shall become fit for the study of scriptures and enter into deeper meditation which would ultimately take him to his final destination, freedom or Liberation (*Mokṣa*).

Aṣṭāvakra is advising here a student, who is on his way to the portal of liberation. As the student enters the higher states of meditation, the teacher wants the student to give up all these limited goals of life which, of course, had their initial blessings to contribute in helping the student to the present state of his awakening. But, in the last lap of the journey, he cannot accomplish the great leap, unless he gets tired of all his mental preoccupations with the ideas and values which were certainly valid in earlier levels of his ego-consciousness.

To a *Vedāntik* student, 'Passion' is his enemy, inasmuch as they will distract his mind towards sense-objects and thus obstruct his final plunge into deeper meditation. 'Wealth' is accompanied by mental anxieties, both in its acquisition and its preservation. And 'Piety', here meaning good and noble acts, both secular and sacred, also is to be given up because they are the cause for conferring upon him more worldly wealth and sense-enjoyments. Later on, we will be told how even the anxiety for Liberation (*Mokṣa*) is also to be given up.

This is the state of highest dispassion (*Vairāgya*) which is to be lived in the meditation-seat while transcending the mind, rather than in the world, while communicating with the other members of the community. This attitude of "total-dispassion" is not a mere physical act of running away from the enjoyments of

1. *Dharma, Artha, Kāma* and *Mokṣa*

objects. This is an attitude that the student discovers in himself as a result of a healthier understanding of the world around him.

स्वप्नेन्द्रजालवत् पश्य दिनानि त्रीणि पञ्च वा ।
मित्रक्षेत्रधनागारदारदायादिसम्पदः ॥ २ ॥

Svapnendra-jālavat-paśya dināni trīṇi pañca vā,
mitra-kṣetra-dhan-āgāra-dāra-dāyādi-sampadaḥ.

स्वप्न-इन्द्रजालवत् *svapna-indrajālavat* = like a dream, or like a magicians' show; पश्य *paśya* = see; दिनानि *dināni* = days; त्रीणि *trīṇi* = three; पञ्च *pañca* = five; वा *vā* = or; मित्र *mitra* = friends; क्षेत्र *kṣetra* = lands; धन *dhana* = wealth; आगार *āgāra* = house; दार *dāra* = wives; दाय-आदि-सम्पदः *dāya-ādi-sampadaḥ* = presents and other such objects of fortune.

2. *Look upon friends, lands, wealth, houses, wives, presents, and other such objects of fortune as a dream, or as a magician's show, lasting only a few days—just three or five.*

As a means of rising above the habitual mental fascinations to live in the pursuit of the traditional 'goals-of-life,' hinted in the above verse, here *Aṣṭāvakra* helps the student in re-educating his view-of-life. In this new understanding, the student can independently come to recognise the hollowness of his generally accepted 'aims-of-existence,' of his relations, of wealth and of all other objects with which we try to enrich our lives and build up our security in existence. All are really illusions of the mind, as insubstantial and false as the dream-objects, or as the world of apparent fantasies created by a magician's wand!! They have only a temporary existence. The ephemeral nature of the world-of-plurality is indicated here by saying : "Lasting only a few days—just three or five."

Constantly keeping this view of the fields-of-experiences, the ego shall cultivate a larger amount of 'dispassion' (*Vairāgya*) for these uncertain factors and their insignificant rewards. The more the student recognises the transitoriness of the joys of achievements in the world-of-plurality, the stronger shall grow in him his 'dispassion' for them.

यत्र यत्र भवेत्तृष्णा संसारं विद्धि तत्र वै ।
प्रौढवैराग्यमाश्रित्य वीततृष्णः सुखी भव ॥ ३ ॥

Yatra yatra bhavet-tṛṣṇā saṁsāraṁ viddhi tatra vai,
prauḍha-vairāgyam-āśritya vīta-tṛṣṇaḥ sukhī bhava.

यत्र यत्र *yatra yatra* = wherever; भवेत् *bhavet* = is; तृष्णा *tṛṣṇā* = desire; संसारम् *saṁsāram* = world; विद्धि *viddhi* = know; तत्र *tatra* = there; वै *vai* = indeed; प्रौढ-वैराग्यम् *prauḍha-vairāgyam* = strong dispassion; आश्रित्य *āśritya* = adopting; वीत-तृष्णः *vīta-tṛṣṇaḥ* = free from desire; सुखी *sukhī* = happy; भव *bhava* = be.

3. *Know that to be the world wherever there is desire. Cultivating strong dispassion, go beyond the desire and be happy.*

Our *Ṛṣī-s* and Masters are never tired of repeating this idea which is a realised truth, a recognised rational fact. If we are not able to stand away from the enchantments of our desires then we would pathetically pursue for their fulfilment, thereby making life a miserable tragedy for ourselves and for others. In *Bhāgavat* (II-8-44) describing *Piṅglā*, the prostitute, the *Ṛṣi* says :

आशा हि परमं दुःखं नैराश्यं परमं सुखम् ।
यथा संछिद्य कान्ताशां सुखं सुष्वाप पिंगलो ॥

Āśā hi paramaṁ duḥkhaṁ nairāśyaṁ paramaṁ sukham,
Yathā saṁchidya kāntāśāṁ sukhaṁ suṣvāpa piṅgalo.

"Desire indeed is the supreme source of sorrow; desirelessness the source of extreme happiness. Just as in the case of *Piṅglā* when she destroyed her passion and anxiety for men, she slept peacefully."

In *Yoga-Vāsiṣṭha* also we find an elaborate metaphor painted in words to drive home the very same truth of life :

> मनोरथ रथारूढं युक्तमिन्द्रियवाजिभिः ।
> भ्राम्यत्येव जगत्कृत्स्नं तृष्णासारथिचोदितम् ॥

> *Manoratha rathā-rūḍhaṁ yuktam-indriya-vājibhiḥ,*
> *bhrāmya-tyeva jagat-kṛtsnaṁ tṛṣṇā-ṣārathi-coditam.*

"The individual-ego, riding in the chariot of the mind, pulled by the horses of sense-organs, wanders all over the world, driven by its charioteer desire."

तृष्णामात्रात्मको बन्धस्तन्नाशो मोक्ष उच्यते ।
भवासंसक्तिमात्रेण प्राप्तितुष्टिर्मुहुर्मुहुः ॥ ४ ॥

Tṛṣṇā-mātrā-tmako bandhas-tannāśo mokṣa ucyate,
bhavā-saṁsakti-mātreṇa prāpti-tuṣṭir-muhur-muhuḥ.

तृष्णा-मात्र-आत्मकः *tṛṣṇāmātra-ātmakaḥ* = consisting of desire alone; बन्धः *bandhaḥ* = bondage; तत्-नाशः *tat-nāśaḥ* = destruction of that; मोक्षः *mokṣaḥ* = liberation; उच्यते *ucyate* = is called; भवासंसक्तिमात्रेण *bava-asaṁsakti-mātreṇa* = through the non-attachment of the world alone; प्राप्ति-तुष्टिः *prāpti-tuṣṭiḥ* = joy from attainment; मुहुर्मुहुः *muhur-muhuḥ* = constantly.

4. *Desire is the soul of bondage and its destruction is said to be 'liberation.' By non-attachment to the world alone does one attain the constant Bliss of the realisation of the Self.*

Where desires have ended, thoughts have ceased—the mind is halted. Where there is no mind, there cannot be any ego, the experiencer of the world-of-plurality and its sorrows. Therefore, "dispassion" (*Vairāgya*) is the only sure and efficient way to reach the Highest State of Bliss.

Mahopaniṣad (V-97) express the same idea :

भोगेच्छामात्रको बन्धः तत्त्यागो मोक्ष उच्यते ।

Bhogecchā-mātrako bandhaḥ tat-tyāgo mokṣa ucyate.

"Sensuous desires alone are bondage;
their renunciation is called liberation."

त्वमेकश्चेतनः शुद्धो जडं विश्वमसत्तथा ।
अविद्यापि न किञ्चित्सा का बुभुत्सा तथापि ते ॥ ५ ॥

Tvam-ekaś-cetanaḥ śuddho jaḍaṁ viśvam-asat-tathā,
avidyāpi na kiñcit-sā kā bubhutsā tathāpi te.

त्वम् *tvam* = you; एकः *ekaḥ* = one; चेतनः *cetanaḥ* = intelligence; शुद्धः *śuddhaḥ* = Pure; जडम् *jaḍam* = material (inert); विश्वम् *viśvam* = universe; असत् *asat* = non-existence; तथा *tathā* = and; अविद्या *Avidyā* = ignorance; अपि *api* = also; न *na* = not; किञ्चित् *kiñcit* = anything; सा *sā* = that; का *kā* = what; बुभुत्सा *bubhutsā* = desire to know; तथापि *tathāpi* = yet; ते *te* = your.

5. *You are the One, Pure Intelligence. The universe is inert and unreal. Ignorance also is non-existent. What then can you yet desire to know?*

By the four earlier verses the teacher indicated to us, in a language of negation, what are the things to be renounced. Here, *Aṣṭāvakra* takes a positive stand, and tries to indicate the student's very Spiritual Centre, to identify with which is to reject everything else.

The essential nature of *being* is the Self, and the Self is Consciousness. Everything else is inert and functions only in the borrowed 'light' of the Self. In the midst of illusory, inert world of names-and-forms, the Self alone is Real. In the 'light' of Pure Intelligence, there cannot be the darkness of 'ignorance.' After making this statement the teacher asks : What more should one intelligently understand? This is all to be understood from the study of the scriptures. To a practical student, who is ready to do *Sādhanā*, and move towards the experience of the Self, no other hair-splitting argumentations and endless logical reasonings are really necessary.

Aṣṭāvakra advises the student to give up his intellectual-gluttony—his ever-growing hunger to study, to discuss, to argue and to investigate. *Mahopaniṣad* (V-69) pointedly indicates what exactly is to be realised :

नाहं न चान्यदस्तीह ब्रह्मैवास्मि निरामयम् ।
इत्थं सदसतोर्मध्यात् यः पश्यति स पश्यति ॥

Nāhaṁ na cānyad-astīha brahmai-vāsmi nirāmayam,
itthaṁ sad-asator-madhyāt yaḥ paśyati sa paśyati.

"Neither I, as an individual, nor others really exist. Unsullied *Brahman* am I. Thus he who sees from a point between Existence and non-existence—the Consciousness that illumines both the Real and unreal—he alone sees the Reality, the Self."

राज्यं सुताः कलत्राणि शरीराणि सुखानि च ।
संसक्तस्यापि नष्टानि तव जन्मनि जन्मनि ॥ ६ ॥

Rājyaṁ sutaḥ kalatrāṇi śarīrāṇi sukhāni ca,
saṁsaktasyāpi naṣṭāni tava janmani janmani.

राज्यम् *rājyam* = kingdom; सुताः *sutāḥ* = sons; कलत्राणि *kalatrāṇi* = wives; शरीराणि *śarīrāṇi* = bodies; सुखानि *sukhāni* = pleasures; च *ca* = and; संसक्तस्य *saṁsaktasya* = attached; अपि *api* = though; नष्टानि *naṣṭāni* = have been lost; तव *tava* = you; जन्मनि जन्मनि *janmani janmani* = life after life.

6. *Kingdoms, sons, wives, bodies and pleasures have all been lost to you, life-after-life, even though you were attached to them.*

In the previous verse a highly metaphysical and philosophical argument was given. An exhaustive definition of the Spiritual Centre in man, the *Ātman* as given out by the *Vedāntik* Masters is :

स्थूलसूक्ष्मकारणशरीरद्-व्यतिरिक्तोऽवस्थात्रयसाक्षी
सच्चिदानन्दस्वरूपो यस्तिष्ठति सः आत्मा ।

Sthūla-sūkṣma-kāraṇa-śarīrad
vayatirikto-'vasthā-traya-sākṣī,
sac-cidā-nanda-svarūpo
yas-tiṣṭhati saḥ ātmā.

"Other than the gross, subtle and causal bodies, the Witness of the three states of waking, dream and deep-sleep, of the Nature of Existence-Knowledge-Bliss—this, which remains in our personality, that is the Self, the *Ātman.*"

The student was shown that he is essentially nothing but the Self, the *Ātman*. And, therefore, what has he to do with the inert and unreal world and with the non-existent 'ignorance'? Here, however, *Aṣṭāvakra* gives us a very rational reason which even a common-man can understand. "Life after life, we must have sought to acquire, to possess and to enjoy kingdoms, sons, wives, bodies and pleasure"; and yet, in every life we had ultimately lost whatever we had. So, it is intelligent not to get ourselves entrapped by the fascinations for these things, because in spite of our attachment, it is their very nature that they must perish. An intelligent man should not therefore, fall a ready victim to such a repeated hallucination.

अलमर्थेन कामेन सुकृतेनापि कर्मणा ।
एभ्यः संसारकान्तारे न विश्रान्तमभून्मनः ॥ ७ ॥

Alam-arthena kāmena sukṛtenāpi karmaṇā,
ebhyaḥ saṁsāra-kāntāre na viśrāntam-abhūn-manaḥ.

अलम् *alam* = no deed; अर्थेन *arthena* = with wealth; कामेन *kāmena* = with desire-fulfilment; कर्मणा सुकृतेन *karmaṇā sukṛtena* = with poius deed; अपि *api* = and; एभ्यः *ebhyaḥ* = from these; संसार-कान्तारे *saṁsāra-*

kāntāre = in the wilderness of the world; न *na* = not; विश्रान्तम् *viśrāntam* = reposed; अभूत् *abhūt* = was; मनः *manaḥ* = mind.

7. *Enough of wealth, desires and pious deeds! In the wilderness of the world, the mind did not find repose in these.*

Repeating the idea, which he had mentioned earlier, *Aṣṭāvakra* insists that the pursuit of 'wealth,' 'desire' and 'piety' is indeed unrewarding from the stand-point of the Highest Goal. Enough with such pursuits. With 'wealth,' mind discovers various avenues of dissipation. 'Desire'—fulfilment have never brought ever a complete contentment to any human-mind: desires only multilply with each fulfilment! 'Pious-deeds' are the very cause that have provided the seeker with his present wealth and desire-fulfilments in the world. In the jungles of world's activities these have never brought peace and repose to the mind. Thus realising, cultivate "dispassion" (*Vairāgya*).

कृतं न कति जन्मानि कायेन मनसा गिरा ।
दुःखमायासदं कर्म तदद्याप्युपरम्यताम् ॥ ८ ॥

Kṛtaṁ na kati janmāni kāyena manasā girā,
duḥkha-māyā-sadaṁ karma tad-adyāpy-uparamyatām.

कृतम् *kṛtam* = undertaken; न *na* = not; कति *kati* = how many; जन्मानि *janmāni* = births; कायेन *kāyena* = with the body; मनसा *manasā* = with the mind; गिरा *girā* = with speech; दुःखम् *duḥkham* = painful; आयासदम् *āyāsadam* = exacting; कर्म *karma* = work (you); तत् *tat* = so; अद्य *adya* = today (at least); अपि *api* = even; उपरम्यताम् *uparamyatām* = cease

8. *For how many births have you not undertaken hard and painful work with your body, mind and speech? Hence, cease them at least even today!*

Gītā clearly points out in its scientific analysis of action how *Tāmasik*-actions performed with utter selfishness bring about sorrows to oneself and to others. The *Rājasik* and *Sāttvik* activities also, when they are unselfish, can reward us with apparent joys. But they, too, are within the category of *Saṁsāra* and, therefore, unreal and painful. No doubt, selfless dedicated activities would increase the *Sāttvik*-content in our inner equipment, and a mind can then come to experience a greater amount of tranquillity and peace. With a mind so purified through selfless dedicated pious-actions, the study of the scriptures and meditations are possible. The grosser rewards of activities are certainly impermanent, and at their best unsatisfactory to an enlightened man.

All our best actions undertaken so diligently and so laboriously with the exacting efficiency have ultimately brought about only sorrows, relieved with patches of impermanent joys!

When this discriminative understanding has dawned in his mind, the student becomes a true spiritual seeker, and addressing such a seeker the teacher here says : "Hence, cease them at least even today."

In *Yoga-Vāsiṣṭha,* we read a similar condemnation of the worldly activities for mature spiritual students:

भुक्त्वा वर्षसहस्राणि दुर्भोगपटलीमिमाम् ।
आब्रह्मस्तम्बपर्यन्तं न तृप्तिरुपजायते ॥
साम्रज्यं सुचिरं कृत्वा तथा भुक्त्वा वधूगणम् ।
भुंक्त्वा परबलान्युच्चैः किमपूर्वमवाप्यते ॥
प्राप्तेन येन नो भूयः प्राप्तव्यमवशिष्यते ।
तत्प्राप्तौ यत्नमातिष्ठेत् कष्ट्यापि हे चेष्टया ॥

Bhuktvā varṣa-sahastrāṇi durbhoga-paṭalīm-imām,
ābrahma-stamba-paryantaṁ na tṛptir-upajāyate.
sāmrajyaṁ suciraṁ kṛtvā tathā bhuktvā vadhūgaṇam,
bhūṁktvā para-balān-yuccaiḥ kim-apūrvam-avāpyate.
prāptena yena no bhūyaḥ prāptavyam-avaśiṣyate,
tat-prāptau yatnamā-tiṣṭhet kaṣṭyāpi he ceṣṭyā.

"Even after enjoying thousands of years the basest of sensuous enjoyments, from the Creator to a tuft of grass, no one has ever reached contentment. Having ruled over vast kingdoms for long years, having enjoyed a harem of wives, having destroyed all enemies around the world— what is the unique thing that one can gain? Laboriously struggle to gain That, having gained. Which, there is nothing more to gain—to gain This, continuously pant and struggle."

Chapter--XI

Self As Pure Intelligence

Introduction

In this Chapter, the Supreme is indicated as Pure Intelligence (*Cid-rūpa*). It is Universal and all-inclusive. There is nothing other than It. And therefore, It is ever at rest, serene and tranquil. No conflict is ever possible in the Self. The universe shines in the Light of the Pure Self. It ever revels in Its own Aloneness (*Kaivalya*). When an intelligent ego rediscovers his identity with this Great Self, he no longer gets himself involved in his external worldly activities.

The *Gītā* doctrine of "inaction in action" has been totally accepted by *Aṣṭāvakra* and he expounds it through the chapters of his Song. This chapter can be considered as *Jñāna-Aṣṭakam*—an Hymn to Pure Knowledge, in eight-verses. True and enduring Peace can be only in the State of Self-hood. Therefore, the preparatory understanding for gaining Self-realisation are here discussed. In fact, this short chapter is full of the qualities of a Man-of-realisation. It explains the nature of the Perfect-man and also indicates the *Sādhanā* to be pursued by the seekers to awake into the Highest Spiritual Awareness of the Universal Infinite Self. Until our perception of the world around is through a clearer perspective, our clinging attachments and mental concern for the world of happenings cannot be ended; there cannot be sufficient inner equipoise for subtler meditations.

Here are the eight lessons for healthier understanding of the world and its play which will bring in peace and tranquillity into the bosom of the seekers.

अष्टावक्र उवाच ।

भावाभावविकारश्च स्वभावादिति निश्चयी ।
निर्विकारो गतक्लेशः सुखेनैवोपशाम्यति ॥ १ ॥

Aṣṭāvakra Uvāca :

Bhāvā-bhāva-vikāraś-ca svabhāvā-diti niścayī,
nirvikāro gata-kleśaḥ sukhe-naivopa-śāmyati.

भाव-अभाव-विकारः *bhāva-abhāva-vikāraḥ* = change in the form of existence and destruction; च *ca* = and; स्वभावात् *svabhāvāt* = from inherent nature; इति *iti* = thus; निश्चयी *niścayī* = one who has understood with certitude; निर्विकारः *nirvikāraḥ* = unperturbed; गत-क्लेशः *gata-kleśaḥ* = free from pains; सुखेन *sukhena* = easily; एव *eva* = indeed; उपशाम्यति *upaśāmyati* = finds peace.

Aṣṭāvakra Said:

1. He who has understood with certitude that change in the form of existence and destruction is inherent in things, he becomes unperturbed and free from this pain—and easily finds his peace.

Intelligent observation with scientific detachment alone can crack the mystery-bound shell of life. Mind and body will act only according to our intellectual understanding and convictions, that one has cultivated in himself. In this chapter *Aṣṭāvakra* gives eight lessons in re-educating the intellectual-values entertained by the student. During this discourse, the sage paints the inner-personality of a Man-of-perfection. *Aṣṭāvakra* invites us to enter into the intellect of a Man-of-Self-realisation and he makes us see things as the wise-man does.

Through the study of the scriptures, and through independent reflection upon the pregnant declarations of the great *Upaniṣad-Ṛṣī-s*, the student must grow into a deep conviction of the spiritual view-points of the world around him. A mere information-gathering-intellect cannot progress on the spiritual journey; nor, can a vague understanding really help us much. The world, as it is, must be understood with an unshakable certitude, that can change the very colour and texture of our view of life and of our mental, intellectual and physical relationships with others.

He who has understood with certitude that existence and destruction are the inherent nature of the things that constitute the universe of change, is the one who can immediately discover a great amount of tranquillity in his bosom. No intelligent man will sit on the sea-shore and complain at the rising and the disappearing of the waves; he knows that this is the inherent nature of the waves. No one will complain at the rising and the setting of the sun each day, because all of us know that this is the inherent nature of the sun.

Similarly, a student of philosophy comes to understand with certitude that, like bubbles in the waters, everything in the universe must constantly keep on changing. His mind, therefore, will not any longer revolt against this inherent nature of the world around him. When this evanescent nature of things is realised, we cannot get ourselves any longer deeply attached to them. Naturally mental peace must come to flood the bosom of such a seeker.

Yoga-Vāsiṣṭha (52-12) thunders:

इमा विचित्राः कलनाः भावाभावमयात्मिकाः ।
दुःखायैव तवोग्राय न सुखाय कदाचन ॥

Imā vicitrāḥ kalanāḥ bhāvābhāva-mayātmikāḥ,
duḥkāyaiva tavogrāya na sukhāya kadācana.

"These endless thought-eruptions, their rising and disappearance, are ever for your terrible sorrows and never, never for your happiness."

ईश्वरः सर्वनिर्माता नेहान्य इति निश्चयी ।
अन्तर्गलितसर्वाशः शान्तः क्वापि न सज्जते ॥ २ ॥

Īśvaraḥ sarva-nirmātā nehānya iti niścayī,
antar-galita-sarvāśaḥ śāntaḥ kvāpi na sajjate.

ईश्वरः *Īśvaraḥ* = God (Self); सर्व-निर्माता *sarva-nirmātā* = Creator of all; न *na* = not; इह *iha* = here; अन्यः *anyaḥ* = other; इति *iti* = this; निश्चयी *niścayī* = one who has understood with certitude; अन्तर्गलित-सर्वाशः *antar-galita-sarvāśaḥ* = with all desires melted away; शान्तः *śāntaḥ* = calm; क्व अपि *kva api* = in anything whatsoever; न *na* = not; सज्जते *sajjate* = is attached.

2. *He who has understood with certitude that God (Self) is the Creator of all, and there is none else here, becomes calm with all his inner desires melted away. He is no longer attached to anything whatsoever.*

If from the great Reality, the world-of-plurality is projected, the created world cannot be other than the material from which it has been created. Thus, the Creator and the created are not two separate factors. The created universe is only yet another form of the Creator. The ornaments made of gold cannot be other than gold.

Thought-disturbances in the mind and the consequent gross perceptions of the outer universe are all existing in the Self illuminated by Its Light of Consciousness. The student who has understood this with certitude, becomes calm, for his desires get melted away. What is there for him to desire, there cannot be any attachment for him—as there is nothing other than himself, for him to covet and to feel entangled with.

In these verses we must not forget that we are given a chance to peep at the world through the intellect of a Man-of-realisation!

आपदः सम्पदः काले दैवादेवेति निश्चयी ।
तृप्तः स्वस्थेन्द्रियो नित्यं न वाञ्छति न शोचति ॥ ३ ॥

Āpadaḥ sampadaḥ kāle daivā-deveti niścayī,
tṛptaḥ svasthendriyo nityaṁ na vāñchati na śocati.

आपदः *āpadaḥ* = misfortunes; सम्पदः *sampadaḥ* = fortune; काले *kāle* = in time; दैवात् *daivāt* = through the effects of past actions; एव *eva* = certainly; इति *iti* = thus; निश्चयी *niścayī* = one who has understood with certitude; तृप्तः *tṛptaḥ* = contented; स्वस्थेन्द्रियः *svasthendriyaḥ* = with all the senses well-controlled; नित्यम् *nityam* = ever; न *na* = not; वाञ्छति *vāñchati* = desires; न *na* = not; शोचति *śocati* = grieves.

3. *He who has understood with certitude that misfortune and fortune come in their own time, through the effects of past actions, becomes ever contented and has all his senses well under-control. He neither desires nor grieves.*

It is all a question of our understanding. Even amidst good fortunes there are people who are in the habit of worrying and growing anxious. There are others who even in the midst of calamitous days of repeated misfortune discover an inner peace born out of unshaken faith.

Fortune and misfortune that happen today in our lives are the rewards and punishments of our own past actions. When this is understood with certitude, man learns to live in contentment, heroically facing whatsoever happens to him in life. He no longer strives or plans for his sense-gratifications; his senses are ever held in check. He desires nothing. He knows not how to grieve over things that had perished in his embrace. Desire is for what is not attained, and grief is generally over what is lost. Both these are happenings according to the rhythm set by our own actions in the past. In this knowledge he discovers an undisturbed peace and unperturbed contentment. This is aptly expressed in *Yoga-Vāsiṣṭa* as follows :

अथापदं प्राप्य सुसंपदं वा महामतिः स्वप्रकृतं स्वभावम् ।
जहाति नो मन्दरवेल्लितोऽपि शौक्ल्यं यथा क्षीरमयांबुराशिः ॥

Athā-padaṁ prāpya susaṁpadaṁ vā
mahā-matiḥ sva-prakṛtaṁ svabhāvam,
jahāti no mandara-vellito'pi śauklyaṁ
yathā kṣīramayāṁbu-rāśīḥ.

"Let misfortune come—or good fortune come. A true sage never leaves his Divine Peaceful Nature (Self), just as the Milky-ocean, in spite of being churned by the *Mandara*-mountain still retains its white-colour!!"

By lifting the mind to a higher vision alone can we withdraw it from its natural habitat consisting of sense-objects. This is the exercise advised by the *Bhagavad Gītā* (VI-25) also:

शनैः शनैरुपरमेद्बुद्ध्या धृतिगृहीतया ।
आत्मसंस्थं मनः कृत्वा न किञ्चिदपि चिन्तयेत् ॥

Śanaiḥ śanai-ruparamed-buddhyā dhṛti-gṛhītayā,
ātma-saṁsthaṁ manaḥ kṛtvā na kiñcid-api cintayet.

"Little by little let him attain quietude by the intellect held in firmness; having made the mind established in the Self, let him not think of anything."

Kaṭhopaniṣad (II-vi-14) reinforces this idea when it declares :

यदा सर्वे प्रमुच्यन्ते कामा येऽस्य हृदि श्रिताः ।
अथ मर्त्योऽमृतो भवत्यत्र ब्रह्म समश्नुते ॥

Yadā sarve pramucyante kāmā ye'sya hṛdi śritāḥ,
atha mrtyo-'mṛto bhavatyatra brahma samaśnute.

"When all desires in the heart are emptied, then the mortal man gains immortality and therein apprehends *Brahman*."

सुखदुःखे जन्म मृत्यू दैवादेवेति निश्चयी ।
साध्यादर्शी निरायासः कुर्वन्नपि न लिप्यते ॥ ४ ॥

Sukha-duḥkhe janma-mṛtyū daivā-deveti niścayī,
sādyā-darśī nirāyāsaḥ kurvann-api na lipyate.

सुख-दुःखे *sukha-duḥkhe* = in happiness and sorrow; जन्म-मृत्यू *janma-mṛtyū* = birth and death; दैवात् *daivāt* = due to the effects of past actions; एव *eva* = certainly; इति *iti* = thus; निश्चयी *niścayī* = one who has understood with certitude; साध्यादर्शी *sādyādarśī* = not seeing after the goals of life; निरायासः *nirāyāsaḥ* = free from care; कुर्वन् *kurvan* = doing; अपि *api* = even; न *na* = not; लिप्यते *lipyate* = tainted.

4. *He who has understood with certitude that happiness and sorrow, birth and death, are all due to the effects of past actions, does no more seek after the ordinary goals of life. He becomes free from care. He is not attached (tainted) even though engaged in action.*

When the understanding has dawned that our present life and all its achievements and sorrows are all effects of the past, he has, thereafter, no more any definite goal to be reached in life except the Infinite Self, which is the Substratum for the entire world and for all the happenings in it. Naturally, he becomes an individualised separate entity; the "ego" in him dies. Therefore, "he is not attached (tainted) even though engaged in action."

This idea of "actionless-ness in action" is the doctrine of the *Bhagavad-Gītā* (V-7) which *Aṣṭāvakra* accepts root and branch:

योगयुक्तो विशुद्धात्मा विजितात्मा जितेन्द्रियः ।
सर्वभूतात्मभूतात्मा कुर्वन्नपि न लिप्यते ॥

Yoga-yukto viśuddhātmā vijitātmā jitendriyaḥ,
sarva-bhūtātma-bhūtātmā kurvann-api na lipyate.

"He who is devoted to the Path-of-actions, whose mind is quite pure, who has conquered the ego, who has subdued his senses, who realises his Self as the Self in all beings—though acting, he is not tainted."

Ego-centric actions alone can leave their impression upon our personality, and thus condition our future thoughts and actions. This is how we get involved in our actions. Mind resting in *Brahman*, and in a spirit of utter dedication to It, when an individual functions, such activities bring about, according to *Gītā*, an exhaustion of the existing *Vāsanā-s*. For one who is revelling in *Brahman*, actions are spontaneous expression of the Divine in the world of beings. He acts not; he is acted through by the Universal Law.

चिन्तया जायते दुःखं नान्यथेहेति निश्चयी ।
तया हीनः सुखी शान्तः सर्वत्र गलितस्पृहः ॥ ५ ॥

Cintayā jāyate duḥkhaṁ nānya-theheti niścayī,
tayā hīnaḥ sukhī śāntaḥ sarvatra galita-spṛhaḥ.

चिन्तया *cintayā* = through anxiety; जायते *jāyate* = is produced; दुःखम् *duḥkham* = sorrow; न *na* = not; अन्यथा *ānyathā* = otherwise; इह *iha* = here; इति *iti* = thus; निश्चयी *niścayī* = one who has understood with certitude; तया हीनः *tayā hinaḥ* = free from that; सुखी *sukhī* = happy; शान्तः *śāntaḥ* = peaceful; सर्वत्र *sarvatra* = everywhere; गलित-स्पृहः *galita-spṛhaḥ* = with desires melted away.

5. *He who has understood with certitude that it is anxiety and nothing else that brings sorrow in the world, becomes free from it and is happy and peaceful everywhere—with his desires melted away.*

Sorrow itself is a mental condition-of-agitation; the more the agitations, the more the sorrow. Where agitations have ceased, mind has become calm, and this alone is the condition of happiness. Therefore, anxiety is that which breeds the sorrows of life. One who learns to leave all anxieties regarding the future, and lives in utter contentment rooted in one's own understanding, he discovers instant happiness and peace. All his desires melt away as he is no more hoping to discover a happiness through the gratification of any desire in himself.

Anxieties can raise storms in the mind only when one allows one's mind to get identified with the world-of-objects outside. Soon the mind cultivates an attachment with the objects. That attachment intensifies to crystalise into a desire for those objects. The desire poisons the mind, and it starts bleeding with its endless sorrows.

Again, we must remember that we are having here, a free show sitting in the intellect of the wise-man, sharing his views of the world throbbing around him.

नाहं देहो न मे देहो बोधोऽहमिति निश्चयी ।
कैवल्यमिव संप्राप्तो न स्मरत्यकृतं कृतम् ॥ ६ ॥

Nāhaṁ deho na me deho bodho'hamiti niścayī,
kaivalya-miva saṁprāpto na smaraty-akṛtaṁ kṛtam.

न *na* = not; अहम् *aham* = I; देहः *dehaḥ* = body; न *na* = not; मे *me* = my; देहः *dehaḥ* = body; बोधः *bodhaḥ* = Pure Intelligence; अहम् *aham* = I; इति *iti* = thus; निश्चयी *niścayī* = one who has understood with certitude; कैवल्यम् *kaivalyam* = the state of Aloneness; इव *iva* = as if; संप्राप्तः *saṁprāptaḥ* = attained; न *na* = not; स्मरति *smarati* = remembers; अकृतम् *akṛtam* = what is not done; कृतम् *kṛtam* = what is done.

6. *"I am not the body, nor is the body mine, I am Pure Intelligence"—he who has understood this with certitude, does no longer remember what he 'has-done' or what he 'has-not-done,' as if he has attained the state of aloneness (*Kaivalya*).*

When a seeker has mentally rejected the not-Self and has ascertained his own nature as the Self—even during the intense moments of his *Sādhanā*, he unconsciously admits to a flood of peace filling him, in which he apparently forgets to worry over what he 'has done,' or what he has 'not yet done.' To worry over what has been done, is the habit of the human-mind, to drag back from the dead-past his memories to muddy the pool of the present. Some not only get worried with regrets of their past, but also are anxious for their future, and this is indicated by the term here "what has not yet been done."

It is a human mind's habit to worry over actions both commited and omitted. When the student has gone through the practice, that has been advised here, he comes to discover within himself such a peaceful state of utter contentment, that therein he learns to live the dynamic present, supremely happy and peaceful and *Aṣṭāvakra* adds: "As though he has reached *Kaivalya*—the Supreme State of the Aloneness of the Self."

Kaṭhopaniṣad (II-vi-10) also advises the same. It guarantees and assures the same condition of inner Peace and Aloneness in the following words :

यदा पञ्चावतिष्ठन्ते ज्ञानानि मनसा सह ।
बुद्धिश्च न विचेष्टति तामाहुः परमां गतिम् ॥

Yadā pañcāva-tiṣṭhante jñānāni manasā saha
buddhiś-ca na viceṣṭati tāmāhuḥ paramāṁ gatim.

"When the five organs-of-knowledge are at rest, together with the mind, and when the intellect ceases functioning (becomes calm), that they call the Highest State."

The ideas of 'I' and 'my' are the expressions of the ego, and when the deeper understanding dawns in a seeker, "I am not the body, nor is the body mine," the ego-centric subject ends, and the ego awakes to the realisation of its Divine Selfhood. Sings *Mahopaniṣad* (IV-72):

द्वे पदे बन्धमोक्षायं निर्ममेति ममेति च ।
ममेति बध्यते जन्तुर्निर्ममेति विमुच्यते ॥

Dve pade bandha-mokṣāyaṁ nir-mameti mameti ca,
mameti badhyate jantur-nirmameti vimucyate.

"The two terms 'bondage' and 'liberation' are nothing but the tyranny of *mine-ness* and the total rejection of this *mine-ness*; by the sense of *mine-ness,* the creature gets bound and it is liberated when the sense of *mine-ness* has ended."

आब्रह्मस्तम्बपर्यन्तमहमेवेति निश्चयी ।
निर्विकल्पः शुचिः शान्तः प्राप्ताप्राप्तविनिर्वृतः ॥ ७ ॥

Ābrahma-stamba-paryantam-aham-eveti niścayī,
nir-vikalpaḥ śuciḥ śāntaḥ prāptā-prāpta-vinir-vṛtaḥ.

आब्रह्म-स्तम्ब-पर्यन्तम् *ābrahma-stamba-paryantam* = from the Creator down to a tuft of grass; अहम् *aham* = I; एव *eva* = indeed (am); इति *iti* = thus; निश्चयी *niścayī* = one who has understood with certitude; निर्विकल्पः *nirvikalpaḥ* = free from all fluctuations (oscillations of thought); शुचिः *śuciḥ* = Pure; शान्तः *śāntaḥ*= serene; प्राप्त-अप्राप्त-विनिर्वृतः *prāpta-aprāpta-vinirvṛtaḥ* = withdrawn from what is attained and what is not attained.

7. *"I am indeed in everything from the Creator down to a tuft of grass"—he who has understood this with certitude becomes free from all thought-oscillations; pure and serene he withdraws from what is attained and what is not attained.*

Limited mind alone gets agitated. The more the limitations, the greater the agitations. The mind completely relinquished and free from all identifications is the mind that has no agitations, and stilled-mind is the Supreme Self.

When the limited identifications of the ego have been transcended, and with certainty when the seekers has understood, "I am indeed the All-pervading Essense behind all names and forms," he is beyond his mind and, therefore, no more can the oscillations of the mind (*Vikalpa*) disturb him. The term '*Nir-vikalpa,*' as applied to *Samādhi* is defined by *Bhartṛhari* as : "an exclusive concentration upon the One entity, without distinct and separate consciousness of the *knower*, the *known* and *knowledge*, an even without Self-consciousness." It is strange, but true, that this familiar term '*Nir-Vikalpa*' taken up and popularised by *Patañjali*, is not at all used either in any of the Principal *Upaniṣad-s* nor in the *Bhagavad-Gītā*. However, *Aṣṭāvakra* freely makes use of it.

नानाश्चर्यमिदं विश्वं न किञ्चिदिति निश्चयी ।
निर्वासनः स्फूर्तिमात्रो न किञ्चिदिव शाम्यति ॥ ८ ॥

Nānāścarya-midaṁ viśvaṁ na kiñciditi niścayī,
nirvāsanaḥ sphūrti-mātro na kiñcidiva śāmyati.

नाना *nānā* = manifold; आश्चर्यम् *āścaryam* = marvellous; इदम् *idam* = this; विश्वम् *viśvam* = universe; न *na* = not; किञ्चित् *kiñcit* = anything; इति *iti* = thus; निश्चयी *niścayī* = one who has understood with certitude; निर्वासनः *nirvāsanaḥ* = free from desire; स्फूर्तिमात्रः *sphūrti-mātraḥ* = Pure Intelligence; न *na* = not; किञ्चित् *kiñcit* = anything; इव *iva* = as if; शाम्यति *śāmyati* = finds peace.

8. *He who has understood with certitude that this manifold and marvellous universe is nothing (unreal), becomes desireless and Pure Intelligence. He finds peace—as if nothing exists.*

In this concluding verse, the negation becomes so complete and total that the student in his reflection understands that the world-of-plurality as interpreted to him, through his body, mind and intellect, has no existence of its own. Having thus realised the illusory nature of the world, he becomes desireless to possess and to enjoy the world-of-objects outside. Without desires the subtle-body withers away, as there are no more thoughts in it; *Vāsanā-s* have already exhausted or else desires would have sprung up; thus causal body also has ceased. Naturally, the ego rediscovers that it is, in its true nature, Pure Intelligence—alone, the Self. He find Absolute peace in the objectless-awareness—at once Infinite and Marvellous.

Chapter XII

How to Abide in the Self

Introduction

In the earlier chapter (XI), considered as an eight-versed hymn to the glory of the Self, Sage *Aṣṭāvakra*, with a rare spontaneity of inspiration, completes a vivid and pulsating picture of the intellectual attitude of a Man-of-Perfection towards happenings in the objective world, and towards his own subjective intellectual reactions to them. Together with that, this chapter gives the view of the world from the silent and quiet bosom of a Man-of-Realisation.

Vedānta being a subjective science, worldly descriptions given out by Masters have no purposeful validity in themselves unless, they are considered as check-posts, in which the student must search his own wiithin. The ideas expounded in the *Vedāntik* philosophy are to be re-read and re-heard by the student himself in his own bosom.

Janaka as a perfect desciple recognises the deep significance of his teacher's words. In this section the royal Saint confesses how he has, in stages, come to abide in himself, in the Blissful Self.

The steps and the stages by which he ascended to this altitude of spiritual experience is being mapped in detail in these eight verses of this section.

Through the ideas provided in this section, when we observe the Man-of-perfection in *Janaka*, continuing his onerous responsibilities of administrating his kingdom and apparently revelling in the luxury and showy sensuousness of his court, we shall gain the glimpse of an unattached mind playing in the world, unaffected by the happenings around it—"like a lotus-leaf in water" (*Padma-patram-iva-ambhasa*) is a famous analogy used in the context by the *Bhagavad-Gītā*.

Emptying the mind of all the thought-disturbances within is the process to attain the spiritual life. To quieten and still even the last traces of thought-disturbance in the mind is the accomplishment of the higher-meditations. This is gained, in different stages, by sealing off the different sources from which these disturbances gurgle into our bosom. These processes of illumination are exhaustively indicated in these eight verses of this section.

जनक उवाच ।

कायकृत्यासहः पूर्वं ततो वाग्विस्तरासहः ।
अथ चिन्तासहस्तस्मादेवमेवाहमास्थितः ॥ १ ॥

Janaka Uvāca :

Kāya-kṛtyā-sahaḥ pūrvaṁ tato vāg-vistarā-sahaḥ,
atha cintā-sahas-tasmā-devam-evāham-āsthitaḥ.

काय-कृत्य-असहः *kāya-kṛtya-asahaḥ* = intolerant of physical action; पूर्वम् *pūrvam* = at first; ततः *tataḥ* = then; वाक्-विस्तर-असहः *vāk-vistara-asahaḥ* = intolerant of extensive speech; अथ *atha* = then; चिन्ता-असहः *citntā-asahaḥ* = intolerant of thought; तस्मात् *tasmāt* = therefore; एवम् *evam* = thus; एव *eva* = indeed; अहम् *aham* = I; आस्थितः *āsthitaḥ* = abide.

Janaka Said :

1. *I became intolerant first of physical action, then of extensive speech and then of thought. Thus do I, therefore, abide in Myself.*

Activities spring forth mainly from three sources—physical, oral and mental. Earlier seekers are advised to discipline their physical activities, their speech and their thoughts in such a way that all of them are geared to the thoughts of the Divine, and thereby the seeker is helped to turn his attention away from its usual pre-occupations with the world of sense-gratifications.

Religious activities like *Yajña*, *Pūjā* etc., and dedicated secular activities as social work, political work etc., are the methods by which the physical activities are divinised. Similarly, singing the glories of the Lord, reading the scriptures aloud, repeating an inspiring-*mantra*, according to the technique of *Japa*, are all accepted methods by which speech can be disciplined to turn towards the spiritual path. Again, thoughts which are generally running out into the world of sense-objects, when turned to contemplate upon the Lord of the Universe, constitutes the thought-discipline for a strict spiritual life.

When a student, having disciplined his body, speech and mind, practises meditation for long, he slowly climbs into the higher scales in meditation. Therein, he discovers that even these prayerful exercises of the body and the study of the scriptures at the speech-level, and all the conscious attempts at concentration in the practice of meditation at the intellectual-level, are all distractions for him in his higher flights into subtler meditation.

In this spiritual autobiography of *Janaka*, the Royal-Saint confesses that he could no longer stand distractions caused by his dedicated physical activities, by prayers, by silent-*Japa*, and even by contemplation. He gave them all up. And he says, "thus do I, therefore, abide in myself."

This is no blasphemy. The earlier *Sādhanā*-s such as services of mankind and rituals, *Kīrtana* and *Pūjā-s*, practice of truthfulness and self-control, concentration and contemplation etc., are all of immense significance to the seeker, because they, in their totality, shall lead the student to the take-off-pad for Higher Meditation. At this stage, in his subtle vision, he gains convincing glimpses of the oneness of the Divine Self everywhere. As *Yoga-Vāsiṣṭha* (Ch. 661-9) says:

कर्मैव देहो ननु देह एव चित्तं तदेवाहमितीह जीवः ।
सः जीव-एवेश्वरचित् स आत्मा सर्वः शिवस्त्वेकपदोक्तमेतद् ॥

Karmeva deho nanu deha eva
cittaṁ tad-evāham-itīḥ jīvaḥ,
saḥ jīva-eveśvara-cit sa ātmā sarvaḥ
śivas-tveka-padoktam-etad.

"The body is nothing but the effects of the past actions; and the mind that prompts the body is itself dynamised by the intelligent-ego (*Jīva*); and this *Jīva* is itself the expression of the Lord; and this Lord is the manifestation of the *Ātman*, the Self—in short, in one word, we say everything is the one *Śiva*." Moments of such understanding are moments when the earlier paths of *Sādhanā* are themselves insufferable mental distractions."

प्रीत्यभावेन शब्दादेरदृश्यत्वेन चात्मनः ।
विक्षेपैकाग्रहृदय एवमेवाहमास्थितः ॥ २ ॥

Prītya-bhāvena śabdāder-adṛśya-tvena cātmanaḥ,
vikṣepai-kāgra-hṛdaya ekame-vāha-māsthitaḥ.

प्रीति-अभावेन *prīti-abhāvena* = for want of satisfaction (attachment); शब्द-आदेः *śabd-ādeḥ* = of sound etc.; अदृश्यत्वेन *adṛsyatvena* = being no object of perception; च *ca* = and; आत्मनः *ātmanaḥ* = of the Self; विक्षेप-एकाग्र-हृदयः *vikṣepa-ekāgra-hṛdayaḥ* = with mind freed from distractions and rendered single-pointed; एवम् *evam* = thus; एव *eva* = indeed; अहम् *aham* = I; आस्थितः *āsthitaḥ* = abide in Myself.

2. *Having no satisfaction (attachment) in sound and the other sense-objects, and the Self being no object of perception, I have my mind freed from distractions and rendered single-pointed. Thus do I, therefore, abide in Myself.*

Explaining the stages by which *Janaka* walked into the Palace of Truth in himself, he confesses here that at this stage he has felt a growing dissatisfaction with "sound etc."—meaning in the study of the scriptures and discussions, in reflection, in *Japa*, etc. and therefore, he dropped them. Again, he found that even contemplation is meaningless, because meditation is a process whereby the mind is trying to visualise, think and experience the Self which is Invisible, Unthinkable. Therefore, he has left even all conscious attempts at contemplation and meditation. Honest to himself, the disciple declares to his teacher: "thus do I, therefore, abide in myself."

समाध्यासादिविक्षिप्तौ व्यवहारः समाधये ।
एवं विलोक्य नियममेवमेवाहमास्थितः ॥ ३ ॥

Samādhyāsa-ādi-vikṣiptau vyavahāraḥ samādhaye,
evaṁ vilokya niyama-meva-mevāham-āsthitaḥ.

सम-अध्यास-आदि-विक्षिप्तौ *sama-adhyāsa-ādi-vikṣiptau* = in the distractions caused by our super-impositions etc.; व्यवहारः *vyavahāraḥ* = activity; समाधये *samādhaye* = for *Samādhi*; एवम् *evam* = thus; विलोक्य *vilokya* = seeing; नियमम् *niyamam* = rule; एवम् *evam* = thus; एव *eva* = indeed; अहम् *aham* = I; आस्थितः *āsthitaḥ* = abiding in myself.

3. *An effort has to be made for Samādhi (for concentration) only when there is distraction of the mind due to one's own super-impositions. Seeing this to be the rule, thus do I, therefore, abide in Myself.*

The efforts at concentration (*Samādhi*) are only for those who have their minds distracted by their own illusory super-impositions. The body, the mind, the ego and their objects are all illusory projections made by the mind, and thereafter the mind gets fascinated by them and, so it is not available for the steady contemplation upon the Self. When this law is clearly understood by me, *Janaka* confesses: "I realised that the practice of meditation is only for those who are in 'ignorance,' suffering from the after-math of their spiritual 'ignorance.' Therefore, I left meditation, and thus do I, therefore, abide in myself." When all super-impositions (*Adhyāsa*) are left, the seeker realises the Self, and the Self-realised, who is awakened to the plane of Infinite Consciousness, can no longer meditate because he has no equipment to meditate with nor any more need for it.

हेयोपादेयविरहादेवं हर्षविषादयोः ।
अभावदद्य हे ब्रह्मन्नेवमेवाहमास्थितः ॥ ४ ॥

Heyopādeya-virahād-evaṁ harṣa-viṣādayoḥ,
abhāvad-adya he Brahman-nevam-evāham-āsthitaḥ.

हेयोपादेय-विरहात् *heyopādeya-virahāt* = in the absence of both the rejectable and acceptable; एवम् *evam* = as well as; हर्ष-विषादयोः *harṣa-viṣādayoḥ* = of joy and sorrow; अभावत् *abhāvat* = because of absence; अद्य *adya* = today; हे *he* = O!; ब्रह्मन् *brahman* = *Brahman*; एवम् *evam* = thus; एव *eva* = indeed; अहम् *aham* = I; आस्थितः *āsthitaḥ* = abide in Myself.

4. *Finding nothing as acceptable and nothing as rejectable, and having neither joy nor sorrow, 'O Brahman' thus do I, therefore, now abide in Myself.*

Addressing his teacher as, 'O *Brahman*'—and, thereby eloquently expressing his gratitude to his teacher, who is, to the disciple, as great as the Self Supreme—the Royal-Saint continues to explain how he scrambled to the next stage of the Higher Meditation.

To a seeker, good is acceptable and evil is rejectable; and the good and the evil are the judgements of the intellect. Having risen above the intellect, the *Yogī* reaches a state wherein there is nothing for him to accept or to reject. He comes to dwell in the Self which illumines both the concepts of the good and the bad, that rise as thoughts at the intellectual level. Having pursued the good, as its reward, we experience our life's joys and as a reward of evil we have life's sorrows. Joys and sorrows are emotions at the mental-level. When the meditator rises above the mind-and-intellect, he transcends both the joys and sorrows of the mind, and the good and the bad concepts of the intellect. "O! *Brahman*! thus do I, now abide in Myself" as Pure Infinite Consciousness Divine.

आश्रमानाश्रमं ध्यानं चित्तस्वीकृतवर्जनम् ।
विकल्पं मम वीक्ष्यैतैरेवमेवाहमास्थितः ॥ ५ ॥

Āśramā-nāśramaṁ dhyānaṁ citta-svīkṛta-varjanam,
vikalpaṁ mama vīkṣyai-taireva-mevāham-āsthitaḥ.

आश्रम-अनाश्रमम् *āśrama-anāśramam* = a particular state-of-life, or no-stage of life; ध्यानम् *dhyānam* = meditation; चित्त-स्वीकृत-वर्जनम् *citta-svīkṛta-varjanam* = control of mental functions; विकल्पम् *vikalpam* = distraction; मम *mama* = my; वीक्ष्य *vikṣyaḥ* = seeing; एतै: *etaiḥ* = by these; एवम् *evam* = thus; एव *eva* = indeed; अहम् *aham* = I; आस्थित: *āsthitaḥ* = abide in Myself.

5. *A particular stage-of-life, or negation of it, meditation, control of mental functions (mind)—recognising these as cause of distractions in me, thus do I, indeed, abide in Myself.*

"A particular stage-of-life" here refers to the traditional divisions of the *Hindū*-life into four stages. These four stages-in-life have each its own distinct duties and disciplines.[1] Each stage in life has its encumbrances of duties and anxieties, which are to *Janaka* distractions in his abiding experience of the Infinite Self. These various stages have a meaning only with reference to the individual's spiritual 'ignorance,' and his consequent identification with his body and the world around.

Similarly, "meditation" to a Man-of-Perfection, whose mind-is-at-rest, is a wasteful exertion. How can he control his mind from wandering into sense-objects, when from his vision

1. Student's life *(Brahmacarya)*; Householder's life *(Gṛhastha)*; Hermit's life *(Vānprastha)*; and Ascetic's life *(Saṁnyāsa)*. These are the four-stages *(Āśramā-s)* in the *Hindū* way-of-life prescribed in our Scriptures.

there is nothing but the Self everywhere. Thus, from his eminence in meditation, he finds all these as distractions and, therefore, he drops them all. And *Janaka* says, "thus, do I, indeed, abide in Myself."

The State *Janaka* indicates now is beyond all the four stages-in-life called in *Hindū* text-books as the *Āśramā-s*. This Trans-*Āśrama*-State is called as *Ati-varṇāśramī*, or the state of the *Avadhūta*. One who is in this state of Super-*Āśrama* has been defined in our *Śāstrā-s* very prescisely as follows:

"यः शरीरेन्द्रियादिभ्यो विभिन्नं सर्वसाक्षिणम् ।
पारमार्थिकविज्ञानं सुखात्मानं च स्वप्रभम् ।
परमतत्त्वं विजानाति सो अतिवर्णाश्रमी भवेत् ॥

Yaḥ śarīrendriy-ādibhyo vibhinnaṁ sarvas-ākṣiṇam,
pārmārthika-vijñānaṁ sukhātmānaṁ ca svaprabham
parama-tattvaṁ vijānāti so ati-varṇāśramī bhavet.

"He who has come to realise that he is the 'Witnessing Consciousness,' the Supreme Self, Blissful and Self-effulgent, entirely separate from the body and the sense-organs— he goes, beyond all castes and creeds, living the Super-State (*Ati-varṇāśramī*)."

कर्मानुष्ठानमज्ञानाद्यथैवोपरमस्तथा ।
बुद्ध्वा सम्यगिदं तत्त्वमेवमेवाहमास्थितः ॥ ६ ॥

Karmānu-ṣṭhānam-ajñānad-yathaivo-parama-stathā,
buddhvā samyag-idaṁ tattvameva-mevāham-āsthitaḥ.

कर्म-अनुष्ठानम् *karma-anuṣṭhānam* = undertaking of actions; अज्ञानात् *ajñānāt* = from ignorance; यथा *yathā* = as; उपरमः *uparamaḥ* = cessation; तथा एव *tathā eva* = even as; बुद्ध्वा *buddhvā* = knowing; सम्यक् *samyak* = fully; इदम् *idam* = this; तत्त्वम् *tattvam* = truth; एवम् *evam* = thus; एव *eva* = indeed; अहम् *aham* = I; आस्थितः *āsthitaḥ* = abide.

6. *Abstention from action is as much the outcome of ignorance as the undertaking of action. Knowing this truth fully well, thus do I, indeed, abide in myself.*

What is to be done and what is not to be done are both judgements of the intellect, and intellect itself has manifested from the spiritual ignorance. As long as the individulised-ego is asserting arrogantly, in order to tame and quieten it, selfless dedicated actions are prescribed, and certain activities which express shamelessly the lower nature of the ego are forbidden, for those who are walking the spiritual path. But these rules of do's and don'ts are made for the ignorant ego —"the Self-forgetful-Self."

So long as one is ill, one should strictly follow the medicines prescribed, and obey the dietetic regulation laid down by his doctor. But when the illness has left and full health has come back, the individual pursues his normal habits of healthy living. Similarly, the disciplines of life, laid down by the kindly Masters, are all meant essentially for the rediscovery of mental equipoise in the agitated bosom of the one who is groping in the darkness of 'ignorance.'

"Knowing this truth fully well," says *Janaka*, in his new-found Wisdom, "thus do I, indeed, abide in Myself."

अचिन्त्यं चिन्त्यमानोऽपि चिन्तारूपं भजत्यसौ ।
त्यक्त्वा तद्भावनं तस्मादेवमेवाहमास्थितः ॥ ७ ॥

Acintyaṁ cintyamāno'pi cintārūpaṁ bhajatyasau,
tyaktvā tad-bhāvanaṁ tasmād-evam-evāham-āsthitaḥ.

अचिन्त्यम् *acintyam* = the unthinkable; चिन्त्यमानः *cintyamānaḥ* = thinking; अपि *api* = even; चिन्तारूपम् *cintārūpam* = a form of thought; भजति *bhajati* = resorts to; असौ *asau* = one; त्यक्त्वा *tyaktvā* = giving up; तत् *tat* = that; भावनम् *bhāvanam* = thought; तस्मात् *tasmāt* = so; एवम् *evam* = thus; एव *eva* = indeed; अहम् *aham* = I; आस्थितः *āsthitaḥ* = abide.

7. *Thinking on the Unthinkable One, one resorts only to a form of (one's own) thought. Therefore, giving up that thought, thus do I, indeed, abide in Myself.*

The Infinite Self, is the very "light" of Consciousness that illumines all our thoughts, and without which our intellect becomes an inert equipment of *matter*. Naturally, the intellect cannot by its activities comprehend the Self, the very essence behind it. The light in the bulb of a torch can never illumine the battery behind it! No telescope can achieve seeing, even dimly, the viewer behind its eye-piece! Therefore, the Self and its Light of Consciousness that enlivens our life in our bosom is declared by the Great *Ṛṣī-s* as Unthinkable.

Lord *Kṛṣṇa* splashes out very clearly in the *Bhagavad Gītā* (XIII-15) :

सूक्ष्मत्वात्तदविज्ञेयम्

Sūkṣmatvāt-tad-vijñeyam.

"Becuase of its subtlity, it is ever incomprehensible."

To reflect and contemplate upon this Self, which is Unthinkable, is itself again a play of our thoughts. In the early stages of *Sādhanā* this method is extremely valid, as all other restlessness of the intellect gets quietened by the thought of the Unthinkable! But to one who has already exploded into the Higher-plane of Consciousness, and who is living vividly the experience of the Infinite Self, for him to sit in meditation, to contemplate upon the Unthinkable is to come out of the thoughtless state into the restlessness of thought! "Therefore," says *Janaka*, "giving up that thought, do I, indeed abide in Myself".

एवमेव कृतं येन स कृतार्थो भवेदसौ ।
एवमेव स्वभावो यः स कृतार्थो भवेदसौ ॥ ८ ॥

Evam-eva kṛtaṁ yena sa kṛtārtho bhavedasau,
evam-eva svabhāvo yaḥ sa kṛtārtho bhavedasau.

एवम् *evam* = thus; एव *eva* = even; कृतम् *kṛtam* = accomplished; येन *yena* = by whom; कृतार्थः *kṛtārthaḥ* = fulfilled; भवेत् *bhavet* = becomes; सः असौ *saḥ asau* = he (the man); एव *eva* = indeed; एवम् स्वभावः *evam-svabhāvaḥ* = by such nature; यः *yaḥ* = who; सः असौ *saḥ asau* = he; कृतार्थः *kṛtārthaḥ* = fulfils himself; भवेत् *bhavet* = becomes.

8. *Blessed is the man who has accomplished this. Blessed is he who thus fulfils himself by his Nature Divine.*

Almost tapping on his own back, as it were, in the ecstasy of his 'Infinite Satisfaction,' *Janaka* blesses himself through his hallelujah for the man who has attained Goodhood even while living (*Jīvan-Mukta*).

Śaṅkara defines *Vedeha-mukti* and *Jivan-mukti* as follows:

देहपातानन्तरं मुक्तिः विदेहमुक्तिः ।

Deha-pātā-nantaraṁ muktiḥ videha-muktiḥ.

"The liberation after the fall of the body is known as *Videha-muktiḥ*.

ब्रह्मैवाहमस्मीत्यपरोक्ष ज्ञानेन
निखिलकर्मबन्ध विनिर्मुक्तो जीवन्मुक्तः ।

Brahmaivā-hamasmītya-parokṣa-jñānena
nikhila-karma-bandhavinir-mukto jīvan-muktaḥ.

"With the *aprokṣa-jñāna* such as : "I am *Brahman*," one gets released from the bondage of past *karmā-s*, is *jīvan-mukti*."

When through *Sādhanā* a seeker comes to a stage when all *Sādhanā*-s drop off in his own achieved experience of the

Infinite Self, he is a unique individual, who, though bodily lives amidst us, has already become the Universal Reality. The experience of the Higher, in him, is spontaneous, effortless, natural. Nothing more can be said of him. He is verily a God living amidst us. He alone is the blessed one! He alone is the blessed one!!

Chapter—XIII

The Bliss Absolute

Introduction

The concluding verse of the previous section opens a vein of poetry in *Janaka*, and the Liberated-in-life, the Royal-Saint expounds, in this section, the Absolute Bliss as the very nature of the Supreme Reality.

It was already explained by the King that one who totally gives up all actions of his body, mind and speech alone can reach to abide in his own Real Nature. In the Pure Infinite Consciousness there is neither action nor inaction—neither joy nor sorrow—neither good nor bad. These are all values at the body, mind and intellect levels. The Consciousness of the Self is the Illuminator of all these and, therefore, is of a different category and order.

These seven pregnant verses have succeeded in giving us an exhaustive estimate of the rewards lived by one who is liberated-in-life, while the *Upaniṣad*-s have perceptibly failed to communicate to the students the magnitude of the bliss and glory experienced by a "*Jīvan-Mukta.*"

Inner renunciation of all our identifications with the perceptions, emotions and thoughts at the body, mind and intellect levels is a much more valid relinquishment than a hasty discarding of one's earthly possessions. The traditional picture of an ascetic is that he has only a single loin-cloth and a begging bowl as his own, and lives under some way-side tree. But even in this condition of voluntary poverty, attachment to that meagre loin-cloth (under-wear) and insignificant coconut-shell (*kamaṇḍalu*) can chain his mind down, refusing him admission into the Highest. *Janaka* seems to remember the stinging words of criticism of his teacher, in the earlier chapter. *Janaka* lives in a palace admist all the apparently wordly luxuries. What has he renounced? Here is the answer from the Royal Saint himself.

From this concept of the State of Supreme Non-dual Self—which remains the same in all the three periods of time, Immutable and Eternal—springs forth the subtle *Vedāntik* doctrine of "Non-origination" (*Ajāt-Vāda*). In fact, the fragrance and beauty of this doctrine, are from the flowers of the *Upaniṣad*-s. We must, as students of the *Hindū* philosophical-thoughts admit that Sage *Aṣṭāvakra* was, perhaps, the first to recognise and express this *Upaniṣadik* suggestion roughly into the form of a *Vedāntik* doctrine. Later on, no doubt, in *Māṇḍūkya Kārikā* we find this doctrine elaborated and expounded into a logical and acceptable philosophical thought.

The state-of-experience expounded here lies beyond the storms and agitations of the *matter*-equipments in man and therefore, this Transcendental State is a State of Bliss, ever undisturbed and Absolute.

जनक उवाच ।

अकिञ्चनभवं स्वास्थ्यं कौपीनत्वेऽपि दुर्लभम् ।
त्यागादाने विहायास्मादहमासे यथासुखम् ॥ १ ॥

Janaka Uvāca :

Akiñcana-bhavaṁ svāsthyaṁ kaupīnatve'pi durlabham,
tyāgādāne vihāyā-smād-ahamāse yathā-sukham.

अकिञ्चन-भवम् *akiñcana-bhavam* = born of the Consciousness that nothing else exists; स्वास्थ्यम् *svāsthyam*= tranquillity; कौपीनत्वे *kaupīnatve* = in the state of wearing just a loin-cloth; अपि *api* = even; दुर्लभम् *durlabham* = rare; त्यागादाने *tyāgādāne* = (ideas of) renunciation and acceptance; विहाय *vihāya* = giving up; अस्मात्

asmāt = therefore; अहम् *aham* = I; आसे *āse* = live; यथा-सुखम् *yathā-sukham* = a true happiness.

Janaka Said :

1. The tranquillity, which is born of the Awareness that there is nothing else but the Self, is rare even for one who wears just a loin-cloth. Therefore, giving up the ideas of renunciation and acceptance, I live in true happiness.

We have already mentioned in the introduction to this section that a mere external relinquishment of our possessions is not true dispassion that can lead us nearer to the state of spiritual tranquillity. Even for one who has thus renounced everything, and has only the barest minimum of even his essential requirements of life, such as food, clothing and shelter, even to such an individual the experience that "there is nothing but the Self (*Akiñcana-bhavam*), and therefore, nothing else have ever been born as the universe"— is indeed rare. To renounce or to accept, there must be the still lingering shades of one's individualised ego. Where the ego has completely ended, there is none in the individual either to accept anything or to renounce anything and that is the State of Supreme Bliss. "Therefore," says *Janaka*, "giving up the ideas of renunciation and acceptance, I live in true happiness."

Although in almost all the *Upaniṣad*-s there is a different theory of Creation expounded by the different *Ṛṣī-s*, any deep student of the *Upaniṣad*-s can very easily detect that the ultimate anxiety of the scriptures is to lead the student to a State, beyond the mind and intellect, to recognise and experience therein the Infinitude of the body, mind and intellect. In all Its Aloneness the Glory of the Self pervades everywhere, Immutable, Eternal and Tranquil.

Thus from the transcendental view-point, gained from the Self, never was there a universe ever projected! This theory of "Non-origination" (*Ajāta-Vāda)* is a doctrine that is inherent in the *Upaniṣad*-s, and it is only very subtly suggested therein. *Aṣṭāvakra* emphasises it to explain it. *Gauḍapāda* later on took it up for an exhaustive treatment and gives a total philosophical exposition of it in his *Kārikā* to *Māṇḍūkya Upaniṣad* (*Advaita Prakaraṇa* III-2):

यथा न जायते किञ्चित् जायमानं समन्ततः ।

Yathā na jāyate kiñcit jāyamānaṁ samantataḥ.

"From which nothing is, in reality, born; though it appears to have manifested in endless forms."

Again, *Gauḍapāda* clarifies in his *Kārikā*, and concludes his chapter on Non-dualism (*Advaita Prakaraṇa* III-48) with the following unambiguous and eloquent verse:

न कश्चिज्जायते जीवः संभवोऽस्य न विद्यते ।
एतत्तदुत्तमं सत्यं यत्र किञ्चिन्न जायते ॥

Na kaścij-jāyate jīvaḥ, saṁbhavo'sya na vidyate,
etat-tad-uttamaṁ satyaṁ yatra kiñcin-na jāyate.

"No *Jīva*, the ego-centric separative-creature, is ever born. There does not exist any cause which can produce them as its effect. This is the highest Truth where nothing is ever born."

कुत्रापि खेदः कायस्य जिह्वा कुत्रापि खिद्यते ।
मनः कुत्रापि तत्त्यक्त्वा पुरुषार्थे स्थितः सुखम् ॥ २ ॥

Kutrāpi khedaḥ kāyasya jihvā kutrāpi khidyate,
manaḥ kutrāpi tat-tyaktvā puruṣārthe sthitaḥ sukham.

कुत्र अपि *kutra-api* = somewhere; खेदः *khedaḥ* = weariness; कायस्य *kāyasya* = of body; जिह्वा *jihvā* = tongue; कुत्र अपि *kutra-api* = somewhere; खिद्यते *khidyate* = is fatigued; मनः *manaḥ* = mind; कुत्र अपि *kutra-api* = somewhere; तत् *tat* = this; त्यक्त्वा *tyaktvā* = having renounced; (अहम् *aham* = I;) पुरुषार्थे *puruṣārthe* = in life's goal;

स्थित: *sthitaḥ* = established; (अस्मि *asmi* = am;) सुखम् *sukham* = in true happiness.

2. *There is weariness of the body here, fatigue of the tongue there, and distress of the mind elsewhere. Having renounced this in life's goal, I live in true happiness.*

The main three sources of weariness, and consequently of restlessness, have already been enumerated earlier as physical, oral and mental. *Janaka* in his wisdom discovers that there is weariness brought to his life by his body. The sense-organs are all channels of sorrow that pour into our bosom restlessness and agitations. In *Yoga Vāsiṣṭha* we read this idea most poetically put :

कुरंगालिपतंगेभमीनास्त्वेकैकशो हताः ।
सर्वैर्युक्तैरनर्थैस्तु व्याप्तस्याज्ञ कुतः सुखम् ॥

Kuraṁgāli-pataṁgebha-mīnās-tvekai-kaśo hatāḥ,
sarvair-yuktair-anarthais-tu vyāptas-yājña kutaḥ sukham.

"The deer, black-bee, butterfly, elephant, fish—each one of these, meets with its death because of its attachment to one or the other of its sense-organs. The ignorant-man is attached to all his five-senses, and how can he ever find happiness in this world."

Physical senses alone are not the sole cause for the sorrows mentioned here, but all physical penance can also bring about weariness of the body for one who is in the Higher States of Meditation, as *Janaka* was.

The study of scriptures and repetition of *mantrā-s* in the pursuit of *Japa-Yoga* can also "make the tongue fatigued." The attempts at meditation is the cause for the distress of the mind, mentioned here. Therefore, *Janaka* renounced all these three in the Supreme Experience of the Infinite Self—"the goal of life," and thereby, "I live in true happiness," declared the King.

कृतं किमपि नैव स्यादिति सञ्चिन्त्य तत्त्वतः ।
यदा यत् कर्तुमायाति तत्कृत्वाऽऽसे यथासुखम् ॥ ३ ॥

Kṛtaṁ kimapi naiva syāditi sañcintya tattvataḥ,
yadā yat kartu-māyāti tat-kṛtvā-''se yathā-sukham.

कृतम् *kṛtam* = done (by the Self); किम्-अपि *kim-api* = nothing whatever; न *na* = not; एव *eva* = certainly; स्यात् *syāt* = is; इति *iti* = thus; सञ्चिन्त्य *sañcintya* = understanding fully; तत्त्वतः *tattvataḥ* = in reality; यदा *yadā* = when; यत् *yat* = what; कर्तुम् *kartum* = to do; आयाति *āyāti* = comes; तत् कृत्वा *tat kṛtvā* = that doing; आसे *āse* = (I) live; यथा-सुखम् *yathā-sukham* = in true happiness.

3. *Understanding fully that nothing whatsoever is really done by the Self, I do whatever presents itself to be done, and so, I live in true happiness.*

Actions are the expressions of thoughts, and they are the disturbances in the mind caused by desires—which are manifestations of our *Vāsanā-s*. Where *Vāsanā-s* have ended, desires cease. Naturally, mind becomes calm of thought-disturbances—and the ego-centric aggressive actions can no longer spring from that Individual. That is the State of Pure Consciousness. The Self is actionless as it is Full and All-pervading. In this great understanding, born out of direct subjective experience, *Janaka* withdraws from all his fields of endeavour and extinguishes the "I-do-mentality" (*Ahaṁkāra*) in him.

However, continues *Janaka*, whenever he is goaded to act in the world outside due to the pressure of his *Prārabdha*, he does it willingly "as an agent" of the Lord, the Self.

With his abdication from the seat of the ego, his entire kingdom of delusion has rolled away from him, and "so", says *Janaka*, "I live in true happiness."

कर्मनैष्कर्म्यनिर्बन्धभावा देहस्थयोगिनः ।
संयोगायोगविरहादहमासे यथासुखम् ॥ ४ ॥

Karma-naiṣkarmya-nirbandha-bhāvā dehastha-yoginaḥ,
saṁyogā-yoga-virahād-ahamāse yathā-sukham.

कर्म-नैष्कर्म्य-निर्बन्ध-भावाः *karma-naiṣkarmya-nirbandha-bhāvāḥ* = who insist upon action or inaction; देहस्थ-योगिनः *dehastha-yoginaḥ* = the *Yogī-s* who are attached to the body; संयोग-अयोग-विरहात् *saṁyoga-ayoga-virahāt* = divorced from association and dis-association; अहम् *aham* = I; आसे *āse* = live; यथा-सुखम् *yathā-sukham* = in true happiness.

4. *The spiritual seekers (*Yogin-s*), who are attached to the body, insist upon action or inaction. Divorced from both association and dis-association, I live in true happiness.*

Even among the great Masters there are some who definitely seem to emphasise a dynamic life of dedicated *Sevā* to the society. There are other Masters who address the student pleading for a life of retirement and utter quietude—inaction at the body, mind and intellect levels. There is *Bhagavad Gītā*, which wants us to see "action in inaction and inaction in actions." Each one of these great advices is addressed to the students at varying levels of their own body-consciousness.

Tāmasik people must undertake vigorous programmes of work, prompted by extreme selfish motives, in order to generate in them the dynamism of *Rajas*. The *Rājasik Sādhakā-s* should learn to act vigorously, in a spirit of selfless dedication, in order to generate the brilliance of *Sattva* in their bosom. Again, the fully developed *Sāttvik* students, in alert and vigilant moments of "actionless action" must have themselves to reach the larger awakening into the Higher Consciousness in them.

Janaka at the peak of his realisation has given up both, his association with the body, and has relinquished all his efforts in dis-associating himself from his body. His ego has ended, and he sees nobody to accept or to reject. Thus, "I live in true happiness," confesses the Royal Saint.

अर्थानर्थौ न मे स्थित्या गत्या वा शयनेन वा ।
तिष्ठन् गच्छन् स्वपन् तस्मादहमासे यथासुखम् ॥ ५ ॥

Arthānarthau na me sthityā gatyā na śayanena vā,
tiṣṭhan gacchan svapan tasmād-ahamāse yathāsukham.

अर्थ-अनर्थौ *artha-anarthau* = good or evil; न *na* = not; मे *me* = my; स्थित्या *sthityā* = by staying; गत्या *gatyā* = by going; वा *vā* = or; शयनेन *śayanena* = by sleeping; वा *vā* = or; तिष्ठन् *tiṣṭhan* = staying; गच्छन् *gacchan* = going; स्वपन् *svapan* = sleeping; तस्मात् *tasmāt* = so; अहम् *aham* = I; आसे *āse* = live; यथासुखम् *yathāsukham* = in true happiness.

5. *No good or evil can be associated with my staying going or sleeping. So whether I stay, or go, or sleep, I live in true happiness.*

No action by itself is either good nor bad. The intention behind the action determines its quality with reference to the *doer*. To an ego-less one, therefore, actions are motivated neither by good nor evil—they are spontaneous expressions of the Divine Will cascading through such perfect Masters. Sitting, or going, or sleeping—in short, under all conditions of stability, movement and rest of the body, such an egoless Master is ever in perfect attunement with the Blissful Self, and *Janaka*, the Man-of-Realisation confesses here, "I live in true happiness."

स्वपतो नास्ति मे हानिः सिद्धिर्यत्नवतो न वा ।
नाशोल्लासौ विहायास्मादहमासे यथासुखम् ॥ ६ ॥

Svapato nāsti me hāniḥ siddhir-yatnavato na vā,
nāśollāsau vihāyā-smād-ahamāse yathā-sukham.

स्वपतः *svapataḥ* = sleeping; न *na* = not; अस्ति *asti* = is; मे *me* = my; हानिः *hāniḥ* = loss; सिद्धिः *siddhiḥ* = success; यत्नवतः *yatnavataḥ* = striving; न *na* = not; वा *vā* = or; नाशोल्लासौ *nāśollāsau* = loss or delight; विहाय *vihāya* = forgoing; अस्मात् *asmāt* = so; अहम् *aham* = I; आसे *āse* = live; यथा-सुखम् *yathā-sukham* = in true happiness.

6. *I do not lose anything by sleeping, nor gain anything by striving. So giving up thoughts of loss and delight, I live in true happiness.*

Having gained the Infinite Bliss, to the Man-of-perfection there is nothing to gain by the diligent and exhausting efforts, nor can anything be taken away from his inner spiritual sovereigntly, if he rests in total peace; apparently undertaking no activities and so living a life of 'sleep.' In his inner state of Fullness there is nothing for him to gain by actions, nor can he lose anything from the treasures of his inner tanquillity, by not acting. All his anxieties for happiness, or his fears for the losses, have been totally given up along with his sense of ego, and thus, declares *Janaka* "I live in true happiness."

सुखादिरूपानियमं भावेष्वालोक्य भूरिशः ।
शुभाशुभे विहायास्मादहमासे यथासुखम् ॥ ७ ॥

Sukhādi-rūpāni-yamaṁ bhāve-ṣvālokya bhuriśaḥ,
śubhā-śubhe vihāyā-smād-ahamāse yathā-sukham.

सुखादि-रूप-अनियमम् *sukhādi-rūpa-aniyamam* = fluctuations of the forms of pleasures etc., भावेषु *bhāveṣu* = in different conditions; आलोक्य *ālokya* = observing; भूरिशः *bhuriśaḥ* = again and again; शुभाशुभे *śubhāśubhe* = good and evil; विहाय *vihāya* = renouncing; अस्मात् *asmat* = so; अहम् *aham* = I; आसे *āse* = live; यथा-सुखम् *yathā-sukham* = in true happiness.

7. *Observing again and again, the fluctuations of the forms of pleasures etc., in different circumstances, I have renounced good and evil, and I live in true happiness.*

An ordinary man is tempted to pursue good and avoid evil, because he is seeking his future happiness. The man of evil is pursuing diligently his evil-ways of life only because he is convinced that he thereby can have his immediate happiness. In short, search for happiness is the spring of all activities, both good and evil.

A little more deeper investigation into the happenings around us can make it vividly clear that the people who pursue the good are seen as often suffering as the evil-minded men enjoying happily in life! So, it is an observed fact, that there are fluctuations of pleasure and pain, depending upon the changes in the external environments and the available circumstances around the individual. Happiness and sorrow, ultimately depend upon our own mental conditions. Transcending the mind and, therefore, renouncing both good and evil, *Janaka* admits, "I live in true happiness"—as the Blissful Infinite Self.

Chapter—XIV

Tranquillity

Introduction

This section consists of only four verses and can be considered as a sacred "Psalm on Peace," wherein the Infinite Peace of the Transcendental State is invoked and glorified. Mind is a thought-flow. In a Liberated-in-Life, there can be no desires, as he is experiencing in his own Self, the Infinite Fullness; and since he has no desires he has no thoughts—naturally, he becomes of an empty-mind : "Void-mind" (*Śūṇya-cittaḥ*). One whose mind is thus completely dissolved in the voiceless experience of the Infinite—He is asleep to the world of objects and its enchantments. He is awake only to the spiritual world of this Peaceful Self.

Janaka concludes this section by declaring that such an awakened Man-of-Wisdom can be fully understood only by another, who like him, has experienced the same State of Pure Consciousness.

जनक उवाच ।

प्रकृत्या शून्यचित्तो यः प्रमादाद्भावभावनः ।
निद्रितो बोधित इव क्षीणसंस्मरणो हि सः ॥ १ ॥

Janaka Uvāca :

Prakṛtyā śūnya-citto yaḥ pramādād-bhāvabhāvanaḥ,
nidrito bodhita iva kṣīṇa-saṁsmaraṇo hi saḥ.

प्रकृत्या *prakṛtyā* = by nature, spontaneously; शून्य-चित्तः *śūnya-cittaḥ* = empty-minded; यः *yaḥ* = who; प्रमादात् *pramādāt* = through inadvertence; भाव-भावनः *bhāva-bhāvanaḥ* = thinking of objects by chance; निद्रितः *nidritaḥ* = asleep; बोधितः *bodhitaḥ* = awake; इव *iva* = as if; क्षीण-संस्मरणः *kṣīṇa-saṁsmaraṇaḥ* = one whose recollections (of wordly life) are extinguished; हि *hi* = indeed; सः *saḥ* = he.

Janaka Said :

1. *He indeed has his recollections of wordly life extinguished—who becomes void-minded spontaneously, who thinks of sense-objects only by chance, and who is, as it were, awake though physically asleep.*

Language can never express experiences beyond the physical level and, therefore, wherever mystic-Sages have tried to communicate their subtle Transcendental spiritual experiences, they have always stammered through their brimful descriptions. Here is a typical example wherein *Janaka* is trying to explain the inner condition and the outer behaviour of one, whose mind has become still and empty of all thought-movements (*Śūnya-cittaḥ*).

The memories of past experiences in the world-of-objects, recorded in our personality for future reference, are called *Vāsanā-s*. It is these *Vāsanā-s* that produce fresh impulses of desires which procreate the mental and the physical disturbances in the individual-ego. The Man-of-Perfection is one who has gone beyond his *Vāsanā-s* and therefore, he is described here as "one who has extinguished all his wordly memories." This state of *Vāsanā*-less-ness is a state of utter mental stillness in Supreme meditation, and this state of total mental-poise is gained by a Man-of-Realisation spontaneously, without any conscious effort (*Prakṛtyā*).

Even though he is constantly in the vivid experience of the Infinite Reality, as long as his physical body exists, forced by its *Prārabdha*, he will be involuntarily forced into some fields of sense-objects. He goes through the world of happenings as though one who is asleep to the enjoyments of the world around him. He is aware and supremely awake only to the State of God-Consciousness.

This is not a mental state that has been reached through pills or drugs, nor is it achieved through effort and *Yoga*. One who is established in his Spiritual Awareness, to him this is a spontaneous vision, constant and effortless. He only becomes casually conscious of the world-of-plurality—a beautiful disturbance, dim and distant, on the horizon of His Infinite Bliss!

क्व धनानि क्व मित्राणि क्व मे विषयदस्यवः ।
क्व शास्त्रं क्व च विज्ञानं यदा मे गलिता स्पृहा ॥ २ ॥

Kva dhanāni kva mitrāṇi kva me viśaya-dasyavaḥ,
kva śāstraṁ kva ca vijñānaṁ yadā me galitā spṛhā.

क्व *kva* = where; धनानि *dhanāni* = riches; क्व *kva* = where; मित्राणि *mitrāṇi* = friends; क्व *kva* = where; मे *me* = my; विषय-दस्यवः *viśaya-dasyavaḥ* = thieves in the form of sense-objects; क्व *kva* = where; शास्त्रम् *śāstram* = scriptures; क्व *kva* = where; च *ca* = and; विज्ञानम् *vijñānam* = knowledge; यदा *yadā* = when; मे *me* = my; गलिता *galitā* = has melted; स्पृहा *spṛhā* = desire.

2. *When once the desires have melted away, where are my riches, where are my friends, where are the thieves in the form of sense-objects—nay, where are the scriptures and knowledge itself.*

Riches (*Dhanāni*), friends (*Mitrāni*), scriptures (*Śāstram*), knowledge (*Vijñānam*)— are all of great value for one's security, comfort and satisfaction while living as an ego amidst the sense-objects. As an ego, when we are living in the world, no doubt, sense-objects with their powerful enchantments can steal into our bosom and plunder away our peace and tranquillity, our discrimination and understanding, even our education and culture. True, very-very true. But, when desires have melted away, to one who has thus come to experience the Infinite Blissful Self, of what value are these external scaffoldings—riches, friends, scriptures or knowledge—which hold together for us, our illusory world of pleasure and pains?

To one who has realised the Self, of what value are the scriptures—of what use is knowledge, spiritual as well as secular? This same idea is much more poetically put in the *Bhagavad Gītā* (II-46) :

> यावानर्थ उदपाने सर्वतः संप्लुतोदके ।
> तावान्सर्वेषु वेदेषु ब्राह्मणस्य विजानतः ॥
>
> *Yāvānartha udapāne sarvataḥ saṁplutodake*
> *tāvān-sarveṣu vedeṣu brāhmaṇasya vijānataḥ.*
>
> "To the *brāhmaṇa*, who has known the Self, all the *Vedā-s* are of so much use as is a reservoir of water in a place where there is flood everywhere."

विज्ञाते साक्षिपुरुषे परमात्मानि चेश्वरे ।
नैराश्ये बन्धमोक्षे च न चिन्ता मुक्तये मम ॥ ३ ॥

Vijñāte sākṣi-puruṣe paramātmāni ceśvare,
nairāśye bandha-mokṣe ca na cintā muktaye mama.

विज्ञाते *vijñāte* = having realised; साक्षि-पुरुषे *sākṣi-puruṣe* = Self who is the 'witness'; परमात्मानि *paramātmāni* = the Supreme Self; च *ca* = and; ईश्वरे *iśvare* = Lord; नैराश्ये *nairāśye* = desirelessness; बन्ध-मोक्षे *bandha-mokṣe* = in bondage and liberation; च *ca* = and; न *na* = not; चिन्ता *cintā* = anxiety; मुक्तये *muktaye* = for emancipation; मम *mama* = my.

3. *As I have realised the Supreme Self who is the 'Witness' and the Lord, the Puruṣa, and have become indifferent both to bondage and liberation, I (now) feel no anxiety for my emancipation.*

In this four versed-chant upon the sense of Infinite Tranquillity (*Śānti-catuṣṭya*), *Janaka* is trying to communicate to us why this Spiritual State is so peaceful and how this State of Tranquillity is never disturbed by the usual storms from the worlds of the body, mind and intellect.

The Supreme Self, the Pure Consciousness, is ever illumining as a "witness" of all that is happening within and without (*Sakṣi-puruṣa*). It is the One Enlivening Presence which orders, governs, regualtes all activities of the whole universe, and as such is the Lord of the Universe (*Īśvara*). On rediscovering that this is the seeker's own Divine Nature, he becomes indifferent to both bondage and liberation. Liberation is only for one who is in bondage. To the liberated, there can be neither the sorrows of bondage nor the bliss of liberation.

Being already emancipated from the sorrowful world, constituted by his own passions of the body, emotions of the mind and agitations of the intellect, the Man-of-Realisation cannot have even the anxiety for "liberation."

This state of Infinite Peace can never be comprehended by us, as the instruments of comprehension that we have at this moment are incapable of conceiving dimensions of the Infinite. By a tea-spoon can we ever empty an entire ocean? Can limited mind comprehend the Unthinkable Self and Its Peace Infinite?

अन्तर्विकल्पशून्यस्य बहिः स्वच्छन्दचारिणः ।
भ्रान्तस्येव दशास्तास्तास्तादृशा एव जानते ॥ ४ ॥

Antar-vikalpa-śūnyasya bahiḥ svacchanda-cāriṇaḥ
bhrāntasyeva daśās-tās-tās-tādṛśā eva jānate.

अन्तः *antaḥ* = within; विकल्प-शून्यस्य *vikalpa-śūnyasya* = devoid of thoughts; बहिः *bahiḥ* = outside; स्वच्छन्द-चारिणः *svacchanda-cāriṇaḥ* = one who roams about at his own pleasure; भ्रान्तस्य इव *bhrāntasya-iva* = like a deluded one; दशाः *daśāḥ* = conditions; ताः ताः *tāḥ tāḥ* = such and such; तादृशाः *tādṛśā* = those like him; एव *eva* = surely; जानते *jānate* = know.

4. *The different conditions of a wise-man, who, devoid of any thoughts within, outwardly roams about at his own pleasure like a deluded man, can only be understood by those like him.*

The Man-of-perfection established in the Higher-planes of Consciousness, has transcended his mind and, therefore, his mind is silent and void of all thoughts (*Śūnya-Cittaḥ*). Naturally, he is free of all hesitations, doubts, uncertainties and confusions. He lives, thereafter, the spontaneous life Divine. In him there is no ego-sense at all. No social or political or religious laws are applicable to him. He lives careless of the consequences. He wants nothing, needs nothing. He has no demands, no desires. He is full in himself. He has become the native of the Divine Fields of Consciousness; He is only a temporary sojourner amidst us! Thus lived all Men-of-wisdom as guiding light for their generations, but at the same time, apparently a threatening danger to the existing social-rules, political systems, religious-traditions!! Always a law unto themselves.

How can such a man be judged except by men of equal vision and, therefore, of equal evolution? It is not in every Man-of-Realisation that we find a definite clue to their inward illumination in their outward behaviour.

Such a Man-of-total-Realisation is extolled in *Yoga Vāsiṣṭha*:

संशान्तान्तःकरणो गलितविकल्पः स्वरूपसारमयः ।
परमशमामृततृप्तस्तिष्ठति विद्वान्निरावरणः ॥

Saṁśānt-āntaḥ-karaṇo galitavikalpaḥ svarūpa-sāramayaḥ
parama-śamāmṛta-tṛptas-tiṣṭhati vidvān-nirā-varaṇaḥ.

"One who has unveiled the Truth in himself, sits ever contented in enjoying the nectar of his own Infinite Peace, his mind and intellect completely at rest, with no inner thought-disturbances—revelling in his own Real Nature."

Chapter—XV

Brahman—The Absolute Reality

Introduction

This is perhaps one of the most pregnant and significant sections in the entire *Aṣṭāvakra-Gītā*. The One Ultimate Reality, the Self, is declared here in unequivocal words: "the One Self in all existence and all existence in the One Self." The Supreme Wisdom, God, indicated in the scriptures by the term 'That,' has no birth, no action, no ego. Such a concept of the Absolute implicitly implies in Itself the doctrine of Non-origination (*Ajāta-Vāda*). All that falls under the cause-effect-system of the mind is nothing but the Self, misapprehended as the illusory world of names-and forms.

Aṣṭāvakra lovingly insists, "have faith, my son, have faith (*Śradhāsva-Śradhāsva*) in this Grand Majestic Truth. The Self is not only Pure Consciousness, which expresses uniformly in all other planes-of-Consciousness, but is also something worshipful, supremely to be revered as God, *Bhagavān*.

In this chapter thus, the natural of *Brahman* is brought out for a direct and imemdiate apprehension of all the seekers. *Aṣṭāvakra* here talks directly from his own mystic experiences. Even in the rich treasure-houses of the Indian mystic literature, we may not find a parallel text-book that can be compared favourably with the sure depth of vision and clarity of expression of this *Gītā*. It is at once profound and practical. It is profound in its powers of suggestiveness which can take a meditative mind to the very peaks. It is practical inasmuch as in other text-books we do not find such subtle instructions to help those who are groping along the summits of the Higher Meditation.

अष्टावक्र उवाच ।

यथातथोपदेशेन कृतार्थः सत्त्वबुद्धिमान् ।
आजीवमपि जिज्ञासुः परस्तत्र विमुह्यति ॥ १ ॥

Aṣṭāvakra Uvāca :

Yathā-tatho-padeśena kṛtārthaḥ sattva-buddhimān,
ājīvam-api jijñāsuḥ paras-tatra vimuhyati.

यथा-तथा *yathā-tathā* = in whatever manner, casually; उपदेशेन *upadeśena* = by instruction; कृतार्थः *kṛtārthaḥ* = gains his end; सत्त्व-बुद्धिमान् *sattva-buddhimān* = a person of Pure Intelligence; आजीवम् *ājīvam* = throughout his life; अपि *api* = even; जिज्ञासुः *jijñāsuḥ* = desirous to know; परः *paraḥ* = the other; तत्र *tatra* = there; विमुह्यति *vimuhyati* = is confused.

Aṣṭāvakra Said :

1. ***A person of Pure Intelligence realises the Self even by instruction casually imparted. A man of impure intellect is confused in trying to realise the Self, even after enquiring throughout his life.***

The text-book remaining the same, and even when the same teacher is explaining and expounding the Truth of *Vedānta*, we find that different students are benefited by the same instructions to different degrees! The *Upaniṣadik* text-books explain this phenomena and attribute the success or failure of the student to the student's own preparedness or un-preparedness in themselves to receive the Great Knowledge Divine.

A mind rich in *Sattva* is calm and serene, and is most receptive to the spiritual ideas discussed in the *Upaniṣad*-s. But when the mind is disturbed by agitations (*Rajas*), or when the intellect is clouded by dullness (*Tamas*), the equipment is not tuned to receive the profound inner secrets of the scriptural declarations. When a mind is stilled and well protected from the onslaughts of passions and desires, it is considered as "Pure Intelligence," which alone will have the required receptivity to apprehend the Truth.

When thus the student is ready to receive the Divine-message, a casual instruction from the teacher is more than sufficient to set the student on the flight to the State of Pure Consciousness.

However, if the student's inner bosom is not disciplined enough, and his mind and intellect are extremely disturbed by the continuous waves of passions and desires, such an individual, even after deep enquiries, throughout his life, remains bewildered and confused in himself, without having even a moment's Spiritual Experience.

That is the reason why *Yoga-Vāsiṣṭha* advises all teachers:

आदौ शमदमप्रायैर्गुणैर्शिष्यं विशोधयेत् ।
पश्चात्सर्वमिदं ब्रह्म शुद्धस्त्वमिति बोधयेत् ॥

Ādau śama-dama-prāyair-guṇair-śiṣyaṁ viśodhayet,
paścāt-sarvam-idaṁ brahma śuddhas-tvamiti bodhayet.

"In the beginning examine the student carefully for qualities of Self-control and inner quietude; thereafter, advise him : 'Thou Art the Pure *Brahman* who is the Essence in all this universe'."

मोक्षो विषयवैरस्यं बन्धो वैषयिको रसः ।
एतावदेव विज्ञानं यथेच्छसि तथा कुरु ॥ २ ॥

Mokṣo viṣaya-vairasyaṁ bandho vaiṣayiko rasaḥ,
etāva-deva vijñānaṁ yathecchasi tathā kuru.

मोक्षः *mokṣaḥ* = liberation; विषय-वैरस्यम् *viṣaya-vairasyam* = distaste for sense-objects; बन्धः *bandhaḥ* = bondage; वैषयिकः *vaiṣayikaḥ* =

sensual; रसः *rasaḥ* = passion; एतावत् *etāvat* = such is; एव *eva* = indeed; विज्ञानम् *vijñānam* = knowledge; यथा *yathā* = as; इच्छसि *icchasi* = you wish; तथा *tathā* = so; कुरु *kuru* = do.

2. *Distaste for sense-object is liberation; passion for sense-objects is bondage., Such indeed is Knowledge. Now you do as you please.*

In a very direct and aphoristic style *Aṣṭāvakra* here defines what constitutes bondage, and what exactly is the nature of liberation—as far as a seeker is concerned. The arrogant-ego, seeking its satisfaction, hungers for sense-gratifications and its entire attention gets dissipated into the world of sense-objects. This is the State-of-bondage.

The ego ends as it awakens to the higher experience of the Universal Spiritual Essence. In the rising waves of fulfilment, not only the ego ends, but it has no more any craving for sense-gratifications. This distaste for sense-objects is a sign of "liberation."

Having explained thus, the *Vedāntik* seer in *Aṣṭāvakra* gives the student full freedom to plan his own life and live his days in complete freedom, as he likes. Those who have yet *Vāsanā-s* to fulfil, they must continue living in the sense-world for exhausting them. There is no other way. Those in whom the vigour of *Vāsanā-s* has calmed down, in them there is a natural sense of growing distaste towards sense-objects.

Force and compulsion can do nothing in this great path of Self-Rediscovery. It is an evolution, and not a revolution. As such, all Masters, after their advice, leave the student to plan out his life, according to his own inner impulses. The concluding verse with which *Kṛṣṇa* ends His main discourse in the *Bhagavat-Gītā* (XVIII-63) we hear again a similar sentiment expressed by the Lord:

इति ते ज्ञानमाख्यातं गुह्याद्गुह्यतरं मया ।
विमृश्यैतदशेषेण यथेच्छसि तथा कुरु ॥

Iti te jñānam-ākhyātaṁ guhyād-guhya-taraṁ mayā,
vimṛśyai-tad-aśeṣeṇa yathe-cchasi tathā kuru.

"Thus has the Wisdom, more secret than all secrets, been declared to you by Me: having reflected over it fully, you act as you choose."

The direction of the mind determines whether the individual is living in bondage or aspiring for liberation, say the wise sages :

मन एव मनुष्याणां कारणं बन्धमोक्षयोः ।
बन्धाय विषयासक्तं मुक्त्यै निर्विषयं स्मृतम् ॥

Mana eva manuṣyāṇāṁ kāraṇaṁ bandha-mokṣayoḥ,
bandhāya viṣayā-saktaṁ muktyai nirviṣayaṁ smṛtam.

"Mind alone is the cause for both bondage and liberation; sensuous mind causes bondage; peaceful mind leads one to liberation."

वाग्मिप्राज्ञामहोद्योगं जनं मूकजडालसम् ।
करोति तत्त्वबोधोऽयमतस्त्यक्तो बुभुक्षुभिः ॥ ३ ॥

Vāgmi-prājñā-mahodyogaṁ janaṁ mūka-jaḍālasam,
karoti tattva-bodho-'yam-atas-tyakto bubhukṣu-bhiḥ.

वाग्मि-प्राज्ञा-महा-उद्योगम् *vāgmi-prājñā-mahā-udyogam* = eloquent, wise and active; जनम् *janam* = man; मूक-जड-अलसम् *mūka-jaḍa-alasam* = mute, inert and passive; करोति *karoti* = makes; तत्त्व-बोधः *tattva-bodhaḥ* = knowledge of the truth; अयम् *ayam* = this; अतः *ataḥ* = so; त्यक्तः *tyaktaḥ* = is shunned; बुभुक्षुभिः *bubhukṣubhiḥ* = by those who want to enjoy.

3. *This knowledge of the Truth makes an eloquent, wise and active person, mute, inert and passive. Therefore, it is shunned by those who wish to enjoy (the world).*

For the material success in the world-of-sensuality, as it is available for us in this competitive world, eloquence, wordly-wisdom and vigorous dynamism are unavoidable. The meditative man, who withdraws from the world of "ignorance" seeking to experience and live the joys of the Self would naturally become unfit for worldly success, during his *Sādhanā* period, because a seeker becomes "mute, inert and passive."

These words should not give us the misconception that spirituality is an undynamic way-of-living. *Buddhā* under the tree will be criticised by the men-of-the world as a useless, idler, a liability to the community, and unfit to live a social life. Only on becoming fully enlightened, *Bhagavān Buddhā* moved out from under the tree, to serve the world, and came to earn the eternal gratitude of mankind as a Prince of Compassion. The profit motivated, impatient man-of-the-world would naturally consider the spiritual-path as too passive and inert for his taste. They, with abhorrence, would reject the path of retirement and steady contemplation, because they want to enjoy the world of sense-objects and thus exhaust their *Vāsanā-s*.

The explanation in this verse justifies what *Aṣṭāvakra* has said to his disciple in the previous verse: "Now do as you please."

न त्वं देहो न ते देहो भोक्ता कर्ता न वा भवान् ।
चिद्रूपोऽसि सदा साक्षी निरपेक्षः सुखं चर ॥ ४ ॥

Na tvaṁ deho na te deho bhoktā kartā na vā bhavān,
cidrūpo'si sadā sākṣī nirapekṣaḥ sukhaṁ cara.

न *na* = not; त्वम् *tvam* = you; देहः *dehaḥ* = body; न *na* = not; ते *te* = your; देहः *dehaḥ* = body; भोक्ता *bhoktā* = enjoyer; कर्ता *kartā* = doer; न *na* = not; वा *vā* = or; भवान् *bhavān* = your; चिद्रूपः *cidrūpaḥ* = Consciousness itself; असि *asi* = are; सदा *sadā* = ever; साक्षी *sākṣī* = witness; निरपेक्षः *nirapekṣaḥ* = indifferent; सुखम् *sukham* = happy; चर *cara* = go about.

4. *You are not the body, nor is the body your's. You are neither the 'doer' nor the 'enjoyer.' You are Consciousness itself, the Eternal, indifferent Witness. You go about happily.*

To those of his students who have the taste to walk the spiritual-path, *Aṣṭāvakra* continues. In the false understanding that we are body, we run after the sense-objects for our satisfaction and happiness. Here the teacher advises us that neither are we the bodies, nor are the bodies ours. We must avoid both our sense of '*I-ness*' and '*mine-ness*' with the body. *One* is not the '*doer*'—who does his activities through the body; nor is *One* the '*enjoyer*'— who enjoys the outer world, again through the body. The '*doer-ship*' and '*enjoyer-ship*' together constitute the ego-sense in us; this is to be completely negated.

After thus negating the gross and the subtle bodies, the sage directly points out what the true Spiritual Nature of man is—"You are Pure Consciousness." And as the Light of Intelligence in the individual, you are a Witness of all the experiences of the body, mind and intellect; and you are ever indifferent to both the joys and sorrows of the equipments. Understanding this, may "you go about happily," thus blesses sage *Aṣṭāvakra*.

रागद्वेषौ मनोधर्मौ न मनस्ते कदाचन ।
निर्विकल्पोऽसि बोधात्मा निर्विकारः सुखं चर ॥५॥

Rāga-dveṣau mano-dharmau na manaste kadācana,
nirviklapo-'si bodhātmā nirvikāraḥ sukhaṁ cara.

राग-द्वेषौ *rāga-dveṣau* = passions and aversions; मनो-धर्मौ *mano-dharmau* = qualities of mind; न *na* = not; मनः *manaḥ* = mind; ते *te* = your; कदाचन *kadācana* = ever; निर्विकल्पः *nirvikalpaḥ* = free from fluctuations; असि *asi* = are; बोधात्मा *bodhātmā* = Intelligence itself; निर्विकारः *nirvikāraḥ* = changeless; सुखम् *sukham* = happily; चर *cara* = go about.

5. *Passions and aversions are the qualities of the mind. The mind is never yours. You are Intelligence itself, free from all fluctuations, and changeless. You go about happily.*

The passions and lusts, like and dislikes, joys and sorrows—these are all fluctuations in the mental-stuff, and they all belong to the mind. As the Pure Infinite Consciousness you are the Illuminator of them all—you are not the mind. Consciousness alone illumines the oscillations of the mind and its inner conflicts. As the Illuminator, you are beyond all restlessness of the mind, ever the same Blissful Self. Having realised thus, *Aṣṭāvakra* says: "You go about happily."

सर्वभूतेषु चात्मानं सर्वभूतानि चात्मानि ।
विज्ञाय निरहंकारो निर्ममस्त्वं सुखी भव ॥ ६ ॥

Sarva-būteṣu cātmānaṁ sarva-bhūtāni cātmāni,
vijñāya nirahaṁkāro nirmamas-tvaṁ sukhī bhava.

सर्वभूतेषु *sarva-būteṣu* = in all beings; च *ca* = also; आत्मानम् *ātmānam* = Self; सर्वभूतानि *sarvabhūtāni* = all beings; च *ca* = also; आत्मानि *ātmāni* = in the Self; विज्ञाय *vijñāya* = knowing (realising); निरहंकारः *nirahaṁkāraḥ* = free from 'I-ness'; निर्ममः *nirmamaḥ* = free from 'mine-ness'; त्वम् *tvam* = you; सुखी *sukhī* = happy; भव *bhava* = be.

6. *Realising the Self in all beings, and all beings in the Self, free from 'I-ness' and free from 'mine-ness,' may you be happy.*

The twin expressions of the ego are the '*I-ness*' and the '*my-ness.*' The arrogance of individuality in our bosom expressing as '*I-ness*' creates the delusory idea of possession towards some of the objects outside expressed as '*my-ness.*' To transcend the ego is to end all the sorrow created by these two illusory concepts of '*I-ness*' and '*my-ness.*' To experience that the Consciousness in each one is the

Consciousness everywhere present, is to understand Infinite Consciousness; and this is the Highest State of Realisation where the sense of ego has totally ended.

Aṣṭāvakra accepts *Gītā*'s concept that the Surpeme is at once transcendental and immanent. The first line of this verse is bodily lifted from *Gītā* (verse VI-29), wherein *Bhagavān* says:

> सर्वभूतस्थमात्मानं सर्वभूतानि चात्मानि ।
> ईक्षते योगयुक्तात्मा सर्वत्र समदर्शनः ॥
>
> *Sarva-bhūta-stham-ātmānaṁ sarva-bhūtāni cātmāni,*
> *īkṣate yoga-yuktātmā sarvatra sama-darśanaḥ.*
>
> "With the mind harmonised by *Yoga* he sees the Self, abiding in all beings and all beings in the Self; he sees the same everywhere."

Thus recognising your oneness with the whole cosmos, released from all tensions and conflicts, advises the sage, "May you be happy."

विश्वं स्फुरति यत्रेदं तरङ्गा इव सागरे ।
तत्त्वमेव न सन्देहश्चिन्मूर्ते विज्वरो भव ॥ ७ ॥

Viśvaṁ sphurati yatredaṁ taraṅgā eva sāgare,
tat-tvam-eva na sandehaś-cinmūrte vijvaro bhava.

विश्वम् *viśvam* = universe; स्फुरति *sphurati* = is manifested; यत्र *yatra* = in which; इदम् *idam* = this; तरङ्गाः *taraṅgāḥ* = waves; इव *eva* = like; सागरे *sāgare* = in the ocean; तत् *tat* = that; त्वम् *tvam* = you; एव *eva* = indeed; न *na* = not; सन्देहः *sandehaḥ* = doubt; चिन्मूर्ते *cinmūrte* = O You, Pure Intelligence!; विज्वरः *vijvaraḥ* = free from fever; भव *bhava* = be.

7. *O You, Pure Intelligence! In you the universe manifests itself like waves in the ocean. Be you free from the fever of the mind.*

One of the four mighty spiritual commandments in the *Hindū Vedā-s* is the declaration : तत्त्वमसि *Tat-tvam-asi* "That Thou Art." This statement is resoundingly echoed in this verse of *Aṣṭāvakra*. The Sage instructs the student, "You are that from which the apparent illusions of the world rise up, play for a while, and disappear, as the waves from the ocean. You are that Pure Intelligence (*Cin-mūrti*)."

To realise our Real Nature to be the Pure Light of Consciousness is to disassociate ourselves from our identifications with our mind, and therefore, from all desires. The outer wordly objects, by themselves, cannot bring any agitation and fevers to the mind. It is our desire to possess and enjoy the sense-objects that lends to the objects the power and the strength to tyrannise us. When the desires have ended, the mind suffers no more any feverish excitements, and can have none of its terrifying deliriums. The mind becomes calm and serenely happy.

श्रद्धस्व तात श्रद्धस्व नात्र मोहं कुरुष्व भोः ।
ज्ञानस्वरूपो भगवानात्मा त्वं प्रकृतेः परः ॥ ८ ॥

Śraddhasva tāta śraddhasva nātra mohaṁ kuruṣva bhoḥ,
jñāna-svarūpo bhagavān-ātmā tvaṁ prakṛteḥ paraḥ.

श्रद्धस्व *śraddhasva* = have faith; भोः तात *bhoḥ tāta* = O son; श्रद्धस्व *śraddhasva* = have faith; न *na* = not; अत्र *atra* = in this; मोहम् *moham* = delusion; कुरुष्व *kuruṣva* = make; ज्ञान-स्वरूपः *jñāna-svarūpaḥ* = knowledge itself; भगवान् *bhagavān* = Lord; आत्मा *ātmā* = Self; त्वम् *tvam* = you; प्रकृतेः परः *prakṛteḥ paraḥ* = beyond nature.

8. *Have faith, my son, have faith! Have no delusion about this! You are knowledge itself. You are the Lord. You are the Self. You are beyond Nature.*

It has been emphasised in the *Bhagavad Gītā* (IV-39) also that a Man-of-faith alone can gain the spiritual wisdom:

श्रद्धावाँल्लभते ज्ञानं तत्परः संयतेन्द्रियः ।
ज्ञानं लब्ध्वा परां शान्तिमचिरेणाधिगच्छति ॥

Śraddhā-vagṁ-llabhate jñānaṁ tatparaḥ saṁyatendriyaḥ
jñānaṁ labdhvā parāṁ śāntim-acireṇādhi-gacchati.

"The man who is full of faith, who is devoted to It, and who has subdued the senses, obtains (this) Knowledge; and having obtained Knowledge, he goes ere long to the Supreme Peace."

Here we must stop for a moment and understand the exact import of this term faith (*Śraddhā*). No other word in the spiritual diction has been, perhaps, so much abused by the organised religions of the world. Faith, as generally understood, is a "blind belief," an empty concurrence with all half-truths! In effect "faith" has come to clamp-on an unhealthy control over the intellect to question and to investigate, to argue and to understand. This is not the sense in which the term '*Śraddhā*' is employed in *Vedāntik* literature. *Śaṅkara* is forced to define in the *Vivekacūḍāmaṇi*-26 indicating that the term '*Śraddhā*' only implies the ability of the human intellect in educating itself through study and direct diligent enquiry, in the following words:

शास्त्रस्य गुरुवाक्यस्य सत्यबुद्ध्यवधारणम् ।
सा श्रद्धा कथिता सद्भिर्यया वस्तूपलभ्यते ॥

Śāstrasya guru-vākyasya satya-buddhya-vadhāraṇam,
sā śraddhā kathitā sadbhiryayā vastū-palabhyate.

"That is called the spirit of faith (*Śraddhā*) by which an individual understands readily the exact import of the Scriptural texts, as well as the pregnant words of advice given by the preceptor—by which alone the Reality of things becomes manifestly clear."

In short, faith is a belief in what I don't know at this moment, so that I may come to know what I merely believe-in today. *Aṣṭāvakra* emphasises the utter need for maintaining brilliant enquiry, to have an alert intellect and mind, and to believe in one's own intellectual and spiritual convictions. Without faith in oneself and in one's own goal, self-unfoldment is impossible.

In this connection, we are reminded of *Yoga-Vāsiṣṭha*'s declaration and the advice: "Have faith and accept the authority of the mystic statements."

यदिदं वच्मि तत्सर्वं ओमित्यादातुमर्हसि ।
अस्माभिश्चिरमन्विष्टं नाऽत्र कार्या विचारणा ॥

Yadidaṁ vacmi tat-sarvaṁ om-ityā-dātum-arhasi,
asmābhiś-ciram-anviṣṭaṁ nā'tra kāryā vicāraṇā.

"You deserve to accept with an "*Oṁ*" all that (what) we are telling you now. We have for long enquired and searched for this Truth, and you need not enquire or discuss."

If this kind of enlightened attitude of faith is not constantly maintained in our bosom, the mind will not be quiet and serene, and therefore, the student's meditation would naturally become in-effectual. Mind-at-rest alone is the "peep-hole" through which the seeker rediscovers his Real Nature. Decalres *Mahopaniṣad* (IV-100):

यत्तुं चञ्चलताहीनं तन्मनोऽमृतमुच्यते ।
तदेव च तपः शास्त्रसिद्धान्ते मोक्ष उच्यते ॥

Yattuṁ cañcalatā-hīnaṁ tanmano'mṛtam-ucyate,
tadeva ca tapaḥ śāstra-siddhānte mokṣa ucyate.

"That mind which is agitation-less, that is Immortality, that alone is *Tapas*. In the *Upaniṣadik* texts, this is what they call as liberation (*Mokṣa*)."

गुणैः संवेष्टितो देहस्तिष्ठत्यायाति याति च ।
आत्मा न गन्ता नागन्ता किमेनमनुशोचसि ॥ ९ ॥

Guṇaiḥ saṁveṣṭito dehas-tiṣṭhatyā-yāti yāti ca,
ātmā na gantā nāgantā kimena-manu-śocasi.

गुणैः *gunaiḥ* = by the constituents of nature;संवेष्टितः *saṁveṣṭitaḥ* = enclosed; देहः *dehaḥ* = body; तिष्ठति *tiṣṭhati* = stays; आयाति *āyāti* = comes; याति *yāti* = goes; च *ca* = and; आत्मा *ātmā* = Self; न *na* = not; गन्ता *gantā* = goes; न *na* = not; आगन्ता *āgantā* = comes; किम् *kim* = why; एनम् *enam* = it; अनुशोचसि *anuśocasi* = lament, mourn.

9. *The body composed of the constituents of nature, comes, stays and goes away. The Self neither comes nor goes. Why, then, do you mourn over it?*

The body made of the five great-elements must necessarily go back to the elements. While the body exists, it functions under its predominant qualities of *Sattva*, *Rajas* and *Tamas*. The body has manifested in order to supply us with our required experiences of the outer and inner worlds. The ego possesses the body, and through it the ego enjoys the world. In all these patterns of existence, the Self, as the Pure Consciousness, is the "illuminator" of them all. The Eternal Self never came, never played, never ended. It was, is and shall ever be. That Supreme Truth is your Real Nature. Then why should you mourn over the death of your body? Should the ocean feel miserable for all the waves that have died?

The tone of expression and the idea expressed both remind us of the *Bhagavad Gītā* chapter II, *ślokā-s* 11 to 13 and 16 to 18.

देहस्तिष्ठतु कल्पान्तं गच्छत्वद्यैव वा पुनः ।
क्व वृद्धिः क्व च वा हानिस्तव चिन्मात्ररूपिणः ॥ १० ॥

Dehastiṣṭhatu kalpāntaṁ gacchatva-dyaiva vā punaḥ,
kva vṛddhiḥ kva ca vā hānis-tava cinmātra-rūpiṇaḥ.

देहः *dehaḥ* = body; तिष्ठतु *tiṣṭhatu* = let remain; कल्पान्तम् *kalpāntam* = till the end of the cycle; गच्छतु *gacchatu* = let go; अद्य *adya* = today;

एव *eva* = itself; वा *vā* = or; पुन: *punaḥ* = again; क्व *kva* = where; वृद्धि: *vṛddhiḥ* = increase; क्व *kva* = where; च *ca* = and; वा *vā* = or; हानि: *hāniḥ* = decrease; तव *tava* = of you; चिन्मात्र-रूपिण: *cinmātra-rūpiṇaḥ* = who are Pure Intelligence.

10. *Let the body last to the end of the 'cycle' (kalpa) or let it go just today itself! Where is there any increase or decrease in you, who are Pure Intelligence.*

The body exists and plays out in the Self, springing from the illusions of the observing mind. The existence of the world, or its dissolution cannot add or take away anything from the Self—just as a *post* is unaffected by the appearance of the *ghost*, or its disappearance. Why then should a sincere seeker ever feel afraid of death? The body has nothing to do with the Self, which is the True Nature of man.

त्वय्यनन्तमहाम्भोधौ विश्ववीचिः स्वभावतः ।
उदेतु वास्तमायातु न ते वृद्धिर्न वा क्षतिः ॥ ११ ॥

Tvayya-nanta-mahām-bhodhau viśva-vīciḥ svabhāvataḥ,
udetu vāstam-āyātu na te vṛddhir-na vā kṣatiḥ.

त्वयि *tvayi* = in you; अनन्त-महाम्भोधौ *ananta-mahām-bhodhau* = in the infinite ocean; विश्व-वीचि: *viśva-vīciḥ* = the waves of the universe; स्वभावत: *svabhāvataḥ* = spontaneously; उदेतु *udetu* = let them rise; वा *vā* = or; अस्तम् आयातु *astam-āyātu* = let them subside, disappear; न *na* = not; ते *te* = your; वृद्धि: *vṛddhiḥ* = gain, increase; न *na* = not; वा *vā* = or; क्षति: *kṣatiḥ* = loss.

11. *In you, who are the Infinite ocean (of Consciousness), let the waves of the universe spontaneously rise and disappear. There can be no gain or loss to you.*

That the universe is spontaneously rising and merging into the Self, is a repetition of the thought already given out in *Janaka*'s discourse on "The Self Supreme" (Ibid. VI-2).

Creations and dissolutions of the universes are the illusions of the mind. They are valid only at the plane of the ego; they have no existence at all in the State of Pure Consciousness. Let dreams come, stay and disappear. How does it add to or take away anything from the waker?

तात चिन्मात्ररूपोऽसि न ते भिन्नमिदं जगत् ।
अतः कस्य कथं कुत्र हेयोपादेयकल्पना ॥ १२ ॥

Tāta cinmātra-rūpo'si na te bhinna-midaṁ jagat,
ataḥ kasya kathaṁ kutra heyopādeya-kalpanā.

तात *tāta* = son! चिन्मात्र-रूपः *cinmātra-rūpaḥ* = Pure Intelligence itself; असि *asi* = you are; न *na* = not; ते *te* = from you; भिन्नम् *bhinnam* = different; इदम् *idam* = this; जगत् *jagat* = world; अतः *ataḥ* = therefore; कस्य *ksya* = whose; कथम् *katham* = how; कुत्र *kutra* = where; हेय-उपादेय-कल्पना *heya-upādeya-kalpanā* = the thought of the rejectable and the acceptable.

12. *O Son! You are Pure Intelligence itself. This universe is nothing different from You. Therefore, how, where and whose can be the ideas of acceptance and rejection?*

How can anyone accept or reject oneself? There is only One Infinite Self everywhere; "That Self am I"; then what is there for Me to accept... other than Myself? How can I reject Myself... as where is anything other than Myself?

The ideas of accepting something as real and rejecting those that are unreal, false or delusory, are all functions of the mind. I am the Pure Intelligence; there is no mind in Me. Therefore, there is no meaning in My accepting anything as real, or rejecting anything as unreal. I alone am the Reality. There is nothing beyond Me.

In *Yoga-Vāsiṣṭha,* we read :

विचित्रवर्णता यद्वद् दृश्यते कठिनातपे ।
विचित्रशक्तिता तद्वद् देवेशे सदसन्मयी ॥

Vicitra-varṇatā yadvad dṛśyate kaṭhinātape,
vicitra-śaktitā tadvad deveśe sada-sanmayī.

"In the bright hot summer noon just as we see different colours in the sky, so too are the infinite powers divine, in Him who is both Existence and Non-existence."

एकस्मिन्नव्यये शान्ते चिदाकाशेऽमले त्वयि ।
कुतो जन्म कुतः कर्म कुतोऽहंकार एव च ॥ १३ ॥

Ekasminn-avyaye śānte cidākāśe-'male tvayi,
kuto janma kutaḥ karma kuto-'haṁkāra eva ca.

एकस्मिन् *ekasmin* = in the One; अव्यये *avyaye* = undecaying; शान्ते *śānte* = serene; चिदाकाशे *cidākāśe* = the space which is Consciousness; अमले *amale* = pure; त्वयि *tvayi* = in You; कुतः *kutaḥ* = from where; जन्म *janma* = birth; कुतः *kutaḥ* = from where; कर्म *karma* = activity; कुतः *kutaḥ* = from where; अहंकारः *ahaṁkāraḥ* = ego; एव *eva* = even; च *ca* = and.

13. *From where will there be birth, activity and even the ego-sense, for You who are the One, Immutable, Serene, Stainless, Pure Consciousness?*

The Non-dual Infinite Reality should be Immutable, for change is the signature of the limited and the many. Since the Consciousness is beyond the realm of the mind, it should be Serene as none of the disturbances of the mind can ever reach the realm of the Self. The Light of Consciousness is that which illumines even the *Vāsanā-s*. Therefore, in the Self there cannot be *Vāsanā-s*—hence it is indicated as Stainless. "Thus the One, Immutable, Stainless, Pure-Consciousness (*Cid-Ākāśa*) .is Your Real Nature," is the declaration of the Sage *Aṣṭāvakra*.

Naturally, there cannot be, in You, either birth or action or ego—all these three are expressions of the "non-apprehension of Reality," which is called the spiritual 'ignorance.'

The term '*Cidākāśa*' is an original phrase used with much dexterity and daring; and in *Yoga-Vāsiṣṭha* and other text-books we find it freely copied and very readily popularised. Space (*Ākāśa*) is that which gives accomodation to things. In space alone *objects* can exist, and they can be perceived. The space in which the worldly-objects exist and in which they are perceived is called *Mahākāśa*. The space in which thoughts exist and are perceivable is called '*citta-ākāśa*'; and the space-of-intelligence is called *cidākāśa*, wherein the Infinitude of the Self is intuitively perceived. In the verse, the Real Nature of the student is indicated as this *Cidākāśa*.

यत्त्वं पश्यसि तत्रैकस्त्वमेव प्रतिभाससे ।
किं पृथग्भासते स्वर्णात् कटकाङ्गदनूपुरम् ॥ १४ ॥

Yattvaṁ paśyasi tatraikas-tvameva pratibhāsase,
kiṁ pṛthag-bhāsate svarṇāt kaṭak-āṅgada-nūpuram.

यत् *yat* = what; त्वम् *tvam* = you; पश्यसि *paśyasi* = see; तत्र *tatra* = there; एकः *ekaḥ* = alone; त्वम् *tvam* = you; एव *eva* = verily; प्रतिभाससे *pratibhāsase* = manifesting or reflecting; किम् *kim* = what; पृथक् *pṛthak* = different; भासते *bhāsate* = appears; स्वर्णात् *svarṇāt* = from gold; कटक-अङ्गद-नूपुरम् *kaṭak-aṅgada-nūpuram* = bangles, armlets and anklets.

14. *You alone manifest as whatever you perceive. Do bangles, armlets and anklets appear different from gold?*

The ornaments are different in names and forms, yet they are not different from gold, the material from which they are made. The universe of names-and-forms has sprung from the Consciousness, which is your True Nature. Therefore, can there be anything in the unvierse which is not Yourself?

The *Chāndogya Upaniṣad* (VI-i-4) also declares in one of her most famous statements:

यथा सोम्यैकेन मृत्पिण्डेन सर्वं मृण्मयं विज्ञातं ।
स्याद् वाचारम्भणं विकारो नामधेयं मृत्तिकेत्येव सत्यम् ॥

Yathā somyaikena mṛt-piṇḍena sarvaṁ mṛṇmayaṁ vijñātaṁ, syād-vācārambhaṇaṁ vikāro nāmadheyaṁ mṛttiketyeva satyam.

"Dear son, by knowing one piece of mud, all things made of mud are understood—in fact, the mud alone is the substance, the names and forms are mere words."

In short, all effects are nothing but the cause itself in another form. As such the universe is nothing but the Infinite Self experienced yet in another form.

अयं सोऽहमयं नाहं विभागमिति सन्त्यज ।
सर्वमात्मेति निश्चित्य निःसङ्कल्पः सुखी भव ॥ १५ ॥

Ayaṁ so'ham-ayaṁ nāhaṁ vibhāga-miti santyaja, sarvam-ātmeti niścitya niḥsaṅkalpaḥ sukhī bhava.

अयम् *ayam* = this; सः *saḥ* = He; अहम् *aham* = I; अयम् *ayam* = this; न *na* = not; अहम् *aham* = I; विभागम् *vibhāgam* = distinction; इति *iti* = this; सन्त्यज *santyaja* = giving up totally; सर्वम् *sarvam* = all; आत्मा *ātmā* = Self; इति *iti* = this; निश्चित्य *niścitya* = realising; निःसङ्कल्पः *niḥsaṅkalpaḥ* = free from desires; सुखी *sukhī* = happy; भव *bhava* = be,

15. *Totally give up all such distinctions as "I am He" and "this I am not." Consider all as the Self, and be desireless and happy.*

According to *Aṣṭāvakra*, the Transcendental Reality and the universe of names-and-forms are not distinct and separate factors. The waves themselves are nothing but the ocean itself, in a state-of-disturbance. Consciousness under the stress of desire "universes" into the multiple names-and-forms. Whatever their apparent nature be, they are all nothing but the Supreme Self.

When thus one has realised that the objects outside are nothing other than one's own Self, how can that one ever have any passion or desire? How can he yearn to possess, to enjoy, and thereby seek his satisfaction in the sense-objects? We are fascinated by the objects only when we consider them as something different from ourselves.

In the awakened state of spiritual experience, the *Ṛṣī-s* of the *Upaniṣad-s* declare :

आत्मैव इदं जगत् सर्वम् ।

Ātmaiva idaṁ jagat sarvam.

"These are all nothing but the Self."

सर्वं ब्रह्मैव जगत् ।

Sarvaṁ brahmaiva jagat.

"The entire universe-of-change is, in essence, nothing but *Brahman.*"

Therefore, the idea that "the Self in Me is He, the supreme Reality," is an assertion which expresses the 'ignorance' of the Self! The negations: "I am not the body, or the objects outside" is an empty childish game—the mad blabberings of the limited, deluded ego!!

"I am the All—there is nothing besides Me. I can neither assert My Nature, nor negate anything in Me. I am the One, the All-Pervading."... Having realised this State-Supreme may you remain, without any mental oscillations of acceptance or rejection of anything—still, calm, serene in your own Self—be happy!

तवैवाज्ञानतो विश्वं त्वमेकः परमार्थतः ।
त्वत्तोऽन्यो नास्ति संसारी नासंसारी च कश्चन ॥ १६ ॥

Tavaivā-jñānato viśvaṁ tvamekaḥ paramārthataḥ,
tvatto'nyo nāsti saṁsārī nāsaṁsārī ca kaścana.

तव *tava* = your; एव *eva* = alone; अज्ञानत: *ajñānataḥ* = through ignorance; विश्वम् *viśvam* = universe; त्वम् *tvam* = you; एक: *ekaḥ* = one; परमार्थत: *paramārthātaḥ* = in Reality; त्वत्त: *tvattaḥ* = than You; अन्य: *anyaḥ* = other; न *na* = not; अस्ति *asti* = is; संसारी *saṁsārī* = transmigratory ego (*Jīva*); न *na* = not; असंसारी *asaṁsārī* = non-transmigratory (Transcendental Self); च *ca* = and; कश्चन *kaścana* = any.

16. *It is through Your 'ignorance' alone that the universe appears to exist. In Reality You are the One. Other than You there is no individual-Self (Jīva)or Supreme-Self (Ātman).*

So long as the mind functions, there is the ego, the perceiver, who perceives the universe. For the universe, there must be a Creator (God); and for the God, there must be a Supreme Consciousness (*Brahman*); and for the individual-ego (*Jīva*), there must be the Consciousness i.e. the Self (*Ātman*) behind it. Thus, once we perceive the world-of-plurality (*Jagat*), we must recognise the Lord (*Iśvara*), the Self (*Ātman*) and the Supreme Reality (*Brahman*). All these distinctions are only to help the individual, step by step, stage by stage, in his unfoldment to realise and awake to the One Infinitude.

"In Reality You are the One; other than You there is neither an individual-ego (*Jīva*) nor a Supreme Self (*Ātman*)." Just as on awakening from a dream there is no more a dreamer, nor a dream-world—all have merged to become the waker's own mind!

The sense of ego and its sorrow (*Saṁsārī*) are all not because of your equipments, but because of your extroverted-ness. Even when the equipments are there—as in the case of great sages when you develop the inward gaze to recognise and experience the presence of the Divine Seat of Consciousness in Yourself, You are ever 'in Bliss. In clear vivid words we read this very idea in the *Saṁkṣepa Śārīrikā*:

तव रूपमेव तव दुःखकरं यदि तन्न पश्यसि बहिर्मुखधीः ।
तव रूपमेव तव तृप्तिकरं यदि तत्प्रपश्यसि निवर्त्य तमः ॥

Tava rūpameva tava duḥkha-karaṁ
yadi tanna paśyasi bahir-mukha-dhīḥ,
tava rūpameva tava tṛptikaraṁ
yadi tat-prapaśyasi nivartya tamaḥ.

"Because of your extroverted-ness if you are not able to recognise Your Own Self, then the equipments that constitute Your "form" indeed becomes a painful calamity. When this veilling of 'ignorance' is removed, and you realise the Self, this very same "form" of Yours, made up of your equipments, becomes completely satisfactory."

भ्रान्तिमात्रमिदं विश्वं न किञ्चिदिति निश्चयी ।
निर्वासनः स्फूर्तिमात्रो न किञ्चिदिव शाम्यति ॥ १७ ॥

Brānti-mātram-idaṁ viśvaṁ na kiñcid-iti niścayī,
nirvāsanaḥ sphūrti-mātro na kiñcid-iva śāmyati.

भ्रान्ति-मात्रम् *bhrānti-mātrām* = mere illusion; इदम् *idam* = this; विश्वम् *viśvam* = universe; न *na* = not; किञ्चित् *kiñcit* = anything; इति *iti* = this; निश्चयी *niścayī* = one who understands with certitude; निर्वासनः *nirvāsanaḥ* = desireless; स्फूर्ति-मात्रः *sphūrti-mātraḥ* = intelligence itself; न *na* = not; किञ्चित् *kiñcit* = anything; इव *iva* = as if; शाम्यति *śāmyati* = finds serenity.

17. *One who understands with certitude that this universe is but an illusion and is nothing, becomes desireless and Pure Intelligence—and finds serenity, as if nothing exists.*

Through one's own direct experience of the Self, when one understands with certitude (*niścayī*) that everything else is delusion—the Self alone is the Reality—he must thereafter become completely desireless. How can he desire anything when there is nothing other than himself? Spontaneously he must come to experience a supreme serenity of the mind, "as if nothing exists" to disturb his mind from the outer world of objects or from the inner-world of passions! A Man-of-Perfection also lives in this world—the world familiar to us, the world of enchanting sense-objects. Whenever the wiseman looks out into the world, through his physical-mental-equipments, certainly, he too will be recognising the world of objects and emotions. He recognises them, but they cannot affect him, as his realisation, that nothing else exists but the Self, is continuous, powerful and constant.

एक एव भवाम्भोधावासीदस्ति भविष्यति ।
न ते बन्धोऽस्ति मोक्षो वा कृतकृत्यः सुखं चर ॥ १८ ॥

Eka eva bhavām-bhodhāv-āsīdasti bhaviṣyati,
na te bandho'sti mokṣo vā kṛta-kṛtyaḥ sukhaṁ cara.

एकः *ekaḥ* = one; एव *eva* = only; भवाम्भोधौ *bhavām-bhodhau* = in the ocean of the existence; आसीत् *āsīt* = was; अस्ति *asti* = is; भविष्यति *bhaviṣyati* = will be; न *na* = not; ते *te* = your; बन्धः *bandhaḥ* = bondage; अस्ति *asti* = is; मोक्षः *mokṣaḥ* = liberation; वा *vā* = or; कृतकृत्यः *kṛtakṛtyaḥ* = contented, fulfilled; सुखम् *sukham* = happily; चर *cara* = roam about.

18. *In the Ocean-of-Existence the One Self only was, is, and will be. There is neither bondage, nor liberation for You. Live fulfilled and roam about happily.*

The names and forms are different to any casual observer; yet, a little deeper contemplation can explain to us that individually every object *exists*—the tree *exists*, the animal *exists*, the man *exists*, I *exist*, You *exist*, He *exists*. The '*Existence*' is apparently a common factor in you, me and he. Individuals may be different from each other: the tree is not the animal, the animal is not the human. But the "*Existence*" in a stone, in a flower, in an animal, in a plant, in the star and in the sun and moon seems to be one and the same. There is One *Existence* (*Satta*) in which things "*exist*." This *Existence* is the expression of the Infinite Reality behind names and forms, and thereafter, It *was*, *is*, and *will be*.

This One Self is your Real Nature. As such there cannot be for you either bondage or liberation. You alone are!! What can then bind you? From what to liberate yourself? Do you mean to say that you have bound yourself with yourself, in yourself, by yourself!! Bondage (*Bandha*) and liberation (*Mokṣa*) have both no meaning at all to one who has realised his one-ness with the Self. "Life, thus fulfilled," "*Aṣṭāvakra* recommends, "roam about happily."

मा सङ्कल्पविकल्पाभ्यां चित्तं क्षोभय चिन्मय ।
उपशाम्य सुखं तिष्ठ स्वात्मन्यानन्दविग्रहे ॥ १९ ॥

Mā saṅkalpa-vikalpābhyāṁ cittaṁ kṣobhaya cinmaya,
upaśāmya sukhaṁ tiṣṭha svātmanyā-nanda-vigrahe.

मा *mā* = not; सङ्कल्प-विकल्पाभ्याम् *saṅkalpa-vikalpābhyām* = by affirming and negating; चित्तम् *cittam* = mind; क्षोभय *kṣobhaya* = disturb; चिन्मय *cinmaya* = O Pure Intelligence; उपशाम्य *upaśāmya* = silencing; सुखम् *sukham* = happily; तिष्ठ *tiṣṭha* = abide; स्वात्मनि *svātmani* = in Your Own Self; आनन्द-विग्रहे *ānanda-vigrahe* = in the embodiment of Bliss.

19. O Pure Intelligence! Do not disturb your mind by affirming and negating things. Silencing them, abide happily in your own Self, which is an Embodiment of the Bliss Absolute.

You are by nature nothing but the Pure Infinite Consciousness. There is nothing for you *to affirm*, nor is there anything for you *to negate*. In the Self there are neither the bodies, nor the mind, nor the intellect—these belong to the realm of delusion. To the Awakened Self, there is nothing to assert or to negate. Therefore, "Silencing them" live happily in your Divine Spiritual Nature. As the Divine Spirit you are a Mass-of-Bliss. None of the disturbances of the pluralistic world can rise to shatter the One Light of Consciousness.

In *Yoga Vāsiṣṭha,* the sage asks :

अहमित्येव बन्धाय नाहमित्येव मुक्तये ।
एतावन्मात्रके बन्धे स्वायत्ते किमशक्तता ॥

Aham-ityeva bandhāya nāham-ityeva muktaye,
etāvan-mātrake bandhe svāyatte kim-śaktatā.

"The idea of '*I am*' takes you to bondage; the idea '*I am not*' leads you to liberation. This is what the bondage is, which is in your own hands—why feel incompetent to reach freedom?"

It is in your own free-will to liberate. *Yoga Vāsiṣṭha* adds:

ममेदमिति बन्धाय नाहमित्येव मुक्तये ।
एतावन्मात्रके वस्तुन्यात्मायत्ते किमज्ञता ॥

Mamedam-iti bandhāya nāham-ityeva muktaye,
etāvan-mātrake vastuny-ātmā-yatte kim-ajñatā.

"The idea of '*this is mine*' takes you to bondage; the idea '*I am not*' lead you to liberation. This is what bondage is, which is in your own hands—why feel you are in 'ignorance'? There is nothing for you to affirm or negate—end this agitation! You are the Self!!"

त्यजैव ध्यानं सर्वत्र मा किञ्चिद्धृदि धारय ।
आत्मा त्वंमुक्त एवासि किं विमृश्य करिष्यसि ॥ २० ॥

Tyajaiva dhyānaṁ sarvatra mā kiñcid-dhṛdi dhāraya,
ātmā tvaṁ-mukta evāsi kiṁ vimṛśya kariṣyasi.

त्यज *tyaja* = give up; एव *eva* = even; ध्यानम् *dhyānam* = contemplation; सर्वत्र *sarvatra* = in every way; मा *mā* = not; किञ्चित् *kiñcit* = anything; *hṛdi* हृदि = in the mind; धारय *dhāraya* = hold; आत्मा *ātmā* = Self; त्वम् *tvam* = you; मुक्तः *muktaḥ* = free; एव *eva* = indeed; असि *asi* = are; किम् *kim* = what; विमृश्य *vimṛśya* = thinking; करिष्यसि *kariṣyasi* = will do.

20. Completely give up even contemplation, and hold nothing in your mind. You are indeed the Self, Ever-Free. What will you do by meditation?

To one who has slept, there can be no more any "*attempt to sleep*." To the sleeper there is no more any anxiety to sleep—he is already asleep. Similarly, once you have realised that "You are indeed the Self—Ever-Free," thereafter, to think, to contemplate, or to meditate upon the nature of the Self, would be to re-crystalise your ego, and disturb your Experience Divine, with the flutterings of your mind.

In short, to give up meditation through meditation is the highest meditation! There is no greater meditation than the meditationless-meditation. It is Infinite fulfilment. It is the end of the way, and the last leap into the goal. Here *Yoga* ends. The dream-of-the ego has rolled away. The Self, as the Self, revels in the Self. The Meditator has become the meditated. Man has stepped onto the Throne of God!

This is no poetic exaggeration of *Aṣṭāvakra*. *Yoga-Vāsiṣṭha* also roars the same naked truth :

अनन्तत्वात् अनन्तस्थ भ्रान्तिर्नास्ति च संप्रति ।
अभ्यास भ्रान्तिरखिलं महाचिद्घनमक्षतम् ॥

Ananta-tvāt anantastha bhrāntir-nāsti ca saṁprati
abhyāsa bhrāntir-akhilaṁ mahācid-ghanam-akṣatam.

"Self being Infinite, delusion in It is impossible; *Sādhanā* to realise the Changeless mass-of-Consciousness is indeed a delusion only."

Chapter—XVI

Self-abidance—Instructions

Introduction

If the previous chapter is a very significant lesson for the highest students in *Vedānta*, the present chapter is the most profitable one for the students of a lesser order, who are yet striving to come out of their delusory misconceptions. Here, in this chapter, we have some special instructions, reliable tips for the great race. Sage *Aṣṭāvakra* suggests some sacred means for Self-abidance.

To end in the Knowledge of the Self all perceptions of the world, and to destroy all our desires for sense-objects, is the unique State of Liberation. Many fail to get established in this Grand State of Consciousness, though it must be admitted, very many seekers do get some exotic glimpses of the Blissful State. What cheats them of their Self-Abidance? Why this tragedy in the life of some seekers? *Aṣṭāvakra* gives us a very satisfactory explanation in this chapter. He also provides us with some very effective tips to correct our ways, to avoid the pit-falls in the path and make a pleasent dash to our Spiritual Goal Divine.

The world is recognised and we communicate with the world by our mind. When this mind is merged in the Self, our world-perceptions must totally disappear into the vision of Supreme Self, the All-Pervading Consciousness. Effortlessness is the essence of the attitude of a Man-of-Perfection. He is a Master Idler (*Ālasya-Dhurīṇaḥ*), in the eyes of men of the world.

The instructions contained in these verses are really most precious tips for the evolved *Sādhakā-s* who are yet struggling in the Higher-levels of meditation. These are meant for those who seem to get themselves, again and again, forcibly necked out from the blazing gateway of the heart's entrance! This chapter is most effective for those stüdents who jerk themselves into their ego-sense at the highest moments of their meditation, all by themselves, most ihvoluntarily.

अष्टावक्र उवाच ।

आचक्ष्व शृणु वा तात नानाशास्त्राण्यनेकशः ।
तथापि न तव स्वास्थ्यं सर्वविस्मरणादृते ॥ १ ॥

Aṣṭāvakra uvāca :

Ācakṣva śṛṇu vā tāta nānā-śāstrāṇya-nekaśaḥ,
tathāpi na tava svāsthyaṁ sarva-vismaraṇādṛte.

आचक्ष्व *ācakṣva* = speak; शृणु *śṛṇu* = hear; वा *vā* = or; तात *tāta* = son; नाना-शास्त्राणि *nānā-śāstrāṇi* = diverse scriptures; अनेकशः *anekaśaḥ* = many times and many ways; तथापि *tathāpi* = still; न *na* = not; तव *tava* = your; स्वास्थ्यम् *svāsthyaṁ* = Self-abidance; सर्व-विस्मरणात् *sarva-vismaraṇāt* = through forgetting all; ऋते *ṛte* = except.

Aṣṭāvakra said:

1. *My son! You may speak many times in many ways, upon the various scriptures, or hear them. But you cannot get established in the Self, unless you forget all.*

As an' Absolutist, sage *Aṣṭāvakra*, does not recognise the existence of anything as God, or the universe, or the ego other than the One Transcendental Self. In the Infinite Self, in Its Homogeneous State, there are no objects or thoughts. The perception of anything, be it without or within the bosom, can be only the delusory imaginations of a confused mind.

Therefore, the teacher says, "you may study all the scriptures of the world, nay, even become so proficient in the contents of the *Upaniṣad*-s that you give eloquent discourses upon all of them; yet; you have only understood the word-meaning of the scriptures, and not the Truth that is indicated by these brilliant statements of the scriptures. Until you realise this Magnificent State of the Peaceful Self, Self-abidance (*Svasthyam*) cannot be gained."

In the Self there is no universe-of-plurality. Hence, the seeker must learn to forget all the memories of illusory objects experienced in the past. This total forgetfulness (*Sarva-vismaraṇa*) alone is the "way." Where the meditator forgets his body, mind and intellect, and his world of objects, emotions and thoughts—the perceiver-ego in him ends, and this is the point wherein the ego disappears into the vision of the Reality. Even the knowledge of the scriptures is only a memory; it also crystallises the ego.

In fact, the ego itself is "a bundle of memories." If a stranger comes and asks you, 'who are you?'—meaning, "please explain the individuality in you," what you would talk from your autobiographical story are all nothing but memories. Wherein all memories are lost—sleep, swooning, under chloroform, or even in the state of madness—therein the ego ends.

Today our mind is constantly preoccupied with the memories of our past experiences and, therefore, we have forgotten our Real Nature. This is the State-of-"bondage." The State-of-"freedom" is the reverse of it. In that State you are not able to grasp any of your phenomenal experiences, because you have merged into the Higher-plane of Consciousness. The dream ends, when the waking comes.

The criticism of the mere book-knowledge of *paṇḍita-s* hinted here in the verse echos the loud condemnation of mere book-knowledge in the *Kaṭhopaniṣad* (I-ii-23):

नायमात्मा प्रवचनेन लभ्यो न मेधया न बहुना श्रुतेन ।
यमेवैष वृणुते तेन लभ्यस्तस्यैष आत्मा विवृणुते तनूं स्वाम् ॥

Nāyam-ātmā pravacanena labhyo
na medhayā na bahunā śrutena,
yamevaiaṣa vṛṇute tena labhyas-
tasyaiṣa ātmā vivṛṇute tanūṁ svām.

"This *Ātman* cannot be attained by study of the *Vedā-s*, nor by intelligence, nor by much hearing. It is gained by him who chooses It alone; to him this *Ātman* reveals Its true nature.

The same idea is vividly put in *Pañcadaśī*:

ग्रन्थमभ्यस्य मेधावि विचार्य च पुनः पुनः ।
पलालमिव ध्यान्यार्थी त्यजेत् ग्रन्थमशेषतः ॥

Grantham-abhyasya medhāvi vicārya ca punaḥ punaḥ,
palālam-iva dhyānyārthī tyajet grantham-aśeṣataḥ.

"An intelligent student after studying the text and after reflecting upon its ideas, again and again, he must throw away all texts, as the seeker of the grains throws away the husk."

Here "throw away" means forget the letter-of-the-text, and accept and live the spirit-of-the-text.

भोगं कर्मसमाधिं वा कुरु विज्ञ तथापि ते ।
चित्तं निरस्तसर्वाशमत्यर्थं रोचयिष्यति ॥ २ ॥

Bhogaṁ karma-samādhiṁ vā kuru vijña tathāpi te,
cittaṁ nirasta-sarvāśam-atyarthaṁ rocayiṣyati.

भोगम् *bhogam* = enjoyment; कर्म *karma* = work; समाधिम् *samādhim* = mental concentration; वा *vā* = or; कुरु *kuru* = do; विज्ञ *vijña* = O Wise-one!; तथापि *tathāpi* = yet; ते *te* = your; चित्तम् *cittam* = mind; निरस्तसर्वाशम् *nirasta-sarvāśam* = in which all desires are extinguished; अत्यर्थम् *atyartham* = that which is beyond objects; रोचयिष्यति *rocayiṣyati* = will you yearn for.

2. *O Wise-one! You may enjoy the world, or undertake work, or practise mental concentration* (Samādhi). *But your mind will still yearn for your own true nature, which is beyond all objects and in which all desires are extinguished.*

The very fact that every man is impatient with his desires and wants to fulfil them shows the inherent demand of the human mind to end desiring and go beyond it. The mind getting restless for the possession and enjoyment of an object is called 'mind desiring for that object.' This condition of the mind invites tremendous disturbances and drags the individual away from his Real Nature of Peace and Tranquillity. Confused and confounded the individualised ego struggles hard to acquire and possess the objects of his desire. When he thus fulfils the desire, there is a burst of peace and joy, and a foolish individual attributes this sense of satisfaction experienced in him to the "object" gained!

Viewed more scientifically, it would become easily clear that by the fulfilment of a desire the mind has become calm and our Real Spiritual Nautre is no more veiled by the thought-curtain that was raised by the mind in agitation.

This silent and eternal yearning of the human mind to realise its Real Nature is the explanation why no man is totally satisfied by all that he possesses. Even if he were to possess the whole universe, still there is in him a sense of discontentment—a bitter taste of non-fulfilment! Keeping this fundamental idea in mind, here the saintly teacher declares that a man may engage himself in sensuous enjoyments, or in fulfilling his duties, or spend his time in a life of secular or sacred contemplation.

Note carefully that here "enjoyment" is at the level of *mind*, "work" at the level of the *body* and "contemplation" at the level of the *intellect*. In spite of his so fully engaging himself at all the levels of his personality, even if he be *totally* successful in all of them, still there will be a residual sense of imperfection, ever nibbling at the vitals of his heart, providing for him a lingering sense of disappointment and dejection.

Man is never satisfied until he rediscovers his Real Nature beyond all equipments and their objects of pleasure—beyond all passions and desires.

आयासात् सकलो दुःखी नैनं जानाति कश्चन ।
अनेनैवोपदेशेन धन्यः प्राप्नोति निर्वृतिम् ॥ ३ ॥

Āyāsāt sakalo duḥkhī nainaṁ jānāti kaścana,
anenaiv-opadeśena dhanyaḥ prāpnoti nirvṛtim.

आयासात् *āyāsāt* = from efforts; सकलः *sakalaḥ* = all; दुःखी *duḥkhī* = miserable; न *na* = not; एनम् *enam* = this; जानाति *jānāti* = knows; कश्चन *kaścana* = anyone; अनेन *anena* = by this; एव *eva* = alone; उपदेशेन *upadeśena* = instruction; धन्यः *dhanyaḥ* = blessed one; प्राप्नोति *prāpnoti* = attains; निर्वृतिम् *nirvṛtim* = liberation.

3. *Because they exert themselves, all are unhappy. But none (knows) appreciates this. Through this instruction alone the Blessed one attains liberation.*

When each member of the community is to scramble in a society to fulfil their unbridled gush of desires, each will have to step on the toes of the many, and the many unconsciously are compelled to dig at the ribs of each one in the community! Every individual is, in honest freedom, striving to discover his happiness. Unfortunately, in the world, desirable objects are less in number; and the desirers are many. If hundred people desire one and the same object, it is evidently clear that ninety-nine of them will have to end in disappointment. This daily struggle, artificially created by the total stupidity of the entire community, has been glorified in the modern secular age, by a glamorous term "healthy, competitive life." Those who stand apart, and with their peaceful bosom, watch the maddening cruelty of this meaningless struggle, they are compelled to call the modern life of self-exhausting competitions as a "rat-race in a trap." In whatever way we may glorify this way-of-life, in essence, it is but the glorification of a tragedy!!

The exhausting exertions of life make every one unhappy, and the paradox is that none understands this. We are reminded of words of the *Yoga-Vāsiṣṭha*:

अज्ञातपरमार्थेन क्रियामात्रे च तिष्ठता ।
फलकार्पण्ययुक्तेन पुंसा तत्त्वं न चिन्त्यते ॥

....

संत्यक्तवासनान्मौनादृते नास्त्युत्तमं पदम् ॥

Ajñāta-paramārthena kriyā-mātre ca tiṣṭhatā,
phala-kārpanya-yuktena puṁsā tattvaṁ na cintyate.

....

Saṁtyakta-vāsanān-maunādṛte nāsty-utmaṁ padam.

"In his ignorance of the Supreme State, ever-exhausting himself in activities, tired with his constant anxiety for results, alas, man never contemplates upon the Reality...There is no greater State of Ẹxistence than the Silence of the Mind, wherein all *Vāsanā-s* have been renounced."

This instruction is more than sufficient for any intelligent student to understand where the harbour of life is and how to pilot the vessel of his life, away from the treacherous sea of passions, into the safety and security of the Self.

व्यापारे खिद्यते यस्तु निमेषोन्मेषयोरपि ।
तस्यालस्यधुरीणस्य सुखं नान्यस्य कस्यचित् ॥ ४ ॥

Vyāpāre khidyate yastu nimeṣon-meṣayor-api,
tasyālasya-dhurīṇasya sukhaṁ nānyasya kasyacit.

व्यापारे *vyāpāre* = in the activity; खिद्यते *khidyate* = feels pain; यः *yaḥ* = who; तु *tu* = indeed; निमेष-उन्मेषयोः *nimeṣa-unmeṣayoḥ* = of closing and opening the eye-lids (winking); अपि *api* = even; तस्य-आलस्य-धुरीणस्य *tasya-ālasya-dhurīṇasya* = of that master idler; सुखम् *sukham* = happiness; न *na* = not; अन्यस्य *anyasya* = other; कस्यचित् *kasyacit* = of anyone.

4. *Happiness belongs to that master-idler who feels distressed even at the effort of opening and closing his eyes! It belongs to none else.*

Activities in the outer world are expressions of inner-thought-disturbances. To the desireless, there is no 'thought-flow'; and to such an individual, who has transcended the mind, no physical activities are ever possible.

He is in the Self—living the Blissful, Infinite. He is unconscious of his body, nor is his consciousness disturbed by the perception of the world-of-plurality. This is the State of *Samādhi.* Spontaneously to maintain this experience as a constant way-of-life is a rare priviledge of the few, and such a spiritual state is termed in *Vedāntik* terminology as '*Sahaja Samādhi.*" In this State of Abidance in Self, to initiate a thought is the most painful fall and hence it is stated here: "Even winking is an insufferable affliction to him."

From the stand-point of a sweating labourer, who is working in the mid-day sun, a doctor in his confortable air-conditioned operation-theatre is an idler! And the Chief Justice of the country, who is working only for five days of the week, and perhaps four hours a day, is an escapist getting exorbitant pay for almost no work at all!!

From the stand-point of the noisy politician, or a busy commercial agent, or a restless social worker, a scientist or a philosopher may appear to be an idler! The subtler the field of investigation, the more the intellect and the mind has to functioon in single-pointed concentration—and the body then seems to relax with no apparent activity outside. From the gross view-point of the thoughtless majority, all such physical relaxations are labelled as idleness.

Thus viewed, a mystic-meditator, at the seat of his meditation experiencing the Infinite Tranquillity, or the Transcendental State, should certainly be considered as the "master-idler." A wheel turning on its oiled ball-bearing at a tremendous velocity of thousands of revolutions per second, would appear to the human-eye as inert and motionless, while the slow-moving water-wheel would appear as constantly in action!

In the most intense activity is an illusion of inaction. In this sense, a man in *Samādhi* would be considered in any society of vigorous material activities as a "colossal idler" (*Ālasya-dhurīṇaḥ*)—to whom even involuntary winking of his eye-lids is an agony, a death-pang!! But we will never understand that this genius of idleness abides in the Absolute Aloneness of the Self-Divine.

इदं कृतमिदं नेति द्वन्द्वैर्मुक्तं यदा मनः ।
धर्मार्थकाममोक्षेषु निरपेक्षं तदा भवेत् ॥ ५ ॥

Idaṁ kṛta-midaṁ neti dvandvair-muktaṁ yadā manaḥ,
dharmārtha-kāma-mokṣeṣu nirpekṣaṁ tadā bhavet.

इदम् *idam* = this; कृतम् *kṛtam* = done; इदम् *idam* = this; न *na* = not; इति *iti* = this; द्वन्द्वैः *dvandvaiḥ* = from the pairs of opposites; मुक्तम् *muktam* = freed; यदा *yadā* = when; मनः *manaḥ* = mind; धर्म-अर्थ-काम-मोक्षेषु *dharma-arth-kāma-mokṣeṣu* = in righteousness (work of religious merit), wealth (wordly prosperity), desire (senual enjoyment) and liberation (spiritual emancipation); निरपेक्षम् *nirpekṣam* = indifferent; तदा *tadā* = then; भवेत् *bhavet* = becomes.

5. *When the mind is free from such pairs-of-opposites as "this is done" and "this is not yet done," it becomes indifferent to righteousness, wealth, desire and liberation.*

So long as we are conditioned by and functioning in the mind, we cannot escape the plurality of experiences. There cannot be joy without sorrow and sorrow has no meaning without joy. A white dot on a white paper is not perceptible. In order to recognise whiteness there must be a black-ground; a black-spot against a white back-ground alone is perceivable. Thus heat and cold, joy and sorrow, and such other pairs-of-opposites are all not quite contrary and different factors, but they are the two "poles" of the same experience. We cannot ever have a magnet without a south and a north pole!

On transcending the mind, these relative fields of experiences are transcended, and to such an individual there are no more any 'goals' to be reached.

In the *Hindū* way-of-life, we have already mentioned earlier, the "goals" to be aspired for, in different stages of man's growth, are laid out as (1) rightousness (Work of religious merit), (2) wealth (wordly prosperity), (3) desire-fulfilments (sensual enjoyment) and (4) liberation (spiritual emancipation). To one who is living in the Self, all these worldly goals have no meaning or purpose. He has no more any duties to, nor has he any rights in, the social systems of human communities. There cannot be a duty without desire; he has become desireless. If he is served by the world, it is only for his wisdom and clarity of vision—the State of Perfection in which he revels in his Higher Consciousness.

विरक्तो विषयद्वेष्टा रागी विषयलोलुपः ।
ग्रहमोक्षविहीनस्तु न विरक्तो न रागवान् ॥ ६ ॥

Virakto viṣaya-dveṣṭā rāgī viṣaya-lolupaḥ,
graha-mokṣa-vihīnas-tu na virakto na rāgavān.

विरक्तः *viraktaḥ* = not-sensual, un-attached; विषय-द्वेष्टा *viṣaya-dveṣṭā* = one who has aversion for sense-objects; रागी *rāgī* = attached, sensual; विषय-लोलुपः *viṣaya-lolupaḥ* = one who hankers after sense-objects; ग्रह-मोक्ष-विहीनः *graha-mokṣa-vihīnaḥ* = one who does not accept or reject; तु *tu* = but; न *na* = not; विरक्तः *viraktaḥ* = unattached; न *na* = not; रागवान् *rāgavān* = attached, sensual.

6. *One who has aversion for sense-objects is considered as 'not-sensual,' and one who covets them is 'sensual." But he who does not accept or reject is neither 'sensual' nor 'not-sensual.'*

From the stand-point of a Man-of-Perfection, since he is awakened to the Pure Consciousness, there is no world-of-plurality, nor a mind in him that should consciously accept the world, or reject it. The play of the mind in the world-of-objects, with passion and lust, is called sesuality. When the mind abhors the sense-objects, and rebounds from them, then the mind is 'not-sensual.' When there are no objects perceivable, nor is there a perceving mind, there can neither be acceptance nor rejection—neither can you label such an individual as 'sensuous' nor as 'not-sensuous'.

हेयोपादेयता तावत् संसार विटपांकुरः ।
स्पृहा जीवति यावद्वै निर्विचारदशास्पदम् ॥ ७ ॥

Heyopādeyatā tāvat saṁsāra viṭapāṁkuraḥ,
spṛhā jīvati yāvad-vai nirvicāra-daśā-spadam.

हेयोपादेयता *heyopādeyatā* = the sense of the acceptance and aversion; तावत् *tāvat* = so long; संसार विटपांकुरः *saṁsāra viṭapāṁkuraḥ* = the branch and sprout of the *Saṁsāra*; स्पृहा *spṛhā* = desire; जीवति *jīvati* = lives; यावत् *yāvat* = as long as; वै *vai* = indeed; निर्विचार-दशा-स्पदम् *nirvicāra-daśā-spadam* = the seat of the state of non-discrimination.

7. *As long as desire, which is the root of the state of non-discrimination, exists, so long there will indeed be the sense of acceptance and aversion—which are the branch and sprout of the tree of Saṁsāra.*

We are reminded of the brilliant examination, of the "path of fall" of man through careless mental life, in the *Bhagavad Gītā* (II-62,63):

ध्यायतो विषयान्पुंसः सङ्गस्तेषूपजायते ।
सङ्गात्संजायते कामः कामात्क्रोधोऽभिजायते ॥
क्रोधाद्भवति संमोहः संमोहात्स्मृतिविभ्रमः ।
स्मृतिभ्रंशाद् बुद्धिनाशो बुद्धिनाशात्प्रणश्यति ॥

Dhyāyato viṣayān-puṁsaḥ saṅgasteṣū-pajāyate,
saṅgāt-saṁjāyate kāmaḥ kāmāt-krodho-'bhijāyate.
krodhāt-bhavâti saṁmohaḥ saṁmohāt-āsmṛti-vibhramaḥ,
smṛti-bhraṁśād buddhi-nāśo buddhi-nāśāt-praṇaśyati.

"When a man thinks of objects, attachment for them arises; from attachment desire is born; from desire arises anger.".............

"From anger comes delusion; from delusion loss of memory; from loss of memory the destruction of discrimination; from destruction of discrimination he perishes."

Desires are the very springs of non-dicrimination, inasmuch as the mind that is stormed by desires loses its ability to judge the situations correctly. When our understanding is weak, we will be tossed about in the confusion of acceptance and aversion, likes and dislikes, towards the available objects around us. *Aṣṭāvakra* describes here that the entire tree of worldly-life (*Saṁsāra*) stems forth from desires; and the branches and twigs of the "tree-of-life" are all constituted of the individual's likes and dislikes, love and aversion.

प्रवृत्तौ जायते रागो निवृत्तौ द्वेष एव हि ।
निर्द्वन्द्वो बालवद्धीमानेवमेव व्यवस्थितः ॥ ८ ॥

Pravṛttau jāyate rāgo nivṛttau dveṣa eva hi,
nirdvandvo bālavad-dhīmāneva-meva vyavasthitaḥ.

प्रवृत्तौ *pravṛttau* = in activity; जायते *jāyate* = is born; रागः *rāgaḥ* = attachment; निवृत्तौ *nivṛttau* = in abstention; द्वेषः *dveṣaḥ* = aversion; एव *eva* = surely; हि *hi* = indeed; निर्द्वन्द्वः *nirdvandvaḥ* = free from the pairs of opposites; बालवत् *bālavat* = like a child; धीमान् *dhīmān* = the wise man; एवम् *evam* = thus; एव *eva* = indeed; व्यवस्थितः *vyavasthitaḥ* = is established.

8. *Activity begets attachment, and abstention from it generates aversion. The Wise-man is free from the pairs-of-opposites, like a child, and indeed, is well-established—in the Self.*

Without desire activity is impossible. The more we act in a field, our desires in that field increase. Mental entanglements with the world outside is attachment. Thus "activity begets attachment."

Certain fields of activities are rejected by us because we know that they are not conducive to us. This rejection or abstention implies our aversion towards certain kinds of experiences. The Liberated is free from all pairs-of-opposites; he has neither attachment nor averstion. He lives in the Infinite Bliss of the Self, and therefore, he meets life head-on, as it comes to greet him! He neither runs after objects, nor runs away from them. Such a man is well-established in the Self Divine.

Here *Aṣṭāvakra* uses the very familiar and popular simile used to describe a Wise-man, "like a child." In almost all the scriptures this simile is used to explain the attitude of a Man-of-Perfection in his dealings with the world around him. This is to be carefully analysed and understood. If once we remove our sentimental prejudices, and come to judge scientifically, it must be confessed that a child is an idiot, as it has not yet developed its powers of judgement and its faculty of rational thinking. To compare a Wise-man to a child is, therefore, obviously unhappy, unbecoming. But in all scriptures we find it repeated; then, there must be, for it, a deeper and valid significance.

A child expresses both anger and love according to its mood of the moment. But the child immediately forgets its earlier mood; meaning, the child refuses to poison the present-moment with the memories of its past-moments! In short, a Wise-man, like a child, meets every moment afresh; he never allows the memories of the past to muddy his present, nor does a Wise-man break the harmony of the present with the discordant notes of his own anxiety for the future. Moment-to-moment he lives happily, dynamically, boldly facing his circumstances around him and his moods within. It is in this sense that we must understand a Wise-man's life, when it is described as 'like a child.'

हातुमिच्छति संसारं रागी दुःखजिहासया ।
वीतरागो हि निर्दुःखस्तस्मिन्नपि न खिद्यति ॥ ९ ॥

Hātum-icchati saṁsāraṁ rāgī duḥkha-jihāsyā,
vīta-rāgo hi nir-duḥkhas-tasminn-api na khidyati.

हातुम् *hātum* = to renounce; इच्छति *icchati* = desires; संसारम् *saṁsāram* = world; रागी *rāgī* = one who is attached; दुःख-जिहासया *duḥkha-jihāsyā* = wishing to avoid sorrow; वीत-रागः *vīta-rāgaḥ* = one who is free from attachment; हि *hi* =

indeed; निर्दुःखः *nirduḥkhaḥ* = free from misery; तस्मिन् *tasmin* = therein; अपि *api* = even; न *na* = not; खिद्यति *khidyati* = feels miserable.

9. *One who is attached to the world, wants to renounce it in order to avoid its miseries; but one without attachment is free from sorrow and does not feel miserable even in the world.*

The general notion of the thoughtless majority is that they are suffering because of the world. The world is constituted of inert matter, and the objects outside can really never convey, all by themselves, any misery or joy to man's mind. An object can give us joy only when it is conducive to our mind; when an object is contrary to our mental demand, that object gives us sorrow. To a smoker cigarette is a joy; to the non-smoker that very same cigarette is a sorrow.

It is the human mind's valuation, demands and cravings that lend the power and the might to the inert objects to molest man with their joys and sorrows. An ordinary worldly-man, living his ego-centric life of passions and desires, feels exhausted and shattered by the miseries that are supplied by the world of circumstances around him. These repeated lashes of sorrows and tragedies goad man to renounce the world, and seek a more satisfactory and happy condition of existence, wherein he can feel a better sense of fulfilment.

A Man-of-Perfection has no demand or desire, and therefore, no attachment with the world around him. When he lives in perfect detachment, there is an extra inner freedom of the mind, and the world around him must then fail to convey to him either joy or sorrow. With his bosom emptied of the monstrous ego-sense, he lives fully in his inner happiness, under all conditions and circumstances. A Wise-man, thus abiding in his Self, is unattached to the world of objects and beings. Even in hell he cannot be miserable; the Bliss in him is Infinite.

यस्याभिमानो मोक्षेऽपि देहेऽपि ममता तथा ।
न च ज्ञानी न वा योगी केवलं दुःखभागसौ ॥ १० ॥

Yasyā-bhimāno mokṣe'pi dehe'pi mamatā tathā,
na ca jñānī na vā yogī kevalaṁ duḥkha-bhāgasau.

यस्य *yasya* = whose; अभिमानः *abhimānaḥ* = vanity, ego-sense; मोक्षे *mokṣe* = in liberation; अपि *api* = even; देहे *dehe* = in the body; अपि *api* = even; ममता *mamatā* = sense of possessive-ness or 'mine'-ness; तथा *tathā* = also; न *na* = not; च *ca* = and; ज्ञानी *jñānī* = wise; न *na* = not; वा *vā* = or; योगी *yogī* = *Yogin*; केवलम् *kevalam* = only; दुःखभाक् *duḥkhabhāk* = sufferer of misery; असौ *asau* = he.

10. *He who has an ego-sense even towards liberation, and he who considers even his body as his own, he is neither a* Jñānī *nor a* Yogin. *He is merely a sufferer of misery.*

Sense of '*doership*' and '*enjoyership*' together constitute the ego and so long as the ego revels in the bosom of a man, he cannot have any spiritual vision, or divine experience. The very vanity that he is a spiritual seeker, or that he has spiritual experiences crystallises his ego-sense, and so, he cannot enter into the total State of Absolute Bliss. Similarly, if there is a vague sense of possession of the body, and even a dim anxiety for its security and comfort, the consequent sense of limitations, fattens the "ego," and the experience-transcendental gets clouded off immediately!

Aṣṭāvakra declares that when one has the ego-sense and the self-conceit towards liberation—"I am liberated"—or when one has a sense of possession even towards his body—"this is my body"—such an individual is neither a *jñānī* nor a *yogin.* As he has not freed himself from his sense of '*I-ness*' and '*my-ness*,' he should get necessarily tossed about, by his own likes and dislikes, in a world of restless miseries.

हरो यद्युपदेष्टा ते हरिः कमलजोऽपि वा ।
तथापि न तव स्वास्थ्यं सर्वविस्मरणादृते ॥ ११ ॥

Haro yadyupadeṣṭā te hariḥ kamalajo'pi vā,
tathāpi na tava svāsthyaṁ sarva-vismaraṇād-ṛte.

हरः *haraḥ* = Śiva; यदि *yadi* = if; उपदेष्टा *upadeṣṭā* = instructor; ते *te* = your; हरिः *hariḥ* = Viṣṇu; कमलजः *kamalajaḥ* = louts-born Creator *Brahmājī*; अपि *api* = even; वा *vā* = or; तथापि *tathāpi* = yet; न *na* = not; तव *tava* = your; स्वास्थ्यम् *svāsthyam* = abidance in the Self; सर्व-विस्मरणात् ऋते *sarva-vismaraṇāt ṛte* = without forgetting all.

11. *Even if* Śiva, Viṣṇu *or the Lotus-born Creator—* Brahmājī *be your instructor, yet, unless you forget all, you cannot achieve abidance in the Self.*

There is no meaning in complaining about the quality and ability of the spiritual teachers. Their capacity to convey experiences to the students are limited—and the grace lies not in the *guru* but in the students themselves. The seekers themselves block their minds from the flood of spiritual grace that reaches them from their teachers. This blockage is built up by the seekers own memories of the past experiences in the world-of-plurality. We had already shown earlier that the bundle of all one's memories together constitutes the "ego."

Unless these are obliterated, destroyed and discarded, the ego cannot be eliminated—and the flight to the Infinite Self can never happen. In order to emphasise this idea, *Aṣṭāvakra* here exclaims that even if you get direct instructions and guidance from the Trinity themselves, yet, the student cannot awake to the Higher-plane of God-hood unless he, himself, cuts off his attachments to his past memories.

Yoga-Vāsiṣṭha (43-10) exclaims:

चिरमाराधितोऽप्येष परमप्रीतिमानपि ।
नाविचारवतो ज्ञानं दातुं शक्नोति माधवः ॥

Ciram-ārādhito-'pyeṣa parama-prītimān-api
nāvicāra-vato jñānaṁ dātuṁ śaknoti mādhavaḥ.

"Even Lord *Mādhava* cannot give wisdom to one who has not contemplated upon the Self, even though he may be one who has for long worshipped the Lord, and is one who has supreme devotion for the Lord."

Chapter XVII

Aloneness of the Self

Introduction

The rhythm in the thought-development here adds an enchanting extra beauty to the Chapter. Verse after verse adds to the total picture of a Man-of-Perfection living amidst us, and yet totally unaffected by the endless miseries, which we are all destined to suffer in this world. Though such descriptions of physical behaviours, mental attitudes and intellectual reactions of a Man-of-Perfection, to the world of objects, emotions and thoughts are met with in our *Upaniṣadik* literature, they are unfortunately lying very much scattered in the gardens of the *Vedā-s*.

Bhagavān Vyāsa did collect them and Lord *Kṛṣṇa* tied them up into an attractive bouquet, and presented it to the *Pāṇḍavā* Prince in the battlefield of *Mahābhārata*, during the close of the second discourse, in His immortal *Bhagavad Gītā*. Here we find in this chapter *Aṣṭāvakra* strings these ideas together, not into a bouquet to be held in the hand or kept in a vase, but as a garland for the student to wear constantly around his neck!

This chapter sings a hymn to the 'Aloneness of the Self' (*Kaivalya*). The One Blissful Self evelopes all. In that State of Bliss, one who has awakened to the Pure Consciousness finds that all his desires have ended; all goals have been reached; even his anxiety for liberation ceases. His mind rolls away; and all its agitations suddenly calm themselves into an Infinite dynamic Peace—all by themselves, spontaneously!! The body and the senses halt in their functions. Far beyond all traces of identifications with the body, mind and intellect, calm and serene, the seeker now comes to experience the *Kaivalya*-State of the Self—All-pervading and Immutable.

To extol this State of Self-realisation, and also to encourage others to walk this noble Path of seeking the Self, the Sage vividly paints here the nature of Man-of-wisdom. The Chapter expounds the fabulous rewards enjoyed by the man who has unfolded himself to experience the Infinite Self. Here is a complete word-picture of the Man-of-Perfection, in a hundred poetic-strokes, on the canvas of the student's mind, held steady in his deep meditations.

अष्टावक्र उवाच ।

तेन ज्ञानफलं प्राप्तं योगाभ्यासफलं तथा ।
तृप्तः स्वच्छेन्द्रियो नित्यमेकाकी रमते तु यः ॥ १ ॥

Aṣṭāvakra Uvāca:

Tena jñāna-phalaṁ prāptaṁ yogābhyāsa-phalaṁ tathā,
tṛptaḥ svacch-endriyo nityam-ekākī ramate tu yaḥ.

तेन *tena* = by whom; ज्ञान-फलम् *jñāna-phalam*= fruit of knowledge; प्राप्तम् *prāptam* = has gained; योग-अभ्यास-फलम् *yoga-abhyāsa-phalam* = the fruit of practice of *Yoga*; तथा *tathā* = as well as; तृप्तः *tṛptaḥ* = contented; स्वच्छेन्द्रियः *svacchendriyaḥ* = purified in his sense; नित्यम् *nityam* = ever; एकाकी *ekākī* = alone; रमते *ramate* = revels; तु *tu* = indeed; यः *yaḥ* = who.

Aṣṭāvakra said:

1. *He has gained the fruit-of-knowledge as well as the fruit-of-practice-of-*Yoga*, who contented and purified in his senses, ever revels in his 'Aloneness' indeed.*

Until the seeker gets awakened to this Transcendental State of Pure Awareness, neither his *Jñāna* nor his *Yoga* is fulfilled. Seeking is fulfilled only in gaining the sought. In its great Awakening, only when the ego merges into the Infinite Self, where nothing else exists, in the State of Aloneness is the goal reached, the destination arrived, the Supreme State of Total Satisfaction gained. In this *Awakening* alone, can all seeking end.

Describing the approach to this gate-way of the State of Perfection, and narrating the experience of Aloneness therein, with a unique beauty of an arresting drama, *Prahlāda* sings in *Yoga-Vāsiṣṭha*. *Prahlāda* describes the experience of his mind as it gets dissolved into *Samādhi*:

विरिंचिभवनात्पारे तत्त्वान्तेऽप्याहरत् पदम् ।
प्रसरत्येव मे रूपमद्यापि न विनर्तते ॥

viriṁci-bhavanāt-pāre tattvānte'pyāharat padam,
prasara-tyeva me rūpam-adyāpi na vinartate.

"Lo, my mind has expanded even beyond the *Brahma-Loka* to embrace the Reality!!...and... even now... it is still expanding—I cannot call it now back again anymore..."

We must carefully note that even at this moment *Prahlāda* is still a *Saṁsārin*, because he is aware of his mind's expansion, and he still claims that he is a mind; he has still the 'ego' in him. This is the State of '*Savikalpa Samādhi*'; residual *ego* is here only panting in its death-agony, but not yet dead!

In the final stage *Yoga-Vāsiṣṭha*, declares the mystic words of the Perfect Master, the fulfilled-God in *Prahlāda*:

हरिः प्रह्लादनामा यो मत्तो नान्यो हरिः पृथक् ।
इति निश्चयवानन्तर्व्यापिकोऽहं च सर्वतः ॥

Hariḥ prahlāda-nāmā yo matto nānyo hariḥ pṛthak,
iti niścayavān-antar-vyāpiko'haṁ ca sarvataḥ.

"Lord *Hari* of the name of *Prahlāda*, is Me alone, and there is no *Hari* other than Me—this is my true realisation. I pervade everywhere and am within everything."

This State of Aloneness (*Kaivalya*) is the State of Supreme and Infinite Consciousness: the State of *Nirvikalpa Samādhi*.

न कदाचिज्जगत्यस्मिन् तत्त्वज्ञो हन्त खिद्यति ।
यत एकेन तेनेदं पूर्णं ब्रह्माण्डमण्डलम् ॥ २ ॥

Na kadācij-jagat-yasmin tattvajño hanta khidyati
yata ekena tenedaṁ pūrṇaṁ brahmāṇḍa-maṇḍalam.

न *na* = not; कदाचित् *kadācit* = ever; जगत् *jagat* = in the world; यस्मिन् *yasmin* = this; तत्त्वज्ञः *tattvajñaḥ* = Knower of Truth; हन्त *hanta* = Oh!; खिद्यति *khidyati* = feels misery; यतः *yataḥ* = for; एकेन *ekena* = alone; तेन *tena* = by himself; इदम् *edam* = this; ब्रह्माण्ड-मण्डलम् *brahmāṇḍa-maṇḍalam* = whole universe; पूर्णम् *pūrṇam* = filled

2. *Oh! The Knower-of-Truth knows no misery in this world, for the whole universe is fileld by himself alone.*

To recognise the world as something different from you is to feel immediately the insignificant existence of yourself in the Total Existence of the cosmos. Thereafter the limited body, mind and intellect feel mercilessly crushed by the crowded universe spread all around. You feel alienated from the grand-total and in this lies the roots of all your miseries. The individual in you then struggles hard to acquire and to possess, at least a part of the universe to be his own, whereby he feels he mitigated much of his growing sense of alientation!

The ego can recognise the world only through its instruments of sense-organs, mind and intellect. As a limited ego it cannot but feel flabbergasted at the force, might and extent of the universe around it. Hence its miseries.

To the Sage who has discovered himself to be the Self, the universe is nothing but waves of disturbances rising in him, the ocean of Consciousness. He realises his oneness with the entire universe. There is no more, in him, any sense of alienation. "The whole universe is filled up by himself alone," and, therefore the "Knower-of-Truth knows no misery ever in this world."

The *Hindū* texts-books are never satisfied by glorifying such a perfect Sage. In *Bhāgavad (Ekādiśa*, XIV-16) we read Lord *Kṛṣṇa* Himself confessing:

निरपेक्षं मुनिं शान्तं निर्वैरं समदर्शनम् ।
अनुव्रजाम्यहं नित्यं पूयेयेत्यंध्रिरेणुभिः ॥

Nirapekṣaṁ muniṁ śāntaṁ nirvairaṁ sama- darśanam,
anuvrajāmy-ahaṁ nityaṁ pūyeyety-aṁghri-reṇubhiḥ.

"The peaceful Sage, who in his equal vision moves about in the world with hatred to none, ever-free—I constantly follow him from behind, seeking to purify Myself, with the dust of his feet!!!"

न जातु विषयाः केऽपि स्वारामं हर्षयन्त्यमी ।
सल्लकीपल्लवप्रीतमिवेभं निम्बपल्लवाः ॥ ३ ॥

Na jātu viṣayāḥ ke'pi svārāmaṁ harṣayanty-amī,
sallakī-pallava-prītam-ivebhaṁ nimba-pallavāḥ.

न *na* = not; जातु *jātu* = at any time; विषयाः *viṣayāḥ* = objects; के अपि *ke api* = any; स्वारामम् *svārāmam* = one contented in the Self; हर्षयन्ति *harṣayanti* = please; अमी *amī* = those; सल्लकी-पल्लव-प्रीतम् *sallakī-pallava-prītam* = who delights in *sallakī* leaves; इव *iva* =

as; इभम् *ibham* = elephant; निम्ब-पल्लवाः *nimba-pallavāḥ* = leaves of the margosa (*nīma*) tree.

3. *No sense-objects ever please the one who is contended in the Self, just as the margosa (*Nīma*) leaves do not please an elephant who delights in* Sallakī-*leaves.*

More delicious in taste are the *Sallakī*-leaves for an elephant. An elephant who is fed on this most satisfying diet, will he ever feel attracted towards the bitter *Neem*-leaves, however green and tender they may be? The Sage, who is living the Infinite Bliss of the Self, is so completely contented and fulfilled in his experience of the Universal Self, how can he ever get enchanted by the bitter-ridden illusory joys of the miserable sense-objects?

In *Yoga-Vāsiṣṭha* we read a brilliant description of the Infinite Bliss experienced by the Sage in his Self:

यथा विविक्तमेकान्ते मनो भवति निर्वृतम् ।
न तथा शशिबिम्बेषु न च ब्रह्मेन्द्रसद्मसु ॥

Yathā viviktam-ekānte mano bhavati nirvṛtam,
na tathā śaśi-bimbeṣu na ca brahmendra-sadamasu.

"The joy that fills a mind, which is thoughtless and undisturbed, such a perfect joy is not found in the pleasing moon, nor in the palace of the Creator, nor for the King-of-gods, *Indra*, himself."

यस्तु भोगेषु भुक्तेषु न भवत्यधिवासितः ।
अभुक्तेषु निराकाङ्क्षी तादृशो भवदुर्लभः ॥ ४ ॥

Yastu bhogeṣu bhukteṣu na bhavatya-dhivāsitaḥ,
abhukteṣu nirākāṅkṣī tādṛśo bhava-durlabhaḥ.

यः *yaḥ* = who; तु *tu* = indeed; भोगेषु *bhogeṣu* = in the object of enjoyment; भुक्तेषु *bhukteṣu* = experienced; न *na* = not; भवति

bhavati = is; अधिवासित: *adhivāsitaḥ* = on whom impressions are left; अभुक्तेषु *abhukteṣu* = in things not yet enjoyed; निराकाङ्क्षी *nirākāṅkṣī* = not hankering after; तादृश: *tādṛśaḥ* = such a one; भव-दुर्लभ: *bhava-durlabhaḥ* = rare in the world.

4. ***Rare in the world is he on whom impressions are not left of things which he had experienced, or one who does not hanker after things not yet enjoyed.***

He is a Sage who has dissolved his ego in the experience of his oneness with the Universal Self. Thereafter he meetsthe world as it turns up, meeting experiences from moment to moment, with a spontaniety which never gets dimmed by his anxiety to enjoy, or his hunger to repeat his experiences. Ego-less actions are always unmotivated, and they are play of body-mind equipments. Ego-less activities cannot leave any impressions; they are expressions of the past (*Prārabdha*). Therefore, *Aṣṭāvakra* indicates that the pseudo-activities of a Man-of-Perfection cannot entangle him with their *Vāsanā-s*.

Being the Infinite Blissful Self himself, the Sage can entertain no restless-desires seeking fulfilments in the empty sense-objects. His bodily functions are all *apparent*-activities seen by the worldly men around, but they cannot entrap the personality of the Sage. He belongs to a category totally different from ours; he is a law unto himself!!

बुभुक्षुरिह संसारे मुमुक्षुरपि दृश्यते ।
भोगमोक्षनिराकाङ्क्षी विरलो हि महाशयः ॥ ५ ॥

Bubhukṣuriha saṁsāre mumuḳṣurapi dṛśyate,
bhoga-mokṣa-nirākāṅkṣī viralo hi mahāśayaḥ.

बुभुक्षु: *bubhukṣuḥ* = one who seeks worldly enjoyments; इह *iha* = here; संसारे *saṁsāre* = in the world; मुमुक्षु: *mumukṣuḥ* = one who desires liberation; अपि *api* = also; दृश्यते *dṛśyate* = is seen; भोग-मोक्ष-निराकाङ्क्षी *bhoga-mokṣa-nirākāṅkṣī* = not desirous of enjoyment or liberation; विरलः *viralaḥ* = rare;. हि *hi* = indeed; महाशयः *mahāśayaḥ.*= noble-minded Sage.

5. *Those who seek worldly enjoyments, and those desirous of liberation, both are found in this world. But rare indeed is the noble-minded Sage who is not desirous of either enjoyment or liberation.*

For one who is hungry, it is natural that he will be anxious to enjoy his dinner. One who is drowning, certainly, he is anxious to be saved. A miserable and imperfect individualised-entity must necessarily seek the satisfaction of his sense-objects. The limited must revolt against his bondages and should be impatient to liberate his own personality. A sage who has already liberated himself from the thraldom of matter, and who has realised the Infinite Bliss, he, thereafter, "is not desirous of either enjoyment or liberation." Of course, such a perfect Sage (*mahāśya*) is indeed very rare.

In *Bhagavad-Gītā* (VII-3) the *Bhagavān* says :

मनुष्याणां सहस्त्रेषु कश्चिद्यतति सिद्धये ।
यततामपि सिद्धानां कश्चिन्मां वेत्ति तत्त्वतः ॥

Manuṣyāṇāṁ sahastreṣu kaścid-yatati siddhaye,
yatatām-api siddhānāṁ kaścin-māṁ vetti tattvataḥ.

"One, perchance, in thousand of men strives for perfection; and one, perchance, among the blessed ones striving thus knows Me in reality."

A similar thought in *Kaṭhopaniṣad* (II-iv-1) brings out the rarity of Self-knowledge:-

पराञ्चि खानि व्यतृणत् स्वयम्भूः तस्मात् पराङ् पश्यति नान्तरात्मन् ।
कश्चिद् धीरः प्रत्यगात्मानमैक्षत् आवृत्तचक्षुरमृतत्वमिच्छन् ॥ १ ॥

Parāñci khāni vyatṛṇat svayambhūḥ
tasmāt parāṅ paśyati nāntarātman;
Kaścid dhīraḥ pratyag-ātmānam-aikṣat
āvṛtta-cakṣur amṛtatvam icchan.

"The Self-existent God has so created the senses that they go outward, and hence man sees the external and not the internal Self. Only, perchance, some wise man desirous of immortality turns his eyes and beholds, the inner *Ātman*."

धर्मार्थकाममोक्षेषु जीविते मरणे तथा ।
कस्याप्युदारचित्तस्य हेयोपादेयता न हि ॥ ६ ॥

Dharmārtha-kāma-mokṣeṣu jīvite maraṇe tathā,
kasyāpy-udāra-cittasya heyo-pādeyatā na hi.

धर्म *dharma* = piety, work of religious merit—duty; अर्थ *artha* = wealth (worldly prosperity); काम *kāma* = desire (sensual enjoyment); मोक्ष *mokṣa* = liberation (spiritual enancipation); जीविते *jīvite* = in life; मरणे *maraṇe* = in death; तथा *tathā* = as well as; कस्य अपि *kasya api* = rare; उदार-चित्तस्य *udāra-cittasya* = of a broad-minded person; हेय-उपादेयता *heya-upādeyatā* = attraction or aversion; न *na* = not; हि *hi* = indeed.

6. *Rare is the broad-minded person who has neither attraction for, nor aversion to Piety, Worldly prosperity, Desire-fulfilment, and liberation as well as life and death.*

The four different 'goals' in life, indicated by the *Hindū Ṛṣī-s* as way-side halting-places enroute the pilgrimage to the Ultimate Self, are all disciplines for the ego to lift itself from its present State of Consciousness onto the Infinite-plane of God-Consciousness. So long as the ego persists, duties pertaining to these four 'goals' of life are to be certainly respected and followed faithfully, as they can prepare the ego for its final merger in the Infinite Self.

Rare indeed, is that Man of Infinite Wisdom, the true-Sage, who has risen above these four worldly 'goals' of life, meaning who has ended his ego and, therefore, has become indifferent to all of them—nay, even to life and death.

Life and death are conditions of the body, over which the ego alone can, in its delusion, grow anxious! To the Immortal Self the existence or the absence of the illusory body is of no consequence at all. Why should the ocean worry over the birth and death of a wave?

वाञ्छा न विश्वविलये न द्वेषस्तस्य च स्थितौ ।
यथा जीविकया तस्माद्धन्य आस्ते यथासुखम् ॥ ७ ॥

Vāñchā na viśva-vilaye na dveṣas-tasya ca sthitau,
yathā jīvikayā tasmād-dhanya āste yathā-sukham.

वाञ्छा *vāñchā* = longing; न *na* = not; विश्व-विलये *viśva-vilaye* = in the dissolution of the universe; न *na* = not; द्वेषः *dveṣaḥ* = aversion; तस्य *tasya* = its; च *ca* = and; स्थितौ *sthitau* = in existence; यथा जीविकया *yathā jīvikayā* = with whatever living (subsistence) turns up by itself; तस्मात् *tasmāt* = so; धन्यः *dhanyaḥ* = the blessed one; आस्ते *āste* = lives; यथासुखम् *yathāsukham* = happily.

7. *The Man-of-Wisdom does not feel any longing for the dissolution of the universe, or any aversion towards its existence. He, the Blessed One, therefore, lives happily in whatever subsistence turns up, as his lot, unasked.*

Living in the Self as the Self, the Man-of-Wisdom has gained all that is to be gained. He has no desires for anything. He demands nothing. He is above all needs. He is full. The whole universe is to him a disturbance in the Infinite Consciousness which is his own Nature. In *That*, this universe is a dust particle; where is then his physical body? Whether it exists or not can be of no concern for him. He has pulled down the veil of 'ignorance' in him, and he has re-discovered his Divine Nature. He has no more any identification with his body.

Such a Sage is not anxious any longer for the dissolution of the universe; he has no aversion towards its play of plurality. The Man-of-Truth has awakened from all his illusions.

Yet from our view-point he is still a member of the community with a physical body, and should not, at least, his body have the bare necessities of existence—food, clothing and shelter? *Aṣṭāvakra* explains that a Man-of-Perfection lives in his own world of Perfect-Bliss, and his body continues its existence living upon whatever comes to him *unasked.* Such a Master, though he lives with us, he is no more a native of this world.

कृतार्थोऽनेन ज्ञानेनेत्येवं गलितधीः कृती ।
पश्यन् शृण्वन् स्पृशन् जिघ्रन्नश्नन्नास्ते यथासुखम् ॥ ८ ॥

Kṛtārtho'nena jñānene-tyevaṁ galita-dhīḥ kṛtī,
paśyan śṛṇvan spṛśan jighran-naśnan-nāste yathāsukham.

कृतार्थः *kṛtārthaḥ* = fulfilled; अनेन *anena* = by this; ज्ञानेन् *jñānen* = by wisdom; इति एवम् *iti evam* = thus; गलित धीः *galita dhīḥ* = with the mind absorbed; कृती *kṛtī* = contented; पश्यन् *paśyan* = seeing; शृण्वन् *śṛṇvan* = hearing; स्पृशन् *spṛśan* = touching; जिघ्रन् *jighran* = smelling; अश्नन् *aśnan* = eating; आस्ते *āste* = lives; यथा-सुखम् *yathā-sukham* = happily.

8. *Being fulfilled by this wisdom of the Self, and with his mind absorbed, and contented in the Self, the Wise-man lives happily—seeing, hearing, touching, smelling and eating.*

Human mind asserts in its restlessness only when it is under the thraldom of its discontentment. When the mind is discontented, desires rise to generate storms in the thought-content of the mind. Seeking fulfilment through its desire-gratifications in the sense-world, the mind dashes into the world-of-objects—to acquire and to enjoy.

The mind of the Man-of-Perfection has discovered a complete sense-of-fulfilment in the experience of the Infinite Self, and, therefore, there is no question of his mind roaming away from him, into the world of sense-pleasures, of its own initiative. He remains at peace with himself and with the world around.

He is in harmony with everything as they are around him, under all circumstances. Externally when the world lashes on him, he receives them—but he never reacts to them! Inwardly, in his supreme happiness he lives—"seeing, hearing, touching, smelling, eating"; in short, he never runs away from the world, nor has he any aversion towards the world. Assimilating sense-experiences he spends his days peacefully: eating in the world through all his mouths! It is not external behaviour, but the state of his inner consciousness that distinguishes a Man-of-Knowledge from an ordinary worldly-sensuous-being. Since the wise-man lives in the same world, externally he must behave as any other human-being. In his inner Wisdom alone he is a Superman, not in anything else.

शून्या दृष्टिर्वृथा चेष्टा विकलानीन्द्रियाणि च ।
न स्पृहा न विरक्तिर्वा क्षीणसंसारसागरे ॥ ९ ॥

Śūnyā dṛṣṭir-vṛthā ceṣṭā vikalānīn-driyāṇi ca,
na spṛhā na viraktir-vā kṣīṇa-saṁsāra-sāgare.

शून्या *śūnyā* = vacant; दृष्टिः *dṛṣṭiḥ* = look; वृथा *vṛthā* = purpose-less; चेष्टा *ceṣṭā* = action; विकलानि *vikalāni* = in-operative; इन्द्रियाणि *indriyāṇi* = senses; च *ca* = and; न *na* = not; स्पृहा *spṛhā* = attachment; न *na* = not; विरक्तिः *viraktiḥ* = aversion; वा *vā* = or; क्षीण-संसार-सागरे *kṣīṇa-saṁsāra-sāgare* = for one in whom the ocean of the world has dried down.

9. *There is no attachment or aversion for one in whom the ocean of the world has dried up. His gaze*

becomes vacant. His bodily actions are purposeless and his senses inoperative.

Even after having awakened to the larger plane of Consciousness, his body has to remain in our plane, and act according to the laws of the human-behaviour in his society. Never does he lose sight of his own inner-kingdom of the experience of the Self. This is a kind of liberated-in-life (*Jīvan-Mukta*). He lives in a state of unbroken *Samādhi* even while he is living and acting as a member of the community.

"His gaze is vacant," because even when he is looking at the world-of-objects, he is seeing nothing but the continuous play of the Infinite Self. His actions are not springing forth from any definite motive or profit, nor have they any purpose to fulfil. They are spontaneous actions—not reactions from the *Vāsanā-s* in himself, because he has none.

His "senses have become in-operative" inasmuch as in the ordinary man the senses bring into his bosom the enchanting informations regarding the fabulous world around. The Man-of-Perfection sees, hears, smells, tastes and touches; his senses are functioning; but none of them can bring their share of storms into the bosom of the Sage, since his mind has already merged in the Universal Consciousness.

In short, in his *Saṁsāra*, the devastating storms of thoughts have ceased. "In him the ocean of the world has dried up." Therefore, he is standing at the bottom of the ocean, and no longer swimming among the heaving bosom of the relentless waves. To such a Wise-man, so firmly established in the substratum, there can be neither any attachment nor aversion towards the outer world of objects, of beings, and of happenings.

न जागर्ति न निद्राति नोन्मीलति न मीलति ।
अहो परदशा क्वापि वर्तते मुक्तचेतसः ॥ १० ॥

Na jāgarti na nidrāti nonmīlati na mīlati,
aho paradaśā kvāpi vartate mukta-cetasaḥ.

न *na* = not; जागर्ति *jāgarti* = keeps awake; न *na* = not; निद्राति *nidrāti* = sleeps; न *na* = not; उन्मीलति *unmīlati* = opens his eyes; न *na* = not; मीलति *mīlati* = close his eyes; अहो *aho* = Oh! परदशा *paradaśā* = the Supreme State of Consciousness; क्व अपि *kva api* = anywhere; वर्तते *vartate* = is; मुक्त-चेतसः *mukta-cetasaḥ* = the liberated soul.

10. *The Man-of-Wisdom neither keeps awake, nor sleeps. He neither opens nor closes his eyes. Oh! the liberated soul anywhere enjoys the Supreme State of Consciousness.*

The inner state of a Man-of-Perfection revelling in his enlightenment is difficult to comprehend and much more difficult to express. Even the most suggestive diction can give us but a set of pleasant contradictions rather than a sustained intelligent description. In the *Bhagavad-Gītā* (II-69) also Lord *Kṛṣṇa* had exhausted Himself in trying to describe the state—and the Lord also had failed as much as the *Upaniṣadik Ṛṣī-s* themselves when he says:

या निशा सर्वभूतानां तस्यां जागर्ति संयमी ।
यस्यां जाग्रति भूतानि सा निशा पश्यतो मुनेः ॥

Yā niśā sarva-bhūtānāṁ tasyāṁ jāgarti saṁyamī,
yasyāṁ jāgrati bhūtāni sā niśā paśyato muneḥ.

"That which is night to all beings, in that Self-controlled man wakes; where all beings are awake, that is the night for the Sage (*Muni*) who sees."

The liberated is identified here with ultimate evershining Self and hence the difficulty for us to comprehend such a Divine Being. He never "keeps awake"—in the sense that in all the waking moments we are living in a world-of-perceptions, with which we react with our likes and dislikes. The wise-man is "never awake" to our world of sensuality and its enchantments; he is 'awake' to the State of Selfhood.

He "never sleeps" meaning inertia (*Tamas*) can no longer affect his Consciousness and make It dull and dim, unable to recognise Itself? We are asleep to the Great and Divine Presence in our bossom; the Wise-man ''never sleeps" like us!

He "never winks." Winking is the physical expression of one's mental and intellectual restlessness. Animals do not wink; intelligent man alone winks. That the Master has not any mental agitations, is all that is meant when Sage *Aṣṭāvakra* characterises a Liberated-man as one who "never winks."

In spite of all these hints, the State of a Man-of-Wisdom cannot be intelligible to us. He is unique. He is understood only by yet another Sage! He is totally dead to the relative world-of-plurality, and yet, cannot be considered as 'sleeping' as he is ever awake to the joyous State of the Blissful Self.

सर्वत्र दृश्यते स्वस्थः सर्वत्र विमलाशयः ।
समस्तवासनामुक्तो मुक्तः सर्वत्र राजते ॥ ११ ॥

Sarvatra dṛṣyate svasthaḥ sarvatra vimalāśayaḥ,
samasta-vāsanā-mukto muktaḥ sarvatra rājate.

सर्वत्र *sarvatra* = everywhere; दृश्यते *dṛśyate* = is seen; स्वस्थः *svasthaḥ* = abiding in the Self; सर्वत्र *sarvatra* = always; विमल-आशयः *vimala-āśayaḥ* = undefiled by desires; समस्त-वासना-मुक्तः *samasta-vāsanā-muktaḥ* = freed from all *Vāsanā-s*; मुक्तः *muktaḥ* = liberated person; सर्वत्र *sarvatra* = under all conditions; राजते *rājate* = revels.

11. *The Liberated-one is found everywhere abiding in the Self, and is undefiled by desires under all conditions. Freed from all* Vāsanā-s, *he revels.*

In the verse, three times, the term '*sarvatra*' is repeated; this is to indicate *at all places, at all times, under all conditions*. A Man-of-Perfection, irrespective of place, time and condition, is untouched by passions and desires. Liberated from all his *Vāsanā*-entanglements, he revels in his own Supreme Glory. He has realised his oneness with All-full Self, and as the Infinite Blissful Self, he has no more any desires. He has no *Vāsanā-s* as he has transcended the causal-body, which is otherwise called as 'ignorance' (*Avidyā*). On realising the Self, the *non-apprehension* of Reality (ignorance) has ended in him.

पश्यन् शृण्वन् स्पृशन् जिघ्रन्नश्नन् गृह्णन् वदन् व्रजन् ।
ईहितानीहितैर्मुक्तो मुक्त एव महाशयः ॥ १२ ॥

Paśyan śṛṇvan spṛśan jighrannaśnan gṛhṇan vadan vrajan,
īhitānī-hitair-mukto mukta eva mahāśayaḥ.

पश्यन् *paśyan* = seeing; शृण्वन् *śṛṇvan* = hearing; स्पृशन् *spṛśan* = touching; जिघ्रन् *jighran* = smelling; अश्नन् *aśnan* = eating; गृह्णन् *gṛhṇan* = accepting; वदन् *vadan* = speaking; व्रजन् *vrajan* = walking; ईहितान् ईहितैः मुक्तः *īhitān īhitaiḥ muktaḥ* = free from attachment and aversion; मुक्तः *muktaḥ* = liberated; एव *eva* = indeed; महाशयः *mahāśayaḥ* = the noble-minded one.

12. *Seeing, hearing, touching, smelling, eating, accepting, speaking and walking, the noble-minded one, free from all attachments and aversions, is indeed liberated.*

The Man-of-Perfection, liberated from the snares of life, does not run away from this world, but he has to continue living in this very same world of ours so long as his physical body lingers about him. He responds to the external stimuli, with all the instruments of action and perception, exactly like any other man in the world. The uniqueness of the Man-of-Perfection is not in the complete cessation of all his activities in the world outside, but in the quality of his heart wherein there will not be even a trace of attachment! Since he has no

Vāsanā-s of his own, he is no more reacting with the world outside as we do, and we cannot but entertain some attachments and, therefore, some aversions.

The expressive language of *Saṁskṛta* has an eloquence of its own, which is never seen in any other language in the world. The term used here "*Īhitan-īhitai*" stems from the root '*Īha*' which mean "ambition" (*vāñchā*), "desire" (*Icchā*), "action" (*ceṣṭā*) and "effort" (*Udyama*). Thus the phrase used by *Aṣṭāvakra* is so commodious that a mountain of meanings can be seen packed into it. The bosom of the Man-of-Perfection is not only free from all attachments and aversions, but he has neither ambitions, nor desires, nor activities, nor efforts. He who recognises the One Self alone everywhere, to him such a state of mind should be natural.

न निन्दति न च स्तौति न हृष्यति न कुप्यति ।
न ददाति न गृह्णति मुक्तः सर्वत्र नीरसः ॥ १३ ॥

Na nindati na ca stauti na hṛṣyati na kupyati,
na dadāti na gṛhṇati muktaḥ sarvatra nīrasaḥ.

न *na* = not; निन्दति *nindati* = abuses; न *na* = not; च *ca* = and; स्तौति *stauti* = praises; न *na* = not; हृष्यति *hṛṣyati* = rejoices; न *na* = not; कुप्यति *kupyati* = is angry; न *na* = not; ददाति *dadāti* = gives; न *na* = not; गृह्णति *gṛhṇati* = receives; मुक्तः *muktaḥ* = the liberated one; सर्वत्र *sarvatra* = in all objects; नीरसः *nīrasaḥ* = free from enjoyment.

13. *The liberated one neither abuses, nor praises. He neither rejoices, nor is he angry. He neither gives nor receives. He is free from enjoyment in all objects.*

Feeling sure that he has not succeeded in painting a Liberated man's mental attitude towards his world around, *Aṣṭāvakra* is making yet another futile attempt at describing the unearthly beauty, balance and brilliancy of the Man-of-

Perfection. He has no *Vāsanā-s*, therefore, no attachments, and naturally, there is no sense-enjoyment left in his bosom, even when he is contacting the sense-objects. Such a man Liberated-in-life (*Jīvan-muktaḥ*) is identified here with the Supreme Self which is never involved in the activities of the body and the mind.

The intellect "abuses and praises." The mind "rejoices and feels angry." The body "receives and gives." None of these activities are his. As the Self, in his Divine Presence, his equipments function, and in them the Wise-man is not in the least involved, nor is he responsible for his own spontaneous actions. The equipments gather their vitality and awareness from the Self and in all of us; they act all by themselves, according to their *Vāsanā-s*; while in the Master there are no *Vāsanā-s*, and therefore, he is not at all affected by the physical activities that are going on around him. These are mere illusions, apparent actions, which can produce no results—cause no reactions in him.

सानुरागां स्त्रियं दृष्ट्वा मृत्युं वा समुपस्थितम् ।
अविह्वलमनाः स्वस्थो मुक्त एव महाशयः ॥ १४ ॥

Sānurāgāṁ striyaṁ dṛṣṭvā mṛtyuṁ vā samupasthitam,
avihvala-manāḥ svastho mukta eva mahāśayaḥ.

सानुरागाम् *sānurāgām* = loving, passionate; स्त्रियम् *striyam* = a woman; दृष्ट्वा *dṛṣṭvā* = seeing; मृत्युम् *mṛtyum* = death; वा *vā* = or; समुपस्थितम् *samupasthitam* = near at hand; अविह्वल-मनाः *avihvala-manāḥ* = unperturbed in mind; स्वस्थः *svasthaḥ* = self-poised; मुक्तः *muktaḥ* = emancipated; एव *eva* = indeed; महाशयः *mahāśayaḥ* = the noble-minded one.

14. *The noble-minded one is not perturbed and remains self-poised at the sight of a woman full of passion, as well as of approaching death. He is, indeed, liberated.*

His Supreme balance-of-mind, under all conditions outside is the final test to know a Liberated-person. If the man is not excited by the presence of a passionate young beautiful woman, nor is he perturbed by the threatening approach of imminent death, then the individual has already transcended the body-mind-intellect equipment and he is awakened to the Infinite Self. Neither the beloved of the dream, nor the tiger of the dream can ever bring any mental disturbance in one who has awakened from his dream!

When the great courtesan, beautifully dressed in muslin and pearls, carrying fruits in a plate, at dead of night approached the temple where Buddha was resting for the day, and knocked at the door, the Lord-of-Compassion woke up, opened the door and met the lusty girl who had reached to tempt the young brilliant man in *Buddhā*. Unperturbed, the Man-of-Peace, smilingly approached her, touched her feet, and with head bent in humble reverence, said: "Mother, how can your son serve you?" With tears falling from her eyes she fell prostrate, apologised and returned to her nearby residence. In time she became one of the greatest workers in the Master's camp.

Here is the example of the serene Tranquillity of the mind of the Liberated-in-life. For such a mind—death has no ferocity; love no enchantment. Power has no satisfaction; wealth has no charm—for the true Man-of-Wisdom.

सुखे दुःखे नरे नार्यं सम्पत्सु च विपत्सु च ।
विशेषो नैव धीरस्य सर्वत्र समदर्शिनः ॥ १५ ॥

Sukhe duḥkhe nare nāryaṁ sampatsu ca vipatsu ca,
viśeṣo naiva dhīrasya sarvatra sama-darśinaḥ.

सुखे *sukhe* = in happiness; दुःखे *duḥkhe* = in misery; नरे *nare* = in man; नार्यम् *nāryam* = in woman; सम्पत्सु *sampatsu* = in fortune; च *ca* = and; विपत्सु *vipatsu* = in misfortune; च *ca* = and; विशेषः

viśeṣaḥ = difference; न *na* = not; एव *eva* = indeed; धीरस्य *dhīrasya* = of the Wise-one; सर्वत्र *sarvatra* = everywhere; सम-दर्शिनः *sama-darśinaḥ* = seeing the same.

15. The Wise-one who sees the same everywhere, sees no difference between happiness and misery, man and woman, fortune and misfortune.

Under all conditions—happiness and misery; among all beings—men or women; amidst all conditions of arrangement-of-things—fortune and misfortune, the Man-of-Perfection is ever-rooted in his own Self, and he never gets disturbed.

The outer objects, by themselves, cannot disturb an individual. Nor can the mind by itself create any restlessness. Only when the mind comes in contact with the world-of-objects and reacts, then alone storms are raised in the bosom. The mind reacts, because of the *Vāsanā-s* in the mind. Man-of-Perfection is one who has emptied his mind of all its memories of the past-*Vāsanā-s*. The serene, tranquil mind of the Liberated can no longer react with the world-around—it has become a true instrument to act with.

The Wise-one is never blind to the Source from which his thoughts arise; the ignorant is never conscious of the Source. Even if the thoughts gurgle out, and among themselves weave the enchanting world of objects, beings and situations, they cannot any longer upset the man, who is continuously conscious of the Source. We can watch a magician's creations with no perplexity, and even wonderment, because we do not forget that it is magic!

He who is thus continuously well-established in the Source, the Consciousness of the Self, even while he is playing in the world-of-plurality, he in his Wisdom knows that all these are the play of the Consciousness Supreme... nothing else.

This verse is to be understood only with reference to the State of the Self; it should not be dragged to the plane of our Consciousness. In our social and communal living—since we are then recognising the plurality—the descriptive declarations of the saints and sages cannot be and should not be practised. If the soldier has the right to shoot and kill, it is only when he is acting as a soldier under the command of his officers. He will be doing a crime if he, in his village, shoots down with his army-weapon his neighbour out of his personal grudge! Do not quote this verse as your excuse for your base, vulgar and immoral life in the community!

न हिंसा नैव कारुण्यं नौद्धत्यं न च दीनता ।
नाश्चर्यं नैव च क्षोभः क्षीणसंसरणे नरे ॥ १६ ॥

Na hiṁsā naiva kāruṇyaṁ nauddhatyaṁ na ca dīnatā,
nāścaryaṁ naiva ca kṣobhaḥ kṣīṇa-saṁsaraṇe nare.

न *na* = not; हिंसा *hiṁsā* = violence, desire to harm; न *na* = not; एव *eva* = surely; कारुण्यम् *kāruṇyam* = mercy, compassion; न *na* = not; उद्धत्यम् *uddhatyam* = pride; न *na* = not; च *ca* = and; दीनता *dīnatā* = humility; न *na* = not; आश्चर्यम् *āścaryam* = wonder; न *na* = not; एव *eva* = surely; च *ca* = and; क्षोभः *kṣobhaḥ* = agitation; क्षीण-संसरणे *kṣīṇa-saṁsaraṇe* = whose worldly life is exhausted; नरे *nare* = in that man.

16. *In the man, whose worldly life is exhausted, there is neither compassion, nor violence, neither humility, nor pride; neither wonder, nor agitation.*

In short, the Illumined one in his new vision of the Infinite Peace in himself does not react at the levels of his body, mind and intellect, as others would in their 'ignorance' of the Higher Reality. Living in the Self, as the Self, the Sage is never involved in his physical, psychological and intellectual contacts with the world around. His body-mind equipment may function in the world in its unchaste impulses, but he, as Consciousness, is only an indifferent Witness of it all. The Liberated-in-life (*Jīvan-mukta*) is not personally involved in the activities of his body or mind; there is no 'he' and 'him'! The Illumined-one is unique, and is ever a law unto Himself. He cannot be compared with anyone—not even with the gods!!

न मुक्तो विषयद्वेष्टा न वा विषयलोलुपः ।
असंसक्तमनाः नित्यं प्राप्ताप्राप्तमुपाश्नुते ॥ १७ ॥

Na mukto viṣaya-dveṣṭā na vā viṣaya-lolupaḥ,
asaṁ-sakta-manāḥ nityaṁ prāptā-prāpta-mupāśnute.

न *na* = not; मुक्तः *muktaḥ* = the liberated one; विषय-द्वेष्टा *viṣaya-dveṣṭā* = has aversion for the objects of the senses; न *na* = not; वा *vā* = or; विषय-लोलुपः *viṣaya-lolupaḥ* = craving for the objects of the senses; असंसक्त-मनाः *asaṁsakta-manāḥ* = with a detached mind; नित्यम् *nityam* = ever; प्राप्त *prāpta* = what is attained; अप्राप्तम् *aprāptam* = what is not attained; उपाश्नुते *upāśnute* = enjoys.

17. *The Liberated-one has neither aversion, nor craving for the objects of the senses. Ever with detached mind, he experiences both what is attained and what is not attained.*

Likes and dislikes, aversion and craving, love and hate—these are emotions that can reach the bosom of one, only when one has a sense of attachment with a particular object or objects around him. The Liberated-one has freed himself from all his sense of attachment, and therefore, he cannot feel any aversion for the world-of-objects, nor can he ever hanker after sense-satisfactions. With a mind detached from all direct involvements, he lives through life meeting with *all that comes to him unasked* in Divine Freedom. He neither enjoys the objects that have come to him, nor does he crave for objects that have not reached him. He meets life directly, head on, accepting nothing, avoiding nothing! His tranquillity is never disturbed.

समाधानासमाधानहिताहितविकल्पनाः ।
शून्यचित्तो न जानाति कैवल्यमिव संस्थितः ॥ १८ ॥

Samādhānā-smādhān-hitā-hita-vikalpanāḥ,
śūnya-citto na jānāti kaivalyam-iva saṁsthitaḥ.

समाधान-असमाधान-हित-अहित-विकल्पनाः *samādhāna-asmādhāna-hita-ahita-vikalpanāḥ* = the mental alternatives of contemplation and non-contemplation, and good and evil; शून्य-चित्तः *śūnya-cittaḥ* = of empty mind (Wise-man); न *na* = not; जानाति *jānāti* = knows; कैवल्यम् *kaivalyam* = in the state of Aloneness; इव *iva* = as it were; संस्थितः *saṁsthitaḥ* = abiding.

18. The Wise-man of empty mind does not know the mental alternatives of contemplation and non-contemplation, and of good and evil. He abides, as it were, in the State of Aloneness.

An ordinary man, as an intelligent being, can never remain without thoughts: he either thinks, or he sleeps. Pure Consciousness experienced in the dynamic state of 'thoughtlessness' is Godhood, and this is not experienced by the average-man. The Wise-man, left to himself, has no thoughts in him, and as such the various mental alternatives, right and wrong, good and evil, beautiful and ugly, heat and cold, joy and sorrow ad infinitum do not at all affect him. He is unattached to the world and as such the world cannot in the least affect him. It is only in the lower, relative-plane that man suffers from his mental agitations. To the Realised, there is no mental disturbance at all. He has transcended his mind and intellect. He is Beyond the beyond (*Parāt-paraḥ*). He abides in the Aloneness of the Absolute One Reality.

निर्ममो निरहङ्कारो न किञ्चिदिति निश्चितः ।
अन्तर्गलितसर्वाशः कुर्वन्नपि करोति न ॥ १९ ॥

Nir-mamo nir-ahaṅkāro na kiñcid-iti niścitaḥ,
antar-galita-sarvāśaḥ kurvann-api karoti na.

निर्ममः *nir-mamaḥ* = devoid of 'my-ness'; निरहंकारः *nir-ahaṁkāraḥ* = devoid of 'I-ness'; न *na* = not; किञ्चित् *kiñcit* = anything; इति *iti* = this; निश्चितः *niścitaḥ* = knowing with certitude; अन्तर्गलित-सर्वाशः *antar-galita-sarvāśaḥ* = with all desires melted away from within; कुर्वन् *kurvan* = doing; अपि *api* = though; करोति *karoti* = does (only appears to do); न *na* = not.

19. Devoid of the feelings of 'I-ness' and 'my-ness', knowing for certain that nothing is, and with all his inner desires melted away, the Wise-man does not act, though he may appear to be acting.

The Liberated-man is one in whom the ego has ended. The ego functions in two ways:

(a) Ego-sense, which is experienced as the *'I'-ness*, and

(b) The ego-feeling experienced as *'my'-ness.'*

When these two are ended, the ego is lifted. The very source of ego is the surge of desires. In the Man-of-Perfection, the ego is ended along with its roots and so. *Aṣṭāvakra* clarifies, "with all his inner desires melted away."

Ego-less activities are no more actions. Impulse for action is desire. The actor is the ego. When there is no actor, nor the impulses of desire, there are only movements of the equipments, and not "action." They can produce no result to the Man-of-Liberation—there is no ego to claim it. An equipment in which this ego has ended, is the empty reed through which the Lord sings His Song-Divine for the benefit of mankind and for the welfare of the world. No more does the individual mind acts through him; the Total-Mind expresses through him as Its chosen equipment-divine. In this sense, One Liberated-in-life is to be considered as God-in-action.

मनः प्रकाशसंमोहस्वप्नजाड्यविवर्जितः ।
दशां कामपि संप्राप्तो भवेद्गलितमानसः ॥ २० ॥

Manaḥ prakāśa-saṁmoha-svapna-jāḍya-vivarjitaḥ,
daśāṁ kāmapi saṁprāpto bhaved-galita-mānasaḥ.

मनः प्रकाश-संमोह-स्वप्न-जाड्य-विवर्जितः *manaḥ prakāśa-saṁmoha-svapna-jāḍya-vivarjitaḥ* = the functions of his mind have ceased to operate and who is free from delusion, dreaming and dullness; (ज्ञानी *jñāni* = the Sage); दशाम् *daśām* = condition; काम् अपि *kām-api* = indescribable; संप्राप्तः भवेत् *saṁprāptaḥ bhavet* = attains; गलित-मानसः *galita-mānasaḥ* = whose mind has melted away.

20. *An indescribable state is attained by the Sage whose mind has melted away, its functions having ceased to operate, and who is free from delusion, dreaming and dullness.*

After nineteen verses of inspired attempt in painting the picture of the Man-of-Perfection, *Aṣṭāvakra* feels, in the last verse here, that he has made only a food of himself! He confesses that this State of Selfhood cannot be described in words.

All these twenty verses are, as it were, so many sign-posts suggesting to the contemplative intellect, a certain direction towards which it may turn its vision. Each student will comprehend this State-of-Perfection to the extent he has prepared his own equipment for the great understanding.

In the Liberated-One, his mind is completely dissolved. Not even *Sattva* expresses through it; *Rajas* that creates delusion and dreams has departed; *Tamas* that veils the intellect from the perception of Reality has been pulled down.

The inertia (*Tamas*) veils the intellect and then the mind becomes agitated (*Rajas*) with its projections and imaginations. Pure "*non-apprehension*" of the Reality is created by *Tamas* and the "*mis-apprehensions*" are produced by the *Rajas*. When these two factors are controlled through *Sādhanā*, the *Sattva* predominates in the mind, and makes it more and more contemplative. In the zenith of meditation, when even the last traces of *Rajas* and *Tamas* are ended, there the Pure *Sāttvik*-mind transcends itself and merges with the Infinite Consciousness. *Māyā* is crossed here. *Avidyā* is ended. In Pure Wisdom revels the Wise-man.

How can such a being be described by words as he transcends the entire world of relative-experiences, where alone is language vehimentaly potent and extremely efficient? At best, language stammers, pants and becomes silent.

Chapter—XVIII

The Goal

Introduction

Even the most potential man of achievement must have been a helpless bundle of living limbs when he was in his mother's womb. Limited by the shells of the mind and intellect, the Infinitely Divine and Omnipotent Reality lives today as a helpless ego chained to our bosom! To release this individuality out of its entanglements is to hatch it out of its shell of time-and-space. It thereafter lives in the realisation of its True Infinite Nature. This is the destination of all evolutions; the Goal to be reached.

This Spiritual-Goal cannot be directly explained as it lies beyond the embrace of words—It transcends the intellect. This Goal is not comprehended by our understanding, but It can be apprehended as our Essential Being. Any discourse upon the Nature of this Reality can only be a futile attempt on the part of the teacher, because the student will never be able to intellectually apprehend That which lies beyond the compass of his intellect's understanding.

And yet, the intellectual students, naturally, demand an explanation, a discourse, an exhaustive description a comprehensive definition, a lucid exposition of the Goal, because the intellectual-man cannot subscribe himself enthusiastically to a path-of-life, without knowing its declared purpose, its final goal, and its true end.

The scriptural Masters, thus compelled to explain the inexplicable, to describe the indescribable, or to define the indefinable, had to adopt various techniques in suggesting the understanding into the contemplative mind of their students. One of the most effective methods adopted, generally, by almost all Masters in India, in bringing to our mind the unique perfections of the Supreme Self, is by helping us to closely observe the physical behaviour and the mental attitude of a Liberated-in-life.

A Sage-in-action is the Infinite Reality visibly demonstrated. The authors of the scriptures, as they explain the behaviour of a Man-of-Perfection, they add copious foot-notes to explain to us how and why the Sage discovers so much of peace and happiness even amidst adverse circumstances, miserable conditions, and even under grave provocations.

This technique of pointing, through a Sage-in-action the unearthly beauties of perfection attained by him, is the modus operandi that is followed in this brilliant eighteenth chapter of the *Aṣṭāvakra Saṁhitā*. As in the *Bhagavad-Gītā*, here also we find this eighteenth chapter serves as a quick summary of all that has been so far said, and serves as a thundrous peroration, richly paving the way to its final conclusions.

The Supreme Goal of Self-hood given out here in this chapter is neither discursive, nor descriptive; all along, in every verse, even at his best, it is demonstrative, inasmuch as the words of *Aṣṭāvakra*, while clearly painting the Sage-in-action, they point to a Divine Reality in and through the Liberated-in-life. In short, these verses are packed with secret instructions to all students of deep meditation upon how they can proceed ahead blasting the fortress of 'ignorance' and bursting into the Blissful Infinitude.

A wealth of thoughts is scattered all along the chapter, rich in their *Upaniṣadik* diction and deep philosophical import. Into this enchanting edifice of majesty and grandeur, the poetic pen of *Aṣṭāvakra* adds an unforgettable charm and beauty with his originally-coined shining terms and blazing phrases. As they light-up our path they spread a constant sweetness with their captivating fragrance of deep mystic-truths. The *Hindū Vedik* assertions... "This Self is *Brahman*" (*Ayam Ātmā Brahma*); "I am *Brahman*" (*Aham-Brahma-Asmi*); "This universe of multiplicity are all nothing but the Self" (*Ātmaiva Jagat sarvam*).... are all echoing and re-echoing in the chambers of these hundred verses. Original phrases—as '*Niṣ-prapañca*' (Beyond relativity); '*nirasa*' (Flavourless); '*Nir-svabhāva*' (Without natural attributes); '*Nirāyāsa*' (Effortless) etc.—enrich and enlighten. All together this chapter serves as sacred-Sanctum, a cherished-chapel consecrated to the Self-Effulgent Universal Consciousness, the One-without-a-second! In it the universe is but a mere hallucination of the restless mind!!

The magic of this chapter smuggles us into the bewitching realm of the Infinite Bliss. No student of contemplative mind can safely stand away from the exotic silence of *Aṣṭāvakra*'s Experience-Divine. The Chapter, with its conclusions, cascades into the Immutable and bewildering statements of deliberate and intentional contradictions—of pleasant and purposeful paradoxes! To ride with them is to end our ego and dash into the lap of Experience-Supreme!

The theme of this chapter is manifestly the life and experience of a Man-of-Wisdom, who is fully established in the Self. Its inescapable witch-craft is not as such in the words employed, but, it lurks somewhere between its words and between its lines. The enchantment of these verses can give us a free-ride to the Spiritual-Goal, if we are accredited pilgrims on the path of deep-meditation.

By the end of this chapter even those students who have failed to arrive at the Goal are left, for all-times to come, with a sense of devotion and reverence towards all Sages, who are living spontaneous *Samādhi*-in-life, enjoying the Infinite Bliss, which is the Nature of the Self (*Pūrṇa-svarasa-vigraha*).

अष्टावक्र उवाच ।

यस्य बोधोदये तावत् स्वप्नवद्भवति भ्रमः ।
तस्मै सुखैकरूपाय नमः शान्ताय तेजसे ॥ १ ॥

Aṣṭāvakra Uvāca:

Yasya bodhodaye tāvat svapna-vad-bhavati bhramaḥ,
tasmai sukhaika-rūpāya namaḥ śāntāya tejase.

यस्य *yasya* = of which; बोध-उदये *bodha-udaye* = at the dawn of Knowledge; तावत् *tāvat* = all; स्वप्नवत् *svapnavat* = like a dream (Unreal); भवति *bhavati* = becomes; भ्रमः *bhramaḥ* = delusion; तस्मै *tasmai* = to That; सुखैक-रूपाय *sukhaika-rūpāya* = which is embodiment of Bliss; नमः *namaḥ* = salutations; शान्ताय *śāntāya* = serene; तेजसे *tejase* = effulgence.

Aṣṭāvakra Said:

1. *Salutations to That, which is the embodiment of Bliss, Serenity, Effulgence, with the dawn of whose knowledge, all delusions become unreal as a dream.*

A mere intellectual study, or reflection, by itself can never lead the student on to the path of real meditation. Meditation is an all-out application of a total integrated personality in the search of Truth. The external marks of religiosity are merely *physical*; deep devotion and reverence are emotional and a clear understanding of the Nature of the Goal and the Path pursued are *intellectual* aspects of the spiritual life. All the three are unavoidable for success in meditation, inasmuch as we have to bring therein our entire personality. Even when *Aṣṭāvakra* is discussing the highest Absolute view-point of the Non-dual *Brahman*, he exemplifies the need for integration in a student of meditation by dramatically adding this opening stanza here, with which he so loudly salutes and so visibly prostrates to the Effulgent Embodiment of Bliss, the Self within.

The Seat of Consciousness, is indicated here as the Substratum for all the imaginary world of the body, mind and intellect and their experiences. When the Substratum (*Adhiṣṭhāna*) is realised, the superimposition (*Adhyāsa*) is instantaneously removed. On seeing the *rope*, the *snake* vision is lost; on recognising the *post*, the fantasy of the *ghost* is gone. On realising the Self, the misconceptions of the ego end immediately. To recognise the apparent illusion to be the real is called 'super-imposition' (*Adhyāsa*). *Śaṅkara* defines *super-imposition* as :

सत्यानृतवस्त्वभेदप्रतीतिरध्यासः ।

Satya-anṛta-vastu-abheda-pratītir-adhyāsaḥ.

"The illusion of seeing no distinction between the Real and the false is *superimposition*."

This reminds us of an equally attractive prostrations to "the power of discrimination' (*Viveka*) offered in *Yoga-Vāsiṣṭha* (II-9-65):

अयमहमिदमागतं ममेति स्फुरितमपास्य बलादसत्यमन्तः ।
रिपुमतिबलिनं मनो निहत्य प्रशममुपैमि नमोऽस्तु ते विवेक ॥

Ayam-aham-idam-āgataṁ mameti
sphuritam-apāsya balād-asatyam-antaḥ,
ripum-ati-balinaṁ mano nihatya,
praśama-mupaimi namo-'stu te viveka.

"O to Thee, *Viveka* , my salutations! Destroying the powerful and strong enemy of my mind—who confused me with the delusions 'I am this,' 'this has come,' 'this is mine' etc.— and has reached me to enjoy the unbroken Serenity of my bosom. *Viveka*! I salute Thee."

अर्जयित्वाऽखिलानर्थान् भोगानाप्नोति पुष्कलान् ।
न हि सर्वपरित्यागमन्तरेण सुखी भवेत् ॥ २ ॥

Arjayitvā-'khilān-arthān bhogān-āpnoti puṣkalān,
na hi sarva-parityāgam-antareṇa sukhī bhavet.

अर्जयित्वा *arjayitvā* = acquiring; अखिलान् *akhilān* = all; अर्थान् *arthān* = worldly objects; भोगान् *bhogān* = enjoyments; आप्नोति *āpnoti* = attains; पुष्कलान् *puṣkalān* = abundant; न *na* = not; हि *hi* = surely; सर्व-परित्यागम्-अन्तरेण *sarva-parityāgam-antareṇa* = without the renunciation of all; सुखी *sukhī* = happy; भवेत् *bhavet* = becomes.

2. *One gets plenty of enjoyments by acquiring the manifold objects of the senses. Surely one cannot be happy without renouncing them all.*

On the first reading it would sound as a contradiction, as the former part of the statement positively declares that there is *joy* in the sense-objects; but it says, in its concluding part, that *happiness* cannot be without renunciation of them all. Here the confusion is generated in our minds only because we are not alert enough to distinguish between '*enjoyment*' and '*happiness*.' *Happiness* is the goal sought by every human-mind and the means employed by everyone is the *enjoyment* of the sense-objects. Generally man misunderstands herein the *means*, sense-enjoyments, to be the *goal*, 'happiness.'

No body denies : there are, but limited and evanescent glimmers of enjoyments when the sense-organs come in contact with the sense-objects. But what man demands is a total-satisfaction, his *happiness*, and not sense-gratification, *enjoyments*. In the renunciation of all sense-pursuits lies the path to permanent and satisfying happiness. Desires create mental agitation—and a mind agitated is a mind in sorrow. By renouncing the desires, the thoughts subside—and a quiet mind is itself the glow of happiness. Thus, lesser the desires, lesser the agitations, and more the joy. Least desires, least agitations, and maximum joy. Therefore, "no-desires" is a state-of-thougthless-ness, which is the State of Infinite Bliss, the Self.

In the absence of all objects, in the deep-sleep-state of Consciousness, there is joy for all, everywhere. In fact, at the moment-of-enjoyment there is no pesence of the object, there is only the experience of the Bliss, which is the very nature of the Self.

कर्तव्यदुःखमार्तण्डज्वालादग्धान्तरात्मनः ।
कुतः प्रशमपीयूषधारासारमृते सुखम् ॥ ३ ॥

Kartavya-duḥkha-mārtaṇḍa-
jvālā-dagdh-āntar-ātmanaḥ,
kutaḥ praśma-pīyūṣa-
dhārā-sāram-ṛte sukham.

कर्तव्य-दुःख-मार्तण्ड-ज्वाला-दग्ध-अन्तरात्मनः *kartavya-duḥkha-mārtaṇḍa-jvālā-dagdha-antarātmanaḥ* = of one whose inner equipment has been scorched by the heat of sun of sorrow of his deeds; कुतः *kutaḥ* = where (is); प्रशम-पीयूष-धारा-सारम्-ऋते *praśma-piyūsa-dhārā-sāram-ṛte* = except in the continuous shower of the ambrosia of desireless-ness; सुखम् *sukham* = happiness.

3. *One whose inner equipment has been scorched by the heat of the sun-of-sorrow arising from his deeds, where can he enjoy happiness, except in the continuous ambrosial shower-of-desireless-ness?*

A mind—that has been stormed by the passionate surge of the continuous lashing waves of desires, and their consequent frothing, noisy deeds—can calm itself only when desireless-ness comes to play therein.

The verse is a typical example of the pictorial style in *Saṁskṛta* literature, especially employed in poetry. Here is an attempt of the poet to communicate philosophical truth in terms of our physical experiences. In the scorching heat of the summer, except a heavy cool-shower, nothing else can cool us into comfort. The desire-ridden bosom is ever in agitation whipping the man into endless endeavours. With the dawn of right knowledge, that the finite objects of the world, with their limited joys, cannnot give what our heart is yearning for, will come the spirit of retirement and relinquishment. Except in this state of intelligent desireless-ness, a storming passionate mind cannot calm itself down. So long as this discriminating knowledge has not dawned in an individual bosom, it has to suffer its endless restlessness. Tranquillity of the mind and inner peace are the rewards of wisdom and right understanding.

भवोऽयं भावनामात्रो न किञ्चित् परमार्थतः ।
नास्त्यभावः स्वभावानां भावाभावविभाविनाम् ॥ ४ ॥

Bhavo'yaṁ bhāvanā mātro na kiñcit paramārthataḥ,
nāsty-abhāvaḥ svabhāvānāṁ bhāvā-bhāva-vibhāvinām.

भवः *bhavaḥ* = universe; अयम् *ayam* = this; भावना-मात्रः *bhāvanā-mātraḥ* = mere mode of thinking; न *na* = not; किञ्चित् *kiñcit* = anything; परमार्थतः *paramārthataḥ* = in reality; न *na* = not; अस्ति *asti* = is; अभावः *abhāvaḥ* = non-existent; स्वभावानाम् *svabhāvānām* = the inherent nature; भाव-अभाव-विभाविनाम् *bhāva-abhāva-vibhāvinām* = in the existent (Self) and the non-existent (universe).

4. *This universe is but a mode of thinking. In reality it is nothing. The inherent nature of the Existent (Self) and of the Non-existent (universe) are never lost.*

Very often statements in *Aṣṭāvakra Gītā* are rendered attractive not only because of their pithy style, but because of their eloquent and ringing diction. Here is a typical example. This universe is but a mode of thinking (*Bhava-ayam bhāvanā-mātraḥ*). This has become a famous saying in the mouths of all *Vedāntik* scholars. On awakening to the Reality, when the mind is hushed up from its thoughts, the magic of the names and forms rolls away and the student realises "In reality it is nothing" (*Na kiñcit paramārthataḥ*). The Sage *Aṣṭāvakra* declares here the great philosophical truth that the Existent Self and the Non-existent universe both can never lose their individual nature.

The Self is Eternal, Permanent, Changeless and Infinite; the universe is non-eternal, impermanent, ever-changing and finite. Neither of them can change their essential nature. In short, the Self alone is Real, and It will ever remain Real. The world-of-plurality is ever unreal, and never can it be real; the Self is Existent. The world is non-existent. They cannot change their nature.

न दूरं न च सङ्कोचाल्लब्धमेवात्मनः पदम् ।
निर्विकल्पं निरायासं निर्विकारं निरञ्जनम् ॥ ५ ॥

Na dūraṁ na ca saṅkocāl-
labdha-mevātmanaḥ padam,
nir-vikalpaṁ nir-āyāsaṁ
nir-vikāraṁ nirañjanam.

न *na* = not; दूरम् *dūram* = far, inaccessible; न *na* = not; च *ca* = and; सङ्कोचात् *saṅkocāt* = limited; लब्धम् *labdham* = ever-attained; एव *eva* = indeed; आत्मनः पदम् *ātmanaḥ padam* = the Nature of the Self; निर्विकल्पम् *nir-vikalpam* = absolute; निरायासम् *nirāyāsam* = effortless; निर्विकारम् *nir-vikāram* = immutable; निरञ्जनम् *nirañjanam* = stainless.

5. *The Self which is Absolute, Effortless, Immutable and Stainless is not far away—inaccessible. Nor is It limited—Unattainable. It is indeed ever-attained.*

The Supreme Consciousness in its Absolute Nature is Stainless meaning "It is beyond all passions and desires—*Vāsanā-s*." 'Perceptions' of the body, 'emotions' of the mind, 'thoughts' of the intellect are all exertions, and therefore, to act with these equipments is always an effort. The *Ātman*, the Reality is explained here as 'Effortless' (*Nirāyāsam*), inasmuch as It is experienced when all equipments are transcended, where the ego surrenders completely and disappears into the vision of the Reality. This Great State is our own Real Nature and, therefore, It is "not far away" from us; It is not inaccessible to anyone.

The limited alone is attainable with our equipments. The Self is Infinite and, therefore, unlimited; naturally It is 'Unattainable.' It is the very being in us, the very Existence-Knowledge in us; as such never is a time when we are away from It. "It is indeed ever-attained." In our delusion we recognise not the constant Presence of this Divine Self.

Roars the *Ṛṣi* in *Muṇḍakopaniṣad* (III-i-7) :

....

दूरात् सुदूरे तदिहान्तिके च
पश्यत्स्विहैव निहितं गुहायाम् ॥

....

Dūrāt sudūre tad-ihāntike ca
paśyat-svihaiva nihitaṁ guhāyām.

"Further than the farthest, It is here within the body. The Sages realize It verily in this life as fixed in the heart."

व्यामोहमात्रविरतौ स्वरूपादानमात्रतः ।
वीतशोका विराजन्ते निरावरणदृष्टयः ॥ ६ ॥

Vyāmoha-mātra-viratau svarūpā-dāna-mātrataḥ,
vīta-śokā virājante nir-āvaraṇa-dṛṣṭayaḥ.

व्यामोह-मात्र-विरतौ *vyāmoha-mātra-viratau* = as soon as illusion ceases; स्वरूप-आदान-मात्रत: *svarūpa-ādāna-mātrataḥ* = as soon as the Self is realised; वीत-शोका: *vīta-śokāḥ* = free from misery; विराजन्ते *virājante* = (they) shine; निरावरण-दृष्टय: *nirāvaraṇa-dṛṣṭayaḥ* = those whose understanding (vision) is fully unveiled i.e. the wise.

6. *Those whose understanding (vision) is fully unveiled, as soon as illusion ceases and the Self is realised, they (the wise) shine free from misery.*

The Self, which is the Essential Nature of the seeker, is not realised by him only because of his ego and its illusion in him. As an ego, he is pre-occupied with his own miseries and his understanding is clouded by *Tamas* and shattered by *Rajas*. When these two moods-of-the-mind are sublimated, contemplative-ness increases in the mind, and the contemplative mind, during moments of its meditation, cannot avoid discovering its own illusions and the Eternal Reality behind them all. Such perfect students shine in inner glory of their directly experienced Spiritual Essence.

समस्तं कल्पनामात्रमात्मा मुक्तः सनातनः ।
इति विज्ञाय धीरो हि किमभ्यस्यति बालवत् ॥ ७ ॥

Samastaṁ kalpanā-mātram-ātmā muktaḥ sanātanaḥ,
iti vijñāya dhīro hi kimbhya-syati bālavat.

समस्तम् *samastam* = all that exists; कल्पना-मात्रम् *kalpanā-mātram* = mere imagination; आत्मा *ātmā* = Self; मुक्तः *muktaḥ* = free; सनातनः *sanātanaḥ* = eternal; इति *iti* = thus; विज्ञाय *vijñāya* = knowing; धीरः *dhīraḥ* = the Wise-man; हि *hi* = indeed; किम् *kim* = does he? अभ्यस्यति *abhyasyati* = acts; बालवत् *bālavat* = like a child.

7. *All that exists is more imagination. The Self is Free and Eternal, Knowing thus, does the Wise-one act like a child?*

On awakening from a dream, the waker realises that the dream that he was seeing was mere imagination and that the waker is the Reality. One who has awakened from the ego's usual plane-of-Consciousness and its endless sorrows, he realises that the worlds of experiences lived at the body, mind and the intellect levels are all imaginations of a mind fluttering in its restlessness. A Wise-man experiences the Infinite Blissful Self. One who has thus awakened to the Higher-plane of Consciousness, can he ever act like a child in the world?

The example 'like a child' employed here, opens up many possible explanations. Commentators differ in their opinions on what exactly is suggested by *Aṣṭāvakra* here. Such a Wise-man certainly will not act in the world thereafter (1) Irresponsibly,

(2) foolishly, (3) mischievously, (4) playfully—as a child! A child in his ignorance may invite harm unto itself, and can innocently cause disastrous calamities to others. A Wise-man, as long as he lives in this world, will never initiate activities which would bring, even unconsciously, sorrows to individuals, or to the community. He is so well-established in the harmony of the Universal Self that all his actions must bring only blessings to others—even activities which look apparently ridiculous, or immoral, can but bring only, in the end, blessings to the community! They can do no wrong, never!!

आत्मा ब्रह्मेति निश्चित्य भावाभावौ च कल्पितौ ।
निष्कामः किं विजानाति किं ब्रूते च करोति किम् ॥८॥

Ātmā brahmeti niścitya bhāvā-bhāvau ca kalpitau,
niṣkāmaḥ kiṁ vijānāti kiṁ brūte ca karoti kim.

आत्मा *ātmā* = Self; ब्रह्म *brahma* = *Brahman*; इति *iti* = thus; निश्चित्य *niścitya* = having known with certitude; भाव-अभावौ *bhāva-abhāvau* = existence and non-existence; च *ca* = and; कल्पितौ *kalpitau* = imagined; निष्कामः *niṣkāmaḥ* = desireless; किम् *kim* = what; विजानाति *vijānāti* = knows; किम् *kim* = what; ब्रूते *brūte* = says; च *ca* = and; करोति *karoti* = does; किम् *kim* = what.

8. *Having known with certitude that the Self is* Brahman, *and the existence and non-existence are mere imaginations, what can one, who is desireless, know, say, or do?*

Here the term "Existence and non-existence" is used as an idiom to indicate the entire world of multiplicity which is recognised in terms of the pairs-of-opposites, such as joy and sorrow, heat and cold, good and bad, right and wrong etc. All of them are at once comprehended by this suggestive term. This is a very popular and much used philosophical idiom in *Vedānta*.

The pairs-of-opposites are expressions of the mind and intellect, and naturally, they are illusions projected by the restless mind upon the Substratum, the Peaceful Self. One who has awakened to the Self, has ended all his illusions—one having seen the *post*, can he get any longer disturbed by the *ghost*-visions?

For such an individual, who has transcended the mind, and therefore, has reached a state of perfect desireless-ness—there can neither be an ego, nor any actions. He has transcended all the three equipments of body, mind and intellect, and naturally, the teacher asks, "what can one, who is *desireless, know, say* or *do?*" Here '*knowing*' is the function of the intellect, '*saying*' represents all activities at the body-level, and '*doing*' all the functions of the mind. In short, there will be no sense of "*doership*" or "*enjoyership*" in that perfected-Master.

An ancient Sage has sung:

शुद्धो मुक्तः सदैवात्मा न वै बध्येत कर्हिचित् ।
बन्धमोक्षौ मनःसंस्थौ तस्मिञ्च्छान्ते प्रशाम्यति ॥

Śuddho muktaḥ sadaivātmā
na vai badhyeta karhicit,
bandha-mokṣau manaḥ-saṁsthau
tasmiñ-cchānte praśāmyati.

"The liberated is ever the Self, beyond the mind and so not bound by anything; bondage and liberation are conditions that depend upon the mind—one whose mind has become hushed up, his entire sense of individuality has ended."

अयं सोऽहमयं नाहमिति क्षीणा विकल्पनाः ।
सर्वमात्मेति निश्चित्य तूष्णीम्भूतस्य योगिनः ॥ ९ ॥

Ayaṁ so'ham-ayaṁ nāha-miti kṣīṇā vikalpanāḥ,
sarvam-ātmeti niścitya tūṣṇīm-bhūtasya yoginaḥ.

अयम् सः *ayam saḥ* = This is that; अहम् *aham* = I; अयम् *ayam* = this; न *na* = not; अहम् *aham* = I; इति *iti* = thus; क्षीणाः *kṣīṇāḥ* =

extinguished (become); विकल्पना: *vikalpanāḥ* = thoughts; सर्वम् *sarvam* = everything; आत्म *ātma* = Self; इति *iti* = thus; निश्चित्य *niścitya* = knowing with certitude; तूष्णीम्-भूतस्य *tūṣṇīm-bhūtasya* = become quiet; योगिन: *yoginaḥ* = of the *Yogin*.

9. *Such thoughts as "This is That," "I am That," and "I am not this"—are existinguished for the* Yogin *who has become quiet, knowing with certitude that everything is Self only.*

On realising the One Infinite Self as All-pervading and Immutable, every kind of mental concept must completely cease. That "I am the body, mind and intellect," or that "I am not the body, mind and the intellect," or the idea that "I am the Self"—all these are conceptual and are, therefore, mere mental disturbances, and at their best only serious intellectual approximations. To become the Self, and to live in the State of Self, is to end all such artificial repetitions and conceptual approximations. The Liberated-in-life directly experiences the Self Immutable.

In one who has Realised, all such thought-agitations are extinguished, and he lives continuously in the awareness that he is the Self—and, therefore, he is the all.

न विक्षेपो न चैकाग्र्यं नातिबोधो न मूढता ।
न सुखं न च वा दुःखमुपशान्तस्य योगिनः ॥ १० ॥

Na vikṣepo na caikāgryaṁ nātibodho na mūḍatā,
na sukhaṁ na ca vā duḥkham-upaśāntasya yoginaḥ.

न *na* = not; विक्षेप: *vikṣepaḥ* = distractions (agitations); न *na* = not; च *ca* = and; एकाग्रयम् *akāgryam* = concentration; न *na* = not; अतिबोध: *atibodhaḥ* = increase of knowledge; न *na* = not; मूढता *mūḍatā* = ignorance; न *na* = not; सुखम् *sukham* = pleasure; न *na* = not; च *ca* = and; वा *vā* = or; दु:खम् *duḥkham* = pain; उपशान्तस्य *upaśāntasya* = who has become serene; योगिन: *yoginaḥ* = of *Yogin*.

10. *The* Yogin *who has attained serenity has no more any distractions, no concentration, no increase in knowledge, no ignorance. He has neither pleasure nor pain.*

The Liberated-in-life has transcended his mind-intellect equipment and therefore, in his serenity there is no fluctuation of knowledge, or feeling, that might come to disturb him ever. 'Distractions' are the experiences of agitations in the mind. 'Concentration' is practised as a discipline of the intellect over the distracted and wild mind. Brilliancy of knowledge or dullness or ignorance are all bright and dull conditions of the intellect. Pleasure and pain are the experiences in the mind.

All these enumerated list-of-factors are to show that there is no stormy state of restlessness in the bosom of a Man-of-Perfection. Nothing disturbs his Infinite Serenity—he experiences what christ describes as, "the Peace, that passeth all understanding."

स्वाराज्ये भैक्ष्यवृत्तौ च लाभालाभे जने वने ।
निर्विकल्पस्वभावस्य न विशेषोऽस्ति योगिनः ॥ ११ ॥

Svārājye bhaikṣya-vṛttau ca lābhā-lābhe jane vane;
nirvikalpa-svabhāvasya na viśeṣo-'sti yoginaḥ.

स्वाराज्ये *svārājye* = in the dominion of heaven; भैक्ष्य-वृत्तौ *bhaikṣya-vṛttau* = in beggary; च *ca* = and; लाभ-अलाभे *lābha-alābhe* = in gain and loss; जने *jane* = in society; वने *vane* = in forest; निर्विकल्प-स्वभावस्य *nirvikalpa-svabhāvasya* = whose nature is without desire-agitations; न *na* = not; विशेषः *viśeṣaḥ* = difference; अस्ति *asti* = is; योगिनः *yoginaḥ* = of the *Yogin.*

11. *Be he in heaven, or be he in beggary—be he in gain or in loss— in company of society or lonely in forest— there is no difference to the* Yogin, *who is free from desire-agitations.*

The previous verse expounded the continuous State of Tranquillity of the inner equipments of the Liberated-in-life. It is very well-known that a Wise-man also will have to certainly live in the very same world of disturbances in which we live. We know that there are thousands of situations, where the outer world can blast our peace within and storm our bosom with hordes of worldly agitations. Here, in this verse, *Aṣṭāvakra* clearly declares that the outer world of happenings—the circumstances and conditions—around a Realised-man will not affect him at all, at any time.

Thus, let him be placed, in a heavenly arrangement of circumstances to give extreme happiness and pleasure, or let him be placed in the midst of poverty and privations forcing him to live a life of beggary, his inward peace and joy is not affected in the least! To him gain and loss are insignificant fluctuations in the outer world. He gains nothing by the worldly gains nor can his spiritual happiness be lost by the loss of worldly objects!

Be he is pleasant company in a city or be he lonely in a forest, it is the same to him—he is ever in the Infinite. The Liberated, who has conquered his desire-agitations, is no more an ego conditioned by its mind, and so he is invulnerable to the persecutions of the world around him.

He lives with his head and heart lost in the Transcendental, though his feet are upon the earth where we crawl about in our misery and self-created illusions of our daily sorrows!!

क्व धर्मः क्व च वा कामः क्व चार्थः क्व विवेकिता।
इदं कृतमिदं नेति द्वन्द्वैर्मुक्तस्य योगिनः ॥ १२ ॥

Kva dharmaḥ kva ca vā kāmaḥ
kva cārthaḥ kva vivekitā,
idaṁ kṛtam-idaṁ neti
dvandvair-muktasya yoginaḥ.

क्व *kva* = where; धर्मः *dharmaḥ* = righteousness; क्व *kva* = where; च *ca* = and; वा *vā* = or; कामः = sense-of-enjoyment; क्व *kva* = where;

च *ca* = and; अर्थः *arthaḥ* = wealth; क्व *kva* = where; विवेकिता *vivekitā* = conscience; इदम् *idam* = this; कृतम् *kṛtam* = done; इदम् *idam* = this; न *na* = not; इति *iti* = thus; द्वन्द्वैः *dvandvaiḥ* = from pairs of opposites; मुक्तस्य *muktasya* = free; योगिनः *yoginaḥ* = of the *Yogin*.

12. For a Yogin, *who has transcended such dual notions as "this is to be done" and "this is not to be done," where is righteousness* (Dharma)*? Where is sense-enjoyment (*Kāma)*? Where is worldly-prosperity (*Artha*)? And where is conscience* (Vivekitā)*?*

In the relative-fields of Consciousness alone can the ego function, and all pairs-of-opposites are the agitations of the ego. The idea that some things are 'to be done' and some are 'not to be done' is based upon the delusion of seeking one's happiness in the world of objects and their arrangements. One, in whom the ego has ended, can no longer have in him the compulsions of the pairs-of-opposites. To such an individual, who has already reached the Supreme Goal, he has no more any use for the various wayside-stations which are the "goals-of-life" (*Puruśārthā-s*), as conceived by the *Hindū* way-of-living—*Dharma*, *Artha* and *Kāma*. He is not moving towards *Mokṣa*—he has reached Liberation-in-life.

Man is often tempted to act at the body and mind levels compromising his own intellectual convictions and ideals. The passing fascination for some immediate gain, forces the mind and the body to revolt against the restraint of the intellect, and rush out to embrace these fanciful sense-objects. When the mind's passion is satisfied, the intellect regains its command, and the mind feels a deep regret at the honest criticisms of the intellect! These shooting pangs of regrets of the mind for having disobeyed the nobler discriminations of the intellect, are popularly called as the "Conscience-pricks."

This is the lot of all educated, cultured people; frequently we are compelled to compromise with our own right understanding. To a Man-of-Perfection there is no such self-criticism that can rise in his intellect, because he has transcended all the equipments! He has no regrets in life, even for "what he has done," or regarding "what he has not yet done." The term '*Vivekitā*' used here for "Conscience" is a very novel term used with its own significant import.

कृत्यं किमपि नैवास्ति न कापि हृदि रञ्जना ।
यथा जीवनमेवेह जीवन्मुक्तस्य योगिनः ॥१३॥

Kṛtyaṁ kimapi naivāsti na kāpi hṛdi rañjanā,
yathā jīvana-meveha jīvan-muktasya yoginaḥ.

कृत्यम् *kṛtyam* = duty; किम् अपि *kim-api* = any; न *na* = not; एव *eva* = surely; अस्ति *asti* = is; न *na* = not; क अपि *ka api* = any; हृदि *hṛdi* = at heart; रञ्जना *rañjanā* = attachment; यथा जीवनम् *yathā jīvanam* = pertaining to present life; एव *eva* = only (is); इह *iha* = in this world; जीवन्-मुक्तस्य *jīvan-muktasya* = liberated-in-life; योगिनः *yoginaḥ* = of the *yogin*.

13. *The Yogin, who is Liberated-in-life, has neither any duty nor any attachment at heart. His actions merely follow the lot of his life.*

On awakening to the Higher-plane, the Self, the Man-of-Perfection has transcended his ego. Not only that he has no more any ego-sense as 'I'; but also has no more any ego-feeling as 'my.' This is the very reason why he has neither desires—no 'I' to entertain them; nor attachments—no sense of possession 'my' to feel attachments for. Generally, when a man desires, then he will have attachments to his desired objects. The Liberated-in-life has neither of them.

In the previous verse the Man-of-Realisation is described as remaining in his Highest-State of experience in *Samādhi*, while here in this verse *Aṣṭāvakra* is describing the liberated-in-life as seen by others, functioning in society. We see a Sage acting in life so long as his body lives. The Sage takes up any work that turns up and lives any kind of life that is available for him.

He is unique, inasmuch as an ordinary man is compelled to choose a particular kind of work and to insist upon a definite type of life that he wants to live. A worldly man insists upon living his own chosen profession. To a Man-of-Perfection there is no choosing; he never plans or demands: he just lives.

He seems to work in any field that comes to him unsaked; he lives upon that whatever comes to him by chance! Under all conditions and circumstances, in all companies, everywhere, at all times, he is supremely serene and blissful in his greater identification with the Infinite Reality. He acts as forced by the *Prārabdha*—resultant of the past actions of his body!!

The body was initiated as a resultant of the past deeds. It has arrived in this world to experience not only the rewards of his past noble life, but also pay for the bad deeds of the past, in terms of exhausting strifes, sorrowful circumstances, miserable diseases, etc. But a Liberated-in-Life, with equal enthusiasm plunges joyously into all such actions that reach him, and his body vigorously functions, wherein he is no 'doer,' but only an indifferent 'observer,' a patient 'witness.' Hence, the deeds of a Sage are termed here as "*Yathā Jīvanam.*"

Even this descriptive explanation is merely to satisfy our ignorant view-point wherein we see the body of the Sage functioning in our plane-of-Consciousness. The Man-of-Realisation is ever in the Self. He has become the Self. In him all activities take place. He himself is ever an observer of his own body functioning through its varied experiences of joys and sorrows! He is never involved in them.

क्व मोहः क्व च वा विश्वं क्व तद्ध्यानं क्व मुक्तता ।
सर्वसङ्कल्पसीमायां विश्रान्तस्य महात्मनः ॥ १४ ॥

Kva mohaḥ kva ca vā viśvaṁ
kva tad-dhānaṁ kva muktatā,
sarva-saṅkalpa-sīmāyāṁ
viśrāntasya mahātmanaḥ.

क्व *kva* = where; मोहः *mohaḥ* = delusion; क्व *kva* = where; च *ca* = and; वा *vā* = or; विश्वम् *viśvam* = universe; क्व *kva* = where; तद्धानम् (तत् हानम् = *tat-hānam*) *tad-dhānam* = its renunciation; क्व *kva* = where; मुक्तता *muktatā* = liberation; सर्व-सङ्कल्प-सीमायाम् *sarva-saṅkalpa-sīmāyām* = beyond the borders of the world of desire-agitations; विश्रान्तस्य *viśrāntasya* = resting; महात्मनः *mahātmanaḥ* = of the noble-minded one.

14. *Where is delusion? Where is the Universe? Where is its renunciation? Or, where is the liberation itself for the noble-minded-one, who rests beyond the world of desire-agitations?*

The 'ignorance' of the Self procreates the delusion of the world of multiplicity. To a Sage who has awakened Himself to the Self, there is no more any delusion, nor does He recognise any world-of-plurality other than the Immutable Self, the One without-a-second. Since He is not recognising the world-of-objects, what is there for Him to renounce? Indeed, he rests in the Self, beyond the world of all passions and cravings and their endless agitations. Calm and serene, he lives the Bliss of the Peaceful Self.

येन विश्वमिदं दृष्टं स नास्तीति करोतु वै ।
निर्वासनः किं कुरुते पश्यन्नपि न पश्यति ॥ १५ ॥

Yena viśva-midaṁ dṛṣṭaṁ sa nāstīti karotu vai,
nirvāsanaḥ kiṁ kurute paśyan-napi na paśyati.

येन *yena* = by whom; विश्वम् *viśvam* = universe; इदम् *idam* = this; दृष्टम् *dṛṣṭam* = is seen; सः *saḥ* = he; न *na* = not; अस्ति *asti* = is; इति *iti* = thus; करोतु *karotu* = may try to obliterate it; वै *vai* = indeed;

निर्वासनः *nirvāsanaḥ* = one who is desireless; किम् *kiṁ* = what; कुरुते *kurute* = has to do; पश्यन् *paśyan* = seeing; अपि *api* = though; न *na* = not; पश्यति *paśyati* = beholds.

15. *He, who sees the universe, may try to obliterate it! What has the desireless to do? He beholds it not, even though he sees!!*

It is the individualised-ego that identifies with the body-mind-intellect equipment and recognises through it the world of objects-emotions-thoughts. When there is a subject to experience, there is also a world-of-objects to be experienced, complete with its joys and sorrows. We are now living at the level of the ego, and as such we see only our projected world of names-of-forms. In our present state-of-Consciousness, we have to accept what we perceive and experience, as the only reality. We have no concept of the subtler realm of the Infinite Self. To the deluded the *ghost* alone is real, there is no *post* at all! And the deluded man must try to negate the *ghost* in his attempt to see the *post*. One who beholds the *post* must necessarily fail to see the *ghost*; one who beholds the Self, fails to see the world.

The desireless-one has no ego in him, which is the 'observer' in the bosom. Where the ego has ended, the Self is realised. Awakened to the perception of the Self, the Sage perceives nothing but the Self everywhere.

'Seeing' is the function of the fleshy eyes. The Man-of-Perfection also sees through his eyes the world-of-objects; yet, he cannot behold our world—which is to us of Infinite enjoyments, powerful fascinations, with its tragic sorcery to bring storms of agitations and sorrows into our bosom, which destroy us completely in exertion, fatigue and disappointment. The awakened Master, though he sees this world with his eyes, fails to behold in it anything unholy and threatening. He sees nothing but the Peaceful Self, the Blissful Reality, spread everywhere within and without, in which the world of names and forms, of joys and sorrows, have no existence at all. The dream has ended; he has Awakened.

We see through our ignorance and understand the world as substantial and real. The sage also sees the same world, but through his understanding recognises it as insubstantial, and unreal. He sees the world as mere 'castles in the sky,' as the 'mirage-water,' as the 'double moon,' as the entertaining 'creations of a magician.' The Man-of-Realisation lives in our world, but his experience of the Self helps him to evaluate life correctly.

येन दृष्टं परं ब्रह्म सोऽहं ब्रह्मेति चिन्तयेत् ।
किं चिन्तयति निश्चिन्तो द्वितीयं यो न पश्यति ॥ १६ ॥

Yena dṛṣṭaṁ paraṁ brahma so'haṁ brahmeti cintayet
kiṁ cintayati niścinto dvitīyaṁ yo na paśyati.

येन *yena* = by whom; दृष्टम् *dṛṣṭam* = is seen; परम् *param* = Supreme; ब्रह्म *brahma* = *Brahman*; सः *saḥ* = he; अहम् ब्रह्म *aham brahma* = 'I am *Brahman*'; इति *iti* = thus; चिन्तयेत् *cintayet* = meditates upon; किम् *kim* = what; चिन्तयति *cintayati* = meditates; निश्चिन्तः *niścintaḥ* = one who has transcended thoughts; द्वितीयम् *dvitīyam* = second; यः *yaḥ* = who; न *na* = not; पश्यति *paśyati* = sees.

16. *He, who sees the Supreme* Brahman, *meditates "I am* Brahman." *He who has transcended all thoughts and when he sees "no second", upon what should he meditate upon?*

In the verse here, *Aṣṭāvakra* points out the subtle distinction between the two Higher-states in meditation. At the earlier stage the student, as a result of his deep-study and long reflection, becomes intellectually convinced of the One Infinite Immutable Reality which is the Substratum for the illusory play of names and forms that constitute the Universe. Here, the students "sees the Supreme *Brahman*"— meaning he intellectually conceives the existence and understands the nature of the Supreme Reality. At this stage the student should strive to meditate, "I am *Brahman*" (*Aham Brahmāsi*). Through this meditation and continuous assertion "I am *Brahman*," he achieves his total detachment from his equipments and discovers his identity with the Infinite Self. This stage is defined as "*Samādhi*-with-thought" (*Savikalpa Samādhi*).

As a result of this spiritual practice and long Self-discipline, the ego ends, the illusory world-of-perceptions cease and the seeker awakes to become the Sage of direct spiritual experience. He transcends his intellect and its thoughts and experiences the One-without-a-second. Having thus reached this State of Consciousness, wherein he has discovered his perfect identity with the *Brahman*, *Aṣṭāvakra* asks very pertinently: "upon what should he meditate?"

Until we sleep, we can try to sleep, but having slept who is there to try? Having reached the State of Self, where is the Seeker to meditate? And try to reach what? On reaching the Goal the pilgrimage has ended. On realising the Self, meditation has culminated. The Meditator has become the Meditated. In this great awakening, the ego has ended along with its dreams. The ego has become the One-Self everywhere.

Describing such a Man-of-Perfection, who has reached his spiritual goal, *Acārya Śaṅkara* sings in his *Vivekacūḍāmaṇi* (554):

लक्ष्यालक्ष्यगितं त्यक्त्वा यस्तिष्ठेत्केवलात्मना ।
शिव एव स्वयं साक्षादयं ब्रह्मविदुत्तमः॥

Lakṣyā-lakṣya-gitaṁ tyaktvā yas-tiṣṭhet-kevalātmanā,
śiva eva svayaṁ sākṣāt-ayaṁ-brahma-viduttamah.

"He who giving up all considerations of the fitness or otherwise of objects of meditation, lives as the Absolute *Ātman*, is indeed *Śiva* Himself—the best among the Knowers-of-*Brahman*."

दृष्टो येनात्मविक्षेपो निरोधं कुरुते त्वसौ ।
उदारस्तु न विक्षिप्तः साध्याभावात्करोति किम् ॥ १७ ॥

Dṛṣṭo yenātma-vikṣepo nirodhaṁ kurute tvasau,
udārastu na vikṣiptaḥ sādhyā-bhāvāt-karoti kim.

दृष्टः *dṛṣṭaḥ* = is seen, experienced; येन *yen* = by whom; आत्म-विक्षेपः *ātma-vikṣepaḥ*= distraction in himself; निरोधम् कुरुते *nirodham kurute* = practises self-control; तु *tu* = indeed; असौ *asau* = he; उदारः *udāraḥ* = the noble-minded great-one; तु *tu* = but; न *na* = not; विक्षिप्तः *vikṣiptaḥ* = distracted; साध्य-अभावात् *sādhya-abhāvāt* = having nothing to accomplish; करोति *karoti* = does; किम् *kim* = what.

17. *He who experiences distractions in himself, indeed must control himself. But the noble-minded great-one is not distracted at all. Having nothing to accomplish, what should he do?*

At the 'non-apprehension' of the Reality 'mis-apprehensions' are entertained by the mind. Spiritual 'ignorance' is, therefore, the cause for the ego and its perceptions of the world. As a limited ego when it recognises the world-of-plurality, it gets distracted with enjoyments of the perceived world. As a spiritual seekers then, the ego-centric *Sādhaka* must necessarily practise 'self-control,' in order to turn his mind away from the fields of his passions, and to persuade it to contemplate upon the Peaceful Self. The imperfect must strive to reach Perfection.

But to the Sage, who is Liberated-in-life, who knows no distractions, who is ever-living the Blissful Peace of the Infinite Perfection, he has nothing to accomplish and, therefore, what has he to do? He has nothing more to gain! He has become the Self. His mind has ended. His ego has merged. The world-dream has rolled away from him. He is the Self—ever All-pervading and Immutable. A Sage knows no meditation.

धीरो लोकविपर्यस्तो वर्तमानोऽपि लोकवत् ।
न समाधिं न विक्षेपं न लेपं स्वस्य पश्यति ॥ १८ ॥

Dhīro loka-viparyasto vartamāno'pi lokavat,
na samādhiṁ na vikṣepaṁ na lepaṁ svasya paśyati.

धीरः *dhīraḥ* = the Wise-man; लोक-विपर्यस्तः *loka-viparyastaḥ* = reverse of the common man; वर्तमानः *vartamānaḥ* = existing; अपि *api* = though; लोकवत् *lokavat* = like an ordinary man; न *na* = not; समाधिम् *samādhim* = absorption; न *na* = not; विक्षेपम् *vikṣepam* = distraction; न *na* = not; लेपम् *lepam* = involvement; स्वस्य *svasya* = of his own; पश्यति *paśyati* = sees.

18. The Wise-man though living like an ordinary person, is the reverse of the common-man. He sees neither absorption, nor distraction nor involvement of himself.

A Sage of Spiritual Vision lives like any other ordinary man in the world, and he pursues normal life. Yet, he is the reverse of the common-man in his estimate of himself and the world around. We, the common folk, consider the world of sense-objects as real, and to us Spiritual-essence is a matter of doubt, a questionable hypothesis of the subtle philosophers. To the Realised Sage, the Self alone is the One Reality and he lives It constantly in his experience. To him the world-of-objects are all illusions of the human mind.

A Sage of inward constant Experience Divine recognises nothing—neither absorption (*Samādhi*), nor distraction (*Vikṣepa*), for he has transcended his mind; and *Samādhi* and *Vikṣepa* are the conditions of the mind. Nor does he himself ever get involved (*Lepam*) in the world of activity. This does not mean that he will not act. He constantly serves the world; but he never gets involved—meaning he never acts with ego and ego-centric desires, and as such, no *Vāsanā-s* are created in him by his activities. Thus "he is the reverse of the common-man."

भावाभावविहीनो यस्तृप्तो निर्वासनो बुधः ।
नैव किञ्चित् कृतं तेन लोकदृष्ट्या विकुर्वता ॥ १९ ॥

Bhāvā-bhāva-vihīno yas-tṛpto nirvāsano budhaḥ,
naiva kiñcit kṛtaṁ tena loka-dṛṣṭyā vikurvatā.

भाव-अभाव-विहीनः *bhāva-abhāva-vihīnaḥ* = transcends existence and non-existence; यः *yaḥ* = who; तृप्तः *tṛptaḥ* = contented; निर्वासनः *nirvāsanaḥ* = free from desire; बुधः *budhaḥ* = wise; न *na* = not; एव *eva* = even; किञ्चित् *kiñcit* = anything; कृतम् *kṛtam* = done; तेन *tena* = by him; लोक-दृष्ट्या *loka-dṛṣṭyā* = in the sight of the world; विकुर्वता *vikurvatā* = acting vigorously.

19. *He, who, transcends existence and non-existence, who is wise, contented, free from desires, does nothing, even if he be acting vigorously in the eyes of the world.*

In the world outside, the public may recognise that the Liberated-in-life is dynamically engaging himself in vigorous programmes of service to the society. Yet, a Man-of-Perfection 'does-nothing,' in the sense that this actions are not actions at all, in the ordinary sense of the word.

We act in the world, motivated by our ego-centric desires. Such actions, undertaken with ego and ego-centric desires, leave their reactions upon us in the form of *Vāsanā-s*. A Man-of-Realisation has ended his ego : "He is contented and free from desires," and therefore, his actions are no more actions.

"He has transcended both existence and non-existence"—*existence* meaning here his identification with the body, mind and intellect and *non-existence* standing for the subtle unmanifested *Vāsanā-s* left in him by his past-actions. Since he has no identification either with his gross, or subtle, or his causal body, his actions can be considered neither as selfish nor self-less works. At best they can be considered only as a sport, a play (*Līlā*).

When a child as at play, we cannot call it "a work," though the child expresses its intelligence, and exhausts its energy. It has nothing to gain by the play, nor will the child lose anything by not-playing. Its play is but a natural explosion of its energy! Thus "*works*" the Liberated-in-life, in any field that comes to him unsaked. There is no impulse of desire behind any of his activities.

These few verses form a beautiful and exhaustive discourse upon the "actionless action" recommended by the *Bhagavad Gītā* (IV-18) :

कर्मण्यकर्म यः पश्येदकर्मणि च कर्म यः ।
स बुद्धिमान्मनुष्येषु स युक्तः कृत्स्नकर्मकृत् ॥

Karmaṇya-karma yaḥ paśyed-akarmaṇi ca karma yaḥ,
sa buddhimān-manuṣyeṣu sa yuktaḥ kṛtsna-karma-kṛta.

"He who recognises inaction in action and action in inaction is wise among men; he is a *Yogī* and a true performer of all actions."

प्रवृत्तौ वा निवृत्तौ वा नैव धीरस्य दुर्ग्रहः ।
यदा यत्कर्तुमायाति तत्कृत्वा तिष्ठतः सुखम् ॥ २० ॥

Pravṛttau vā nivṛttau vā naiva dhīrasya durgraḥ,
yadā yat-kartum-āyāti tat-kṛtvā tiṣṭhataḥ sukham.

प्रवृत्तौ *pravṛttau* = in activity; वा *vā* = or; निवृत्तौ *nivṛttau* = in inactivity; वा *vā* = or; न *na* = not; एव *eva* = surely; धीरस्य *dhīrasya* = of the Wise-one; दुर्ग्रहः *durgraḥ* = trouble, uneasiness; यदा *yadā* = when; यत् *yat* = what; कर्तुम् *kartum* = to do; आयाति *āyāti* = comes; तत् *tat* = that; कृत्वा *kṛtvā* = doing; तिष्ठतः *tiṣṭhataḥ* = living; सुखम् *sukham* = happily.

20. *The Wise-one, who lives on happily, doing what comes to him to be done, does not feel trouble (uneasy) either in activity or in inactivity.*

The Man-of-Realisation has nothing to gain for himself by undertaking an activity, nor has he to lose anything by not doing, yet, he is seen to be constantly engaged in various programmes of service. This is explained in the following verse by Lord *Kṛṣṇa* in *Gītā* (III-22) :

नानवाप्तमवाप्तव्यं वर्त एव च कर्मणि ।

Nānavāptam-avāptavyaṁ varta eva ca karmaṇi.

"....... Nor is there anything unattained that should be attained by Me; yet, I engage Myself in action."

Aṣṭāvakra here explains that into the activities, that reach him uninvited—as demanded by his age, for the benefit of the community—he plunges fully, recognising them as his *Prārabdha.*

While his body, mind and intellect are functioning in their respective fields, he remains unaffected, constantly rooted in his experience of the Divine Self, observing, along with the universe around him, his own equipments expressing in the field-of-action. Since he is so fully established in the experience of the One-Self everywhere, his equipments can never dance except to the melody of Life Divine. No discordant note can ever come into the songful actions of such a Perfect Master.

Be he in the fields of activity, or be he in retirement, he is equally peaceful, contented, blissful. In no activity is he ever a '*doer*' or an '*enjoyer.*' There is no ego in him. He revels as the Self: his equipments act in His Divine Presence within!!

निर्वासनो निरालम्बः स्वच्छन्दो मुक्तबन्धनः ।
क्षिप्तः संस्कारवातेन चेष्टते शुष्कपर्णवत् ॥ २१ ॥

Nir-vāsano nir-ālambaḥ svacchando mukta-bandhanaḥ,
kṣiptaḥ saṁskāra-vātena ceṣṭate śuṣka-parṇavat.

निर्वासनः *nir-vāsanaḥ* = desireless; निरालम्बः *nir-ālambaḥ* = autonomous (independent); स्वच्छन्दः *svacchandaḥ* = free; मुक्त-बन्धनः *mukta-bandhanaḥ* = free from bondage; क्षिप्तः *kṣiptaḥ* = blown, cast; संस्कार-वातेन *saṁskāra-vātena* = by the wind of effects of past actions; चेष्टते *ceṣṭate* = moves; शुष्क-पर्णवत् *śuṣka-parṇavat* = like a dry leaf.

21. *Blown by the wind of effects of the past actions (Saṁskārā-s), the desireless, independent, free and liberated person moves about like a dry leaf.*

To one who has realised the Infinitude, he has no more any vanity of his body—in fact, he has no more any use for it. It is something like a dry-leaf that has fallen away from a tree, when its functions are ended for the tree! The body-mind-intellect equipments have already dried up, curled and fallen away from the Wise-man; they are of no use to him, the Self-Realised.

Not only the leaf dances on the branches of the tree, but the fallen-leaf again, apparently seems to be very dynamic and active when it is blown hither and thither by the passing breeze! To the ignorant eyes of men, a Sage also seems to be acting in the world outside. The body of the Enlightened, when it functions in the world, does so not prompted by his ego and ego-centric desires. *Aṣṭāvakra* explains that, like a dry-leaf that is blown here and there by the whimsical breeze, so too, the equipments of a Man-of-Perfection moves about in different directions—set by its *Prārabdha*.

The past actions leave deep and powerful *Vāsanā-s*, which channelise all the thought-flow into definite directions, in each individual. These thought-channels, that determine the character of an individual, made by the cumulative effects of his entire past, are called *Saṁskārā-s*. One *Yogī* may spend all his life-time in quietude, in a solitary cave plunged in *Samādhi*. Another one may move about in the society, like a mad-man, miserably clad, careless of his food, sleeping perhaps on the foot-path, exposed to the sun and rain! Yet another, may take great programmes for the cultural revival of a country, and for the moral rehabilitation of his community! One may found a religion, and another may float a Mission! None of them is responsible for any of his actions, because there is no *doer*-ego in any one of them. Their actions are determined by their *Prārabdha*—and they are never involved in any of their activities. They live in a realm where our praises and abuses cannot even reach them!

The analogy of the dry-leaf moving without any purpose, shunted here and there, by the amorous breeze, is a very striking example for the propelling force working behind a Spiritual Master in his life after his Self-rediscovery.

असंसारस्य तु क्वापि न हर्षो न विषादता ।
स शीतलमना नित्यं विदेह इव राजते ॥ २२ ॥

Asaṁsārasya tu kvāpi na harṣo na viṣādatā,
sa śītala-manā nityaṁ videha iva rājate.

असंसारस्य *asaṁsārasya* = one who has transcended worldly experience; तु *tu* = indeed; क्व अपि *kva api* = anywhere; न *na* = not; हर्षः *harṣaḥ* = joy; न *na* = not; विषादता *viṣādatā* = sorrow; सः *saḥ* = he; शीतल-मनाः *śītala-manāḥ* = tranquil minded; नित्यम् *nityam* = ever; विदेहः *videhaḥ* = one without a body; इव *iva* = as if; राजते *rājate* = exists.

22. *Never is joy or sorrow, for one who has transcended the worldly experiences. Tranquil in mind, he lives like one without a body.*

Once the ego is transcended, the identifications with the body and the mind have also ended. In the mind alone the sensations of joy and sorrow can arise. These are different modifications of the mind. These disturbances can reach the mind only with reference to a desire-fulfilled, or a desire-flouted. To the realised Saint there are neither ego nor desires and, therefore, his mind is ever tranquil—as thought-agitations cannot rise to disturb his bosom.

In this Divine Inner Peace, the Man-of-Perfection constantly experiences the Supreme State of Infinite Consciousness, and his body, as explained earlier, unmotivated by personal desires, moves about prompted by its own *Prārabdha*. In his physical reactions with the world around, he seems to be so careless about his body, as he is not himself constantly conscious of his equipments. *Aṣṭāvakra* here points out the step-motherly attitude of a Man-of-Perfection towards his own body and its destiny, and the Sage exclaims in his Song, that the Liberated-in-life "lives like one without a body."

This Supreme State is practically described in *Yoga Vāsiṣṭha*:

पश्चात् पावनपावनं पदमजं तत्प्राप्य तच्छीतलं ।
तत्संस्थेन न शोच्यते पुनरलं पुंसा महापत्स्वपि ॥

Paścāt pāvana-pāvanam padam-ajaṁ tat-prāpya tacchī-talaṁ,
tat-saṁsthena na śocyate punaralaṁ puṁsā mahā-patsvapi.

"....Later, having reached the Holy-of-holies, this Unborn State, his tranquil-mind established in It, he never grieves even amidst the greatest calamities."

कुत्रापि न जिहासाऽस्ति नाशो वाऽपि न कुत्रचित् ।
आत्मारामस्य धीरस्य शीतलाच्छतरात्मनः ॥ २३ ॥

Kutrāpi na jihāsā'sti nāśo vā'pi na kutracit,
ātmā-rāmasya dhīrasya śītalā-cchatar-ātmanaḥ.

कुत्रापि *kutrāpi* = anywhere; न *na* = not; जिहासा *jihāsā* = desire to renounce; अस्ति *asti* = is; नाशः *nāśaḥ* = loss; वा *vā* = or; अपि *api* = even; न *na* = not; कुत्रचित् *kutracit* = anywhere; आत्मा-रामस्य *ātmā-rāmasya* = one who delights in the Self; धीरस्य *dhīrasya* = of the Wise-man; शीतल-अच्छतर-आत्मनः *śītala-acchatara-ātmanaḥ* = whose mind is serene and pure.

23. *The wise, who delights in the Self, whose mind is serene and pure, has no desire to renounce anything whatsoever, nor does he feel any loss anywhere.*

On transcending the mind alone is the State of Self realised. The thought-flow that constitutes the mind cannot dry up until its source, the ego-centric desire, has been completely eliminated. When thus the ego has ended, and the mind flouted, the delusory vision of the world should completely end and therefore, to the "the Wise-man who delights in the Self," there can be "no desire to renounce anything whatsoever." He sees nothing to be renounced! His mind is serene and pure (*Śītala-acchatara-ātmanah*).[1]

This does not mean that he will hold on to everything in the world! For, a worldly man also does not want to renounce anything! To clarify this position the Sage continues: "Nor does he feel any loss anywhere." The Man-of-Enlightenment comes to live in such a different dimension altogether that no loss in the relative-world of finite objects around him, nor within him, can affect, even in the least, the Infinite joys of the Immutable Self. Transcending the body-and-mind, the ego in the Wise-man, has now awakened to the Blissful Self.

प्रकृत्या शून्यचित्तस्य कुर्वतोऽस्य यदृच्छया ।
प्राकृतस्येव धीरस्य न मानो नावमानता ॥ २४ ॥

Prakṛtyā sūnya-cittasya kurvato'sya yadṛcchayā,
prākṛta-syeva dhīrasya na māno nāva-mānatā.

प्रकृत्या *prakṛtyā* = by nature; शून्य-चित्तस्य *sūnya-cittasya* = void in mind; कुर्वतः *kurvataḥ* = undertaking to do; अस्य *asya* = this; यदृच्छया *yadṛcchayā* = what comes of itself unasked; प्राकृतस्य इव *prākṛtasya iva* = like a common man; धीरस्य *dhīrasya* = of the Wise-one; न *na* = not; मानः *mānaḥ* = honour; न *na* = not; अवमानता *avamānatā* = dishonour.

24. *By nature of void-in-mind and undertaking to do what comes of itself unasked, the Wise-one, unlike a common-man, is not affected by honour or dishonour.*

1. शीतलाच्छतरात्मनः = अच्छतर–स्वच्छतर ... serene and extremely pure—meaning completely agitation-less.

The Liberated-in-life by his very nature becomes "void-in-mind" as the thought-flow in him has ceased. He has transcended his mind. No modifications can disturb the mental-stuff in him. He spends his time performing whatever work comes to him unasked, prompted by his *Prārabdha*! Though he is thus living in our world, functioning like any one of us, unlike us, it is immaterial for him whether he is revered or cursed for his activities. His body acts on the stage of the world as the dry-leaves are blown here and there by the passing breeze. The Wise-man's actions are all prompted by a Higher Will, ever Divinely Kind and always Sweetly Merciful. The Lord of the Universe (*Jagadīśvara*) functions through him. Honour and dishonour are judgements of the intellect; to one who has transcended his intellect, where is honour? What is dishonour?

कृतं देहेन कर्मेदं न मया शुद्धरूपिणा ।
इति चिन्तानुरोधी यः कुर्वन्नपि करोति न ॥ २५ ॥

Kṛtaṁ dehena karmedaṁ na mayā śuddha-rūpiṇā,
iti cintā-nurodhī yaḥ kurvan-napi karoti na.

कृतम् *kṛtam* = done; देहेन *dehena* = by the body; कर्म *karma* = work; इदम् *idam* = this; न *na* = not; मया *mayā* = by Me; शुद्ध-रूपिणा *śuddha-rūpiṇā* = of Pure Nature; इति चिन्ता-अनुरोधी *iti cintā-anurodhī* = thus conforming to such thoughts; यः *yaḥ* = who; कुर्वन् *kurvan* = acting; अपि *api* = though; करोति *karoti* = acts; न *na* = not.

25. *One who acts in conformity with thoughts such as: "This is done by the body and not by Me, the Pure Self"— such a person even though acting does not act.*

An action is not a mere movement of limbs. Without a wilful ego an action is never performed. In deep-sleep, if you kick with your foot, even your own *Guru*, it is not an act. Whatever, a child does is not considered as an action. Action is an action where there is an ego-centric wilfulness.

A liberated-in-life is one who lives constantly in the experience that he is the Self, and that all activities done in the world are done by his body and mind, drawing their vitality from Me, the Self, all by themselves, and that I am not involved in these activities. Thus, there is no ego to receive the results of those actions of the body, and therefore, *Aṣṭāvakra Gītā* here declares: "even though acting he does not act" (*Kurvann-api karoti na*).

This idea is one of the vibrant thoughts running through and through the *Bhagavad-Gītā*.[1] *Upaniṣad*-s repeatedly thunder this idea. Mystic Master of all eras in India have again and again confirmed the Truth of this statement with their own inward experiences.

अतद्वादीव कुरुते न भवेदपि बालिशः ।
जीवन्मुक्तः सुखी श्रीमान् संसरन्नपि शोभते ॥ २६ ॥

Atadvādīva kurute na bhavedapi bāliśaḥ,
jīvan-muktaḥ sukhī śrīmān saṁsarann-api śobhate.

अतद्-वादी-इव *atad-vādī-iva* = like one who does not say why; कुरुते *kurute* = acts; न *na* = not; भवेत् *bhavet* = is; अपि *api* = even though; बालिशः *bāliśaḥ* = dullard, fool; जीवन्-मुक्तः *jīvan-muktaḥ* = one who is liberated even while living; सुखी *sukhī* = happy; श्रीमान् *śrīmān* = blessed; संसरन् *saṁsaran* = being in the world; अपि *api* = even; शोभते *śobhate* = flourishes.

26. *The Liberated-in-life acts like one, who does not say why he is acting so. But he is not, thereby, a fool. Even though in the world, he is ever-happy and blessed.*

An intelligent man plans his activities and expects to achieve his chosen goal, or earn his purpose. He is clear of his

1. Refer chapter III, 26-28; chapter IV, 20-21; chapter V, 8-9 and 13; chapter XIII, 9; and chapter XVIII, 58—all these verses of the *Bhagavad Gītā*, often directly, sometimes indirectly, declare the Truth of what *Aṣṭāvakra* is emphasising here.

motives. He is precise of his intentions. But an unintelligent fool, if he is questioned, due to his foolishness, cannot say for what purpose he is doing a piece of work. He is unconscious of his intentions. He is not intelligent enough to recognise that his activities are to achieve a definite goal of his. If such a fool were to be asked why he has undertaken a certain activity, he is not able to state his motive (*Atad-vādī*)[1].

The Liberated-in-life, under the force of the *Prārabdha* of his body, spontaneously acts in the world, mainly to establish good-will among mankind. But if we were to ask him why he is undertaking such endeavours, he has no answer to give, he can only smile. His actions are without any personal motives; they are all programmes of activities expressing through him as ordained by the Lord of the Universe.

Here the fool is not able to answer because he is far below the average in his Mind and intellect. The Wise-man is not able to answer the same questions because he is so much arisen above the mind-intellect equipment.

Even though living in this world, wherein we suffer our daily tensions, stresses and conflicts, the Liberated-in-life, as he has no ego in him, "is ever happy and blessed."

नानाविचारसुश्रान्तो धीरो विश्रान्तिमागतः ।
न कल्पते न जानाति न शृणोति न पश्यति ॥ २७ ॥

Nānā-vicāra-suśrānto dhīro viśrānti-māgataḥ,
na kalpate na jānāti na śṛṇoti na paśyati.

नाना-विचार-सुश्रान्तः *nānā-vicāra-suśrāntaḥ* = withdrawing from diverse reasonings; धीरः *dhīraḥ* = the Wise-one; विश्रान्तिम् *viśrāntim* = complete repose; आगतः *āgataḥ* = attains; न *na* = not; कल्पते

1. *Atad-vādī* (अतद्वादी)—not a *tat-vādī* (तत्वादी)—one who can explain clearly what it is. He who can explain the goal, to gain which he is pursuing all his efforts, he is described as a *tat-vādī* (तत्वादी)–a Sage has no motive to explain and so is an *Atad-vādī* (अतद्वादी)–like a fool!!

kalpate = thinks; न *na* = not; जानाति *jānāti* = knows; न *na* = not; शृणोति *śṛṇoti* = hears; न *na* = not; पश्यति *paśyati* = sees.

27. *The Wise-man who has withdrawn himself from diverse reasonings, and has attained complete repose, neither thinks, nor knows, nor hears, nor sees.*

The divine experience of the Infinite Self is beyond all reason. It is not intellectual appreciation, but it is a spiritual apprehension, gained when the meditator transcends his intellect. Once the Man-of-Perfection has reached this Blissful State of Total Repose, it being the State of the Immutable Self, never again can he ever be shunted out of It into the realm of the mind, to be mercilessly tossed about there, amidst its endless agitations.

The ego in him has ended, and therefore, there cannot be in him either the sense of '*doership*' or the sense of '*enjoyership.*' Therefore, "he neither thinks nor knows, nor hears, nor sees." It is the subject-ego who identifies with the intellect, mind and the sense-organs and arrogates the sense of individuality as the '*thinker*'— I, or a '*feeler*'—I, or a '*knower*'—I, or a '*perceiver*'—I. With the end of the ego all these functions have ended. The Enlightened One has attained the *peaceful-repose* of the Infinite Self.

असमाधेरविक्षेपान्न मुमुक्षुर्न चेतरः ।
निश्चित्य कल्पितं पश्यन् ब्रह्मैवास्ते महाशयः ॥ २८ ॥

asamādher-avikṣepān-na mumukṣur-na cetaraḥ,
niścitya kalpitaṁ paśyan brahmai-vāste mahāśayaḥ.

असमाधेः *asamādheḥ* = not practising meditation; अविक्षेपात् *avikṣepāt* = for having no agitations; न *na* = not; मुमुक्षुः *mumukṣuḥ* = aspirant-for-liberation; न *na* = not; च *ca* = and; इतरः *itaraḥ* = the other (bound); निश्चित्य *niścitya* = knowing for certain; कल्पितम् *kalpitam* = figment of imagination; पश्यन् *paśyan* = seeing; ब्रह्म *brahma* =

Brahman; एव *eva* = as; आस्ते *āste* = lives; महाशयः *mahāśayaḥ* = the Wise-one.

28. *Since the Wise-one has no agitations and does not practise meditation, he is not an aspirant-for-liberation—nor is he, in bondage. Having known the universe to be a figment of his imagination, even though he sees it, he exists as* Brahman *Itself.*

The causes for agitations in man's bosom are ego and his ego-centric desires. In the Wise-man, the *Vāsanā-s* have ended, and his ego has sublimated. He lives in the *Brahmik*-Consciousness and experiences It as his own Real Nature.

Since there are no agitations, he will not be any longer trying to control the mind's out-going tendencies, through diligent practice of meditation. The hungry alone needs to eat food; the thirsty alone needs to drink—the agitated mind alone needs to practice meditation. The Sage who has already reached the Goal, and has thus awakened to the Divine Nature, Infinite and Immutable, does not need do any more meditation. Since he is not meditating, he cannot be considered any longer as an "aspirant-for-liberation" (*Mumukṣu*)—the fact is, he has already liberated (*Mukta*) himself from all his delusory entanglements with his body, mind and intellect.

On awakening to the Blissful-Self, he has realised that the world of names and forms that he has experienced was nothing but a figment of his own imagination. He has awakened from the dream of the *subject-object*-world. Even if he now perceives the world, he recognises it as a magic-show. He has now become *Brahman*, "he exists as *Brahman* itself."

यस्यान्तः स्यादहङ्कारो न करोति करोति सः ।
निरहङ्कारधीरेण न किञ्चिदकृतं कृतम् ॥ २९ ॥

Yasyāntaḥ syād-ahaṅkāro na karoti karoti saḥ,
nirahaṅkāra-dhīreṇa na kiñcid-akṛtaṁ kṛtam.

यस्य *yasya* = whose; अन्तः *antaḥ* = within; स्यात् *syāt* = is; अहङ्कारः *ahaṅkāraḥ* = sense of ego; न *na* = not; करोति *karoti* = acts; (अपि *api* = though); करोति *karoti* = acts; सः *saḥ* = he; निरहङ्कार-धीरेण *nir-ahaṅkāra-dhīreṇa* = by the Wise-one who is free from the sense of ego; न *na* = not; किञ्चित् *kiñcit* = anything; अकृतम् *akṛtam* = undone; कृतम् *kṛtam* = doing (and).

29. *He who has the ego-sense in him within, acts (mentally), even though he does not act (physically). Surely, the Wise-one, who is free from the sense of ego, does not act (mentally), even though he acts (physically).*

All actions spring from man's ego and his ego-centric desires. One who is conscious of his separate individuality cannot avoid his ego-sense, and truly, even if he is not physically working in the world outside, says *Aṣṭāvakra*, "he acts" (*karoti saḥ*). One who is extremely conscious of his body and mind, even when he is sitting down for meditation, though he is not apparently working in the world-outside, cannot quieten his mind, and therefore, is in a state of dynamic activity in his within.

On the other hand, the sage, who has conquered his ego, is ever revelling in the Infinite Self, and so is not acting at any time—be he in a field of *Sevā*, visibly functioning or be he at rest, sitting quietly, without acting (*Na kiñcid-akṛtam kṛtam*[1]).

This verse under commentary would be apparently contradicting a later verse in this very same chapter.[2] This contradiction is only apparent. Sage is beyond both action and inaction—he has transcended the equipments, and therefore, he is beyond the influences of the pairs-of-opposites.

1. There is another reading of this verse which we find in some editions wherein it is spelt as *Na kiñcid-dhi kṛtaṁ kṛtam* (न किंचिद्धि कृतं कृतम्) meaning "one who has no ego, indeed even what he does is not an act." The reading that we have selected has a deeper transcendetal significance and hence our choice.

2. The wise-one does freely whatever comes to be done, whether good or evil; for his actions are like those of a child.

And this cannot mean that a Sage can do anything. By his very nature he has become Perfect in his activities and thoughts. A Sage cannot really do wrong, as he is free from ego. All activities springing from the sense-of-ego are selfish activities, which are what we consider as immoral acts. He acts from a point above the moral-level—his very vision is universal, and therefore, actions springing from him always carry the fragrance of his Universal Love. He has no concern for good or evil, with morality or immorality. Whatever he does constitutes the moral code for us to follow! The qualities of his actions are the standards by which the world determines its sense of righteousness; its concept of *Dharma*!

When one performs his duties from his ego-centre, it becomes work, and in work there can be good and evil, morality and immorality. When a man performs in the outer world with a bosom that has no ego to vitiate, he does not 'work' but he merely 'acts.' In a spontaneous inspired act there is no ego, and as such divine acts cannot create any *Vāsanā-s*, positive or negative in the personality of the Sage. Such actions are to be considered as inactions— or to distinguish it clearly, we may call them as "actionless actions."

नोद्विग्नं न च संतुष्टमकर्तृ स्पन्दवर्जितम् ।
निराशं गतसन्देहं चित्तं मुक्तस्य राजते ॥ ३० ॥

Nodvignaṁ na ca saṁtuṣṭam-akartṛ spanda-varjitam,
nirāśaṁ gata-sandehaṁ cittaṁ muktasya rājate.

न *na* = not; उद्विग्नम् *udvignam* = troubled; न *na* = not; च *ca* = and; संतुष्टम् *saṁtuṣṭam* = pleased; अकर्तृ *akartṛ* = actionless; स्पन्द-वर्जितम् *spanda-varjitam* = free from fluctuations; निराशम् *nirāśam* = desireless; गत-सन्देहम् *gata-sandeham* = purged of doubts; चित्तम् *cittam* = mind; मुक्तस्य *muktasya* = of the liberated-one; राजते *rājate* = shines.

30. *The mind of the Liberated is neither troubled, nor pleased. It is actionless, free from fluctuations, desireless, and purged of all doubts.*

The Liberated-in-life is one who has directly experienced the Self and has, therefore, awakened to be Pure Consciousness. As such he has arisen above the mind-intellect equipment and their oscillations. Naturally, he is free from passions, attachments, ego-thoughts and desires.

This verse marshals a team of arguments justifying the declaration made in the previous verse. An individual, who has thus emptied himself in the within, is a Sage, who acts and even when he is acting, is not "troubled" by passions (*Na-udvigam*), because, he is free from love and hatred. He has no attachments and, therefore, he is contented and "pleased" (*Saṁtuṣṭaḥ*). Since there is no ego in him he is "actionless" *(A-kartṛ)*. He has risen above his mind-intellect equipment and, therefore, thought-agitations cannot disturb him at all—"he is free from fluctuations" (*Spanda-varjitam*). He has gained all that is to be gained and in the fullness of his supreme satisfaction he has become "desireless" (*Nirāśam*). In the vivid experience of the Infinitude he has no more any doubts regarding the nature of the Absolute Goal (*Gata-Sandeham*).

निर्ध्यातुं चेष्टितुं वापि यच्चित्तं न प्रवर्तते ।
निर्निमित्तमिदं किन्तु निर्ध्यायति विचेष्टते ॥ ३१ ॥

Nir-dhyātuṁ ceṣṭituṁ vāpi yaccitaṁ na pravartate,
nir-nimitta-midaṁ kintu nirdhyāyati viceṣṭate.

निर्ध्यातुम् *nirdhyātum* = to meditate; चेष्टितुम् *ceṣṭitum* = to act; वा *vā* = or; अपि *api* = also; यत् चित्तम् *yat-cittam* = whose mind; न *na* = not; प्रवर्तते *pravartate* = engages itself; निर्निमित्तम् *nir-nimittam* = without any motive; इदम् *idam* = this; किन्तु *kintu* = but; निर्ध्यायति *nirdhyāyati* = meditates; विचेष्टते *viceṣṭate* = acts.

31. *The mind of the Liberated-one does not engage itself either in meditation or in activity. It becomes meditative and active without any motive—spontaneously.*

The Liberated-in-life lives as the Self, in the Self. He dwells above the mind. From where he is, he cannot even recognise the clamorous mind or his functioning body. Therefore, he cannot continue meditation, either for the purpose of withdrawing his sense-organs, or to calm down the pulsations of thoughts in his mind. Meditation is the function that an ego can undertake for its awakening. The already awakened, can no longer pursue meditation. Having reached the destination how can we continue walking the route by which we reach our destination?

At the same time we should not misunderstand that a Man-of-Perfection is living a life as we live: a victim of the lusts of his body, of the passions of his mind and of the restlessness of his intellect. The Enlightened-one is constantly established in the State of his Highest-meditation, ever-revelling in the Self, be he in meditation or in apparent activities. Spontaneity is the essence of his entire living. When he is quiet, in him we see the Divine-at-rest. When he acts, in him we watch the Divine-in-action.

तत्त्वं यथार्थमाकर्ण्य मन्दः प्राप्नोति मूढताम् ।
अथवाऽऽयाति सङ्कोचममूढः कोऽपि मूढवत् ॥ ३२ ॥

Tattvaṁ yathārtha-mākarṇya mandaḥ prāpnoti muḍhatām,
athavā''yāti saṅkocama-mūḍhaḥ ko'pi mūḍhavat.

तत्त्वम् *tattvam* = Truth; यथार्थम् *yathārtham* = real; आकर्ण्य *ākarṇya* = hearing; मन्दः *mandaḥ* = the unintelligent person; प्राप्नोति *prāpnoti* = gets; मूढताम् *muḍhatām* = confused; अथवा *athavā* = or; सङ्कोचम् आयाति *saṅkocam āyāti* = withdraws within; अमूढः *amūḍhaḥ* = intelligent man; कः अपि *kaḥ api* = some; मूढवत् *mūḍhavat* = like a fool.

32. *An un-intelligent person becomes confused on hearing the Real Truth, but some intelligent man withdraws within (and lives) like a fool.*

A subtle intellect trained to meditate and move within, exploring the depths of one's own personality, is absolutely necessary for a spiritual seeker in order to digest what the scriptures talk about the Absolute Nature of the Supreme Self. A primary school student, in his immaturity, may become completely confused and extremely disturbed if he were taught Einstein's Relativity theory, with all its subtle mathematical and scientific implications. The same student if he is allowed to cultivate scientific knowledge and having educated himself upto his graduate standard, thereafter if he is given a course in Einstein's Theory, it should not be difficult for the same student to grasp its implications in the entirety of its real depths.

The 'unintelligent' (*Mandaḥ*)— means one whose thoughts are turned towards sense-gratifications, and therefore, not available for serene and deep reflections. Such an individual if he were to listen to a discourse given out by a Sage upon the Highest Transcendental Truth in all its Absolute Glory, such an unprepared, student is sure to get confused.

The same discourse when listened to by a student who has prepared himself with all the disciplines necessary for the comprehension of the Infinite Self, gets himself rocketted into his own within, to experiences therein the Peaceful Self. At this juncture, that student, may be considered by the worldly people as a "fool" (*Mūḍhaḥ*), who is not taking any active part in the competitive world, acquiring wealth, running after objects, panting in passions indulging in mad revelry and generally getting torn apart between like and dislikes, through joy and sorrow, amidst pleasure and pain!!

Hence, *Aṣṭāvakra* uses the simili here 'like a fool'— he is not a fool, but he is like a fool. A fool is incapable of taking any activity in the outer world and, is ever an idler. Yet, he is never quiet as he is full of desires and, so, his mind would be constantly in agitation. A Wise-man also remains without activities, but his mind is ever quiet and serene within, because in him there are no desires.

Emphasising the need for preparation of the student before he enters the Halls-of-*Vedānta*, *Yoga-Vāsiṣṭha* humorously declares:

वयं तु वक्तुं मूर्खाणामजितात्मीयचेतसाम् ।
भोगकर्दममग्नानां न विद्मोऽभिमतं मतम् ॥

....

तेषामभिमता नार्यः भावाभावविभूषिताः ॥

Vayaṁ tu vaktuṁ mūrkhāṇām-ajitātmīya-cetasām,
bhoga-kardama-magnānāṁ na vidmo'bhimataṁ matam.

....

teṣām-abhimatā nāryaḥ bhāvābhāva-vibhūṣitāḥ.

"We don't know how to explain Saving-Truth of Spiritual Life to persons who are gross, with uncontrolled senses, or passions, who are drowned in lusty enjoyments. Let them learn it all from women who are dressed in their lack-of-intelligence!"

एकाग्रता निरोधो वा मूढैरभ्यस्यते भृशम् ।
धीराः कृत्यं न पश्यन्ति सुप्तवत् स्वपदे स्थिताः ॥ ३३ ॥

Ekāgratā nirodho vā mūdair-abhyasyate bhṛśam,
dhīrāḥ kṛtyaṁ na paśyanti suptavat-svapade sthitāḥ.

एकाग्रता *ekāgratā* = concentration; निरोधः *nirodhaḥ* = control of the mind; वा *vā* = or; मूढैः *mūdaiḥ* = by the fools, ignorant; अभ्यस्यते *abhyasyate* = is practised; भृशम् *bhṛśam* = repeatedly; धीराः *dhīrāḥ* = the wise; कृत्यम् *kṛtyam* = anything to be attained (done); न *na* = not; पश्यन्ति *paśyanti* = see; सुप्तवत् *suptavat* = like persons in sleep; स्वपदे *svapade* = in one's own Self; स्थिताः *sthitāḥ* = abiding.

33. *The fools constantly practise concentration and control of the mind. The Wise, abiding in his own Self, like persons in deep-sleep, do not find anything to be attained.*

Here the term 'fool' is used to indicate those who are still conscious of their body and mind, and therefore, in whom the ego is very aggressive. One who is conscious of his body and mind, so long as he is in this ego-state of Consciousness, will and must practise Self-control of the sense-organs and concentration of his mind. But the Liberated-in-life, who is already revelling in his own Self, has his mind flouted, his ego driven out, finds nothing more to be attained! He is, *Aṣṭāvakra* explains, "like a person in deep-sleep." One who is in dreamless-sleep in not conscious of his body, or of the world-of-plurality. There is no *mis-apprehension* in him. The Sage who is apprehending the Self, also does not see or experience any '*mis-apprehensions*' of the equipments, or their fields of experiences.

The Liberated-Sage lives in a world of his own, away from our natural fields-of-experiences, ever-awakened to the Infinite Presence of the Blissful Self everywhere. To such an individual, who is constantly living as the Self, in the Self, upon what is he to meditate?....With what? What is he to withdraw from? He has reached his Goal Surpeme.

If *Aṣṭāvakra* is giving us a direct flight to the Realm of Reality in this verse, *Yoga-Vāsiṣṭha* at one point is kind enough to indicate to us the various stages enroute to this benign destination:

पूर्वं विवेकेन तनुत्वमेति रागोऽथ वैरं च समूलमेव ।
पश्चात्परिक्षीयत एव यत्नः सः पावनो यत्र विवेकितास्ति ॥

Pūrvaṁ vivekena tanu-tvameti
rāgo'tha vairaṁ ca samūlameva
paścāt-parikṣīyata eva yatnaḥ
saḥ pāvano yatra vivekitāsti.

"First through cultivated discrimination our attachment dies away. Thereafter aversions are removed from us along with their roots (the ego). Thereafter slowly the very effort of meditation calms down, when he reaches that Glorious State where True Discrimination (Self) really is!!

अप्रयत्नात् प्रयत्नाद्वा मूढो नाप्नोति निर्वृतिम् ।
तत्त्वनिश्चयमात्रेण प्राज्ञो भवति निर्वृतः ॥ ३४ ॥

Aprayatnāt-prayatnād-vā mūḍho nāpnoti nirvṛtim,
tattva-niścaya-mātreṇa prājño bhavati nirvṛtaḥ.

अप्रयत्नात् *aprayatnāt* = from inaction; प्रयत्नात् *prayatnāt* = from action; वा *vā* = or; मूढः *mūḍhaḥ* = the fool; न *na* = not; आप्नोति *āpnoti* = attains; निर्वृतिम् *nirvṛtim* = tranquillity; तत्त्व-निश्चय-मात्रेण *tattva-niścaya-mātreṇa* = simply by knowing the Truth; प्राज्ञः *prājñaḥ* = the Wise-one; भवति *bhavati* = becomes; निर्वृतः *nirvṛtaḥ* = tranquil.

34. *The fool does not attain tranquillity either by action or by inaction. The Wise-one becomes tranquil merely by knowing the Truth.*

The ego-centric person—who is extremely conscious of his body, mind and intellect, and naturally, whose attention is always turned in catering to the endless gross and subtle demands of the body and mind—is indicated here by the term 'fool.' And such a person can never reach mental tranquillity, either by "doing actions" (*Prayatnāt*), nor by suppression of them—by "not doing" (*Aprayatnāt*). For a time, every seeker can, by his sheer will-power, suppress the flood of his desires, and look apparently a disciplined entity pursuing his path of spiritual seeking. But he cannot awake to the State of Pure Consciousness by these methods. Activity in the sensuous world, or apparent inactivity towards them, are no criterion for the spiritual realisation.

One who has eliminated his ego, and purified his mind of his sensuous *Vāsanā-s*, such a seeker (*Prājñaḥ*) alone has cultivated in himself a mind which is ready for a flight in meditation. Such a student is able to move in the direction indicated in the scriptures, and therefore, as he is listening to his teacher, or reflecting upon these great truths, comes to experience the State of Selfhood.

Here the term 'action' (*Prayatna*) is used to indicate activities prompted by desires. The term 'in-action' (*A-prayatna*) is used here to indicate the apparent state of quietude that we see in an individual, attained through his mental suppressions! By either method we cannot reach the State of Tranquillity to be experienced in Spiritual realisation.

The deep import of this verse reminds us of a similar statement in the *Bhagavad-Gītā* (III-17) where the Lord is careful to explain that the Bliss of the Self-realised is not due to any forced and artificial suppression of desires:

यस्त्वात्मरतिरेव स्यादात्मतृप्तश्च मानवः ।
आत्मन्येव च सन्तुष्टस्तस्य कार्यं न विद्यते ॥

Yastv-ātma-ratir-eva syād-ātma-tṛptaś-ca mānavaḥ,
ātmanyeva ca santuṣṭas-tasya kāryaṁ na vidyate.

"But the man who rejoices only in the Self, who is satisfied with the Self, who is content in the Self alone, for him, indeed, there is nothing (more) to be done."

शुद्धं बुद्धं प्रियं पूर्णं निष्प्रपञ्चं निरामयम् ।
आत्मानं तं न जानन्ति तत्राभ्यासपरा जनाः ॥ ३५ ॥

Śuddhaṁ buddhaṁ priyaṁ pūrṇaṁ
niṣ-prapañcaṁ nirāmayam,
ātmānaṁ taṁ na jānanti
tatrā-bhyāsa-parā janāḥ.

शुद्धम् *śuddham* = pure; बुद्धम् *buddham* = enlightened; प्रियम् *priyam* = beloved; पूर्णम् *pūrṇam* = perfect; निष्प्रपञ्चम् *niṣprapañcam* = beyond the visible universe (transcendental); निरामयम् *nirāmayam* = stainless; आत्मानम् *ātmānam* = Self; तम् *tam* = that; न *na* = not; जानन्ति *jānanti* = know; तत्र *tatra* = in this world; अभ्यासपराः *abhyāsaparāḥ* = devoted to diverse practices; जनाः *janāḥ* = men.

35. *In this world those who devote themselves to diverse practices do not know the Self which is*

Pure, Enlightened, Beloved, Perfect, Transcendental and Stainless.

These verses are not to be misunderstood to mean that *Sādhanā* is unnecessary. Those who have not done *Sādhanā*, *Aṣṭāvakra* indicates them by the derogatory term 'fool' (*Mūḍhaḥ*). But a *Sādhaka* must know that the *Sādhanā* is the means, and the direct experience of the Infinite is the goal. Very often the seeker comes to confuse the means for the very goal. In ordinary life this often happens. Money is the means for happy-living, but there are fools who mistake the means for the end, and get exhausted in their worry for and anxiety of collecting money, and, in their miserliness, they live but a miserable life!

In the Spiritual life, do not be such a miserable fool! The various practices of devotion to the Lord, service to the society, study of the scriptures, reflection upon the truths and even meditation—are all means to awaken ourselves from the dreams of the ego, and realise our True Nature. To students of Higher-meditation this warning is appropriate and very necessary. *Aṣṭāvakra Gītā* is a dialogue between the great Sage, and an equally great student, *Janaka*. And hence, the discussion is at this high level. Early seekers should not get confused.

नाप्नोति कर्मणा मोक्षं विमूढोऽभ्यासरूपिणा ।
धन्यो विज्ञानमात्रेण मुक्तस्तिष्ठत्यविक्रियः ॥ ३६ ॥

Nāpnoti karmāṇā mokṣaṁ vimūḍho-'bhyāsa-rūpiṇā,
dhanyo vijñāna-mātreṇa muktas-tiṣṭhatya-vikriyaḥ.

न *na* = not; आप्नोति *āpnoti* = attains; कर्मणा *karmāṇā* = by action; मोक्षम् *mokṣam* = liberation; विमूढः *vimūḍhaḥ* = an highly unintelligent person; अभ्यास-रूपिणा *abhyāsa-rūpiṇā* = in the form of *Yoga*-practice (Control of mind); धन्यः *dhanyaḥ* = the blessed; विज्ञान-मात्रेण *vijñāna-mātreṇa* = by mere intuitive enlightenment; मुक्तः *muktaḥ* = liberated; तिष्ठति *tiṣṭhati* = remains; अविक्रियः *avikriyaḥ* = Immutable.

36. *An highly unintelligent person never attains (the Self) through the repeated practices of controlling his mind. The Blessed-one, through mere intuitive enlightenment, remains Liberated, and Immutable.*

The statement made by *Aṣṭāvakra* in the previous verse must have confused the student, as he has shaken the very bottom of the student's faith! Just as in the *Karma-kāṇḍa* portion of *Vedā-s* students get often attached to their rituals and they are made to leave them when they step into the *Upaniṣadik* portion. The teacher has to jerk them out, so that, the mind of the student which has been trained already in the ritual, may come to play in a higher and subtler field of the "study-of-the-scriptures." Later on, the student is advised to "meditate" upon the Self, in order to make his mind still subtler, for a deeper penetration of his enquiry into the secret chambers of the pulsating "Universal Life."

Now the Sage here in this song is giving, as it were, that last kick to the student, who is attached to his pursuit in the path-of-meditation. The very act of meditation nourishes the ego in the student, and compels him to maintain a sense of meaningless distinction between himself—the meditator, and the Truth—that is meditated upon.

The revered Sage has already demonstrated that he can wield a sharp pen, and mercilessly scratch to wound the student and smear it with ridicule so as to scorch away the student's stupidity out of his personality once forever.[1]

Here again the teacher adopts his usual style. He says: 'an highly intelligent person (*Vimūḍhaḥ*) does not attain realisation through his *Yoga*-practices by which he is trying to control his mind" While "a blessed-one" (*Dhanyaḥ*), meaning an intelligent and true seeker, by the right apprehension of the Nature of the Self, ends all his *Sādhanā* and remains continuously revelling in

1. This particular style in thought of *Aṣṭāvakra* is seen in the entire, Chapter III, Ibid entitled "Self in All–All in Self."

the Self. Meditation is the means, experience of the Self is the end. To mechanically repeat and to unintelligently hold on to the different practices is to maintain a sense of distinction between the seeker and the Reality. These last traces of the ego, the sense of individuality in the meditator, must end. Then the *subject* merges with the *object*, and the One Self alone shines in all its Infinite Bliss.

मूढो नाप्नोति तद्ब्रह्म यतो भवितुमिच्छति ।
अनिच्छन्नपि धीरो हि परब्रह्मस्वरूपभाक् ॥ ३७ ॥

Mūḍho nāpnoti tad-brahma yato bhavitum-icchati,
anicchan-napi dhīro hi parabrahma-svarūpa-bhāk.

मूढः *mūḍhaḥ* = the fool; न *na* = not; आप्नोति *āpnoti* = attains; तत् *tat* = that; ब्रह्म *brahma* = *Brahman*; यतः *yataḥ* = as; भवितुम *bhavitum* = to become; इच्छति *icchati* = desires; अनिच्छन् *anicchan* = without desiring; अपि *api* = even; धीरः *dhīraḥ* = the Wise-one; हि *hi* = surely; पर-ब्रह्म-स्वरूप-भाक् *para-brahma-svarūpa-bhāk* = enjoys the Nature of the Supreme *Brahman*.

37. *The fool does not attain Brahman, for he desires to become It! The Wise-one certainly realises the Nature of the Supreme Brahman even without desiring to do so.*

The impulse behind all meditation is the desire to realise, and this very desire is the last link that holds the student on to the seat of his struggles without allowing him to glide peacefully into the realm of the Pure Self. Therefore, this burning desire to realise (*Mumukṣutva*) is being removed from the bosom of the mature student by a painless surgery in this verse. In the beginning the desire to again the spiritual vision is encouraged in the student because thereby his mind, naturally and without effort, rolls away from all other *objective* desires—in order to fulfil this great desire for the *subjective* illumination. When the student has become completely introvert, he has to again lift himself from the scalding material world of the mind. The mind is to be transcended. Thoughtless mind is the arbour for Enlightenment. So long as there is even the "desire-to-realise," the student cannot fold-up his mind.

This is exactly like the one who complains that he can't sleep, because of his very anxiety to sleep!

Thus, in the process of *Vedānta*, through efforts we give up our desires for the world-outside, and for this the mind is mounted with one sincere and deep desire-to-liberate. To give up this very "desire" is the last effortless-act, and in this effortlessness is the *Awakening*. That you want to become *Brahman* is a "wrong idea." "You can never *become Brahman*" this is a "false notion." You are already *Brahman*. Never desire to become *Brahman*—you may desire to *Be Brahman*!!

Such an individual, who has accomplished this last conscious act of renunciation—of the very desire-to-realise—is the blessed one, who attains the total unveiling of the Truth. *Yoga-Vāsiṣṭha* roars :

....

भारूपैकस्वरूपेऽस्मिन् स्वरूपेण जयाम्यहम् ॥

....

Bhārūpaika-svarūpe-'smin svarūpeṇa jayāmy-aham.

"I victoriously live in this Effulgent Consciousness as my own sole Essence."

In short, direct experience is gained through '*Vijñāna*' only. This direct path to enlightenment does not recognise, at this moment, any need for mental control brought about by the deep desire-to-liberate. Even this *spiritual desire* feeds the ego and nourishes the sense of separateness between the meditator and the meditated. At this stage, when the student has already fulfilled all the previous trainings, he must strive to remain in the Divine State of *just* "*Be*."

निराधारा ग्रहव्यग्रा मूढाः संसारपोषकाः ।
एतस्यानर्थमूलस्य मूलच्छेदः कृतो बुधैः ॥ ३८ ॥

Nirādhārā graha-vyagrā mūḍhāḥ saṁsāra-poṣakāḥ,
etasyā-nartha-mūlasya mūla-cchedaḥ kṛto budhaiḥ.

निराधाराः *nirādhārāḥ* = supportless; ग्रह-व्यग्राः *graha-vyagrāḥ* = eager for attainment of freedom; मूढाः *mūḍhāḥ* = fools; संसार-पोषकाः *saṁsāra-poṣakāḥ* = sustainer of the world; एतस्य *etasya* = of this; अनर्थ-मूलस्य *anartha-mūlasya* = the root of misery; मूल-च्छेदः *mūla-cchedaḥ* = cutting at the root; कृतः *kṛtaḥ* = is done; बुधैः *budhaiḥ* = by the wise.

38. *Without any support and eager for the attainment of freedom, the fools only keep up the world! The Wise cut at the very root of this world, which is the source of all misery.*

The perception of the pluralistic world of phenomena stems forth from the 'ignorance,' and the Wise-one cuts at the very root of this tree-of-*Saṁsāra*. The *non-apprehension*-of-the-Reality (*ignorance*) ends only in the *apprehension*-of-the-Reality (*Knowledge*). Compared to these Wise-ones, who thus strive to experience directly that which lies beyond the hushed mind, *Aṣṭāvakra* here ridicules, those who, in their eagerness for gaining this revelation, spend their entire time and energy in mental control and suppressions. Mind itself is false, and it roams about in its illusions of plurality. Instead of destroying the very source of the mind, to strive to control the mind is a waste of energy to a matured *Sādhaka*.

These instructions are given not to the beginners; *Janaka* is a spiritual student trembling on the verge of realisation. To him is addressed the entire song by Sage *Aṣṭāvakra*.

Without any support (*Nirādhāra*)—the very mind and its projections are all supported by the Pure Infinite Consciousness that illumines all experiences. To try to control the mind from its fascinations is like trying to control the dreamer in his behaviour in the dream—it is like beating with a stick to kill the *serpent in the rope*!!

On waking up, the dreamer is completely controlled; on seeing the *rope* there is no serpent to be killed. On realising the Self, there is no mind to control, nor a world of *objects* to be denied!

"The source of all misery" is the *ignorance* of the Self; the very conscious effort in meditation indicates that the meditator is still in the realm of *ignorance* perceiving his world-of-delusions. That is the reason why *Aṣṭāvakra* declares that the foolish in their attachment to meditation maintain in themselves the illusion of the world-of-plurality.

Mental control is unavoidable in order to start meditation. In the intense moments of meditation, the meditator must end in the meditated. This take off can occur only when even the last withering whiffs of the insubstantial ego are surrendered by the meditator. He must heave to experience the Effulgent Self. This is the Goal of the great Sage—across the frontiers of the Real and the unreal—of the True and the false—of the Permanent and impermanent. The student is now on the verge of *ignorance*, hesitating to leap into the Infinite Reality. Students with the tempo and purity of *Janaka* alone can understand the true import and significance of what the mystic Master in *Aṣṭāvakra* is communicating here.

न शान्तिं लभते मूढो यतः शमितुमिच्छति ।
धीरस्तत्त्वं विनिश्चित्य सर्वदा शान्तमानसः ॥ ३९ ॥

Na śāntiṁ labhate mūḍho yataḥ śamitum-icchati,
dhīras-tattvaṁ viniścitya sarvadā śānta-mānasaḥ.

न *na* = not; शान्तिम् *śāntim* = peace; लभते *labhate* = gains; मूढः *mūḍhaḥ* = the fool; यतः *yataḥ* = as; शमितुम् *śamitum* = to be calm; इच्छति *icchati* = wants to get; धीरः *dhīraḥ* = the Wise-one; तत्त्वम्

tattvam = Truth; विनिश्चित्य *viniścitya* = knowing for certain; सर्वदा *sarvadā* = ever; शान्त-मानसः *śānta-mānasaḥ* = tranquil in mind.

39. *Since the fool wants to get peace through control of his mind, he does not gain it. The Wise-one knowing for certain the Truth, is ever tranquil in mind.*

The knowledge of the post alone can bring peace to the mind that is agitated with the *illusion of the ghost.* Realisation of the Self alone can fill the personality of a Sage with "peace that passeth all understanding." The fool wants to "get peace," and therefore, he struggles to control his mind. He misses it totally. The very struggle in him brings conflicts in himself. If peace is something to be attained, it will then, certainly, be lost also! The fool desires to gain peace, as though it has to be gained as a reward for his efforts in controlling his mind! The very struggle in controlling the mind feeds the mind and makes it strong. It is like trying to put down fire with petrol, misunderstanding it to be waters! Mind can never be controlled by the mind. By rising above the mind-intellect alone can the equipments be controlled. The Wise-one, experiencing for certain the Self, in his direct vision, "is ever tranquil in his mind"—because he has transcended his mind.

क्वात्मनो दर्शनं तस्य यद्दृष्टमवलम्बते ।
धीरास्तं तं न पश्यन्ति पश्यन्त्यात्मानमव्ययम् ॥ ४० ॥

Kvātmano darśanaṁ tasya
yad-dṛṣṭam-avalambate,
dhīrāstaṁ taṁ na paśyanti
paśyanty-ātmānam-avyayam.

क्व *kva* = where; आत्मनः *ātmanaḥ* = of the Self; दर्शनम् *darśanam* = knowledge; तस्य *tasya* = whose; यत् *yat* = who; दृष्टम् *dṛṣṭam* = seeing the manifested world; अवलम्बते *avalambate* = resorts to; धीराः *dhīrāḥ* = the Wise; तम् तम् *tam tam* = this and that; न *na* = not; पश्यन्ति

paśyanti = see (but); पश्यन्ति *paśyanti* = see; आत्मानम् *ātmānam* = Immutable; अव्ययम् *avyayam* = Self.

40. Where is the vision-of-the-Self to one who resorts to seeing the manifested world? The Wise do not see this and that, but see only the Immutable Self.

Without transcending the mind, the experience of the Self is impossible, is the idea that is emphasised in this verse. The perceptions of the body, the emotions of the mind and the thoughts of the intellect together constitute an individual's manifested world-of-experiences. So long as our awareness is thus turned outward, we can be conscious of the world of multiplicity alone. Such an individual can never come to be awake to the Infinite glory of the Pure Self.

The Realised Saints and Sages—"the Wise do not see this and that"—see the Immutable Reality alone. The true meditator rises above the awareness of his equipments, and therefore, he no longer apprehends the world of objects, emotions and thoughts. At such moments of intense meditation, when the mind-intellect is completely halted, the meditator plunges into the "meditated" to be the Self. Here he experiences the Immutable Reality Supreme.

The idea of the previous verse is expanded and emphasised here, in saying that, so long as the seeker is trying to control the wanderings of his mind with his mind, he may relatively quieten his mind, but can never totally succeed. Rising above the mind is the only method. "Renounce even the last lingering sense of identification in the meditator"—this is the call sent out through the pregnant suggestions of this fabulous verse!

In the worldly perception, there is always the *subject-object*-relationship. The One Immutable Self is experienced only when the *objects* merge into the *subject*.

क्व निरोधो विमूढस्य यो निर्बन्धं करोति वै ।
स्वारामस्यैव धीरस्य सर्वदाऽसावकृत्रिमः ॥ ४१ ॥

Kva nirodho vimūḍhasya yo nirbandhaṁ karoti vai,
svārāmasyaiva dhīrasya sarvadā-'sāv-akṛtrimaḥ.

क्व *kva* = where; निरोधः *nirodhaḥ* = control of mind; विमूढस्य *vimūḍhasya* = of the supreme fool; यः *yaḥ* = who; निर्बन्धम् करोति *nirbandham karoti* = strives; वै *vai* = indeed; स्वारामस्य *svārāmasya* = who delights in the Self; एव *eva* = surely; धीरस्य *dhīrasya* = the Wise-one; सर्वदा *sarvadā* = always; असौ *asau* = that; अकृत्रिमः *akṛtrimaḥ*.= spontaneous.

41. *Where is the control of the mind for the fool, who strives for it? To the Wise-one who delights in the Self, it is indeed spontaneous and perennial.*

Aṣṭāvakra has not yet finished explaining why he had made a criticism of all attempts at mental controls. To control the mind with the mind is ineffectual—it is as laughable an attempt as to straighten a dog's tail! It is the very nature of the mind that it should gush out to embrace the sense-objects. Divorced from sense-objects mind has no existence at all!

Fools alone continue striving in the control of the mind. So long as the striving exists, the mind continues and, therefore, such an individual is characterised here as a fool. As a contrast to the foolish *Sādhaka*, the Sage now indicates the condition of the Wise-man.

After controlling the mind from its wildest passions and lusts for the sense-objects, with that relatively quietened mind we must start our sincere meditations. Meditation quietens the mind and his extremely be-calmed mind should be finally ignored by the meditator, when he heaves into the field of his spiritual-experience. "One who thus delights in the Self," to such an Enlightened One mental control is "spontaneous and perential" inasmuch as he has risen above the mind, and in his realisation has understood that the mind itself was an illusion!

All activities at controlling the mind strengthen the seeker's identification with the mind. The mind continues its existence fed by its own recognition of this delusion. On awakening to the Self, the mental control fulfils itself inasmuch as no more control of the mind is possible, because, the illusion of the mind itself has been lifted from the awareness of the Man-of-Realisation.

Early *Sādhakā*-s should control the mind. It has been all along repeated by us that this text is addressed to those who have already risen to the outer frontiers of the unreal, and are hesitating to take the last step for the total merger of the individual-Self with the Universal-Self.

भावस्य भावकः कश्चिन्न किञ्चिद्भावकोऽपरः ।
उभयाऽभावकः कश्चिदेवमेव निराकुलः ॥४२॥

Bhāvasya bhāvakaḥ kaścinna kiñcid-bhāvako-'paraḥ,
ubhayā-'bhāvakaḥ kaścid-eva-meva nirākulaḥ.

भावस्य *bhāvasya* = of existence; भावकः *bhāvakaḥ* = who thinks; कश्चित् *kaścit* = someone; न *na* = not; किञ्चित् भावकः *kiñcit-bhāvakaḥ* = who thinks that nothing is; अपरः *aparaḥ* = someone else; उभया-अभावकः *ubhayā-abhāvakaḥ* = who thinks neither; कश्चित् एव *kaścit eva* = rarely one; एवम् *evam* = thus; निराकुलः *nirākulaḥ* = free from distractions.

42. *Some think that 'existence' is, and others that 'nothing' is. Rare is the one who thinks neither. He is perfectly serene—free from all distractions.*

To The *Cārvakā-s,*[1] the world is 'existence.' It is real. The manifested world alone is the only 'reality.' Some other thinkers, meaning a group of Budhists called the *Madhyamikā-s*, consider "nothing is." Applied to *Sādhanā,* some consider that the Self is to be meditated upon as "Existence-Knowledge-Bliss" (*Sat-cit-Ānanda*); others recommend that the Infinite is realised when the mind has no existent-thoughts. According to them

1. Pure materialists in Indian Philosophy—the Supreme Atheists.

consciousness-of-an-object is the "Knowledge of that object." Therefore, objectless-consciousness is the Pure Infinite Self.

Hence *Aṣṭāvakra* exclaims, "rare is the one, who thinks neither," and adds "he is perfectly serene." The Calm Self is the illuminator of both the "existence" of the mind, which is the source of the world-of-plurality, and the same Consciousness illumines the absence of mind, and therefore, the "non-existence" of the world-of-experiences.

The Self is ever Peaceful. Never was a world ever created in it; nor can we say that the world has been eliminated. The *post* remains as the *post*: the *ghost* was only an illusion—its presence or absence is of no concern to the *post*.

शुद्धमद्वयमात्मानं भावयन्ति कुबुद्धयः ।
न तु जानन्ति संमोहाद्यावज्जीवमनिर्वृताः ॥ ४३ ॥

Śuddham-advayam-ātmānaṁ
bhāvayanti ku-buddhayaḥ,
na tu jānanti saṁmohād-
yāvaj-jīvam-anir-vṛtāḥ.

शुद्धम् *śuddham* = Pure; अद्वयम् *advayam* = without-a-second; आत्मानम् *ātmānam* = the Self; भावयन्ति *bhāvayanti* = meditate; कुबुद्धयः *kubuddhayaḥ* = men of dull intellect; न *na* = not; तु *tu* = but; जानन्ति *jānanti* = realise; संमोहात् *saṁmohāt* = due to delusion; यावत् जीवम् *yāvat-jīvam* = as long as they live; अनिर्वृताः *anirvṛtāḥ* = unhappy.

43. *Those of dull intellectual meditate upon the* Ātman *as Pure and One-without-a-second, but they do not realise It. Through delusion they remain unhappy as long as they live.*

Our identification with the intellect is so powerful and strong at this moment that even a student at meditation remains as a mere intellectual being, toying with the ideas of the Pure Self, the One-without-a-second. With these terms of meditation they do not really meditate, but they only tie themselves down with the suggestive ideas with which the *Upaniṣad*-s have, in Infinite mercy, indicated the Truth to us. No doubt the meditation is the *means* to awake and to realise. To 'Be' the Self is the *Goal*.

The dull intellects, some how or other, retain, deep in themselves, the unconscious idea that the Self is something to be perceived—to be gained, to be achieved! *Ātman* is the "Subject," the very being in the meditator, and it can never, never be objectified. It does not mean that we should not think of the Self. Thinking about the nature of the Self is the only way by which one can turn one's mind away from all its preoccupations. But the final leap is not to *become Brahman*—but just to *Be Brahman*.

Brahman is not a state to *become*.... it is just to *Be*. The dullards apprehend. It not, because of this delusion in them, that the Self is to be gained through meditation! They continue their meditation all through their life, yet, they remain ever unhappy, bound within the mind-intellect-entanglements.

मुमुक्षोर्बुद्धिरालम्बमन्तरेण न विद्यते ।
निरालम्बैव निष्कामा बुद्धिर्मुक्तस्य सर्वदा ॥ ४४ ॥

Mumukṣor-buddhir-ālambam-antareṇa na vidyate,
nirālambaiva niṣkāmā buddhir-muktasya sarvadā.

मुमुक्षोः *mumukṣoḥ* = of one aspiring for liberation; बुद्धिः *buddhiḥ* = intellect; आलम्बम् *ālambam* = support; अन्तरेण *antareṇa* = without; न *na* = not; विद्यते *vidyate* = remains; निरालम्बा *nirālambā* = without any support; एव *eva* = surely; निष्कामा *niṣkāmā* = free from desires; बुद्धिः *buddhiḥ* = intellect; मुक्तस्य *muktasya* = of the liberated one; सर्वदा *sarvadā* = ever.

44. *The intellect of one who aspires for liberation cannot function without a supporting-object. But the*

desireless intellect of the Liberated-one is, indeed, ever without any support (in meditation).

"The desire for Liberation" (*Mumukṣutvam*) is a mighty power to be used by a student in his early days of spiritual *Sādhanā*. It maintains the student in the spiritual field, encourages him to pursue the Path-of-meditation. But here the teacher is pointing to a stage in meditation wherein even this anxiety-to-realise the Self is a shackle, that ties him down to the relative-field of his intellect. "One who aspires for liberation" is the one who has not yet gained the Self and, therefore, is still an ego living in the field of the *subject-object*-experiences. As such the ego-centric intellect in the seeker consciously holds on to the Self, upon which he is meditating, as an "*object*" other than himself!

The Liberated-one has cleansed his intellect of even this "desire-to-liberate," and therefore, he is in his meditation, "without any support," inasmuch as he is the Self!

We may meditate upon the Self, but the fulfilment of meditation is in the direct-experience of the Self—wherein the experiencer and the experienced are not two factors. To be awakened to the Self is to be the Self. The *dreamer* when he awakes, he becomes the very *waker*.

विषयाद्वीपिनो वीक्ष्य चकिताः शरणार्थिनः ।
विशन्ति झटिति क्रोडं निरोधैकाग्र्यसिद्धये ॥ ४५ ॥

Viṣayā-dvīpino vīkṣya cakitāḥ śaraṇ-ārthinaḥ,
viśanti jhaṭiti kroḍaṁ nirodhai-kāgrya-siddhaye.

विषयाः *viṣayāḥ* = sense-objects; द्वीपिनः *dvīpinaḥ* = tigers; वीक्ष्य *vīkṣya* = encountering; चकिताः *cakitāḥ* = the frightened one; शरणार्थिनः *śaraṇ-ārthinaḥ* = seeking refuge; विशन्ति *viśanti* = enter; झटिति *jhaṭiti* = at once; क्रोडम् *kroḍham* = the cave; निरोध-एकाग्र्य-सिद्धये *nirodha-ekāgraya-siddhaye* = for attaining control and concentration.

45. *Encountering the tigers of sense-objects, the frightened ones seeking refuge at once enter the cave of the mind, for the attainment of control and concentration.*

An ego-centric personality can never escape perceiving the sense-objects. The very instrument, by which they perceive the sense-objects, is the mind, and the mind is fed by the sense-objects, as they bring storms of agitations into the mind and distract the mind from its poise and concentration. Seekers in the beginning should try to turn their attention away from all sense-enjoyments, by remembering the Lord and entering the 'cave' within—meaning their mind-intellect equipments. Withdrawing the sense-attention from the enchanting objects and re-directing the mind to the Greater Reality is one of the antidote for the sensuous excitements. No doubt, in their early days, seekers have no other remedy, available for them.

Here *Aṣṭāvakra* is advising the students who have gained sufficient equipoise in themselves. He says the Liberated-in-life are never frightened of the sense-objects, nor do they escape into the "cave"...... for, they, in fact, perceive no plurality at all! The *Bṛhadāraṇyaka Upaniṣad* (I-iv-2) thunders:

द्वितीयात् वै भयं भवति ।

Dvitīyāt vai bhayaṁ bhavati.

"The perception of the other is, indeed, the source of all fear."

There is an inherent contradiction in this scheme followed as an early *Sādhanā*. Mind is that which projects the sense-objects, and it is the mind, again, that is running towards the *objects*. To run into the mind is in fact equivalent to running into the mouth of the sense-objects themselves! In short, we cannot avoid the world-of-plurality and its undivine enchantments by any horizontal movement. Wherever you run, you are still a captive of your mind. Only by lifting ourselves—in the vertical movement to the Higher-plane of Consciousness—can we rise above the shackles of the mind.

निर्वासनं हरिं दृष्ट्वा तूष्णीं विषयदन्तिनः ।
पलायन्ते न शक्तास्ते सेवन्ते कृतचाटवः ॥ ४६ ॥

Nir-vāsanaṁ hariṁ dṛṣṭvā tūṣṇīṁ viṣaya-dantinaḥ,
palāyante na śaktāste sevante kṛta-cāṭavaḥ.

निर्वासनम् *nir-vāsanam* = desireless; हरिम् *harim* = lion; दृष्ट्वा *dṛṣṭvā* = encountering; तूष्णीम् *tūṣṇīm* = quietly; विषय-दन्तिनः *viṣaya-dantinaḥ* = the elephants of sense-objects; पलायन्ते *palāyante* = run away; न *na* = not; शक्ताः *śaktāḥ* = able; ते *te* = they; सेवन्ते *sevante* = serve; कृत-चाटवः *kṛta-cāṭavaḥ* = flattering courtiers; (इव *iva* = like).

46. Encountering the desireless man-lion, the elephants of sense-objects, quietly run away; or, if unable to run away, serve him like flattering courtiers!!

The glory of the Man-of-Perfection is pointed out here, indicating how he lives amidst the sense-objects, unmolested by them. In fact, *Aṣṭāvakra* says that the sense-objects run after him to serve him faithfully, as flattering courtiers rush to serve their royal master.

Desires are expressions of *Vāsanā-s* in-our-intellect. One who has no *Vāsanā-s* has no desires. It is the desire-to-enjoy in us that entangles us with the sense-objects. A desireless man perceives the *objects* but he is not affected by them. Child in a toy-shop is excited, certainly not its father! Both of them are surrounded by toys, but the child has the desire to possess them; its father has no more those *Vāsanā-s* in him.

The Liberated-man moves about in the world, without any *Vāsanā* in him, and therefore, the sense-objects cannot enchant him. The consort of *Indra* may come and dance around Lord *Parameśvara*, but the Lord of *Kailāśa*, gets least disturbed! In our mythology we find many instances wherein the grey-haired toothless Sages, plunged in meditation, woke up to dance with these enchanting dancers of *Indra's* court and thereby, the Sages lost their mental equanimity and balance, which they cultivated with their long years of *Tapas*.

In short, the sense-objects can entrap only a mind that is seduced with its own desires. The desireless man is a lion among the elephants of sense-objects—declares Sage *Aṣṭāvakra*, though elephants are powerful creatures, they cannot encounter the king-of-beasts and they take to their heels. *Bhagavad-Gītā* (II-59) declares the same:

विषया विनिवर्तन्ते निराहारस्य देहिनः ।
रसवर्जं रसोऽप्यस्य परं दृष्ट्वा निवर्तते ॥

Viṣayā vinivartante nirāhārasya dehinaḥ,
rasa-varjaṁ raso'pyasya paraṁ dṛṣṭvā nivartate.

"The objects of the senses turn away from the abstinent man leaving the longing (behind); but his longing also turns away on *seeing* the Supreme."

Here the Sage adds one more thought. In case the sense-objects are unable to run away from the Master, they surrender completely to the will of the Master, and they seek to serve him as sycophants in an imperial court of a tyrant king!

न मुक्तिकारिकां धत्ते निःशङ्को युक्तमानसः ।
पश्यन् शृण्वन् स्पृशन् जिघ्रन्नश्नन्नास्ते यथासुखम् ॥४७॥

Na mukti-kārikāṁ dhatte niḥśaṅko yukta-mānasaḥ,
paśyan śṛṇvan spṛśan jighrann-aśnann-āste yathā-sukham.

न *na* = not; मुक्ति-कारिकाम् *mukti-kārikām* = practices of control as a means to liberation; धत्ते *dhatte* = adopts; निःशङ्कः *niḥ-śaṅkaḥ* = free from doubts; युक्त-मानसः *yukta-mānasaḥ* = one whose mind is identified with the Self; पश्यन् *paśyan* = seeing; शृण्वन् *śṛṇvan* = hearing; स्पृशन् *spṛśan* = touching; जिघ्रन् *jighran* = smelling; अश्नन् *aśnan* = eating; आस्ते *āste* = lives; यथा-सुखम् *yathā-sukham* = happily.

47. *He who is free from doubts and has his mind identified completely with the Self, never resorts to the practices of control as a means to liberation. Seeing, hearing, touching, smelling and eating, he lives happily.*

One who has identified himself completely to the Self is an Awakened-soul, and in him there is no more any ego-centric individually. Without ego and desires, actions in the world outside are no more actions that can bind him with their *Vāsanā*-results. They are no more actions; they are pseudo-acts.

The Liberated-in-life is untainted, ever-untouched by such natural functions of sense-organs as "seeing, hearing, touching smelling and eating." They are the functions of the senses. The inert *matter*-composed sense-organs are themselves acting only by drawing their enlivening energy from the very Self, which is the nature of the Man-of-Perfection. Such activities of the sense-organs cannot affect him. With the heat of the sun, water evaporates, forms into masses of clouds, and the clouds rain down; can the rain ever wet the sun? Can we say that the sun has created the rain? Yet, would their be rain if the sun were not there? The Liberated-Sage is unaffected by the normal activities of his sense-organs. He is not in his body—his mind is in him.

वस्तुश्रवणमात्रेण शुद्धबुद्धिर्निराकुलः ।
नैवाचारमनाचारमौदास्यं वा प्रपश्यति ॥ ४८ ॥

Vastu-śravaṇa-mātreṇa śuddha-buddhir-nirākulaḥ,
naiv-ācāram-anācāram-audāsyaṁ vā prapaśyati.

वस्तु-श्रवण-मात्रेण *vastu-śravaṇa-mātreṇa* = by mere listening to the Real; शुद्ध-बुद्धिः *śuddha-buddhiḥ* = who nas attained Pure Intellect;

निराकुलः *nirākulaḥ* = serene; न *na* = not; एव *eva* = indeed; आचारम् *ācāram* = proper conduct; अनाचारम् *anācāram* = improper conduct; औदास्यम् *audāsyaṁ* = indifference; वा *vā* = or; प्रपश्यति *prapaśyati* = sees.

48. *Having established in his Pure Intellect and having become serene—by a mere listening to the Real, the Wise-one, no more sees what is proper and improper action—or even what is inaction.*

By eliminating the desire and the ego, the intellect becomes calm and serene, and such a quietened bosom is considered, in the spiritual literature of India, as the "Pure-intellect" (*Śuddha-buddhi*).

One who has cultivated such a steady mind of continuous equipoise, to him a mere listening to a Master's discourse about the Reality is sufficient to turn his entire mind in the direction pointed out by the scriptures. Since the seeker has no desires in him, no ray-of-his-mind is entangled with the world-of-objects. With his entire mind thus turned towards the Higher Reality, he spontaneously awakes to the Experience Transcendental. He becomes the Liberated-in-life.

Such a Wise-one thereafter knows not what is proper and improper actions, not even what is inaction! He is no more the "*doer*" or the "*enjoyer.*" His ego is dead. He no more does any activity. All activities are taking place in him. The proper and improper actions of his dream, are no more of any consequence! The Liberated, living in the Higher Consciousness, does not belong any longer to this world; he is no more a native of our globe—he is just a sojourner here!

यदा यत्कर्तुमायाति तदा तत्कुरुते ऋजुः ।
शुभं वाप्यशुभं वापि तस्य चेष्टा हि बालवत् ॥ ४९ ॥

Yadā yat-kartum-āyāti tadā tat-kurute ṛjuḥ,
śubhaṁ vāpya-śubhaṁ vāpi tasya ceṣṭā hi bālavat.

यदा *yadā* = when; यत् *yat* = which; कर्तुम् *kartum* = to do (as his lot); आयाति *āyāti* = comes; तदा *tadā* = then; तत् *tat* = that; कुरुते *kurute* = does; ऋजुः *ṛjuḥ* = freely; शुभम् *śubham* = good; वा अपि *vā api* = or; अशुभम् *aśubham* = evil; वा *vā* = or; अपि *api* = even; तस्य *tasya* = his; चेष्टा *ceṣṭā* = action; हि *hi* = for; बालवत् *bālavat* = like that of a child.

49. *The Wise-one does freely whatever comes to his lot, whether good or evil; his actions are like those of a child.*

The Man-of-Realisation lives in total freedom at all times, and under all conditions and circumstances. He knows no limitations. He puts no curb upon himself. He does not seek fields of activities. Whatever circumstances reach him, he accepts it without any anxiety or hesitation. He lives meeting his *Prārabdha* openly, without any fear or favour. Nothing affects him. Nothing entangles him. In no activity does he entertain the idea that he is the "doer."

"The Wise does freely," meaning without the shackles of ego and ego-centric desires. He has neither the ego-sense within, nor has he the ego-feelings towards the world-of-objects; he has neither 'I-ness' nor 'my-ness.' Whatever comes to him, good or evil, he meets them heroically, seeing in and through them all, the same One, Infinite Self. The intellect—the equipment that discriminates the good and the evil—has been transcended by him.

In this way, living moment to moment dynamically, facing life as it comes, both in its raw beauty and naked abhorrence, the actions of the Wise are compared to the innocent actions of children. This example has already been exhaustively analysed.

This verse apparently contradicts the thought expressed earlier[1]: "He who has egoism in him acts even though he does not act. Surely the Wise-one is free from egoism does not act even though he acts."

1. Ibid. XVIII-29.

स्वातन्त्र्यात् सुखमाप्नोति स्वातन्त्र्याल्लभते परम् ।
स्वातन्त्र्यान्निर्वृतिं गच्छेत् स्वातन्त्र्यात् परमं पदम् ॥ ५० ॥

Svātantryāt sukham-āpnoti svātantryāl-labhate param,
svātantryān-nirvṛtiṁ gacchet svātantryāt paramaṁ padam.

स्वातन्त्र्यात् *svātantryāt* = from freedom; सुखम् *sukham* = happiness; आप्नोति *āpnoti* = attains; स्वातन्त्र्यात् *svātantryāt* = from freedom; लभते *labhate* = attains; परम् *param* = the highest; स्वातन्त्र्यात् *svātantryāt* = from freedom; निर्वृतिम् *nirvṛtim* = peaceful state, tranquillity, repose; गच्छेत् *gacchet*= attains; स्वातन्त्र्यात् *svātantryāt* = from freedom; परमम् *paramam* = supreme; पदम् *padam* = state (attains).

50. *Through freedom one attains to happiness; through freedom to the highest; through freedom to repose; and through freedom to the Supreme State.*

With a free and unshackled mind alone the Spiritual Awakening can be accomplished. Any thought, good or bad, is 'a stress in the Infinite." Without a disturbance the placid and clear surface of a lake cannot have ripples. Any discipline, any value of life, even trying to maintain the mind in meditation is a disturbance in the Consciousness! Thoughtless-state is the "no-mind"; it is the State of Pure Consciousness, without any stress in It. With this idea in mind *Aṣṭāvakra* addresses students, who have moved to the Highest-state in meditation.

This does not mean that a fool, who lives a sensous life of indiscipline is in any way reaching near the Truth. There are unintelligent and unprepared students who vociferously declare such a licentious life of freedom as a means for Realisation! They become *Maharṣī-s* and Sages to spread such ideas among the innocent masses of the world, they twist and pervert the already ugly face of the community. They are a real peril to the society. We have repeatedly warned, that this text-book is meant only for students, who have risen above in their spiritual pursuit, after having undergone all the unavoidable preliminary disciplines, which alone can bring about inner purifications.

अकर्तृत्वमभोक्तृत्वं स्वात्मनो मन्यते यदा ।
तदा क्षीणा भवन्त्येव समस्ताश्चित्तवृत्तयः ॥ ५१ ॥

Akartṛtvam-abhoktṛtvaṁ svātmano manyate yadā,
tadā kṣīṇā bhavan-tyeva samastāś-citta-vṛttayaḥ.

अकर्तृत्वम् *akartṛtvam* = that one is not the *doer*; अभोक्तृत्वम् *abhoktṛtvam* = that one is not the *enjoyer*; स्वात्मनः *svātmanaḥ* = of one's own Self; मन्यते *manyate* = perceives; यदा *yadā* = when; तदा *tadā* = then; क्षीणाः *kṣīṇāḥ* = destroyed; भवन्ति *bhavanti* = become; एव *eva* = indeed; समस्ताः *samastāḥ* = all; चित्त-वृत्तयः *citta-vṛttayaḥ* = modifications of the mind.

51. *All the modifications of the mind are indeed destroyed, when a man realises that the Self in him, is neither the doer nor the enjoyer.*

In the last stages of the spiritual practices, the attention is more and more upon the Self, rather than upon the equipments of experiences and their endless fields. To continuously contemplate upon the Self, as one's own Real Nature, and to meditate that as the Self, one is neither the *doer*, nor the *enjoyer*, in any of the activities of one's body, mind and intellect—is to quieten the mind most effectively. This attitude spells death to the ego.

This dwelling upon the Self and Its nature-divine is also, no doubt, "a thought." There is newly-risen 'school-of-thought' in India led by a gang of incorrigibles, rather than by men of any spiritual unfoldment. They have no knowledge of the *Upaniṣad*-s, nor have they lived the spiritual life. They laugh at all spiritual practices—nay, even at the attempt of the seeker to quieten his mind and compose himself for contemplation upon the Self! Their arguments are quite tantalising to any superficially intellectual man, indeed! But they are certainly false prophets when judged from the State of Realisation.

The thought "*I am the Self*" or the thought that "the Infinite Self is neither the *doer* nor the *enjoyer*" is indeed a "thought." But this "thought" has a magic of its own and it annihilates all other thoughts of the ego. It is the ego which arrogates to itself the false attitudes of the *doership* and the *enjoyership*. This "thought" when held on for a sufficiently long time within the meditator, it shall not only destroy all other thoughts, but also disappear itself into the Thoughtless State of direct-Experience. This is not said by us for gaining an argument. This is not something that the students of *Vedānta* should bitterly swallow down their throats in a helpless blind-faith! It is supremely rational and entirely satisfying to any enquiring intellect.

"Thought" upon the Self, dear children, is not, in fact, a "thought." A thought must have necessarily an object. The *thought of the Self* is a "thought" on the *subject* and therefore, it has no *object*. "Objectless-thought" *is not a thought*. And yet, for the last withering mind, contemplation upon the Self is an unavoidable staff—helping him along the last few steps to the Threshold of Reality.

When the sense of *doership* and *enjoyership* is completely eradicated, the ego disappears into the vision of the Self. The meditator merges in the meditated—the river has reached the ocean—there to be the ocean: no more can the river remain separate.

उच्छृङ्खलाप्यकृतिका स्थितिर्धीरस्य राजते ।
न तु संस्पृहचित्तस्य शान्तिर्मूढस्य कृत्रिमा ॥ ५२ ॥

Ucchṛṅkha-lāpya-kṛtikā sthitir-dhīrasya rājate,
na tu saṁspṛha-cittasya śāntir-mūḍhasya kṛtrimā.

उच्छृङ्खला *ucchṛṅkhalā* = unrestricted; अपि *api* = though; अकृतिका *akṛtikā* = spontaneous (natural); स्थितिः *sthitiḥ* = life; धीरस्य

dhīrasya = of the Wise; राजते *rājate* = shines; न *na* = not; तु *tu* = but; संस्पृह-चित्तस्य *saṁspṛha-cittasya* = whose mind is attached; शान्तिः *śāntiḥ* = calmness; मूढस्य *mūḍhasya* = of the foolish, deluded person; कृत्रिमा *kṛtrimā* = deliberate (unnatural, feigned).

52. *The conduct of the Wise-one, which is unrestricted (by motive) shines, being spontaneous, i.e. free from pretence; but not the deliberate calmness of the foolish, whose mind is attached (i.e. full of desires).*

The Liberated-one has in him no more any urge to fulfil his happiness through sense-gratifications. He has no desires. He lives a spontaneous and natural life, unrestricted and free, ever-rooted in the Experience-Divine and therefore, shines in the Effulgence of his inner Peace and Enlightenment.

Such a Man-of-Realisation is contrasted here with the ignorant fool, whose mind is full of passions and desires, and yet, for a show, he suppresses them all, and externally exhibits a false attitude of an artificial calmness! This deliberate and unnatural pose may deceive the onlookers, but as for as the individual entity is concerned, he cannot come to revel in the positive experience of the Peaceful Self. Pretences cannot lead us to the Kingdom of the Self within.

Such false pretences become terrible mile-stones tied to weigh down the neck of a seeker! No seeker should feel satisfied with such pretences. True Peace can come only in the direct experience of the Self, reached through right knowledge, with which we end our stupid ego.

विलसन्ति महाभोगैर्विशन्ति गिरिगह्वरान् ।
निरस्तकल्पना धीरा अबद्धा मुक्तबुद्धयः ॥ ५३ ॥

Vilasanti mahā-bhogair-viśanti giri-gahvarān,
nirasta-kalpanā dhīrā abaddhā mukta-buddhayaḥ.

विलसन्ति *vilasanti* = sport (कदाचित् *kadācit* = sometimes); महाभोगैः *mahā-bhogaiḥ* = with great enjoyments; विशन्ति *viśanti* = enter, retire, resort to (कदाचित् *kadācit* = sometimes); गिरि-गह्वरान् *giri-gahvarān* = caves of mountains; निरस्त-कल्पनाः *nirasta-kalpanāḥ*= one who is free from mental imagining; धीराः *dhīrāḥ* = the Wise; अबद्धाः *abaddhāḥ* = unbound; मुक्त-बुद्धयः *mukta-buddhayaḥ* = of liberated intellect.

53. *The Wise—who are free from mental imagining, unbound and liberated in intellect, sometimes sport in the midst of great enjoyments and at other times retire to the mountain-caves.*

In the entire chapter *Aṣṭāvakra* was continuously singing the joys and perfections experienced by the Liberated-in-life. Here he explains how the Man-of-Realisation would live in this world and what would be his reactions to the outer world.

Man-of-Perfection has eliminated his ego, has transcended his intellect and mind, and therefore, has ended all his imaginings. His mind is completely at rest because he has withdrawn from his mental projections. His intellect is released from the shackles of the ego. He is no more limited by desires. Thus his mind has scaled to its own heights, through contemplation—a mind that is unbound and unshackled by its usual restlessness.

With such a peaceful and conquered mind and intellect within, the Man-of-Perfection lives in the world like an uncrowned king, a Sovereign-of-sovereigns. He sometimes sports with all enjoyments and sometimes he is seen retired to the mountain-retreats, on the Ganges banks, and there lives lost in *Samādhi*.

It is immaterial to him where his body happens to be. Its *Prārabdha* may drag it into the world of sense-objects. From the ordinary view-point of the common-man, a Man-of-Realisation may be seen amidst luxurious environments, fascinatingly rich, and surrounded by objects of pleasure. But since his inner equipments are rendered impotent, and since his ego has been transcended, the outer joys of the sense-objects cannot add even a wee-bit to the Infinite Bliss of the Sage. The fields of sensuality never disturb him as he has neither the sense of doership nor enjoyership in him.

At times he may be found completely retired from the fields of activities and enjoyments, living in some silent cave in the *Himālayās*, maintaining himself on fruits and roots, apparently lost in total *Samādhi*. This is from our frail view-point! Whether his body is amidst sense-objects, or in a solitary cave, it is immaterial to the Liberated-in-life: he is ever the Self experiencing the Infinite Bliss of the Self, in the Self! To the Awakened it does not matter if his dream-world is still continuing, and how his dream-body is still functioning in the presence of the other members of his past dream!

श्रोत्रियं देवतां तीर्थमङ्गनां भूपतिं प्रियम् ।
दृष्ट्वा सम्पूज्य धीरस्य न कापि हृदि वासना ॥५४॥

Śrotriyaṁ devatāṁ tīrtham
aṅganām bhūpatiṁ priyam,
dṛṣṭvā sampūjya dhīrasya
na kāpi hṛdi vāsanā.

श्रोत्रियम् *śrotriyam* = one versed in the *Vedā-s*; देवताम् *devatām* = gods; तीर्थम् *tīrtham* = holy places; अङ्गनाम् *aṅganām* = woman; भूपतिम् *bhūpatim* = king; प्रियम् *priyam* = beloved one; दृष्ट्वा *dṛṣṭvā* = seeing; सम्पूज्य *sampūjya* = honouring; धीरस्य *dhīrasya* = of the Wise-one; न *na* = not; का अपि *kā api* = not a bit; हृदि *hṛdi* = in the heart; वासना *vāsanā* = desire.

54. *Whether he is honouring a Vedik scholar, the gods, or the holy places—or seeing a woman, a king or a beloved one, not a bit of desire ever springs in the heart of the Wise-one.*

It is natural in India that we honour a learned scholar of the *Vedā-s*, or worship gods in the various fabulous temples of India, or visit enchanting and peaceful places of pilgrimage. None of these activities can engender any desire in the Man-of-Perfection. Let him see a beautiful-woman, let him visit a mighty-monarch, let him meet a beloved-one—none of these contacts can precipitate any desire in him.

Transcending his own ego, he has come to experience the One Self everywhere, and thus, under all conditions, in all places in every contact, his attention is consistently engaged in experiencing the Infinite Bliss of the All-pervading Self. He becomes a man of "equal vision" (*Sama-dṛṣṭi*).

भृत्यैः पुत्रैः कलत्रैश्च दौहित्रैश्चापि गोत्रजैः ।
विहस्य धिक्कृतो योगी न याति विकृतिं मनाक् ॥५५॥

Bhṛtyaiḥ putraiḥ kalatraiśca dauhitraiścāpi gotrajaiḥ,
vihasya dhikkṛto yogī na yāti vikṛtiṁ manāk.

भृत्यैः *bhṛtyaiḥ* = by servants; पुत्रैः *putraiḥ* = by sons; कलत्रैः *kalatraiḥ* = by wives; च *ca* = and; दौहित्रैः *dauhitraiḥ* = by daughter's sons; च *ca* = and; अपि *api* = also; गोत्रजैः *gotrajaiḥ* = by relatives; विहस्य *vihasya* = ridiculing, scoffed; धिक्कृतः *dhikkṛtaḥ* = despised, abused; योगी *yogī* = the Realised-one; न *na* = not; याति *yāti* = undergoes; विकृतिम् *vikṛtim* = perturbation; मनाक् *manāk* = in the least.

55. *The Liberated is not at all perturbed even when scoffed and despised by his servants, sons, wives, daughter's sons and other relations.*

Insults and abuses wound but the ego. To the Wise-one both praises and abuses are sounds in the air expressing two different conditions of the speaker's mind! A happy mind makes pleasant sounds, called "sweet words"; and an unhappy mind makes cruel noices, called "abuses." Both are disturbances created in the atmosphere around the speaker's mouth! The Liberated-Man is not at all affected by them. Ordinarily the ego in us gets wounded by understanding the significance of what the other says, and then reacts, and invariably similar abuses disturb the *same* atmosphere, now springing from our mouth!

Once, we are told, *Bhagavān Buddhā* was abused and insulted in the market-place. Lord *Buddhā* stopped and listened to all the abuses—but his serene smile never left his lips. When the market-man was tired and stopped making noises, *Buddhā* majestically continued on His way. Now a young disciple, who was with the Master at that time, said: "Lord, give me the permission, I will go and show him ... I will give back to him!... How dare he abuse my Master?" Then ever-smiling *Buddhā* pitifully looked at the ignorant disciple, and sweetly replied: "Son, no doubt that man gave us a lot of abuses, but I did not receive them! Therefore, I have nothing to give back to him! In case you had received them, please go and give them back to him!!" This is called the perfect "state of intellectual-equanimity" (*Sama-buddhi*).

The one who has Realised the Self sees nothing but the Self-in-action everywhere. He has no ego in him, and therefore, he neither likes nor hates; to him honour and dis-honour are equal; he is neither attached, nor has he any aversion. Everywhere, at all times, and in everything, he watches and sees nothing but his own Self revelling in Its Peaceful Effulgence.

सन्तुष्टोऽपि न सन्तुष्टः खिन्नोपि न च खिद्यते ।
तस्याश्चर्यदशां तां तां तादृशा एव जानते ॥ ५६ ॥

Santuṣṭo'pi na santuṣṭaḥ khinnopi na ca khidyate,
tasyā-ścarya-daśāṁ tāṁ tāṁ tādṛśā eva jānate.

सन्तुष्टः *santuṣṭaḥ* = delighted; अपि *api* = though; न *na* = not; सन्तुष्टः *santuṣṭaḥ* = delighted; खिन्नः *khinnaḥ* = afflicted; अपि *api* = though; न *na* = not; च *ca* = and; खिद्यते *khidyate* = feels afflicted;

तस्य *tasya* = his; आश्चर्य-दशाम् *ascarya-daśām* = stupendous state; ताम् ताम् *tām tām* = that and that; तादृशा: *tādṛśāḥ* = those like him; एव *eva* = alone; जानते *jānate* = know.

56. *Though delighted, he is not delighted. Though afflicted, he is not afflicted. Only those who are like him, understand this Stupendous State.*

The one who lives in the Self, as the Self, has transcended his mind, and therefore, if the mind is pleased, he is not pleased. It is the mind that feels "afflicted," and why should he feel afflicted? The mind, the intellect and the body belong to us. We are their owners, possessors, properietors (*Śvāmin-s*). If my buffalo gets dysentery, do I run to the hospital? No doubt, the buffalo belongs to me! Possessor is not the possessed. The joys and afflictions of my body, of my intellect and of my mind cannot be joys and afflictions of me!

Wherever the Sage be, under all conditions, he lives the experience of the Effulgent Self. He has become the Self. This "Stupendous State" (*Āścarya-daśā*) cannot be described in words, or communicated in any other way to the ego-centric man. There is no language by which it can be expressed.

Only on transcending the mind and intellect do we awaken to the Self, and the experience of the Self is not known at all by those who are still in the web of the mind and intellect! Whatever the Sage does or does not—whatever we do or do not do to the Sage—it is all the same to the Sage; for, to him there is only the Infinite Consciousness everywhere. How can the pleasures and sorrows of the dream affect any more the one who has awakened?

कर्तव्यतैव संसारो न तां पश्यन्ति सूरयः ।
शून्याकारा निराकारा निर्विकारा निरामयाः ॥ ५७ ॥

Kartavya-taiva saṁsāro na tāṁ paśyanti sūrayaḥ,
śūnyā-kārā nirā-kārā nir-vikārā nirā-mayāḥ.

कर्तव्यता *kartavyatā* = sense of duty; एव *eva* = indeed; संसारः *saṁsāraḥ* = mundane world; न *na* = not; ताम् *tam* = that; पश्यन्ति *paśyanti* = sees; सूरयः *sūrayaḥ* = the Wise; शून्याकाराः *śūnyākārāḥ* = of the form of void (All-pervading); निराकाराः *nirākārāḥ* = formless; निर्विकाराः *nirvikārāḥ* = immutable; निरामयाः *nirāmayāḥ* = untainted.

57. *The sense-of-duty, indeed, is the mundane world. This is not acknowledged by the Wise-one, who has realised himself as the All-pervading formless, Immutable, Untainted Self.*

Of course I have a sacred duty to look after, protect, serve and help my wife and children, and also my community, that I see around me in my dream!

The *dream-I* while dreaming believes that the dream-world is real. In this, sense-of-Reality, are born all my duties and responsibilities. When I have awakened to the *waker-I*, what duties are there towards my dream-family and dream-community? The Wise-one, Liberated-in-life, is the Awakened-one. He has "awakened" to the Infinite Consciousness. He cannot be touched by the laws of duties and responsibilities projected and maintained by the mind-in-disturbance. No sense-of-duty can arise without attachments; attachments cannot be unless we permit a sense-of-reality to the world-of-plurality. To the awakened, the illusory world of objects and beings are no more and therefore, he, living as the "All-pervading, Formless, Immutable and untainted" Self, has no more any sense-of-duty towards anyone.

अकुर्वन्नपि संक्षोभात् व्यग्रः सर्वत्र मूढधीः ।
कुर्वन्नपि तु कृत्यानि कुशलो हि निराकुलः ॥ ५८ ॥

Akurvannapi saṁkṣobhāt vyagraḥ sarvatra mūḍhadhīḥ
kurvann-api tu kṛtyāni kuśalo hi nirākulaḥ.

अकुर्वन् *akurvan* = without doing anything, in inaction; अपि *api* = even; संक्षोभात् *saṁkṣobhāt* = owing to commotion within; व्यग्रः

vyagraḥ= agitated; सर्वत्र *sarvatra* = at all times; मूढधीः *mūḍhadhīḥ* = one of dull intellect, the fool; कुर्वन् *kurvan* = performing; अपि *api* = even; तु *tu* = but; कृत्यानि *kṛtyāni* = duties; कुशलः *kuśalaḥ* = the adept (Wise); हि *hi* = indeed; निराकुलः *nirākulaḥ* = unperturbed.

58. *The fool, even in 'inaction', is ever-agitated by his commotion within. But the adept (Wise) even when perfroming his duties, indeed, is unperturbed.*

Although in the previous verse it has been said that the Man-of-Perfection has no more duties to perform, it does not mean that a Perfect-Master will remain in life as a log of wood!! He serves the society in his own way, with utter freedom of his own personality. The difference between the activities of a Man-of-Perfection, and an imperfect ego, is in the conditions of their minds. The bosom of a fool, even while sitting apparently at rest in his meditation-seat, is in storms with the passion-promted commotions! His ego bleeds with its imaginations!

A Sage ever calm and serene within, with his ego sublimated, his mind revelling in the Self, undertakes mighty human programmes of moral rehabilitation of the entire humanity. Mighty programmes are launched, and they guide and lead such programmes as though it is an entertaining game and engaging sport, a mighty relaxation, a glorious holiday! In the serenity of their minds they generate a mightier dynamism, and thus, their actions become almost super-human, materially benefial, morally spectacular, spiritually a blessing!!

Bhagavad-Gītā (II-48) underscores this idea, when *Kṛṣṇa* laughs at Arjuna's pseudo-religion which makes him declare his unwillingness to enter the field of activity. In the crisp statement of *mantrik*-beauty *Kṛṣṇa* summarises his entire philosophy when he says:

समत्वं योग उच्यते ।

Samatvaṁ yoga ucyate.

"Evenness if mind is *Yoga*" i.e. Equanimity within is spiritual life.

The Lord of the *Bhagavad-Gītā* (in Ch. II-50) emphasises this idea, again, almost in the same breath, when He declares:

योगः कर्मसु कौशलम् ।

Yogaḥ karmasu kauśalam.

"*Yoga* is the dexterity in action" i.e. Efficiency and dexterity in action is spiritual life."

सुखमास्ते सुखं शेते सुखमायाति याति च ।
सुखं वक्ति सुखं भुङ्क्ते व्यवहारेऽपि शान्तधीः ॥ ५९ ॥

Sukham-āste sukhaṁ śete sukham-āyāti yāti ca,
sukhaṁ vakti sukhaṁ bhuṅkte vyavahāre-'pi śāntadhīḥ.

सुखम् *sukham* = happily; आस्ते *āste* = sits; सुखम् *sukham* = happily; शेते *śete* = sleeps; सुखम् *sukham* = happily; आयाति *āyāti* = comes; याति *yāti* = goes; च *ca* = and; सुखम् *sukham* = happily; वक्ति *vakti* = speaks; सुखम् *sukham* = happily; भुङ्क्ते *bhuṅkte* = eats (enjoys); व्यवहारे *vyavahāre* = in practical affairs of life; अपि *api* = even; शान्तधीः *śāntadhīḥ*. = of peaceful mind (the Wise-one).

59. *Even in practical affairs of life, the Wise-one, of peaceful mind, sits happily, sleeps happily, moves happily, speaks happily and eats happily.*

To the Saint the distinction between the inner Divine Experience and the outer wordly experiences merge in the All-comprehensive Infinite of the Experienced-Self. He is ever peaceful in his mind, and no disturbance ever reaches his bosom, because everywhere he recognises but the play of the One Self. Thus he is even-minded towards all beings and things, and his equanimity cannot be disturbed whatever be the circumstances.

The *Vāsanā*-inflicted sense of separative-ego (*Jīva*) in us is that which brings about all sense-of-conflicts in life. One who has risen above the ego has awakened to the Aloneness of the Self, wherein there is no distinction at all between *subject* and *object*.

The outer world of multiplicity, no doubt, apparently looks totally different from the *subjective* entity in the observer. Ordinarily we consider, these two factors as completely different from each other. In this unholy divorce between the *subject* and the *object*, we create for ourselves our conflicts within and the world-outside becomes for us a field of incorrigible challenges.

The face of a cow looks, certainly, different from the view of the same cow from its hind-part. Because a cow looks differently from the front and from the back, no sane one would say that the same cow is two different animals!! We cannot separate the front-part of the cow from its hind-part without destroying the cow! The *subject* and *object* are two aspects of the One Reality, which the Liberated-in-life, is continuously experiencing. Hence their minds are ever peaceful (*Śānta-dhīḥ*).

Having experienced this One Universal Reality, thereafter, without ego and ego-centric-desires, they allow themselves to come in contact with the world outside at all levels, ever-happy, under all circumstances! "The Wise-one sits happily, sleeps happily, moves happily, speaks happily and eats happily." Says *Bhagavad-Gītā* (IV-22):

यदृच्छालाभसन्तुष्ट ......।

Yad-ṛcchā-lābha-santuṣṭaḥ ....

He enjoys that "whatever comes to him unasked."

स्वभावाद्यस्य नैवार्तिर्लोकवद् व्यवहारिणः ।
महाह्रद इवाक्षोभ्यो गतक्लेशः सुशोभते ॥ ६० ॥

svabhāvād-yasya naivārtir-lokavad vyava-hāriṇaḥ,
mahāhṛda ivākṣobhyo gata-kleśaḥ suśobhate.

स्वभावात् एव *svabhāvāt eva* = by his inner disposition; यस्य *yasya* = whose; न *na* = not; आर्तिः *ārtiḥ* = distress; लोकवत् *lokavat* = like ordinary people; व्यवहारिणः *vyavahāriṇaḥ* = acting; महाहृदः *mahāhṛdaḥ* = vast lake; इव *iva*= like; अक्षोभ्यः *akṣobhyaḥ* = unagitated; गत-क्लेशः *gata-kleśaḥ* = with sorrows extinguished; सुशोभते *suśobhate* = shines.

60. One who, due to his inner disposition even when engaged in practical affairs of life does not have any distress like ordinary people, he remains unagitated, like a vast lake, with all his sorrows extinguished— he, indeed, shines.

The lakes of our minds are disturbed with thought-ripples mainly from two sources. The outer-objects can enter our bosom through our sense-openings and create disturbances therein. Again, even in the absence of outer-objects of temptations, the inner mind, through its own stored up memories of past experiences, and its fresh imaginations of future indulgences, can create storms within all by itself! In the case of one who has conquered himself and reached the State of Self-realisation, in him the ego and ego-centric desires are completely absent, and therefore, neither the outer world, nor his own subjective mind, can bring about any disturbance at all into the serene lake of his mind.

Such a Master has already transcended his mind-intellect equipment. He directly experiences the Tranquil Self at all times, under all circumstances. He has become an '*Ātmārāma.*' His mental disposition, thereafter, is to recognise and experience the Self everywhere. Hence he is ever unagitated. Even when he is engaged in the practical affairs of life, he is not disturbed at all in his constant experience of the life. Neither desires, nor ego, ever rises in his mind to disturb his bosom. He shines.... with the Glory of the Divine Self in him!

निवृत्तिरपि मूढस्य प्रवृत्तिरुपजायते ।
प्रवृत्तिरपि धीरस्य निवृत्तिफलभागिनी ॥ ६१ ॥

Nivṛttir-api mūḍhasya pravṛttir-upajāyate,
pravṛttir-api dhīrasya nivṛtti-phala-bhāginī.

निवृत्तिः *nivṛttiḥ* = withdrawal; अपि *api* = even; मूढस्य *mūḍhasya* = of the fool; प्रवृत्तिः *pravṛttiḥ* = action; उपजायते *upajāyate* = becomes; प्रवृत्तिः *pravṛttiḥ* = action; अपि *api* = even; धीरस्य *dhīrasya* = of the Wise-one; निवृत्ति-फल-भागिनी *nivṛtti-phala-bhāginī* = shares the fruits of withdrawal (in-action).

61. *With the fool, even withdrawal (inaction) becomes action. With the Wise, even action results in the fruit of withdrawal (in-action).*

Action and inaction—the dynamic-life of acquisition of wealth and the passive-life of renunciation of objects—both depend not merely upon the physical movements of the limbs or their indolent rest. They both depend upon the presence or the absence of ego and its desires. It is the sense of "*doership*" and "*enjoyership*" that makes actions full of agitations and restlessness. Once these false concepts are removed, the Man-of-Wisdom, transcending his ego and ego-centric desires, inspiredly works. Such spontaneous activities can provide for the Wise-man, the rewards of total-renunciation, and complete retirement. Self-withdrawal (*nivṛtti*) brings serenity of the mind; it is the outgoing tendencies of the mind (*Pravṛtti*) that breeds its restlessness.

A fool, who is ego-centric, even when he is withdrawing himself from all activities, in his quiet hut-of-meditation on the Ganges banks, feels mentally restless and unhappy. The Liberated-in-life even when he is in the midst of activities, serving the world and its humanity, is ever-serene and happy—nothing disturbs him, because he acts in the world from his seat in the Self!

परिग्रहेषु वैराग्यं प्रायो मूढस्य दृश्यते ।
देहे विगलिताशस्य क्व रागः क्व विरागता ॥ ६२ ॥

Parigraheṣu vairāgyaṁ prāyo mūḍhasya dṛśyate,
dehe vigalit-āśasya kva rāgaḥ kva virāgatā.

परिग्रहेषु *parigraheṣu* = in possessions; वैराग्यम् *vairāgyam* = aversion; प्राय: *prāyaḥ* = often; मूढस्य *mūḍhasya* = of the fool; दृश्यते *dṛśyate* = is seen; देहे *dehe* = in body; विगलित-आशस्य *vigalita-āśasya* = of one whose attachment has vanished; क्व *kva* = where; राग: *rāgaḥ* = attachment; क्व *kva* = where; विरागता *virāgatā* = aversion.

62. *The fool often shows aversion to his possessions. Where is attachment, and where is aversion for him whose love for the body has vanished?*

An ordinary man would like to get away from his field of activities and conflicts, if not every week-end, at least once a year on a long vacation. He gets tired of the struggles of acquisition; he gets exhausted by the continuous indulgence. Even in his moment to moment enjoyments also, say after eating two or three bars of chocolates, he shows aversion to eating more. This "desireless-ness" (*Vairāgya*) for the chocolate is after-all a temporary phase, and by evening he would like to have another bar; certainly by tomorrow, he will anxiously seek for some chocolates himself!

As long as we are identified with our physical body, we cannot really grow "desireless" towards objects that are conducive for the happiness of our physical body. This body-consciousness cultivates in us tremendous attachments, endless desires, vulgar passions and incorrigible lusts. Temporary "aversion and desireless-ness" (*Vairāgya*) is of no avail in the spiritual world.

As a contrast to such a foolish man, *Aṣṭāvakra* describes the attitude of the Liberated-in-life. His entire love for the body has vanished. To him the body has become a dry-leaf that has fallen away from him! To him, thereafter, there is neither attachment (*Rāga*), nor lust for the objects of the world. Nor has he any "aversion nor desireless-ness" (*Vairāgya*). He has neither *Rāgā*, nor *Vairāgya*. He rises above both of these attitudes of the mind. He has no identification with the body, and therefore, he is not aware of the objects-of pleasures at all.

भावनाभावनासक्ता दृष्टिर्मूढस्य सर्वदा ।
भाव्यभावनया सा तु स्वस्थस्यादृष्टिरूपिणी ॥ ६३ ॥

Bhāvanā-bhāvanā-saktā dṛṣṭir-mūḍhasya sarvadā,
bhāvya-bhāvanayā sā tu svasthasyā-dṛṣṭi-rūpiṇī.

भावना-अभावना-आसक्ता *bhāvanā-abhāvanā-āsaktā* = attached to ideation (thinking) and non-ideation (non-thinking); दृष्टिः *dṛṣṭiḥ* = view; मूढस्य *mūḍhasya* = of the fool or deluded one; सर्वदा *sarvadā* = always; भाव्य-भावनया *bhāvya-bhāvanayā* = engaged in the ideation of objects; सा *sā* = that; तु *tu* = but; स्वस्थस्य *svasthasya* = of one established in the Self; अदृष्टि-रूपिणी *adṛṣṭi-rūpiṇī* = of the nature of non-ideation.

63. *The view of the fool is always attached to ideation and non-ideation. But the view of one established in the Self, though engaged in the ideation of objects, is of the nature of non-ideation.*

It is the seeker, who is yet ignorant of the Supreme Experience, that must have the discipline of maintaining noble and divine thoughts in the mind, and must learn to eliminate all negative, agitation-producing thoughts of passions and lusts. It is an early seeker, who must withdraw his mind from the contemplation of body, mind and intellect, and turn his thoughts into a steady meditation upon the nature of the Self. The Seeker strives to reach a state of non-ideation by regulating, controlling and ending ultimately all his voluntary and involuntary ideations.

One who is established in the experience of the Self, to him even while "he is engaged in ideation of objects"—

even while thoughts are running fast and vigorous in his mind—he is enjoying the "state of non-ideation"—the State-of-Thoughtless-ness!

It is not a question of whether there are thoughts in the mind or not; the question is, whether we are ourselves identified with the thoughts in the mind. The Sage is one who has withdrawn his identifications, and therefore, the existence or non-existence of the thoughts is of no consequence to him! So long as I am standing on the beach, how can the waves of the ocean ever affect me?

We play the part of a fool not because the thoughts are rising in our minds, but because we identify with them so much that we totally come to forget the source from which the thought-ripples have risen up. The Man-of-Realisation is one, who even while observing the noisy thought-waves rising in his mind, is never totally unconscious of the "source" from which they arise. From the Infinite Consciousness, due to desire-stresses, thoughts 'wave-up'—these very thoughts are nothing but Consciousness expressed at the mental level. Hence *Aṣṭāvakra* points out that even during ideations, when once he is established in the Self, he is ever in a "State of non-ideation."

सर्वारम्भेषु निष्कामो यश्चरेद् बालवन्मुनिः ।
न लेपस्तस्य शुद्धस्य क्रियमाणेऽपि कर्मणि ॥ ६४ ॥

Sarvā-rambheṣu niṣkāmo yaś-cared bālavan-muniḥ,
na lepas-tasya śuddhasya kriyamāṇe-'pi karmaṇi.

सर्व-आरम्भेषु *sarva-ārambheṣu* = in all undertakings, or actions; निष्काम: *niṣkāmaḥ* = without desire or motive, unattached; (सन् *san* = being); य: मुनि: *yaḥ muniḥ* = the Wise-one who; चरेत् *caret* = moves; बालवत् *bālavat* = like a child; न *na* = not; लेप: *lepaḥ* = attachment, involvement; तस्य *tasya* = of whom; शुद्धस्य *śuddhasya* = pure; क्रियमाणे *kriyamāṇe* = which is being done; अपि *api* = even; कर्मणि *karmaṇi* = actions; (भवति *bhavati* = is).

64. *The Wise-one, who has no motive in all his actions, moves like a child, and is pure, has no attachments even in the action that is being done by him.*

One in whom the ego is no more, that individual cannot have the sense of "*doership*." A child is not accused when a disastrous tragedy is ultimately caused by the innocent activities of a child. There are instances where a child playing with a loaded-gun has killed one of its parents! Here the child is not accused of murder, because its action is not motivated. The Sage is one in whom there is neither an ego, nor any selfish desire. Therefore his actions are considered as always innocent. Hence a Sage-in-action is readily compared here with a child-at-play.

It is the ego and its selfish motives that entangle us in the world outside. These unhealthy involvements breed all the sorrows in every field of activity. A Man-of-Realisation acts inspiredly in any field of endeavour, that comes to him as his lot, without ever getting himself shackled by the duties attached to it. To him, all activities become an engaging sport—a joyous relaxation—an entertaining play.

This expressive phrase *Sarvārambha* (सर्वारम्भ) reminds us of its affective use in the *Bhagavad-Gītā* (XII-16):

....

सर्वारम्भपरित्यगी यो मद्भक्तः स मे प्रियः ।

....

Sarva-ārambha-parityagī yo mad-bhaktaḥ sa me priyaḥ.

"Renouncing all undertakings (or commencements) he who is (thus) devoted to me, is dear to Me.".

....

सर्वारम्भपरित्यागी गुणातीतः स उच्यते ।

(*Bhagavad Gītā,* XIV-25)

....

Sarva-ārambha-parityāgī guṇātītaḥ sa ucyate.

"Abandoning all undertakings, he is said to have crossed beyond the *Guṇā-s*."

....

सर्वारम्भा हि दोषेण धूमेनाग्निरिवावृताः ।

(Bhagavad Gītā, XVIII-48*)*

....

Sarva-ārambhā hi doṣeṇa dhūmena-agnir-iva-āvṛtāḥ.

".... For, all undertakings are enveloped by evil, as fire by smoke."

According to Lord *Kṛṣṇa,* the idea is not that the Man-of-Perfection will not undertake any work, but in all undertakings he has no vanity of "*doership*" Hence a man of devotion and knowledge is described by the Lord, "as one who has renounced completely all undertakings" (*Sarva-ārmbha-parityāgī*).

स एव धन्य आत्मज्ञः सर्वभावेषु यः समः ।
पश्यन् शृण्वन् स्पृशन् जिघ्रन्नश्नन्निस्तर्षमानसः ॥ ६५ ॥

Sa eva dhanya ātmajñaḥ
sarva-bhāveṣu yaḥ samaḥ,
paśyan śṛṇvan spṛśan jighrann
aśnan-nistarṣa-mānasaḥ.

स *sa* = that; एव *eva* = indeed; धन्यः *dhanyaḥ* = blessed; आत्मज्ञः *ātmajñaḥ* = knower of the Self; सर्वभावेषु *sarva-bhāveṣu* = in all conditions; यः *yaḥ* = who; समः *samaḥ* = the same; पश्यन् *paśyan* = seeing; शृण्वन् *śṛṇvan* = hearing; स्पृशन् *spṛśan* = touching; जिघ्रन् *jighran* = smelling; अश्नन् *aśnan* = eating; निस्तर्ष-मानसः *nistarṣa-mānasaḥ* = whose mind is free from thirst (desire).

65. *Blessed indeed is that Knower of the Self, who, with his mind free from thirst, even though seeing, hearing, touching, smelling or eating, remains the same under all conditions.*

In the fields of activities it is inconceivable for us how an individual can continuously maintain his equanimity without being troubled by the endless tossings that the world should necessarily provide even to a Man-of-Wisdom. Here, *Aṣṭāvakra*, explains the secret by which the Man-of-Perfection maintains his unbroken serenity under all conditions, in the outer world.

The secret lies in the special orientation that he has brought about in his mental-field. He has removed from his mind all thirst—all its craving for sense-gratifications. Once the mind is de-hypnotised of its hunger to seek fulfilment in sense-objects, that dispassionate mind becomes completely neutral to the empty charms in the world of happenings around him. Not that the Man-of-Realisation runs away from the world of sense-objects. He lives fully, freely.

The world around us is a gift of the Lord. Our delicate sense-organs are a grace of the almighty. A Man-of-Realisation would not dare to insult the Lord of the Universe either by destroying the instruments-of-Perception, or by rejecting the sense-objects. "Seeing, hearing, touching, smelling, and eating," he shows his gratitude to the Creator of the Universe, and honours Him by accepting His invitations to this feast of delusion, in his stupendous fairs of illusion!

He is a free soul, free to live in the world, absolutely uninhibited, without tensions and conflicts, apparently indulging. But the world of sense-objects cannot entangle him. He sees the world as great entertainment by a fabulous magician! Even while looking at them, he perceives but the Supreme Reality behind. He lives life in a ceaseless mood of breathless wonderments, but never, ever a victim of its hallucinations!

क्व संसारः क्व चाभासः क्व साध्यं क्व च साधनम् ।
आकाशस्येव धीरस्य निर्विकल्पस्य सर्वदा ॥ ६६ ॥

Kva saṁsāraḥ kva cā-bhāsaḥ
kva sādhyaṁ kva ca sādhanam
ākāśasyeva dhīrasya
nir-vikalpasya sarvadā.

क्व *kva* = where; संसारः *saṁsāraḥ* = world; क्व *kva* = where; च *ca* = indeed; आभासः *ābhāsaḥ* = ego (appearance); क्व *kva* = where; साध्यम् *sādhyam* = end (goal i.e. liberation); क्व *kva* = where; च *ca* = and; साधनम् *sādhanam* = means (path i.e. spiritual practices); आकाशस्य एव *ākāśasya eva* = like the universal space; धीरस्य *dhīrasya* = of the Wise-one; निर्विकल्पस्य *nir-vikalpasya* = changeless; सर्वदा *sarvadā* = always.

66. *Where is the world and where is its ego, where is the end and where are the means—for the Wise-one, who is ever-changeless like the universal space?*

We must here, again repeat, the warning that we have been giving all through this text. Early seekers should not quote these verses and their basis drop their practices! These are intended for One who has already achieved his Goal—who has fulfilled his life—who has awakened to the Pure Infinite Self. These verses are not addressed to the early seekers. These are addressed to a *Janaka*-like student, who is on the outermost verges of the finitude, yet hesitating to step into the Realm of the Infinite.

To the Man-of-Perfection, who has already realised the Self, there is for him nothing but the Self. To him there is no world-of-*objects*, nor is there in him an *experiencer* of the world, the ego. He has already achieved the Goal, and therefore, he has no more any Goal to gain, no more an end to achieve. What 'path' should he follow, or what 'means' he must adopt? And for what? The Man-of-Realisation is ever in the Infinite, wherein he has become Changeless, All-pervading like the Universal Space. He has ended all his limitations. The pot has broken and the pot-space has become one with the eternal universal space!

The wave has merged in the ocean. The pot has been crushed and has become the mud. The dreamer has awakened.

The Liberated-in-life is the Supreme Self-in-action.

Man-hood has ended in sheer God-hood.

स जयत्यर्थसंन्यासी पूर्णस्वरसविग्रहः ।
अकृत्रिमोऽनवच्छिन्ने समाधिर्यस्य वर्तते ॥ ६७ ॥

Sa jayaty-artha-saṁnyāsī pūrṇa-svarasa-vigrahḥ,
akṛtrimo-'navacchinne samādhir-yasya vartate.

सः *saḥ* = he; जयति *jayati* = cry hallelujah; अर्थ-संन्यासी *artha-saṁnyāsī* = who has renounced all desires; पूर्ण-स्वरस-विग्रहः *pūrṇa-svarasa-vigrah* = who is the perfect embodiment of all Bliss, which is his own nature; अकृत्रिमः *akṛtrimaḥ* = spontaneous; अनवच्छिन्ने *anavacchinne* = in the unlimited; समाधिः *samādhiḥ* = absorption; यस्य *yasya* = whose; वर्तते *vartate* = is.

67. *Hallelujah to him who has renounced all desires, who is the embodiment of Perfect Bliss, which is his own nature, and who is spontaneously absorbed in the unlimited space.*

Even the serene tranquillity of the revered Sage *Aṣṭāvakra* seems to heave up into emotions of adoration and love. To that individual man, who has successfully broken the shackles of his delusion and has merged to be the Infinite Self, he crises *Jai-jai.* Hallelujah, to the victorious person who has freed himself from his ego-shackles, to experience his Immutable, Divine Glory, as the boundless Substratum for the whole universe!

The Liberated-in-life having renounced all the desires in him has now come to experience himself as the "embodiment of Perfect Bliss which is his own nature" (*Pūrṇa-svarasa-vigrahaḥ*). Here this term used by *Aṣṭāvakra* is one of the precious jem-like phrases that has unconsciously, crystallised in the Sage's mind during his contemplation upon the theme of his glorious Song. Many such enchanting phrases of fabulous significance have been minted and sent out into circulation by the Sage in this *Saṁhitā.* The phrase evidently screams the *Advaitik* realisation, wherein the meditator is not separate from the meditated: wherein the subject has merged in the object-of-contemplation: wherein the river has reached the ocean!

This merger of the individuality with the universal Reality is effortless—is spontaneous. This great awakening into the Spiritual Experience is automatic and natural. There is no strain or struggle in it. All efforts are in ending the ego, in weaning the mind away from its fascination for sense-objects. *Śaṅkara* expresses the spontaneity and effortless-ness of the final stage of Self-Realisation in his *Vivekacūḍāmaṇi* (V-533):

देवदत्तोऽहमित्येतद् विज्ञानं निरपेक्षकम् ।
तद्वद् ब्रह्मविदोऽप्यस्य ब्रह्माहमिति वेदनम् ॥

Devadatto'hamity-etad vijñānaṁ nir-apekṣakam,
tadvad brahma-vido-'pyasya brahmāham-iti vedanam.

"The clear knowledge 'I am *Devadatta*' is independent of everything; similar is the case with the realisation in the Knower-of-*Brahman* that 'I am *Brahman*'."

बहुनात्र किमुक्तेन ज्ञाततत्त्वो महाशयः ।
भोगमोक्षनिराकाङ्क्षी सदा सर्वत्र नीरसः ॥ ६८ ॥

Bahunātra kim-uktena jñāta-tattvo mahā-śayaḥ,
bhoga-mokṣa-nirā-kāṅkṣī sadā sarvatra nīrasaḥ.

बहुना *bahunā* = much; अत्र *atra* = here; किम् *kim* = what use? उक्तेन *uktena* = by saying; ज्ञाततत्त्वः *jñāta-tattvaḥ* = who has realised the Truth; महाशयः *mahāśayaḥ* = the great-souled one; भोग-मोक्ष-निराकांक्षी *bhoga-mokṣa-nirākāṅkṣī* = free from the desire of enjoyment and liberation; सदा *sadā* = at all times; सर्वत्र *sarvatra* = in all places; नीरसः *nīrasaḥ* = devoid of passions (is).

68. *In short, here there is no need to say more. The great souled-one, who has realised the Truth, is free from desire for sense-enjoyments and for spiritual liberation. He is devoid of all passions, in all places, and at all times.*

On summarising what has been said so far, in this chapter, the Sage is evidently feeling that he has not completely expressed what he wants to. In this verse he is, in a way, summarising his thoughts. All great Masters have followed this very same method. Even the *Vedā-s* despair in her inability to communicate the State of Perfection, and she has to satisfy herself by merely indicating the Goal which is beyond all expressions.

"In short, here there is no need to say more" meaning, that for those who have purified their inner-equipment, what has been said so far is more than sufficient. And to others, any amount of such discussions will not bring even a glimmer of understanding. The Great Teacher means that if *Janaka* has been restless enough in his mind, and thus has *not realised the Self* even after listening to what has been said so far, then it is useless for the Master to keep on disturbing the student's mind!

This is not an expression of the teacher's despair at the brilliant student *Janaka*, but an open confession that language is utterly imcompetent to communicate this knowledge. The intellect of the listener is no vessel to receive what the teacher wants to give. The student has to transcend his individuality, and come to be awake to the State of Pure Consciousness, all by himself.

In this great flight across the frontiers of the limited, the meditator is not allowed to smuggle anything through the barriers of Consciousness. Even the noblest aspirations have to be renounced. All *mantrā-s* and prayers, all devotions and *Yoga*, all meditations and even "the anxiety to realise the Truth" (*Mumukṣutva*), is not allowed to be smuggled into the Supreme State of Consciousness.

The Liberated-in-life is free from desires—both for the sense-enjoyments and for spiritual liberation. He is indeed devoid of all passions—at all times, under all circumstances. Passions and desires are the attributes of the ego. One who has transcended the mind and intellect (*Mahāśayaḥ*), to him where are these outgoing tendencies—which are essentially of the nature of the mind? He has already transcended his mind!

महदादि जगद्द्वैतं नाममात्रविजृम्भितम् ।
विहाय शुद्धबोधस्य किं कृत्यमवशिष्यते ॥ ६९ ॥

Mahad-ādi jagad-dvaitaṁ nāma-mātra-vijṛmbhitam,
vihāya śuddha-bodhasya kiṁ kṛtyama-vaśiṣyate.

महदादि *mahad-ādi* = beginning with *Mahat* (total intellect); जगद् द्वैतम् *jagad dvaitam* = the pluralistic world; नाम-मात्र-विजृम्भितम् *nāma-mātra-vijṛmbhitam* = manifested merely by name; विहाय *vihāya* = renouncing; शुद्ध-बोधस्य *śuddha-bodhasya* = of one who is Pure Consciousness; किम् *kim* = what; कृत्यम् *kṛtyam* = to be done; अवशिष्यते *avaśiṣyate* = remains.

69. *What remains to be done by one who is Pure Consciousness? He has renounced the pluralistic world, which begins with Mahat (total intellect) and is manifested merely by names.*

The entire phenomenal world-of-plurality is the expression of the "macro-cosmic-intellect" indicated in the *Sāṅkhayan* philosophy as *Mahat*. According to them *Prakṛti* is the material-*cause* from which evolves the *Mahat*. From *Mahat* in logical steps evolves the sense-of-ego (*Ahaṅkāra*), mind (*Mana*), the five organs-of-perception (*jñāna-Indriyā-s*) and the five organs-of-action (*Karma-indriyā-s*), the five 'subtle'-elements (*Tanmātrā-s*), the five 'gross'–elements (*Mahā-bhūtā-s*)—by the combinations of which, in different proportions, the world-of-plurality manifests. When out of gold, the gold-smith beats out a bar, pulls wires, cuts it into bits, hammers them into tiny rings and makes them into a chain, the ornament so made is to be nothing but gold! The bar, the wire, the bits, the rings and the chain are all merely 'names'; they are all, in essence, nothing but gold itself. Phenomenal world-of-plurality is nothing but the expressions of the *Prakṛti*—all the rest is nothing but mere distinctions in names.

It is the "ego" in us, the *subject*, that experiences, through the mind and the sense-organs, the perceptions of the world-of-multiplicity expressed as obejcts, emotions and thoughts. The Liberated-in-life is one who has transcended his ego and has awakened to the Infinitude of the Self. From this standpoint therefore, where is the world for him? Then what duties can bind him to the world? There is nothing to be done by him—there is nothing for him to achieve!

In this Supreme State of Fulfilment—experienced when, as the Self, he has already done all that is to be done—the Man-of-Perfection has nothing more to achieve in the world of names-and-forms. Even though it was the very day that my daughter was to be given away in marriage, if I wake up, have I any more duties towards my daughter and the arrangements already made for her marriage in my last night's dream? What duty have I towards my dream-family?

The verse does not mean that there is no duty for a *Sādhaka* towards the world around him. This is meant for those who are no more seeing the phenomenal-world—those who are revelling in the experience of the Self.

In this context, we are reminded of the famous description of *Mahopaniṣad* (V-72) wherein the *Ṛṣi* explains to us how such a Man-of-Wisdom views the phenomenal-world:

अशङ्किताऽपि संप्राप्ता ग्रामयात्रा यथाऽध्वगैः ।
प्रेक्ष्यते तद्वदेव ज्ञैर्भोगश्रीरवलोक्यते ॥

Aśaṅkitā'pi samprāptā grāma-yātrā yathā-'dhavagaiḥ,
prekṣyate tadvad-eva jñair-bhogaśrīr-avalokyate

"Just as the villagers watch a team of tourists passing through the village-street, so does the Wise-man watch the daily parade of the world in front of him!!"

The villagers, certainly, see the pilgrims (or the tourists) who are passing through the village, but the residents of the village are not at all affected by what they see—except that they are entertained by the crowd that is pasing by!! The Liberated-in-life with perfect detachment watches the parade of the world that marches in front of his awareness!!

भ्रमभूतमिदं सर्वं किञ्चिन्नास्तीति निश्चयी ।
अलक्ष्यस्फुरणः शुद्धः स्वभावेनैव शाम्यति ॥ ७० ॥

Bhrama-būtam-idaṁ sarvaṁ kiñcin-nāstīti niścayī,
alakṣya-sphuraṇaḥ śuddhaḥ svabhāve-naiva śāmyati.

भ्रम-भूतम् *bhrama-būtam* = produced by illusion; इदम् *idam* = this; सर्वम् *sarvam* = all; किञ्चित् *kiñcit* = anything; न *na* = not; अस्ति *asti* = exists इति *iti* = thus; निश्चयी *niścayī* = knowing with certitude; अलक्ष्य-स्फुरणः *alakṣya-sphuraṇaḥ* = to whom the Imperceptible is revealed; शुद्धः *śuddhaḥ* = the Pure One; स्वभावेन् *svabhāven* = naturally; एव *eva* = indeed; शाम्यति *śāmyati* = becomes tranquil.

70. *The Pure One knows with certitude that this universe is the product of illusion, and that nothing really exists. The Imperceptible Self is revealed to him and he, naturally, becomes tranquil.*

After the direct experience of the Self, there cannot be even a trace of doubt, because he has actually woken up. Such a Wise-man continuously experiences the Effulgent Self.

Here, the experiences does not mean that the Self is an 'object' of the experiences. The Infinite Consciousness is the *Absolute Subject*—It can never be an object. Objects can only be perceived by the body, mind or the intellect. *Aṣṭāvakra* in order to point out that the *Self is the final and only Subject*, uses the adjective "The Imperishable Self." The Knowledge of the Self is not emerging out of the activities of the sense-organs, mind or the intellect. In Self-realisation, the process is unique inasmuch as it is gained when "the ego disappears into the vision of the Reality."

With this realisation the individual becomes Pure—Completely free from his ignorance-of-Reality. It is this 'ignorance' that precipitates the inner-equipments and the ego. It is the ego that crystallise the required physical body and projects the appropriate world-of-objects through its imaginations in order to experience among them its chosen joys and sorrows! The Self-Realised Sage is one who has ended the "non-apprehensions of Reality" (*ignorance*) in the direct experience of the 'Imperceptible.'

Aṣṭāvakra concludes "naturally he becomes tranquil." In the Self, revelling as the Self, what disturbance can reach the Divine? All disturbances arise from either the body, or the mind, or the intellect—transcending these equipments the Sage revels in the Blissful Self.

शुद्धस्फुरणरूपस्य दृश्यभावमपश्यतः ।
क्व विधिः क्व च वैराग्यं क्व त्यागः क्व शमोऽपि वा ॥७१॥

Śuddha-sphuraṇa-rūpasya
dṛśya-bhāvam-apaśyataḥ,
kva vidhiḥ kva ca vairāgyaṁ
kva tyāgaḥ kva śamo'pi vā.

शुद्ध-स्फुरण-रूपस्य *śuddha-sphuraṇa-rūpasya* = of the nature of Pure Effulgence; दृश्य-भावम् *dṛśya-bhāvam* = the phenomenal world; अपश्यतः *apaśyataḥ* = not seeing; क्व *kva* = where; विधिः *vidhiḥ* = the rules of life (conduct); क्व *kva* = where; च *ca* = and; वैराग्यम् *vairāgyam* = dispassion; क्व *kva* = where; त्यागः *tyāgaḥ* = renunciation, relinquishment; क्व *kva* = where; शमः *śamaḥ* = control of the mind; अपि *api* = also; वा *vā* = or.

71. *Rules of life, dispassion, relinquishment, control of the mind—what are all these to one who is of the Nature of Pure Effulgence, and who does not perceive the phenomenal-world at all.*

Medicines, strict diet, confinement to bed; a nurse to attend, bed-pan in the bed—what are these for one who has come out of the hospital and is living a normal healthy, social life? The limited-ego—suffering from its "*ignorance*," entangled by the fascination of the world around him, chained and shackled by his emotions and passions, tossed about by his own mental agitations—to such a suffering ego-centric man, in his delirium, the *Upaniṣad*-s prescribe retirement, quietude, contemplation, self-control and rules of righteous conduct and the disciplines of moral and ethical living.

But to one who has awakened to the Nature of the Pure Infinite Consciousness, wherein he, as the Self, cannot-perceive any world-of-phenomena, to such a Man of complete Self-realisation there cannot be any rules of conduct. His actions are spontaneous and divine and they are what constitute the very "standard"—which are declared by the scriptures of the world as *Dharma* or righteousness. His conduct is *Dharma*; he is not following *Dharma*. Men-of-Realisation prescribe *Dharma* with their life, by their conduct; we, seekers of Perfection must implicity abide and follow the pattern-of-life and the standard-of-living that such Masters have demonstrated in their life.

Aṣṭāvakra is dissecting the nature of the Man-of-Perfection, for the education of a brilliant spiritual student, who is on the seat of his meditation—the Royal-Saint *Janaka*. To misunderstand its import and to wrongly apply this verse in life would be suicidal to the spiritual life of any seeker. You are warned!!

स्फुरतोऽनन्तरूपेण प्रकृतिं च न पश्यतः ।
क्व बन्धः क्व च वा मोक्षः क्व हर्ष क्व विषादिता ॥७२ ॥

Sphurato-'nanta-rūpeṇa,
prakṛtiṁ ca na paśyataḥ.,
kva bandhaḥ kva ca vā mokṣaḥ
kva harṣa kva viṣāditā.

स्फुरत: *sphurataḥ* = shining; अनन्त-रूपेण *ananta-rūpeṇa* = in endless forms; प्रकृतिम् *prakṛtim* = nature (relative existence); च *ca* = and; न पश्यत: *na paśyataḥ* = one who is not seeing the pluralistic world; क्व *kva* = where; बन्ध: *bandhaḥ* = bondage; क्व *kva* = where; च *ca* = and; वा *vā* = or; मोक्ष: *mokṣaḥ* = liberation; क्व *kva* = where; हर्ष: *harṣaḥ* = joy; क्व *kva* = where; विषादिता *viṣāditā* = sorrow.

72. *Where is bondage? Where is liberation? Where is joy? Where is sorrow?.... for one who does not perceive Nature—the relative existence—but sees only the Self shining in endless forms.*

The individualised subjective-ego (*Jīva*) looking out, through its *Vasanā*-layers, sees the delusory world of names-and-forms, and deliberately divides the world as things that it likes, and things that it dislikes. To this deluded-ego, there is nothing but the world of names-and-forms, which is real, substantial, true. To the ego there is nothing greater, nobler, diviner, more eternal. As a limited-self, certainly, the ego comes to feel its sense of limitation, and therefore it complains of its bondages. It is the ego that grows anxious to liberate itself from the entanglements of its own sorrows! The ego, in its identification with the body, is happy or unhappy, and it suffers in a self-created life of joy and sorrow.

The Sage who has risen above the ego, and has, therefore transcended his intellect and awakened to the Self, from his Divine State, sees no plurality at all. He is the one, who is Liberated-in-life. Such a Sage, even when his mind interprets to him the phenomenal-world of names-and-forms, from his deep inner experience, realises that the apparent illusion of plurality in front of him, are all nothing but the Consciousness Itself playing in different forms.

To one who has the knowledge of the nature of the ocean, can the waves and the bubbles be separate from it? To one who has the wisdom of gold, can the gold-ornaments, irrespective of its shape and beauty, be anything really different from gold? On awakening from the dream, could the dream that we saw before, anything different from our own mind? To the awakened Man-of-Perfection even when he views the world-of-plurality, can he ever forget the essential Truth, that shimmers in and through the names-and forms.

Joys and sorrows are the ultimate result of '*ignorance.*' On the '*non-apprehension* of Reality' we take the '*mis-apprehensions*' to be Real, and in this lies the essence of bondage. Says *Śaṅkara* in the *Vivekacūḍāmaṇi* (V-139):

> अत्रानात्मन्यहमिति मतिर्बन्ध ....।
>
> *Atrāna-atmany-aham-iti matir-bandha....... .*
>
> "To identify the Self with the not-self—this is bondage of man."

बुद्धिपर्यन्तसंसारे मायामात्रं विवर्तते ।
निर्ममो निरहङ्कारो निष्कामः शोभते बुधः ॥ ७३ ॥

Buddhi-paryanta-saṁsāre māyā-mātraṁ vivartate,
nirmamo nir-ahaṅkāro niṣkāmaḥ śobhate budhaḥ.

बुद्धि-पर्यन्त-संसारे *buddhi-paryanta-saṁsāre* = in the phenomenal world, which lasts until Self-knowledge; माया-मात्रम् *māyā-mātram* = mere illusion; विवर्तते *vivartate* = prevails; निर्ममः *nirmamaḥ* = devoid of 'mine-ness'; निरहङ्कारः *nir-ahaṅkāraḥ* = devoid of 'I-ness'; निष्कामः *niṣkāmaḥ* = free from passions, attachments; शोभते *śobhate* = excels; बुधः *budhaḥ* = the Wise-one.

73. *The illusion of this phenomental-world prevails until Self-knowledge. The Wise-one lives devoid of 'I-ness,' devoid of 'mine-ness,' and free from passions.*

According to the "categories" of *Vedānta* (*Prakṛyā*), the *apprehension* of Reality alone can destroy all *mis-apprehensions*. Hence we have translated "the phenomenal-world which lasts until Self-knowledge" (*Buddhir-paryanta-saṁsāre*). But the subtle intellect of *Janaka* must have grasped the delicate import when Sage *Aṣṭāvakra* had deliberately used the term *Buddhi* (Intelligence) in his phrase. The illusion of *Saṁsāra* can end permanently only with the direct-perception of Reality; an illusion can exist in our mind only so long as we are not prepared to look at it intelligently. To re-view the world-of-plurality with a sharp, steady, discriminative intellect is to recognise the illusory nature of the world-of-objects that we now, so readily, take for granted.

Even physically the world of names-and-forms is almost conclusively proved by physics and chemistry as having no basis at all, at least, in the laboratory! Chemistry reduces all the names and forms into energy. Physics declares to me that all that I perceive are ordered by, governed by the relativity of time and space. Thus, in the presence of intelligent observation, *Saṁsāra* can never stand. It persists in our stupidity, and it is nurtured and nourished only by our idle imaginations. The acceptance of this illusory world-of-plurality, and the consequent sorrows and suffering in it, are all true until the student diligently investigates it.

On enquiry it becomes easily clear that it is the ego-sense in us which perceives the phenomenal world. The ego-sense in us is the "perceiver" of the world-illusion, and the ego-feeling in us is our sense-of-possession in the world. In short, the ego-sense, as the perceiver accepts the illusion of names-and-forms are true and the ego-feeling clings to the illusion with its possessiveness. He who has transcended this ego has transcended both, his ego-sense and his ego-feeling.

Where the subject is no more, the world-of-objects perceived by him, rolls away, curls up and disappears! In the Perfect Master the ego has been removed entirely, permanently, by its very roots—the ego, which stems up from passions. Indeed, such a Sage, established in his Self-realisation, excels not only among the humanity, but even among the gods! He has become the very substratum for the 'Creator,' the 'created world,' and the 'individual ego' that have mysteriously sprung up during the state of delusion—from the One Immutable Self.

अक्षयं गतसन्तापमात्मानं पश्यतो मुनेः ।
क्व विद्या च क्व वा विश्वं क्व देहोऽहं ममेति वा ॥७४॥

Akṣayaṁ gata-santāpam-ātmānaṁ paśyato muneḥ,
kva vidyā ca kva vā viśvaṁ kva deho'haṁ mameti vā.

अक्षयम् *akṣayam* = Imperishable; गत-सन्तापम् *gata-santāpam* = free from grief; आत्मानम् *ātmānam* = Self; पश्यतः *paśyataḥ* = seeing; मुनेः *muneḥ* = to the Wise-one; क्व *kva* = where; विद्या *vidyā* = knowledge; च *ca* = and; क्व *kva* = where; वा *vā* = or; विश्वम् *viśvam* = universe; क्व *kva* = where; अहम् देहः *Aham dehaḥ* = I am the body; मम (देहः) *mama (dehaḥ)* = mine is the body; इति *iti* = thus; वा *vā* = or;

74. *To the Wise-one who perceives the Self as both Imperishable and free-from-grief, where is knowledge, and where is the universe? Where is the feeling 'body am I', or the feeling 'mine is the body.'*

Continuing to paint the picture of Man-of-Perfection for the edification of the great student, the Royal Saint *Janaka*, again and again, Sage *Aṣṭāvakra*, grows more and more eloquent, as though he is honestly feeling that, inspite of his brilliant exposition he has not communicated even a vague picture of the inner experience of the Liberated-one!

To misunderstand '*I am the body*' is the very seed from which breeds all confusions of the mind. the destinies of the body thereafter become the destinies of the individual because of his extreme identification with his body. Such a sense of "possessiveness" (*mine-ness*) comes towards all things related to the comfort and happiness of the body. Thus the mistaken identity that my body is myself sets me into a false relationship with the world around me. In this web of delusory values the individual suffers—and this is called *Saṁsāra.*

The Sage who has risen above the ego, and realised that the Self in him is Imperishable and Free-from-grief, how can there be in him any more anxiety to know anything? He alone is. All knowledges are "objects" of his awareness. He, as the Self, illumines all intellectual conclusions, called 'Knowledges.' Having realised the Self there is nothing more to know. This question of *Aṣṭāvakra* here, echoes the question with which the student approached the Master in the *Muṇḍak*a *Upaniṣad* (I-i-3):

....

कस्मिन्नु भगवो विज्ञाते सर्वमिदं विज्ञातं भवतीति ॥

....

Kasminnu bhagavo vijñāte sarvam-idaṁ vijñātaṁ bhavatīti.

"Sire what is that Knowledge by knowing which all other knowledges become known?"

The Self is "Knowledge-of-all-knowledges" inasmuch as It is in the Light of Consciousness, by which, all conclusions, arrived at by the rational intellect are awared by us.

We must come to know the greater Reality only when we are perceiving the unreal world of names-and-forms. To the one who has awakened to the Real, how can there be for him the perception of the unreal? To him where is the Universe?

निरोधादीनि कर्माणि जहाति जडधीर्यदि ।
मनोरथान् प्रलापांश्च कर्तुमाप्नोत्यतत् क्षणात् ॥ ७५ ॥

Nirodhādīni karmāṇi jahāti jaḍa-dhīr-yadi,
manorathān pralāpāṁś-ca kartum-āpnotyatat kṣaṇāt.

निरोध-आदीनि *nirodha-ādīni* = control etc.; कर्माणि *karmāṇi* = practices; जहाति *jahāti* = leaves; जड-धीः *jaḍa-dhīḥ* = one of dull intellect; यदि *yadi* = if; मनोरथान् *manorathān* = desires; प्रलापान्

pralāpān = fancies; च *ca* = and; कर्तुम् *kartum* = to do; अप्नोति *āpnoti* = begins, arrives at; अतत् क्षणात् *atat kṣaṇāt* = from that very moment.

75. *No sooner does a man of dull intellect give up the practices of mental control, than he becomes a prey to desires and fancies, from that very moment.*

Here is a verse through which *Aṣṭāvakra* talks to the unprepared students, encouraging them to continue their *Sādhanā*, while at the same time the Sage has a subtle message in it for students struggling in their higher meditations.

So long as there are *Vāsanā-s* in an individual, he is "one of dull intellect," and he cannot stop practising mental-control. For, the instant he allows his mind to roam about, the released mind would immediately jump into desire-ruts and fly into its fancies. The *Vāsanā-s*, expressing in the intellect, are called "desires"; and desires expressed in the mind are called "thoughts"; and the mind so agitated soon gets losts in its own fancies and imaginations. Thus, early seekers, should never give up their rugular practices of control at their body, mind and intellect levels—regulating the immoral and unethical living at the body-level; control of the low-emotions and baser passions at the mental level, and attempts at settling the thought-flow of the intellect through study, reflections and meditations.

The same verse has a deeper significance to all students who are already struggling on the higher-levels of intense meditation. To them *Aṣṭāvakra* is asking a pertinent question. How can you expect to control your mind with your own mind? This is illogical. Mind can be controlled and brought under our command only when we rise above the mind.

Our equipments will continue their efficient functioning; they are only serving us in expressing our "*ignorance*' (*Vāsanā-s*). When the mind is gushing forth efficiently into the sense-objects, the spiritual seeker, in the beginning considers this efficiency of his mind, as an obstacle for the meditations. Therefore, he curbs the mind's royal enthusiasm in its own functioning. Here the Sage is indicating to the student that mental-control is a means—it is the path. The 'end' is Self-realisation—the 'goal' is awakening to the Self. So long as we are pursuing the 'means,' we will not reach the 'end.' When we reach the 'goal,' we must have left the 'path.'

Thus, the foolish seeker should understand that the moment he stops his mental-control, his desire-ridden ego will drive his mind towards the sense-objects. The desires in him manifest, and his power of imagination brings storms of disturbances into his mind. In short, in the dull seeker the ego is not ended—his desires are only suppressed and not sublimated.

From this dissection of the inner bosom of the struggling *Sādhaka*, the teacher points out that mere self-control and *Yogik* practices alone, by themselves, cannot help in lifting man to Godhood. He must grow to altitudes beyond the peaks of desires. We have already mentioned very often that all *Yogik*-practices in the early stages are horizontal flights from sense-objects and mental-quakes. Here the call of *Aṣṭāvakra* to the students is that he had run almost across the entire 'run-way,' and now he must 'take off'!

Vertical flight through self-upliftment is the only way to detach ourselves from the realms of delusion and mental illusions. The various *Yogā-s* pursued by a student can no doubt quieten the mind, calm the intellect and thus generate maximum tranquillity and serenity in the bosom. To misunderstand these passing moods of inner peace and joy for the ultimate realisation is a tragic mistake. Many do. The Sage has warned us.

The tranquil-mind rendered temporarily peaceful as a result of spiritual practices, is the "pad' from which the meditation must rocket up into the higher Infinite Consciousness. In the Realisation of the Self alone complete transcendance can be achieved. The Supreme is *not gained as a result of Yoga*; the Infinite is with us—we have only to realise it. *Just be.*

मन्दः श्रुत्वापि तद्वस्तु न जहाति विमूढताम् ।
निर्विकल्पो बहिर्यत्नादन्तर्विषयलालसः ॥ ७६ ॥

Mandaḥ śrutvāpi tadvastu na jahāti vimūḍhatām,
nirvikalpo bahir-yatnād-antar-viṣaya-lālasaḥ.

मन्दः *mandaḥ* = the dull one; श्रुत्वा *śrutvā* = hearing; अपि *api* = even; तत् *tat* = that; वस्तु *vastu* = Reality; न *na* = not; जहाति *jahāti* = gives up; विमूढताम् *vimūḍhatām* = delusion; निर्विकल्पः *nirvikalpaḥ* = with mental fluctuations suppressed; बहिः *bahiḥ* = outwardly; यत्नात् *yatnāt* = through effort; अन्तः *antaḥ* = within; विषय-लालसः *viṣaya-lālasaḥ* = cravings for sense-objects (is).

76. *A man of dull intellect even after hearing the Truth does not give up his delusion. Though outwardly, through suppression he may appear to be without mental fluctuations, a craving for sense-objects shall linger in him.*

The seeker here is significantly described as "of dull intellect,' because he is one, who has yet no direct experience of the Self, and so is continuing his mental control exercises, in the false hope that the *Yoga*-practices will one day reward him with the gift of Self-Realisation! Self is something that is already with us. No one can give It. No body can gift It. Our own ego veils It from us. Ending the ego is to be achieved not through *Yoga*, but by direct Experience. *Jñāna* cannot help at this juncture; it has served us upto the threshold of Reality. Now the seeker must heave into the state of Self in himself—all by himself; *Vijñāna* is the goal.

One, who is ready for this leap into the Unknown, will no more have the delusion of ego and its passions. The "dull-witted" *Sādhaka* through suppression, might put up a saintly appearance of tranquillity, and may even experience, honestly in himself, a certain amount of mental equipoise and serenity. But when the challenge is too severe, he would find himself riddled with passions, lusts, greeds—often of the lowest and basest types. Here the student gets extremely desperate, supremely disappointed—his entire faith shatters, both in himself and in the *Śāstrā-s.*

Aṣṭāvakra here shows a clean mirror for the seeker to recognise the ugliness and crookedness of his inner personality! Deep in the student lurks the subtle *Vāsanā-s* for sense-pleasure.

We are reminded of *Śrī Kṛṣṇa*'s beautiful words in *Bhagavad-Gītā* (II-59) where he consoles the seekers of the lesser order, when he says:

विषया विनिवर्तन्ते निराहारस्य देहिनः ।
रसवर्जं रसोऽप्यस्य परं दृष्ट्वा निवर्तते ॥

Viṣayā vinivarnante nirāhārasya dehinaḥ,
rasa-varjaṁ raso'pyasya paraṁ dṛṣṭvā nivartate.

"The objects of the sense turn away from the abstinent man, leaving the longing (behind); but his longing also turns away on seeing the Supreme."

Historically *Aṣṭāvakra-Gītā* has been attributed to a period soon after the *Bhagavad-Gītā*. That was perhaps the main reason that these twenty chapters are together called as *Aṣṭāvakra-Saṁhitā*, to make a subtle contrast with the content, theme and style of the *Gītā*. Lord *Kṛṣṇa*'s *Bhagavad-Gītā* addresses to the dynamic men-of-action—of the order of Arjuna. *Aṣṭāvakra Saṁhitā* whispers to only meditators of the *Janaka*-order. *Kṛṣṇa*'s eighteen chapters are songs sung to quieten the agitations in the deluded man-of-action, the despondent *Arjuna* on the battle-field, while, the twenty chapters here are the thunderous roars whispered in the ears of the intelligent seeker in his seat-of-meditation.

In short, both the verses suggest, in unequivocal words, that control and suppression may help in the early stages, in relatively quietening the bosom, but they must necessarily fail in completely eliminating the tossings of the mind. Direct Self-realisation alone is the only baptism that can purify the ego and divinise man into the awareness of the Supreme Self.

ज्ञानाद्गलितकर्मा यो लोकदृष्ट्यापि कर्मकृत् ।
नाप्नोत्यवसरं कर्तुं वक्तुमेव न किञ्चन ॥ ७७ ॥

Jñānād-galita-karmā yo loka-dṛṣṭyāpi karma-kṛt,
nāpnotya-vasaraṁ kartuṁ vaktu-meva na kiñcana.

ज्ञानात् *jñānāt* = owing to wisdom; गलित-कर्मा *galita-karmā* = whose work has dropped; यः *yaḥ* = who; लोक-दृष्ट्या *loka-dṛṣṭyā* = in the sight of the ordinary people; अपि *api* = even; कर्म-कृत् *karma-kṛt* = doing work; न *na* = not; आप्नोति *āpnoti* = gets; अवसरम् *avasaram* = occasion; कर्तुम् *kartum* = to do; वक्तुम् *vaktum* = to say; एव *eva* = even; न *na* = not; किञ्चन *kiñcana* = anything.

77. *He, whose work has dropped off with the dawn of Wisdom, gets no occasion to do or to say anything even though in the eyes of the ordinay people he is doing work.*

Earlier *Aṣṭāvakra* had described the Man-of-Wisdom and his relationship with his own physical body. He compared it with a dry-leaf that has fallen down from the tree. The dry-leaf under the compulsion of the passing breeze may apparently look more dynamic than when it was on the tree, going about, fluttering, curling up, swirling down, dancing along—here and there—all under the whims of the passing breeze. The Sage then declared that the body of the Liberated-in-life moves about, functions and apparently serves the humanity—all under the compulstion of its *Prārabdha*.

To the Realised Sage there is no ego. He has neither the *sense of doership*, nor has he the *attitude of enjoyership*. Since he is, thus, above his ego, he himself has not the vanity that he is doing the work, nor is he conscious of the glory of the mighty work he may have inaugurated and accomplished. He works in the society, only from the view-point of the ordinary people. Stop him on his path, and ask him: "what more should we do to add an extra momentum to your mighty work?" He is surprised, and gets rather confused!

You are awakened from a dream and your entire family anxiously questions you: What happened? What was the tragedy? Why did you cry out for help? You, to now awakened, are in a fix—and indeed ashamed of your dream!! What can the awakened Master say—how can he answer?

The Liberated-in-life "gets no occasion to do or say anything"—there is no individual-ego in him. The *Upaniṣad*-s explain that through the Sage, the total-*Vāsanā-s* of his era work. Can the telescope of Nelson explain what he saw? Can the *Kodaṇḍā*-bow of *Śrī Rāma* give a description of *Rāmāyaṇa*—though it was always at the shoulders of *Dāśarathi* and must have witnessed everything! The Sage is only an *instrument*. He is not responsible for what his body does. He is not conscious of it at all. Is the tree responsible for its dry-leaf reaching your room in the passing-breeze? He has no sense of *doer-ship*, and therefore, he has no autobiography, after his Self-Realisation.

क्व तमः क्व प्रकाशो वा हानं क्व च न किञ्चन ।
निर्विकारस्य धीरस्य निरातङ्कस्य सर्वदा ॥ ७८ ॥

Kva tamaḥ kva prakāśo vā hānaṁ kva ca na kiñcan,
nir-vikārasya dhīrasya nirā-taṅkasya sarvadā.

क्व *kva* = where; तमः *tamaḥ* = darkness; क्व *kva* = where; प्रकाशः *prakāśaḥ* = light; वा *vā* = or; हानम् *hānam* = loss; क्व *kva* = where; च *ca* = and; न *na* = not; किञ्चन *kiñcan* = anything; निर्विकारस्य *nir-vikārasya* = unperturbed; धीरस्य *dhīrasya* = of the Wise-one; निरातङ्कस्य *nir-ātaṅkasya* = fearless; सर्वदा *sarvadā* = ever.

78. *To the Wise-one, who is ever unperturbed and fearless, where is darkness? Where is light? Where is loss?.... There is nothing whatsoever.*

Knowledge and ignorance, Light and darkness, loss and gain, are all expressions of duality experienced at the level of the mind and the intellect. To one, who has transcended the mind, where are these pairs-of-opposites? He has no *ignorance*, because he has gained *Knowledge*. But in the Man-of-Wisdom where is *Knowledge*? Knowledge has a meaning only with reference to *ignorance*. One, who has awakened to the Pure-Self and become the Illuminator of the both *Knowledge* and *ignorance*, he, as the Supreme Self, can neither be defined in term of *ignorance* nor *Knowledge*.

In the Infinite Bliss of his All-full nature, how can anything be added so that he may profit by it; nor can anything be taken away from him, so that he may suffer a loss. Nothing can be added to the Infinite. Nothing can be taken away form the Infinite. Infinite is ever the Infinite. The profits gained in the dream, or the losses suffered in the dream, are both of no significance at all to the dreamer who has now awakened!

क्व धैर्यं क्व विवेकित्वं क्व निराङ्कतापि वा ।
अनिर्वाच्यस्वभावस्य निःस्वभावस्य योगिनः ॥ ७९ ॥

Kva dhairyaṁ kva vivekitvaṁ kva nirāṅkatāpi vā,
anir-vācya-svabhāvasya niḥ-svabhāvasya yoginaḥ.

क्व *kva* = where; धैर्यम् *dhairyam* = patience; क्व *kva* = where; विवेकित्वम् *vivekitvam* = discrimination; क्व *kva* = where; निराङ्कता *nir-āṅkata* = fearlessness; अपि *api* = even; वा *vā* = or; अनिर्वाच्य-स्वभावस्य *anirvācya-svabhāvasya* = of indescribable nature (indefinable); निःस्वभावस्य *niḥ-svabhāvasya* = impersonal, attributeless; योगिनः *yoginaḥ* = of the *Yogin*.

79. *For the fulfilled seeker (*Yogin*), who is attributeless and of undefinable nature, where is patience? Where is discrimination? Where is even fearlessness?*

These three qualities are essential for any seeker who dares to walk the spiritual path: (1) patience, (2) discrimination and (3) fearlessness. Lack of anyone of them can cause the student's fall on the path. Everywhere all Masters have emphasized, again and again, the need for cultivating these essential mental qualities in a seeker undertaking the great pilgrimage.

A long staff, a water-pot and, probably, a couple of blankets are essential for one who is going on a trek up a mountain. But when he has returned after his trip, and has reached his home, should he still carry the staff, the water-pot and the blankets? They are all necessary for his pilgrimage. But when he has reached the destination, these things are naturally, dropped down. They are, now, of no use to him at all. So long as we are struggling in the delusory world of happenings—as miserable toys, being played about by the whimsical fancies of the mind—at that time, to keep our balance and swim to the shore we need the help of a piece of wood floating down the river. When once we have reached safely the banks of the river, should we carry that piece of wood on our shoulders, all the way, when we are dragging ourselves home?

Patience, to continue meditations in spite of repeated failures among waves of disturbances; *ability to discriminate* clearly, between the inert matter vestures around us and the clear spiritual Light of Consciousness in our bosom; the *daring heroism to face fearlessly* the total *extinction* of our limited-ego during our plunge into the Infinite State of Blissful Self—all these are the unavoidable and necessary equipments to help the seekers on his path.

The Liberated-in-life, having already reached the Goal, has no use for these. And *Aṣṭāvakra* confesses here that this "characterless character" (*Niḥ-svabhāvaḥ*) of a Self-Realised Master is indeed indescribable. The Sage apologises himself to his student at his own total inability to communicate the real Nature of one who is truly Liberated-in-life.

न स्वर्गो नैव नरको जीवन्मुक्तिर्न चैव हि ।
बहुनात्र किमुक्तेन योगदृष्ट्या न किञ्चन ॥ ८० ॥

Na svargo naiva narako jīvan-muktir-na caiva hi,
bahu-nātra kim-uktena yoga-dṛṣṭyā na kiñcana.

न *na* = not; स्वर्गः *svargaḥ* = heaven; न *na* = not; एव *eva* = also; नरकः *narakaḥ* = hell; जीवन्-मुक्तिः *jīvan-muktiḥ* = the state of liberation-in-life; न *na* = not; च *ca* = and; एव *eva* = even; हि *hi* = indeed; बहुना *bahunā* = much; अत्र *atra* = here; किम् *kim* = what need; उक्तेन *uktena* = by saying; योग-दृष्ट्या *yoga-dṛṣṭyā* = in the *Yogik* vision; न *na* = not; किञ्चन *kiñcana* = anything.

80. There is no heaven, nor is there a hell—there is not even the State-of-Liberation. In short, in the Yogik *vision nothing exists.*

This does not mean that *Aṣṭāvakra* is nodding at the theory of non-existence (*Sūnya-vāda*) scaffolded up by the arguments of a group of Buddhists. What he means here is certainly that in the awareness of a Perfected Master "nothing exists"—nothing that you and I, from our view-point, experience as existing. To a Realised Saint "nothing exists" except the one Infinite *Saccidānanda*—the Self.

Heaven and hell are imaginary realms of experiences, conceived by the deluded-mind for its own pleasures and pains, under the throes of its own good and bad *Vāsanā-s*. To the ego if, the world is real, heaven and hell can also be equally real! We are reminded of the same Sage *Aṣṭāvakra*'s reply to king *Janaka*, when he wanted to know which is real: the king dreamt that he was a beggar and on waking up, he saw himself to be the king. Now is the beggar, the king's dream; or the king, the beggar's dream? *Aṣṭāvakra*'s reply was typical. The Sage replied: "O king, if you think that the beggar was real, the throne and the crown of yours is as real as the beggar of your dream!" If this world is real, to him heaven and hell shall be equally real. These are all experiences at the ego-level. The Liberated-in-life is one who has risen above the ego. To him even this world and his own body are never constantly in his awareness. He has realised their illusory nature. How can he then, ever, conceive of a heaven and a hell?

In him the God, the world and the ego—all have merged into the very Substratum, the Self... and That he is!

नैव प्रार्थयते लाभं नालाभेनानुशोचति ।
धीरस्य शीतलं चित्तममृतेनैव पूरितम् ॥ ८१ ॥

Naiva prārthayate lābhaṁ nālābhen-ānuśocati,
dhīrasya śītalaṁ cittam-amṛte-naiva pūritam.

न *na* = not; एव *eva* = surely; प्रार्थयते *prārthayate* = long for; लाभम् *lābham* = gain; न *na* = not; अलाभेन *alābhena* = at the loss; अनुशोचति *anuśocati* = grieves; धीरस्य *dhīrasya* = of the Wise-one; शीतलम् *śītalam* = cool (serene); चित्तम् *cittam* = mind; अमृतेन *amṛtena* = with nectar; एव *eva* = indeed; पूरितम् *pūritam* = filled.

81. *A Wise-man neither longs for gain, nor grieves at the loss. His serene mind is indeed filled with the nectar—the Supreme Bliss.*

The limited alone can seek for a greater fulfilment, because of the essential sense-of-imperfection in the limited. One, who is conditioned by his own identifications with the body, mind and intellect, alone can seek his temporary sense-gratifications in the fields of objects, emotions and thoughts. The hungry will seek food. The thirsty will seek water. The limited must come to seek a greater joy and satisfaction.

The Liberated-in-life has discovered his identity with the Infinite Blissful Self and, therefore, he has no sense of imperfections in him. The All-full cannot feel any gain from the delusory world-of-plurality, nor can he ever experience sorrows at any loss. We have already pointed out earlier that nothing can be added to the Infinite, nor can anything be substracted from the Infinite. The *Upaniṣadik* 'Peace invocation' (*Śānti Pāṭha*) declares it clearly :

पूर्णस्य पूर्णमादाय पूर्णमेवावशिष्यते ।

Pūrṇasya pūrṇam-ādāya pūrṇam-evāva-śiṣyate.

"From the Whole, when the Whole is negated, what remains is, again the Whole."

The bosom of the Man-of-Perfection is ever serene and tranquil—absolutely "cool." Compared with him our bosoms are always surging and seething, boiling and gurgling with the lava-of-desires. Being tranquil, the heart of the Man-of-Perfection is filled with nectar (*Amṛtam*). In the *Hindū* mythology, *Amṛtam* (nectar) is considered a pleasant and glorious drink of the heavens! Picturisation of the subtle philosophical Truth is the style of the *Purāṇā-s*. The term *Amṛtam* means "Immortality," "deathlessness." Death is nothing but change; the death of the previous condition culminating in the birth of a new condition is called "change." Deathless-ness, therefore, means the "state of changeless-ness." Change is experienced in and by the human-mind, and therefore, one who has transcended the mind has also crossed over the seething waters of change.

Aṣṭāvakra in this verse clearly illustrates that his pen can write the poetic language of the *Purāṇā-s*.

न शान्तं स्तौति निष्कामो न दुष्टमपि निन्दति ।
समदुःखसुखस्तृप्तः किञ्चित् कृत्यं न पश्यति ॥८२॥

Na śāntaṁ stauti niṣkāmo na duṣṭam-api nindati,
sama-duḥkha-sukhas-tṛptaḥ kiñcit kṛtyaṁ na paśyati.

न *na* = not; शान्तम् *śāntam*= one who is calm; स्तौति *stauti* = praise; निष्कामः *niṣkāmaḥ* = one who is completely free from desire; न *na* = not; दुष्टम् *duṣṭam* = one who is wicked; अपि *api* = even; निन्दति *nindati* = blame; सम-दुःख-सुखः *sama-duḥkha-sukhaḥ* = same in happiness and sorrow; तृप्तः *tṛptaḥ* = contented; किञ्चित् *kiñcit* = anything; कृत्यम् *kṛtyam* = to be achieved; न *na* = not; पश्यति *paśyati* = sees.

82. *The desireless-one has neither praise for the calm, nor even blame for the wicked. Contented and the same in happiness and misery, he finds nothing to be achieved.*

The State of Perfection as conceived by the Great *Ṛṣī-s* of India, is a state-of-desirelessness reached in the *direct experience* of Infinite, unearthly, inward peace—the Self. It is not suppression of desires, it is not even sublimation of desires. It is a state wherein the individual, in his own inner experience of immeasurable satisfaction and happiness, is rendered incapable of entertaining any more desires! Light and darkness cannot remain at one and the same time and at one and the same place. Light is not absence of darkness, but light is a state wherein darkness in incapable of playing about. Thus, the state-of-desirelessness is not a condition arrived at by omission. It is a state that is achieved by the positive experience of the Master, when he awakens onto the larger dimension of the Pure Self.

In the fullness of his Conscious Bliss, the Liberated-in-life has come to a state-of-desirelessness. Desires procreate thoughts, and "thought-flow" is mind. In the Self-realised Master, there is no mind; and therefore there must be absence of thought-agitations. Mind gives the delusory sense of ego; in *a state of mind-lessness*, there cannot be an ego.

It is the ego-centric-individuality in me that praises the beautiful in life and condemns the wickedness of life. Where ego is not, neither can that Man-of-Peace praise anything nor condemn anything. From this view-point there is nothing other than the Self.

He is at peace with himself, calm and serene—and no happenings around him can ever gate-crash into his realm to agitate him there is his Kingdom Divine. Naturally, he will be observed by us as *equal* both in facing misery and in meeting happiness. We have already explained how the Man-of-Realisation no more reacts with the world of challenges. He has no ego to react with. Man-of-Perfection knows only *how to act* spontaneously; he *never reacts*. This is the secret of his unshakable 'balance' under all conditions.

He has achieved all that is to be achieved. We strive to achieve something in order to complete ourselves. The sense of incompleteness has ended in the glorious one who has exploded the suffocating walls of his ego, and has entered into the Limitless Bliss of the Self. What more has he there-after to achieve in life?

धीरो न द्वेष्टि संसारमात्मानं न दिदृक्षति ।
हर्षामर्षविनिर्मुक्तो न मृतो न च जीवति ॥ ८३ ॥

Dhīro na dveṣṭi saṁsāram-ātmānaṁ na didṛakṣati,
harṣāmarṣa-vinirmukto na mṛto na ca jīvati.

धीरः *dhīraḥ* = the Wise-one; न *na* = not; द्वेष्टि *dveṣṭi* = hates; संसारम् *saṁsāram* = the world of change; आत्मानम् *ātmānam* = the Self; न *na* = not; दिदृक्षति *didṛakṣati* = wishes to see; हर्ष-अमर्ष-विनिर्मुक्तः *harṣa-amarṣa-vinirmuktaḥ* = free from joy and sorrow; न *na* = not; मृतः *mṛtaḥ* = dead; न *na* = not; च *ca* = and; जीवति *jīvati* = lives.

83. *This Wise-one neither hates the world-of-change, nor wishes to "see" the Self. Free from joy and sorrow, he is neither dead nor alive.*

The kindly paternal anxiety of *Aṣṭāvakra* to explain in words and communicate to his disciple the condition of the Man-of-Perfection makes the Sage stammer into these verses. No doubt, *Aṣṭāvakra* is the most eloquent Master—but alas, only to the few. He is not a mass-preacher as *Śrī Kṛṣṇa* is in the *Bhagavad-Gītā*. In this lies the difference in the 'altitudes' at which *Gītā* serenades in and *Saṁhitā* cascades from.

It is the seeker who revolts against the realm-of-change (*Saṁsāra*m)—for all its perturbations and disturbances that shatter the seeker's mental peace and his intellectual poise. Again, it is a seeker who is conscious of his imperfections, that revolts against his ego and yearns to experience the Unlimited, Eternal Self. It is one, who has not yet slept, who struggles to sleep!

The Wise-one, who has already realised the Self, to him there is no more any anxiety to experience (see) the *Ātman*. Nor has he any quarrel with the realm-of-change (*Saṁsāra*), because, from his stand-point there is nothing but the Self everywhere. Thus, he has nothing to reject, nor has he anything to accept in life. Physically he appears to be with us living in the world, but certainly he is no more a native in this globe!!

We cannot say that he is dead—he moves about, talks, eats sleeps as any other living human-being. Therefore, certainly he is not dead. But is he living? Whatever it be, he is not living like us. He seems quite dead to the enchantments of the world around, to the joys and sorrows of the world—he has no desires, no passions; he never *reacts* to the external world. If an organism is incapable of reacting to the external world, we generally consider that organism as dead. A Man-of-Perfection is "*dead*" because he never *reacts*. But he is *alive*, for he *acts*. Thus, ordinary terms, with which we categorise and, therefore, determine things, are all of no avail in the description of the Liberated-in-life.

निःस्नेहः पुत्रदारादौ निष्कामो विषयेषु च ।
निश्चिन्तः स्वशरीरेऽपि निराशः शोभते बुधः ॥ ८४ ॥

Niḥ-snehaḥ putra-dārādau niṣkāmo viṣayeṣu ca,
niścintaḥ sva-śarīre-'pi nirāśaḥ śobhate budhaḥ.

निःस्नेहः *niḥ-snehaḥ* = without attachment; पुत्र-दारा-आदौ *putra-dārā-ādau* = in the son, wife and others; निष्कामः *niṣkāmaḥ* = without desire; विषयेषु *viṣayeṣu* = in sense-objects; च *ca* = and; निश्चिन्तः *niścintaḥ* = free from care; स्वशरीरे *svaśarīre* = for his own body; अपि *api* = even; निराशः *nirāśaḥ* = free from expectation; शोभते *śobhate* = lives in glory, shines; बुधः *budhaḥ* = the Wise-one.

84. *Shining (glorious) is the life of the Wise-man, free from all expectations, without any attachment for children, wife and others, free from desire for the sense-objects, and without care even for his own body.*

These terms employed here is describing the physical and mental reactions of the Man-of-Perfection to the world outside, should appear to the uninitiated as the descriptions of some horrible and terrible Satanic Power! Without any attachment, with no desire, no expectations, and without even a care for his own body—here is a congenital idiot, insentient to everything fine and beautiful in life!

This is the reason why *Aṣṭāvakra* has more than once already explained that the inner experience of a Man-of-Wisdom can be appreciated and understood only by another, who has the similar experience. Words can only belie him. Our imperfect mind cannot comprehend the majestic glory, the divine harmony, the brilliant perfections of a Man of Self-realisation.

"Shining" (Glorious-*Śobhate*) with the Effulgence of Perfection is the life of the Wise-man, which is not disturbed by his mental pre-occupations either with the future (expectations) or with the present: he has neither "expectations" nor "desires." He is not disturbed by the memories of his past; all attachments spring from the pleasant memories of the past. You can never get attached to the son who is not yet born, nor with a wife whom you have not yet married. How can one have attachment to wealth that one has not yet earned and saved?

The desire to seek *happiness in sense-objects, attachment to the dear and near ones*, and great expectations for the larger *joys*, to be fulfilled *in the future*—all these three have a direct reference to the *body-consciousness* in the individual. The embodied, who is living in identification with his own body, can never escape these three sources of restlessness and sorrow. A Man-of-Perfection as described here is above these three natural human weaknesses, only because "he is without care, even for his own body."

"Identification with the body, the not-self," is *bondage*; the Man-of-Perfection has freed himself from the enmeshment of *matter*. He has risen to a new dimension of living, where at this moment we have no admission. And hence we are not able to recognise the beauty and glory of the State in which live the Spiritual Masters.

तुष्टिः सर्वत्र धीरस्य यथापतितवर्तिनः ।
स्वच्छन्दं चरतो देशान्यत्रास्तमितशायिनः ॥ ८५ ॥

Tuṣṭiḥ sarvatra dhīrasya yathā-patita-vartinaḥ,
svacchandaṁ carato deśān-yatrā-stamita-śāyinaḥ.

तुष्टिः *tuṣṭiḥ* = (he is) contented; सर्वत्र *sarvatra* = everywhere; धीरस्य *dhīrasya* = of the Wise-one; यथा-पतित-वर्तिनः *yathā-patita-vartinaḥ* = who lives on whatever that comes to his lot; स्वच्छन्दम् *svacchandam* = at pleasure; चरतः *carataḥ* = roaming about; देशान् *deśān* = countries; यत्र-अस्तमित-शायिनः *yatra-astamita-śāyinaḥ* = resting wherever the sun sets.

85. Contenment ever dwells in the heart of the Wise-men, who lives upon whatever happens to come unasked as his lot, and who roams about at pleasure, resting wherever he is, when the sun sets!

Expectation of a greater happiness through acquisition and re-arrangement of things around us is the cause for all discontentment. Seeking comfort from outside, man unfortunately creates a miserable world for himself and for others. However much, we may glorify this way-of-life by high-sounding and noble-looking terms—like "healthy competitive living" or "progressive living" or "high standards of living"—we all know it is an unavoidable tragedy. We may not declare so from political platforms, and admit it in our economic text-books, but we know it alright in the depth of our hearts. The Man-of-Wisdom alone knows what true contentment is, because he has discovered the Source of All-Bliss in himself. He is no more a beggar, begging for his happiness and satisfaction at the hovels of sense-objects. His Palace of Bliss is built within himself, with the marbles of peace and joy.

Revelling ever in the luxurious bliss of the Self, the Master has no demands for the world-outside—nothing in the Infinite world can add to his satisfaction, which he has already conquered in himself. Yet, his body moving amidst the manifested world continues to live and function by its own momentum, gathered by it in the past. In him there is no ego to give the equipment a propulsion of its own. The body exists and moves about until its *Prārabdha* is over.

This unmotivated apparent existence of the physical body is being described here in this verse by *Aṣṭāvakra*. The Self-realised roams about singing within him the glory of Glory that he is himself—with no particular destination to reach, no itinerary to fulfil, no great-grand programme to complete. Rich in inward peace, fabulous in his wisdom, he scatters his knowledge all about him, careless of whether his generation is benefited by his Infinite bounty or not.

As far as he himself is concerned, he has no demand upon the community for his sustenance. The barest minimum needs of man have been defined by socialist economists as food, clothing and shelther. The Perfect Master has no expectation of even these three fundamental needs. Under the way-side trees he has his shelter. Every day he is clothed in fresh, new space (*Digambara*)! Whatever unasked comes to him as his lot, he enjoy them thoroughly!

Wealth or disease, worship or insults, abuses or praises, he expects none of them. He faces them all with equanimity. For whatever he sees is nothing but the Self. Whatever he hears is but a ripple in the Consciousness. What does he lose if his generation insults him? What has he to gain if others glorify him? He needs no vote. He needs no throne. He is the Lord of all lords. He is the Sovereign of all soverəigns....self-appointed for all times to come.

पततूदेतु वा देहो नास्य चिन्ता महात्मनः ।
स्वभावभूमिविश्रान्तिविस्मृताशेषसंसृतेः ॥ ८६ ॥

Patatūdetu vā deho nāsya cintā mahātmanaḥ,
svabhāva-būmi-viśrānti-vismṛtā-śeṣa-saṁsṛteḥ.

पततु *patatu* = may drop down dead; उदेतु *udhetu* = may rise up to live; वा *vā* = or; देहः *dehaḥ* = body; न *na* = not; अस्य *asya* = this; चिन्ता *cintā* = care; महात्मनः *mahātmanaḥ* = of the great one; स्वभाव-भूमि-विश्रान्ति-विस्मृत-अशेष-संसृतेः *svabhāva-būmi-viśrānti-vismṛta-aśeṣa-saṁsṛteḥ* = who has completely transcended birth and rebirth due to his repose upon the floor (foundation) of his own Being.

86. Reposing upon the floor (foundation) of his own Being and completely transcending birth and rebirth, the Great-one does not care whether his body drops down dead or rises up to live.

The entire world of phenomenon constituting the fields of experiences, and all the equipments of experiences in us, are all superimposed upon the Infinite Self, which is the Great Grand Ground upon which the universes rise up and play out their history. Having awakened to this Immutable Substratum Infinite, how can he ever worry about the destinies of his insignificant, illusory body? From his Infinite altitude he can only view and see that universes are all minute stresses in Consciousness. In one of such a universe is an insignificant dot which represents our world of seven continents. Among them one continent is Asia; in it is the sub-continent *Bhārat*. In *Bhārat* is a little town or a village, where again in one street is a house, and in one corner of its *varāndā* rests a miscroscopic dust-particle called "my-body!" Now "whether it rises to live or drops down to die," how can it affect Me who am the Substratum for all the Universes?

The Spiritual Master ever lives in his perfect identity with the "flood" of Truth, and therefore, he is careless of his own physical existence in the world-of-delusion. Having woken up from the dream, what is your attitude towards the beautiful young body that you had in the dream? Certainly you "do not care whether your body drops down dead or rises up to live" —for you are now awake!!

अकिञ्चनः कामचारो निर्द्वन्द्वश्छिन्नसंशयः ।
असक्तः सर्वभावेषु केवलो रमते बुधः ॥ ८७ ॥

Akiñcanaḥ kāmacāro nir-dvandvaś-chinna-saṁśayaḥ,
asaktaḥ sarva-bhāveṣu kevalo ramate budhaḥ.

अकिञ्चनः *akiñcanaḥ* = without any possession; कामचारः *kāmacāraḥ* = moving at pleasure; निर्द्वन्द्वः *nirdvandvaḥ* = free from the pairs-of-opposites; छिन्न-संशयः *chinna-saṁśayaḥ* = whose doubts have been cut asunder; असक्तः *asaktaḥ* = unattached; सर्वभावेषु *sarvabhāveṣu* = in all things; केवलः *kevalaḥ* = alone; रमते *ramate* = rejoices; बुधः *budhaḥ* = the Wise-one.

87. *The Wise-one stands alone, unattached to anything. He is without any possession and moves at his will and pleasure. He is free from the pairs-of-opposites, and his doubts have been cut asunder. He, indeed, is the Blessed-one.*

The world-of-objects by themselves can never become a shackle upon man. It is his sense of possesssion in them that reduces him to an ego; the ego then suffers with its desires and passions for the world-of-objects. This sense of possession can be towards objects, towards beings or towards places. There are some who are attached to their teachers; there are others who are attached to the *Ganges*-banks or to some other holy places. These are all certainly very essential for the early seekers. The right place and the right environments have a magic of their own, under the charm of which the unbridled mind may, in the early stages, become available for the taming and training necesary for it to take up a serious study of the scriptures. Here in the case of a Man-of-Perfection, *Aṣṭāvakra* explains, how the Master has no sense of possession at all and the Liberated-in-life moves from place to place without any attachment to the places. Mentally he is no more living at the ego-centre and therefore, is not buffeted among the common agitations and torn between joy and sorrow, honour and dishonour and such other pairs-of-opposites.

Thus, physically he has no possessions; he is not attached to any particular place. Mentally he is pacified enough not to be disturbed by the pairs-of-opposites. The Master moves about freely in the world. Even intellectually he is not disturbed by any doubts regarding the Reality, since he is living, with every breath of his life, the experience of the Self and, therefore, he has cut asunder all his doubts. He is not only detached from 'places,' but also detached completely from 'things and beings.' It is this attachment to places, things and beings that is a source for all mental disturbances in the worldly men.

Thus, the Man-of-Realisation revels alone is the 'alone' all-alone (*Kevalaḥ Ramate*). The Aloneness of the Self indicates the Absolute State and its All-Pervasiveness. In the *post* there cannot be any trace of the *ghost*! Never can the illusory-*snake* leave its scales upon the *rope*!! Awakened to the Self, the Infinite Consciousness, there cannot be any trace of the world-of-illusions. The Truth ever alone is. This State of Aloneness, is the goal, indicated in *Vedānta* as the State of '*Kaivalya*.'

The term employed by *Aṣṭāvakra*, to describe the Man-of-Perfection, "whose doubts has been cut asunder" (*Chinna-saṁśayaḥ*) reminds us of the *Muṇḍakopaniṣad* (II-ii-8):

भिद्यते हृदयग्रन्थिः छिद्यन्ते सर्वसंशयाः ।
क्षीयन्ते चास्य कर्माणि तस्मिन् दृष्टे परावरे ॥

Bhidyate hṛdya-granthiḥ chidyante sarva-saṁśayāḥ,
kṣīyante cāsya karmāṇi tasmin dṛṣṭe parāvare.

"When he has seen both the Higher and the Lower, the knots of his heart become untied; all doubts are cut asunder; and all his *Karmā-s* are consumed."

निर्ममः शोभते धीरः समलोष्टाश्मकाञ्चनः ।
सुभिन्नहृदयग्रन्थिर्विनिर्धूतरजस्तमः ॥ ८८ ॥

Nirmamaḥ śobhate dhīraḥ sama-loṣṭāśma-kāñcanaḥ,
subhinna-hṛdya-granthir-vinir-dhūta-rajas-tamaḥ.

निर्मम: *nirmamaḥ* = devoid of '*my-ness*'; शोभते *śobhate* = excels (shines); धीर: *dhīraḥ* = the Wise-one; सम-लोष्ट-अश्म-काञ्चन: *sama-loṣṭa-aśma-kāñcanaḥ* = to whom a clod of earth, a previous stone or the lump of gold is the same; सुभिन्न-हृदय-ग्रन्थि: *subhinna-hṛdya-granthiḥ* = in whom the knots of the hearts are completely cut off; विनिर्धूत-रज:-तम: *vinirdhūta-rajaḥ-tamaḥ* = who has cleansed himself of both *Rajas* and *Tamas*.

88. The Wise-one who is devoid of his ego, and to whom a clod of earth, a precious stone and a bar of gold are all the same, whose knots of the heart have been cut asunder and who has cleansed himself of all his Rajas and Tamas—shines.

The verse under review serves as a rich museum exhibiting some of the most precious phrases in our ancient literature. The verse shines in its beauty, set with the fabulous thoughts of the *Upaniṣad*-s and the eloquent phrases of the *Gītā*.

The Self-Realised Sage shines with an unearthly glow of godly perfections! He has eliminated his limited mortal-ego—the cancer of the personality, that provides all the agonies of existence. Intellectually he sees no plurality; even when he sees the wrold-of-objects, they are all to him but ripplings in the Self, which is his own Nature. Therefore, to him things which are considered as precious and covetable by the '*ignorant*' worldly-men are of no consequence.[1] To him a clod-of-earth or a previous-stone or a bar-of-gold are all nothing but "*matter*" in

1. In this connection, it is very interesting to observe that among some tribes in deep Africa, we are told that the canine-teeth of the wild-dogs are very precious in as much as the ladies there string them together to wear as a necklace. To them, perhaps diamound is not of such a great value; pearls are of no significance, but the dog's teeth are precious. Some of the hippies in the modern cities move about hanging a beli from their necks; they consider it very precious and covetable; while in India only grazing cows wear such bells in their necks!! The things by themselves are not precious, it is the possessor that gives them their values.

different forms and colours, and they are essentially of no value. This phrase is bodily lifted from the famous 'Song of the Lord.'[2]

The human personality is considered by the great *Ṛṣī-s* in their analysis as being bound by three powerful chords and these are called as the "knots-of-the-heart" (*Hṛdya-granthi*). The heart of human-personality is conditioned by three essential but delusory factors—'*ignorance*' (*Avidyā*), 'desire' (*Kāma*) and 'work' (*Karma*). The spiritual '*ignorance*' of our Real Nature causes us to feel, in ourselves a sense of imperfection, and the suggestions that the intellect gives to complete this sense of imperfection are called 'desires.' The intellectual desires breed agitations in the mind, which express as vigorous 'activities' at the body level (*Karma*). All these three : *ignorance, desire* and *work* limit us, curtail our freedom, shackle us to pits of sorrow and pain, all through our physical existence in this world.

The source of this triple personality-entanglement is certainly the "*non-apprehension* of the Reality," the spiritual '*ignorance*' (*Avidyā*). Man-of-Perfection is one who has destroyed his '*ignorance*' by his direct, personal experience of the Self, and therefore, he has "cut asunder" all the painful knots upon the heart of his personality. This expression echoes the ample significance roared in its original use in *Muṇḍakopaniṣad* (II-ii-8) quoted in *Śloka*-87 and *Kaṭhopaniṣad* (II-iii-15):

यदा सर्वे प्रभिद्यन्ते हृदयस्येह ग्रन्थयः ।
अथ मर्त्योऽमृतो भवत्येतावदनुशासनम् ॥

yadā sarve prabhidyante hṛdaya-syeha granthayaḥ,
atha martyo-'mṛto bhavaty-etāvad-anuśāsanam.

"When all the knots-of-the hearts are severed here on earth, then the mortal becomes immortal, so far is the instruction (of all *Vedānta*)."

The spiritual '*ignorance*' in us is expressed in our psychological personality as three different mental climates

2. *Bhagavad-Gītā*, VI-8.

called *Sattva*, *Rajas* and *Tamas*. All these three, obstruct our vision of the spiritual Reality. *Tamas* veils the intellect from its direct perception of the Self (*Āvaraṇa*). Then the mind gets affected by *Rajas*; consequently the mind starts projecting the world-of-plurality through its agitations (*Vikṣepa*). The veiling of the intellect (*Tamas*) and the agitations of the mind (*Rajas*) together make us what we are—an ego-centric non-entity, capable of only desire, sorrows, sighs and tears!!

He, in whom the *Rajas* and *Tamas* have been completely cleaned off, is one whose mind is serene, and the veiling gets completely lifted. It is to lift the *Rajas* thus from our mind, that we have the "outer" spiritual practices (*Bāhya-sādhanā*). It is to eliminate the *Tamas* from the intellect that the seekers are advised to practise meditation, which is the "inner" spiritual practice (*Ābhyantara-sādhanā*).

Janaka is a disciple who has now only a very vague, thin misty film of '*ignorance*' in him. He stands at the threshold; hence the advice of *Aṣṭāvakra* sounds strange to us, perhaps, unfamiliar, and even, foreign—when he criticises the student for entertaining even "an anxiety for liberation" (*Mumukṣutva*), and discourages him from pursuing even the "goals-of-life" as recommended by the *Ṛṣī-s* (*Puruśārtha*). These advices addressed to such a student, who is already reaching the summit, need not confuse the resolve, determination, consistency and sincerity of the early seekers, who have yet to walk the path—that sharp and narrow path. *Kaṭhopaniṣad* (I-iii-14) calls it : "the razor's edge" in the following words :

....

क्षुरस्य धारा निशिता दुरत्यया दुर्गं पथस्तत्कवयो वदन्ति ॥

....

Kṣurasya dhārā niśitā duratyayā
durgaṁ pathas-tat-kavayo vadanti.

....

"Like the sharp edge of a razor is that path difficult to cross and hard to tread—thus say the wise."

सर्वत्रानवधानस्य न किञ्चिद्वासना हृदि ।
मुक्तात्मनो वितृप्तस्य तुलना केन जायते ॥ ८९ ॥

Sarvatrān-avadhānasya na kiñcid-vāsanā hṛdi,
muktāt-mano vitṛp-tasya tulanā kena jāyate.

सर्वत्र-अनवधानस्य *sarvatra-anavadhānasya* = indifferent to all objects; न *na* = not; किञ्चित् *kiñcit* = any; वासना *vāsanā* = desire; हृदि *hṛdi* = in the heart; मुक्त-आत्मनः *mukta-ātmanaḥ* = of the Liberated-one; वितृप्तस्य *vitṛptasya* = completely contented; तुलना *tulanā* = comparison; केन *kena* = with whom; जायते *jāyate* = is.

89. *Who can be compared with a Liberated-one, who has no desires at all lingering in his heart, who is contented and totally indifferent to everything?*

In these few closing verses of the chapter *Aṣṭāvakra* is admitting that however much we may explain the inner nature of the Man-of-Perfection, in fact, we must necessarily fail to give a complete, and exhaustive report of his Divine Nature. He is indescribable. There is none to whom he can be compared with. The unique beauty of the Man-of-Perfection and his incomparable glory will ever be a wonder to the human intellect. One who has emptied himself of all desires, which are the impulses in all ego-centric actions, who is so completely contented in his own Infinite Inner-Peace, and therefore, he who has become "totally indifferent to the enchanting world of sense-objects"—that individual though anatomically has still the shape of a man, he has reached a new evolutionary height wherein he cannot be considered any longer as a finite, mortal creature. His inner life of thoughts and emotions is incomparable with anyone in the universe. His inner experience is of the Absolute Self, which is the Substratum for the Universe. *Aṣṭāvakra* despairs and cries out: "Who can be compared with the Liberated-man?"

जानन्नपि न जानाति पश्यन्नपि न पश्यति ।
ब्रुवन्नपि न च ब्रूते कोऽन्यो निर्वासनादृते ॥ ९० ॥

Jānan-napi na jānāti paśyan-napi na paśyati,
bruvan-napi na ca brūte ko'nyo nir-vāsanād-ṛte.

जानन् *jānan* = knowing; अपि *api* = even; न *na* = not; जानाति *jānāti* = knows; पश्यन् *paśyan* = seeing; अपि *api* = even; न *na* = not; पश्यति *pasyati* = sees; ब्रुवन् *bruvan* = speaking; अपि *api* = even; न *na* = not; च *ca* = and; ब्रूते *brūte* = speaks; कः *kaḥ* = who; अन्यः *anyaḥ* = other; निर्वासनात् ऋते *nirvāsanāt ṛte* = except the desireless one.

90. Who, but the desireless-one knows not though knowing, sees not though seeing, and speaks not though speaking?

The Sage is trying to justify his exclamation in the previous verse that the unique nature of the Man-of-Perfection is incomparable. Not only that he is rid of all desires, but in the Liberated-in-life there is no ego at all. All our descriptions of another personality are always the discription of his ego. Here is one who has transcended his sense of individuality and has merged with the Universal Substratum. We cannot describe him as we would describe another man in the community, in terms of what he thinks, or what he perceives, or what he does. This is how we write autobiographies of great men. The life-history of a Saint is impossible to write. He cannot be measured by the activities of his mind and intellect, nor can be be evaluated in terms of what he has gained through his organs-of-perception, nor by what he has given to the world through his organs-of-action.

A Man-of-Perfection has a highly developed and a completely disciplined outer and inner equipments as any other normal man, yet *Aṣṭāvakra* despairs here that we cannot describe him in term of his activities by the equipments in him. The Wise-man in his Self-Realisation has ended completely his sense of *doership* and *enjoyership*, and, therefore, even though he is *knowing*, there is *no knower* in him; though he is *seeing* there is *no seer* in him; though he is *speaking* there is no *speaker* in him. We are reminded of the famous words of the *Kaivalya Upaniṣad* (*mantra*-21).

...... पश्याम्यचक्षुः स शृणोम्यकर्णः ।

...... *Paśyāmy-acakṣuḥ sa śṛṇomy-akarṇaḥ.*

"..... I see without eyes, hear without ears."

भिक्षुर्वा भूपतिर्वापि यो निष्कामः स शोभते ।
भावेषु गलिता यस्य शोभनाऽशोभना मतिः ॥ ९१ ॥

Bhikṣur-vā bhūpatir-vāpi yo niṣkāmaḥ sa śobhate,
bhāveṣu galitā yasya śobhanā-'śobhanā matiḥ.

भिक्षुः *bhikṣuḥ* = beggar; वा *vā* = or; भूपतिः *bhūpatiḥ* = king; वा *vā* = or; अपि *api* = indeed; यः *yaḥ*= who; निष्कामः *niṣkāmaḥ* = unattached; सः *saḥ* = he; शोभते *śobhate*= excels; भावेषु *bhāveṣu* = at existent things; गलिता *galitā*= dropped; यस्य *yasya* = whose; शोभना-अशोभना *śobhanā-aśobhanā* = good and evil; मतिः *matiḥ*. = view.

91. May he be a beggar or a king, he indeed excels who is unattached and whose view of existent things has been freed from the sense of good and evil.

From the Self and through the Self, the Self-Realised man can only be conscious of the Self, that is everywhere. The goldsmith sees but gold whatever be the form of the ornaments. It is only the ego, that perceives the pluralistic world of phenomena and gets entrapped by their false charms. One who is enslaved at the level of the ego, prompted by his desires, gushes out to embrace the sense-objects, and seeks his enjoyment among the un-satisfactory sense-gratifications. The very same world-of-objects is viewed from the Self by the Master, who sees in and through them all the brilliancy and glow, the beauty and effulgence of the Ever-Present Self everywhere. Just as when we enter a mirrored-hall, everywhere and at all points we see but ourselves reflected, the spiritually Awakened-one sees nothing but the Self, inherent in all names and forms—everywhere and at all times.

Mahopaniṣad (V-169) also declares this fact of the spiritual life:

यैरेव जायते रागो मूर्खस्याधिकतां गतैः ।
तैरेव भोगैः प्राज्ञस्य विराग उपजायते ॥

Yaireva jāyate rāgo mūrkhasyā-dhikatāṁ gataiḥ,
taireva bhogaiḥ prājñasya virāga upajāyate.

"The very same objects that increase desires and passions in the foolish mind, those very same objects-of-enjoyments provide the Man-of-Wisdom with total dispassion."

Since the Man-of-Realisation recognises nothing but the Absolute Reality everywhere, in all things, and at all places, he comes to rise above the sense of good and evil. He is no more living in our level of Consciousness. He has awakened to be the Infinite Self, himself.

क्व स्वाच्छन्द्यं क्व सङ्कोचः क्व वा तत्त्वविनिश्चयः ।
निर्व्याजार्जवभूतस्य चरितार्थस्य योगिनः ॥ ९२ ॥

Kva svācchandyaṁ kva saṅkocaḥ kva vā tattva-viniścayaḥ
nirvyā-jārjava-bhūtasya caritār-thasya yoginaḥ.

क्व *kva* = where; स्वाच्छन्द्यम् *svācchandyam* = licentiousness; क्व *kva* = where; संङ्कोचः *saṅkocaḥ* = restraint; क्व *kva* = where; वा *vā* = or; तत्त्व-विनिश्चयः *tattva-viniścayaḥ* = determination of Truth; निर्व्याजार्जव-भूतस्य *nir-vyājārjava-bhūtasya* = who is the embodiment of guileless sincerity; चरितार्थस्य *caritārthasya* = who has fulfilled his desired end; योगिनः *yoginaḥ* = of the *Yogin*.

92. ***For the Yogin, who has attained his fulfilment, and who is an embodiment of guileless sincerity, where is licentiousness? Where is restraint? Where is determination of the Truth of the Self?***

The Realised-Saint is one who is constantly living in the Self, as the Self. He has risen above his ego, and therefore, he is always away from the vanity of *doership*. Naturally, what charm is it to him to be licentious? How can he live a wanton-life of sense-indulgence? For whose enjoyment? And where is meaning in his life now for 'restraint of sense-organs.' These are all the activities of the ego. If there is, for one, any sense of enjoyment in the pleasure of the objects in the world around, certainly that ego must learn to live in restraint, so that his mental energies are not wasted in the unproductive and exhausting pursuits of sense-gratifications. How can one, who has awakened from a dream, practise either indulgence or restraint in the dream-world?

The Master who has risen above his ego, cannot be judged with our ethical standards. He transcends every law. He is a law unto Himself! To the Awakened Man, the Transcendental Reality stands revealed in all Its Infinite Splendour and Absolute Beauty; where is for him "the pursuit in search of Truth?"

He has conquered himself and reached the Supreme Goal of Life. He has crowned himself with the State-of-Perfection. There is nothing more for him to gain. He is the Truth. Where is the "determination of Truth of the Self" for him?

आत्मविश्रान्तितृप्तेन निराशेन गतार्तिना ।
अन्तर्यदनुभूयते तत्कथं कस्य कथ्यते ॥ ९३ ॥

Ātma-viśrānti-tṛptena nirāśena gatārtinā,
antar-yad-anubhūyate tat-kathaṁ kasya kathyate.

आत्म-विश्रान्ति-तृप्तेन *ātma-viśrānti-tṛptena* = one who is contented with the repose in the Self; निराशेन *nirāśena* = desireless; गत-अर्तिना *gata-artinā* = who transcends his sorrows; अन्तः *antaḥ* = within; यत् *yat* = which; अनुभूयते *anubhūyate* = is experienced; तत् *tat* = that; कथम् *katham* = how; कस्य *kasya* = to whom; कथ्यते *kathyate* = can be said.

93. *How and to whom can be described, the inner experience of one who is desireless, who transcends all his sorrows, and who is contented with his repose in the Self?*

The despair of the Sage *Aṣṭāvakra* rises to a screaming crescendo as he realises, more and more, his inability to communicate to his brilliant student the True Nature of the Liberated-in-life, even though the Sage himself is fully experiencing It. The State of Perfection refuses to come within the embrace of language. This Transcendental Experience Divine can never be forced to crystallise as an idea in the limited finite intellect, and therefore, words cannot picturise this Experience Unique—wherein the *subject* and the *object* merged into One-Homogeneous-Whole!!

The *Upaniṣad*-s themselves despair in their inability to express this transcendental nature of the Supreme Reality. In utter despair the *Ṛṣi* cries out in *Taittirīya Upaniṣad* (II-4):

यतो वाचो निवर्तन्ते अप्राप्य मनसा सह ।......................॥

Yato vāco nivartante, aprāpya manasā saha, ...

The Realm of Reality is there from where the mind along with speech returns disappointed. ....

The Truth transcends the mind and other equipments, and therefore, these equipments are of no use in the "perceptions" of the Self. The Self-Realised Master, liberated from the vehicles of *matter*, on awakening to the Pure Consciousness becomes the Self *Muṇḍaka Upaniṣad* (III-ii-9).

ब्रह्मवेद ब्रह्मैव भवति ।

Brahmaveda brahmaiva bhavati

"Knower of the *Brahman* becomes the *Brahman*."

Naturally, the teacher asks how we can describe such a Master and to whom can we describe him—who will understand that State of Transcendence?

सुप्तोऽपि न सुषुप्तौ च स्वप्नेऽपि शयितो न च ।
जागरेऽपि न जागर्ति धीरस्तृप्तः पदे पदे ॥ ९४ ॥

Supto'pi na suṣuptau ca svapne'pi śayito na ca,
jāgare'pi na jāgarti dhīras-tṛptaḥ pade pade.

सुप्तः *suptaḥ* = asleep; अपि *api* = even; न *na* = not; सुषुप्तौ *suṣuptau* = in deep sleep; च *ca* = also; स्वप्ने *svapne* = in dream; अपि *api* = even; शयितः *śayitaḥ* = lying; न *na* = not; च *ca* = and; जागरे *jāgare* = in waking state; अपि *api* = even; न *na* = not; जागर्ति *jāgarti* = is awake; धीरः *dhīraḥ* = the Wise-one; तृप्तः *tṛptaḥ* = contented; पदे पदे *pade pade* = under all conditions.

94. The Wise-one is not asleep, even when in deep-sleep. He is not lying down even when dreaming. And he is not awake even in his waking-state. He is contented under all conditions.

For the first time in the *Saṁhitā, Aṣṭāvakra* is making an attempt to describe the Man-of-Perfection with reference to our common experiences in the three different planes-of-Consciousness. Ordinarily a man gathers his total experiences of life from the planes of the waking, dream and dreamless-sleep. The Liberated-in-life is one who has transcended all these usual planes, wherein we function through our gross, subtle and causal bodies. The Self-Realised, lives awakened to the "fourth plane-of-Consciousness" (*Turīya*), in a state of unbroken 'ecstasy.' He has identified himself with the Pure Consciousness here, which is the very Consciousness that illumines all the experiences in the three lesser states of awareness in all creatures, everywhere.

We, in our 'ignorance' identify ourselves totally with our gross, subtle and causal bodies, and thus come to live intensely and exclusively either the experience of the "waking" or of the "dream" or of the "deep-sleep." One who has transcended these three equipments, and has realised his Essence in the Self, he too, though continues to be in the waking, dream and deep-sleep states, cannot be considered as a waker, dreamer, and deep-sleeper—inasmuch as his identifications with the realms of the not-self have been completely eliminated, and consequently, there is no *sense of ego* in him. He has become a '*Witness*'[1] of all that is happening, through the three bodies, in the three states-of-Consciousness.

Therefore, *Aṣṭāvakra* explains "the Wise-one is not asleep, even when in deep sleep; is not lying down even when dreaming; and is not awake, even when in the waking-state." The *ego alone can experience*, in its vanity, that "I am the waker, dreamer, or the deep-sleeper," and directly lives the joys and sorrows in all these three planes.

'*Ignorance*' expresses itself in two ways :

(a) the "*non-apprehension* of Reality," and

(b) the "*mis-apprehensions* of the same."

The state of "*non-apprehension* of Reality" is the *state-of-sleep*, wherein the sleeper is not comprehending anything at all.

The state of "*mis-apprehension* of the Reality" is the *state-of-dream*, when the dreamer has experiences but his entire world is made up of the fancies of his own mind.

According to the higher *Vedāntik* text-books, in the above sense of these terms, the *Ācāryā-s* consider that the entire human-life is composed of only two states—*dream* and *deep-sleep*. The waking also is a kind of "dream" inasmuch as therein also we have not got the knowledge of the Reality : the perceived world-of-plurality is also made up of our "*mis-apprehensions*."

This *Upaniṣadik* usage of these familiar terms—waking, dream and deep-sleep—is employed by *Aṣṭāvakra* in the verse under our review. Though apparently the physical body is

---

1. अवस्था-त्रय-साक्षी (*Avasthā-traya-sākṣī*)—Witness of all happenings in all the three states-of-Consciousness: Waking, dream and deep-sleep—is the Self.

resting in *deep-sleep*, the *Yogin* has never "the *non-apprehension* of Reality" (Self). Similarly, even while the *Yogin* is "dreaming"—be it the projected world outside his body (waking), or inside his bosom (dream)— his ego never crystallises and therefore, revelling ever in the Experience of the Self, never perceives "any *mis-apprehensions* of Reality." "He is not awake," even while he is awake to the phenomenal world, as he has no sense of *I-ness* and *my-ness* in his waking-world. He is not 'awake', he is really *Awake* i.e. he is not 'awake' to the world of names-and-forms, but is really *Awake* to the Transcendental Self.

ज्ञः सचिन्तोऽपि निश्चिन्तः सेन्द्रियोऽपि निरिन्द्रियः ।
सबुद्धिरपि निर्बुद्धिः साहङ्कारोऽनहंकृतिः ॥ ९५ ॥

Jñaḥ sacinto-'pi niścintaḥ sendriyo-'pi nir-indriyaḥ,
sabuddhir-api nir-buddhiḥ sāhaṅkāro-'nahaṁ-kṛtiḥ.

ज्ञः *jñaḥ* = the Man-of-Wisdom; सचिन्तः *sacintaḥ* = thinks; अपि *api* = though; निश्चिन्तः *niścintaḥ* = devoid of thought; सेन्द्रियः (स + इन्द्रियः) *sendriyaḥ (sa + indriyaḥ)* = possessed of sense-organs; अपि *api* = though; निर-इन्द्रियः *nir-indriyaḥ* = devoid of sense-organs; सबुद्धिः *sabuddhiḥ* = possessed of intelligence; अपि *api* = though; निर्बुद्धिः *nir-buddhiḥ* = devoid of intelligence; साहङ्कारः *sāhaṅkāraḥ* = possessed of egoism (अपि *api* = though); अनहंकृतिः *anahaṁkṛtiḥ* = devoid of ego.

95. *The Man-of-Wisdom is devoid of thoughts even when he thinks. He is devoid of sense-organs, even though he possessses them. He is devoid of intelligence even though endowed with an intellect. He is devoid of egoism, even though he possesses an ego.*

The Liberated-in-life has got mind and its thoughts—sense-organs and their sense-perceptions—an intellect and its intelligence. He has certainly a sense of individuality, ego and therefore, he must have "egoism." Yet, in this miserable complex, together called 'a living mortal personality,' the Wise-man has no sense of identification, and so, *Aṣṭāvakra* is compelled to described him, in a maddening language of contradictions, as he has employed in this verse. The Realised-One has all equipments in him, but there is no sense of "*doership*" in him. From an ordinary observer's stand-point, a Sage is apparently making use of all his equipments, and living a normal life just as anyone else. The only distinction that lifts him to be a unique divine creature in the community of men is in that, he has no sense of "*doership*" or "*enjoyership*" in his pulsating vigorous equipments.

Without the sense of ego, even the life in the equipments is nothing but a continuous experience of the Self! The "non-apprehension of Reality" (*Tamas*) has no sorrows in it (deep-sleep). The "mis-apprehensions that are projected by the mind" (dream and waking) have really no sorrows in themselves. But having projected, when the mind identifies with its own imaginations, in this unholy wed-lock between the mind and its projections, is born the ego, and it is this ego, as the *subject*, that experiences the joys and sorrows of its delusory world.

Right at the moment of perception, there is, in fact, no experience at all. The experience is registered by the ego, only as a memory. 'I saw' is an experience; 'I see' is a spontaneous flare of Consciousness! Every experience is a thought. Every thought entertained is a subtle memory of the past. *Thought-bundle is the ego*—therefore, the *ego is nothing but a heap of dead experiences*!...... a mass of memories!!

The Man-of-Perfection lives in the immediate experiences. He refuses to drag the past to muddy the present. He lives eternally in Consciousness, which illumines all experiences, in all bosoms, at all times, in all places.

न सुखी न च वा दुःखी न विरक्तो न सङ्गवान् ।
न मुमुक्षुर्न वा मुक्तो न किञ्चिन्न च किञ्चन ॥ ९६ ॥

Na sukhī na ca vā duḥkhī na virakto na saṅgavān,
na mumukṣur-na vā mukto na kiñcinna ca kiñcana.

न *na* = not; सुखी *sukhī* = happy; न *na* = not; च *ca* = and; वा *vā* = or; दुःखी *duḥkhī* = miserable; न *na* = not; विरक्तः *viraktaḥ* = unattached; न *na* = not; सङ्गवान् *saṅgavān* = attached; न *na* = not; मुमुक्षुः *mumukṣuḥ* = aspirant for liberation; न *na* = not; वा *vā* = or; मुक्तः *muktaḥ* = liberated; न *na* = not; किञ्चित् *kiñcit* = something; न *na* = not; च *ca* = and; किञ्चन *kiñcana* = anything.

96. The Wise-one is neither happy nor miserable, neither attached nor unattached, neither liberated nor an aspirant for liberation—he is neither this nor that.

In so many words, through repeated verses, the Sage is confessing that it is impossible to explain, to another, the nature of the Man-of-Perfection, and his attitude towards life. He lives beyond the equipments, and views the world from his giddy heights; and we, who are still in the entanglements of our own intellect, can never even vaguely comprehend the State of the Experience-Transcendental.

Joy and sorrow are experiences at the realm of the mind. The Man-of-Self-realisation is neither happy nor miserable—meaning he is never identified with his mind.

The sense of attachment and non-attachment are experiences judged and maintained at the intellectual level—a true Saint is not identified with his intellect and therefore, we cannnot describe him in terms of either his attachments or his non-attachments.

From the spiritual level we can define one person as liberated and another one, who is a serious student, as one aspiring to get himself liberated—a Man-of-Perfection is neither liberated nor is he an aspirant-for-liberation, because he has "awakened" to the Supreme— and from his new heights of Wisdom, he looks back to realise, that never was he ever in bondage and, so has never been liberated!! Having awakened from the dream, will you strive to escape the prison in which you were, during the dream?

In short, nothing can be predicated of the Master, who has become one with the Self: "He is neither this nor that" (*Na kiñcit-na ca kiñcana*).

Even the most voluminous classic in *Vedānta, Yoga-Vāsiṣṭha,* when it comes to the point of explaining the mental attitude and inner experience of the Liberated-in-life, loudly despairs:

ततस्तेजस्तमोनिद्रामोहादि परिवर्जिताम् ।
कामप्यवस्थामास्थाय विशश्राम मनः क्षणम् ॥

Tatas-tejas-tamo-nidrā-mohādi pari-varjitām
kāmapy-avasthām-āsthāya viśaśrāma manaḥ kṣaṇam.

"When the mind leaves perceptions and delusions, ignorance and illusions, it comes immediately to rest in some inexplicable and unique State."

विक्षेपेऽपि न विक्षिप्तः समाधौ न समाधिमान् ।
जाड्येऽपि न जडो धन्यः पाण्डित्येऽपि न पण्डितः ॥९७॥

Vikṣepe-'pi na vikṣiptaḥ samādhau na samādhimān,
jāḍye-'pi na jaḍo dhanyaḥ pāṇḍitye-'pi na paṇḍitaḥ.

विक्षेपे *vikṣepe* = in distraction; अपि *api* = even; न *na* = not; विक्षिप्तः *vikṣiptaḥ* = distracted; समाधौ *samādhau* = in *Samādhi*; न *na* = not; समाधिमान् *samādhimān* = in meditation; जाड्ये *jāḍye* = in dullness; अपि *api* = even; न *na* = not; जडः *jaḍaḥ* = dull; धन्यः *dhanyaḥ* = the blessed-one; पण्डित्ये *paṇḍitye* = in learning; अपि *api* = even; न *na* = not; पण्डितः *paṇḍitaḥ* = learned.

97. *The Blessed-one is not distracted even in distraction. He is not in meditation even in Samādhi. He is not dull even in a state of dullness. And he is not learned, even though possessed of learning.*

This is not an exceptional style characteristic of only *Aṣṭāvakra.* All Masters have to employ "the language of contradictions" when they come to explain the inexplicable! This is the only way in which an attempt can be made to "describe the indescribable." This can read as confusions, only to those who are trying to understand it with their intellect. This is not a thing that is to be understood by the intellect. All confusions will end when the seeker transcends his body-consciousness. Experience alone can reveal the Truth. The *Śāstrā-s* can only point out the path—the way. The seeker must earn his own direct-experience.

Man-of-Wisdom is in essence other than what he appears to be. In his realisation he stands distinctly separate from, and as something other than, "the ever-changing complex," constituted of his *matter*-vestures. He is extremely unconcerned with his mental conditions—nay, even with his physical destinies. Distractions, the poise-of-meditation, the slumberous dullness, the erudition and scholarship of learning—all these are only attributes of the mind and intellect. One who has transcended these equipments, how can he be affected by these attributes?

From verse ninety-four onwards it is a brilliant lyrical cry expressing the inability of man's intellectual judgement and of his poetic-sentiment to comprehend and understand the glory and grandeur that is the Man-of-Realisation. Indeed, it is but most appropriate to call this eloquent chapter as "The Goal," wherein we have hundred beautiful and precise indications each pointing to the unique Beauty and inexpressible Glory of the Liberated-in-life.

मुक्तो यथास्थितिस्वस्थः कृतकर्तव्यनिर्वृतः ।
समः सर्वत्र वैतृष्ण्यान्न स्मरत्यकृतं कृतम् ॥ ९८ ॥

Mukto yathā-sthiti-svasthaḥ kṛta-kartavya-nirvṛtaḥ,
samaḥ sarvatra vai-tṛṣṇyān-na smaraty-akṛtaṁ kṛtam.

मुक्तः *muktaḥ* = liberated-one; यथा-स्थिति-स्वस्थः *yathā-sthiti-svasthaḥ* = abiding in the Self in all conditions; कृत-कर्तव्य-निर्वृतः *kṛta-kartavya-nirvṛtaḥ* = free from the idea of action and duty; समः *samaḥ*= same; सर्वत्र *sarvatra* = everywhere; वैतृष्ण्यात् *vaitṛṣṇyāt* = due to the absence of desires; न *na* = not; स्मरति *smarati* = broods over; अकृतम् *akṛtam* = what has not been done; कृतम् *kṛtam* = what has been done.

98. *The Liberated-one, who abides in the Self, under all conditions, is released from the idea of actions and of duty. He is the same everywhere, and due to the absence of desires in him, does not brood over what he has done and what he has not done.*

The main idea that has been hammered all through the chapter is again being hinted at, lest the student should overlook its significance. The Man-of-Perfection has neither the ego-sense (*I-ness*), nor the ego-feeling (*my-ness*). Since he has no ego, he has no sense of action or duty. "Due to the absence of desires in him," he has no regrets in life. He refuses to look back to remember what he has accomplished in life, or not-accomplished in life. Neither by commission nor by omission can the mind of the Master ever get disturbed. He never broods over the past, or upon the future. He lives in the 'eternal-present.' He is a law unto himself—he is unique.[1]

न प्रीयते वन्द्यमानो निन्द्यमानो न कुप्यति ।
नैवोद्विजति मरणे जीवने नाभिनन्दति ॥ ९९ ॥

Na prīyate vandyamāno nindyamāno na kupyati,
naivodvijati maraṇe jīvane nābhinandati.

न *na* = not; प्रीयते *prīyate* = is pleased; वन्द्यमानः *vandyamānaḥ* = praised; निन्द्यमानः *nindyamānaḥ* = blamed; न *na* = not; कुप्यति *kupyati* = annoyed; न *na* = not; उद्विजति *udvijati* = fears; मरणे *maraṇe* = at death; जीवने *jīvane* = in life; न *na* = not; अभिनन्दति *abhinandati* = rejoices.

1. विलक्षणः *Vilakṣanaḥ* = Unique

99. The Liberated-in-Life does not feel pleased when praised; nor does he feel annoyed when blamed. He neither rejoices in life, nor fears death.

Having awakened to the Absolute Consciousness Divine, he no more dwells in the physical body, and therefore relative experiences are no more his. The world cannot touch him. The storms and clouds, the thunders and lightenings of the passionate world-of-*matter* can play only at the feet of his gigantic Divine Colossus. He dwells on the peaks, which is lost to our vision among the heavens.

The praise and insults, honour and dishonour of the pygmies of the world are all of no concern to him. He neither feels elevated by our appreciations, nor is he dejected and despaired at our insults. He needs no compliments of his age. He is self-sufficient unto himself. He lives in this world to give and not to take. He accepts nothing, desires nothing.

He neither rejoices in life, nor is he, when threatened with destruction, afraid of death! Calm and serene he faces life. To him the existence in the body is but a play. He has become the True-Existence which is the Substratum for the whole universe.

The diction used in this verse is reminiscent of the lingering phrases of the brilliant *Bhagavad-Gītā* :

....

नाभिनन्दति न द्वेष्टि तस्य प्रज्ञा प्रतिष्ठिता । (*Bh.Gītā* II-57)

....

Na-abhinandati na dveṣṭi tasya prajñā pratiṣṭhitā.

"...... who neither rejoices nor hates, his Wisdom is firm."

..................लोकान्नोद्विजते च यः । (*Bh.Gītā* XII-15)

..................*Lokān-nodvijate ca yaḥ.*

"........And who cannot be agitated by the world."

न धावति जनाकीर्णं नारण्यमुपशान्तधीः ।
यथा तथा यत्र तत्र सम एवावतिष्ठते ॥ १०० ॥

Na dhāvati janā-kīrṇaṁ nāraṇyam-upaśānta-dhīḥ,
yathā tathā yatra tatra sama evāva-tiṣṭhate.

न *na* = not; धावति *dhāvati* = runs after; जन-अकीर्णम् *jana-akīrṇam* = crowded places; न *na* = not; अरण्यम् *araṇyam* = solitude of a forest; उपशान्त-धीः *upaśānta-dhīḥ* = one whose mind is serene; यथा तथा *yathā tathā* = in any way; यत्र तत्र *yatra tatra* = anywhere; सम *sama* = the same; एव *eva* = indeed; अवतिष्ठते *avatiṣṭhate* = lives.

100. The serene-minded Master seeks neither the crowded place, nor the solitude of the forest. He remains the same under any conditions—in any place.

Established as he is in the Experience Transcendental, nothing affects him at all, wherever he be. He is not affected by the environments. He is the one who influences the entire atmosphere by his presence and glory. To him it is immaterial whether he is in a crowded town or in a solitary cave of the *Himālayan* forests!

Whether he be amidst the majestic objects of the market-places, amidst the din and roar of human frailities, he is ever-established in the Self. Even in the lonely forest of the mighty *Himālayās* he is the same. To him there is no distinction. His inner Experience of Perfection cannot be obstructed under any conditions. He is ever in the Infinite Bliss, which is the nature of the Self.

Bhagavad Gītā (V-19) thunders:

....

निर्दोषं हि समं ब्रह्म .... ॥

....

Nirdoṣaṁ hi samaṁ brahma ....

"The Supreme is the flawless state, the same everywhere."

Wherever he is, under whatever conditions, he remains the same, unaffected by his physical experiences which are ordered by his *Prārabdha* (Ibid, VIII-21).

This concluding verse of this chapter, now under review, echoes an idea which *Janaka* gave earlier in Ibid II-21:

"Oh! I do not find any duality; even the multitude of human-beings, therefore, has become like a forest. Towards what should I then feel attachment?"

A statement in *Annapūrṇopaniṣad* (V-99) throws a flood of light, explaining why the Master feels so readily indifferent under all conditions. Declares the *Upaniṣad*:

विहरन् जनतावृन्दे देवकीर्तनपूजनैः ।
खेदाह्लादौ न जानाति प्रतिबिम्बगतैरिव ॥

Viharan janatā-vṛnde deva-kīrtana-pūjanaiḥ
khed-āhlādau na jānāti pratibimba-gatair-iva.

"Let him revel in the midst of the populace, or let him spend his time in the glorification and the worship of the Lord. He knows neither his sorrows nor his joys—just as a sun that is reflected."

The reflection of the sun in the waters may dance, may break up, but the sun in the heaven is not affected by the conditions of the reflected-sun. Similarly, the Pure Infinite Consciousness, which is now the Nature of the Man-of-Perfection, is not affected by the experiences of the "ego" in him—the Light-of-Consciousness playing in his mind! Master is ego-less, hence he is unaffected by the outer environments.

Chapter XIX

The Grandeur of the Self

Introduction

The thundrous eloquence of *Aṣṭāvakra* in the previous chapter expounded the 'Spiritual Goal' of human-life and painted, as vividly as words could, the nature of the Liberated-in-life (*Jīvan-mukta*). When Perfect Masters, like *Aṣṭāvakra*, inspiredly talk on spiritual themes, they do not aim at public applauses. Theirs' is the mission of not only communicating the Spiritual Knowledge to their listeners, but also strive to help the seekers to gain a direct experience of the Goal indicated.

All seekers are not able to immediately gain a vision of the Reality, because of their inherent mental unpreparedness for the revelation. But perfect students like *Janaka* understand the words of the Masters to be "pointers on the road," and as seekers, they have the mental subtlety to lift themselves in the directions so clearly pointed out. This process of 'hearing' the teacher, and at the same time lifting our mind into those marvellous heights of Perfection, is called the process of "listening" (*Śravaṇa*). The *Upaniṣad-s* are never tired of indicating the infallibility of the process of "listening."

To a true student revelation of the Self comes instantaneously, during his intense *listening* in rapt attention. Here, *Janaka* has accomplised the true *listening*, and, hence, when his Master has concluded his previous discourse, in this chapter, the student rises to mould in words his Self-Experience. Communication of a joy is a way of intensifying and enlarging the bliss experienced. *Janaka* exclaims over the grandeur of his repose in the Self, for his teacher's satisfaction. The fulfilment of Knowledge in *direct vision and wisdom* is the unique goal of true "*Vedāntik*-listening" (*Śravaṇa*).

If the previous chapter is listened to, or ardently studied, with *Janaka*'s attention, the result would be the same in any spiritual student. In eight verses *Janaka* here explains the majestic peace which is the State of the Self : the majestic Grandeur of the Pure Consciousness.

Beyond the ordinary goals-of-life (*Puruṣārtha*), beyond all metaphysical speculations, transcending all the concepts of time and space, far removed from the tumults of life and death, dwells the majestic glory of the Infinite Self in its own unique majesty. This, in short, is *Janaka*'s narration in the chapter.

The *Tejobindu Upaniṣad* (I-45) endorses:

येषां वृत्तिः समा वृद्धा परिपक्वा च सा पुनः ।
ते वै सद्ब्रह्मतां प्राप्ता नेतरे शब्दवादिनः ॥

Yeṣāṁ vṛttiḥ samā vṛddhā paripakvā ca sā punaḥ,
te vai sad-brahmatām prāptā netare śabda-vādinaḥ.

"Those who have purified their minds and cultivated the alertness necessary to comprehend the Self, they alone apprehend the Pure *Brahman*—not others who merely prattle the dialects and quote the letter of the *Śāstrā-s*."

जनक उवाच ।

तत्त्वविज्ञानसन्दंशमादाय हृदयोदरात् ।
नानाविधपरामर्शशल्योद्धारः कृतो मया ॥ १ ॥

Janaka Uvāca:

Tattva-vijñāna-sandaṁśam-ādāya hṛdyo-darāt,
nānā-vidha-parāmarśa-śalyod-dhāraḥ kṛto mayā.

तत्त्व-विज्ञान-सन्दंशम् *tattva-vijñāna-sandaṁśam* = the pincers of the knowledge of Truth; आदाय *ādāya* = taking; हृदय-उदरात् *hṛdya-udarāt* = from the innermost recesses of the heart; नाना-विध-परामर्श-शल्य-उद्धार: *nānā-vidha-parāmarśa-śalya-uddhāraḥ* = the extraction of the thorn of diverse judgements; कृत: *kṛtaḥ*= is done; मया *mayā* = by me.

Janaka said:

1. Using the pincers-of-knowledge of Truth, from the innermost recesses of my heart, I have extracted the thorn of adverse opinions.

Vedā-s emphatically say : *Ekaṁ sat viprāḥ bahudā vadanti* (एकं सत् विप्रा: बहुधा वदन्ति) : "Though Truth is one, Sages call it differently"—and this is because in the past, every Master in India talked only *to teach*—unlike philosophers in the west who strive now to *propound* their 'new' philosophy, or declare their 'fresh' definitions of Truth. The *Ṛṣī-s* always taught to a student, or a team of students, who had approached them requesting for guidance in their spiritual pilgrimage. Each Master thus analysed the student, and guided from where he was, to the same Grand-peak. The different philosophies thus expound but different approaches—all of them in the end, arrive at the same *subjective* experience, at the same Temple of Reality.

Each Master, in advocating his thoughts, was excrutiatingly logical, and each carried an irresistible intellectual charm. To enter into these diverse arguments, for a mere intellectual entertainment, would unavoidably produce, in the student, a lot of unnecessary mental agitations, breeding unnatural doubts and their unhealthy restlessness. *Ācārya Śaṅkara* has warned the students against this hazard on the path of study, in his *Vivekacūḍāmaṇi* (V-62) :

शब्दजालं महारण्यं चित्तभ्रमणकारणम् ।
अत: प्रयत्नाज्ज्ञातव्यं तत्त्वज्ञात्तत्त्वमात्मन: ॥

Śabda-jālaṁ mahāraṇyaṁ citta-bhramaṇa-kāraṇam,
ataḥ prayatnāj-jñātavyaṁ tattva-jñais-tattvam-ātmanaḥ.

"Commentaries on philosophies constitute a thick jungle in which a roaming mind may easily get lost, in its own delusion. Therefore, true seekers of *Brahman* should, through right efforts, come to *experience* the Real Nature of the Self."

All these confusions in the mind can really end with the direct perception of the Self. With a sense of utter gratitude, the student here, the Royal Sage *Janaka*, confesses that he has cleared his mind of all its doubts. Only with the "forceps" of direct-knowledge can we remove the "thorns" of doubts, that ulcerate in the deepest depths of our personality.

Study can guide us, but the knowledge of the text cannot gift us with the Reality. The *Upaniṣad-s* repeatedly warn us that mere study of the text, and repeated listening to various Masters, cannot by themselves, take us near the Truth until we decide to move towards it :

नायमात्मा प्रवचनेन लभ्यो
न मेधया न बहुना श्रुतेन ॥
.... (*Kaṭhopaniṣad, I-ii-23*)

Nāyam-ātmā pravacanena labhyo
na medhayā na bahunā śrutena.,
....

"This *Ātman* cannot be attained by study of *Vedā-s*, nor by intelligence, nor by much hearing."

The entire verse echoes with the natural sentiments of gratitude that every student feels towards the Master who guided him to his own Self and thereby helped him to escape the Self-created tortures of endless sorrows. We read such sentiments expressed by the students of the *Upaniṣad*-s both in the *Bṛhadāraṇyakopaniṣad* and in the *Praśnopaniṣad* (VI-8).

......त्वं हि नः पिता योऽस्माकम्
अविद्यायाः परं पारं तारयसीति ।........

.... *tvaṁ hi naḥ pitā yo'smākam*
avidyāyāḥ paraṁ pāraṁ tārayasīti, ...

"Thou art our father who helps to go across the ocean of our thick ignorance."

क्व धर्मः क्व च वा कामः क्व चार्थः क्व विवेकिता ।
क्व द्वैतं क्व च वाऽद्वैतं स्वमहिम्नि स्थितस्य मे ॥ २ ॥

Kva dharmaḥ kva ca vā kāmaḥ
kva cārthaḥ kva vivekitā,
kva dvaitaṁ kva ca vā'dvaitaṁ
svamahimni sthitasya me.

क्व *kva* = where; धर्मः *dharmaḥ* = piety, meritorious deeds; क्व *kva* = where; च *ca* = and; वा *vā* = or; कामः *kāmaḥ* = desire, sense enjoyments; क्व *kva* = where; च *ca* = and; अर्थः *arthaḥ* = prosperity; क्व *kva* = where; विवेकिता *vivekita* = conscience, discrimination; क्व *kva* = where; द्वैतम् *dvaitam* = duality; क्व *kva* = where; च *ca* = and; वा *vā* = or; अद्वैतम् *advaitam* = non-duality; स्व-महिम्नि *sva-mahimni* = in my own grandeur; स्थितस्य *sthitasya* = abiding; मे *me* = my.

2. *Where is piety? Where is desire? Where is wealth? Where indeed is conscience? Where is duality and where, again, is non-duality?—for me who abides in my own grandeur?*

From his unique State of Infinite Self, *Janaka* exclaims that he cannot recognise, from where he is, the significance, or even the glory, of the various lesser 'goals-of-life'—'piety' (*Dharma*), 'wealth' (*Artha*) and 'desire' (*Kāma*). As there is no conflict between his own knowledge and his ego-centric activities, there is no question of any 'pangs of conscience' (*Vivekitā*) in him.

As a means of directing the mind of the student from the disturbing realm-of-plurality, the *Upaniṣadik* Masters had directed their students towards the non-dual Self, One without-a-second. This non-duality is an illusory attribute of the Self, no doubt, endorsed and accepted by the *Ṛṣī-s*, as it would help the students to walk out of their greater illusions of the world-of-multiplicity. Once the seeker transcends his mind, even the concept of non-duality will become meaningless. The Self alone is. In this universal state of Pure Existence nothing can be predicated. Every attempt at verbalisation of the Absolute Self is an unforgivable blasphemy against Truth. Declares *Avadhūta Gītā* (I-35):

अद्वैतं केचिदिच्छन्ति द्वैतमिच्छन्ति चापरे ।
समं तत्त्वं न विन्दन्ति द्वैताद्वैतविवर्जितम् ॥

Avaitaṁ kecid-icchanti dvaitam-icchanti cāpare,
samaṁ tattvaṁ na vindanti dvaitā-dvait-vivarjitam.

"Some want duality, others want non-duality. They do not apprehend the Truth. It is neither duality nor non-duality."

Chāndogyopaniṣad (VII-xxiv-1) calls this state, which is transcending both duality and non-duality, as *Brahman*. In this discussion the question came up as to where does the *Bhūmā* abide? "It abides in its own grandeur—which is non-grandeur," was the answer :

यत्र नान्यत् पश्यति नान्यत् शृणोति
नान्यत् विजानाति स भूमाऽथ ।
यत्र अन्यत् पश्यति अन्यत् शृणोति
अन्यत् विजानाति तदल्पं ।
यो वै भूमा तदमृतम्
अथ तदल्पं तन्मर्त्यं ।
स भगवः कस्मिन् प्रतिष्ठित इति
स्वे महिम्नि यदि वा न महिम्नीति ॥ १ ॥

Yatra nānyat paśyati nānyat śṛṇoti
nānyad vijānāti sa bhūmā-'tha.
yatra anyat paśyati sṛṇoti
anyat vijānāti tad-alpaṁ
yo vai bhūmā tad-amṛtam
atha tad-alpaṁ tan-martyaṁ,
sa bhagavaḥ kasmin pratiṣṭhita iti
sve mahimni yadi vā na mahimnīti.

"There where nothing is perceived as other, nothing is heard as other, nothing is known as other that is Infinite (*Bhūmā*); where something is perceived as other, something is heard as other, something is known as other that is finite (*Alpam*); That which is Infinite (*Bhūmā*), that is Immortal; what is finite (*Alpam*), that is mortal." Where is, Sir, this *Bhūmā* abiding? "It abides in its own grandeur—which is non-grandeur."

क्व भूतं क्व भविष्यद्वा वर्तमानमपि क्व वा ।
क्व देशः क्व च वा नित्यं स्वमहिम्नि स्थितस्य मे ॥३॥

Kva bhūtaṁ kva bhaviṣyad-vā vartamānamapi kva vā,
kva deśaḥ kva ca vā nityaṁ svamahimni sthitasya me.

क्व *kva* = where; भूतम् *bhūtam* = past; क्व *kva* = where; भविष्यत् *bhaviṣyat* = future; वा *vā* = or; वर्तमानम् *vartamānam* = present; अपि *api* = even; क्व *kva* = where; वा *vā* = or; क्व *kva* = where; देशः *deśaḥ* = space; क्व *kva* = where; च *ca* = and; वा *vā* = or; नित्यम् *nityam* = eternity; स्व-महिम्नि स्थितस्य मे *sva-mahimni sthitasya me* = for me abiding in my own grandeur.

3. *Where is the past? Where is the future? Where, even, is the present? Where is space? Where, even, is eternity for me who abide in my own grandeur?*

Time and space are really the concepts of the mind and intellect. Where the mind-intellect is not functioning, as in deep-sleep, or under chloroform, the individual has no such measurements in his experience. Time and its duration are as much the creation of the human-mind as the concept of space and its distances.

Distances are measured in space between two relative points, let us say between two points—A and B. From A to B the distance may be any linear measurement; but in all these cases we know, that at point A the distance is always zero, whatever be the distance measured at point B.

In the same way the duration of time is measured as "the interval between any two successive experiences." You, perhaps, started reading this book at 10-00 a.m., and you stopped reading at 11-00 a.m. Then the interval between these two different experiences is called the measurement of time. Every experience is entertained by the mind in terms of its thoughts. Thus the interval between thoughts is the unit-measurement of time. If there is no other experience-B, then the time ceases; at experience-A time is zero!

In the seeker, who has transcended his mind, there can be no thoughts, and therefore, the concepts of both 'time and space' cannot be in him, when he is abiding beyond his mind, in the Self.

In 'time' the mind again entertains the illusory ideas of the past, present and future. In the Self these illusions can have no valid existence. For one, who has thus transcended the cocnepts of both 'time and space,' the very idea of "eternity" has no meaning, because the very concepts of eternity is : "non-stop-time."

On transcending the mind, *Janaka* confesses, he has arrived at a realm of experience, where the world-of-plurality cannot come to play, as it has not got the 'time-space' frame-work for the names and forms to exists.

क्व चात्मा क्व च वाऽनात्मा क्व शुभं क्वाशुभं तथा ।
क्व चिन्ता क्व च वाऽचिन्ता स्वमहिम्नि स्थितस्य मे ॥४॥

Kva cātmā kva ca vā'nātmā
kva śubhaṁ kvāśubhaṁ tathā,
kva cintā kva ca vā'cintā
sva-mahimni sthitasya me.

क्व *kva* = where; च *ca* = also; आत्मा *ātmā* = Self; क्व *kva* = where; च *ca* = and; वा *vā* = or; अनात्मा *anātmā* = not-self; क्व *kva* = where; शुभम् *śubham* = good; क्व *kva* = where; अशुभम् *aśubham* = evil; तथा *tathā* = similarly; क्व *kva* = where; चिन्ता *cintā* = anxiety; क्व *kva* = where; च *ca* = and; वा *vā* = or; अचिन्ता *acintā* = anxiety; स्व-महिम्नि स्थितस्य मे *sva-mahimni sthitasya me* = for me abiding in my own grandeur.

4. *Where is the Self? Where is the non-Self? Where, similarly, are good and evil? Where is anxiety or non-anxiety—for me, who abide in my own grandeur?*

On awakening from the dream the entire *subject-object*-world of the dream disappears to merge with the very essence and substance of the waker's mind. In the same way on awakening, from the present state of our existence, into the Infinite State of the Self, *Janaka* exclaims, that he, in his new State, cannot conceive the distinction between the Self and the non-self, or between the good and evil, or between the condition of anxiety and non-anxiety. All these are sustained and interpreted by the human-mind. On transcending the mind one rediscovers the Self and in the Self, where are these illusions of the mind?

The *Saṁskṛta* terms *Cintā* and *Acintā* are translated here as 'anxiety' and 'non-anxiety'. Some commentators, however, have interpreted these two terms as 'meditation' and 'non-meditation.' This rendering is equally acceptable. In one's delusory state, when the ego is trying to transcend the mind, there is a "state-of-meditation." When the ego, is turned outward, fattening the mind and pre-occupied with its joys of sense-gratifications, there is the "state-of-non-meditation." Both these have a reference to the introvertedness and the extrovertedness of the mind. On transcending the mind and reaching the Self, there can be neither meditation-state nor the non-meditation-state.

क्व स्वप्नः क्व सुषुप्तिर्वा क्व च जागरणं तथा ।
क्व तुरीयं भयं वापि स्वमहिम्नि स्थितस्य मे ॥ ५ ॥

Kva svapnaḥ kva suṣuptirvā kva ca jāgaraṇaṁ tatha,
kva turīyaṁ bhayaṁ vāpi sva-mahimni sthitasya me.

क्व *kva* = where; स्वप्नः *svapnaḥ* = dream; क्व *kva* = where; सुषुप्तिः *suṣuptiḥ* = deep sleep; वा *vā* = or; क्व *kva* = where; च *ca* = and; जागरणम् *jāgaraṇam* = wakefulness; तथा *tathā* = as also; क्व *kva* = where; तुरीयम् *turīyam* = fourth state of Consciousnes; भयम् *bhayam* = fear; वा *vā* = or (where); अपि *api* = even; स्वमहिम्नि स्थितस्य मे *svamahimni sthitasya me* = for me abiding in my own grandeur.

5. *Where is dream, where is deep-sleep, where is wakefulness, and also where is the fourth-state of Cosnciousness; where is even fear for me, who abide in my own grandeur.*

Māṇḍūkyopaniṣad, for the first time, has scientifically observed and philosophically analysed an individual's experience in the three fields-of-Consciousness—the waking, the dream and the deep-sleep. With reference to these three fields—of the waker, of the dreamer and of the deep-sleeper—on transcending the gross, subtle and the causal bodies, the ego disappears into the vision of the fourth-plane of Consciousness (*Turīya*). In terms of the known alone the unknown can be defined and indicated. In *Māṇḍūkyopaniṣad,* the *Ṛṣi* has kindly indicated this Pure State of Consciousness, from our world of experiences, in the relative field.

Just as on awakening from the dream, the dreamer and his dream-world merge into the waker, so too, on reaching this Fourth-Plane, we transcend the earlier three states of delusion and therefore, the experience of the Pure Self cannot be called as the Fourth-Plane. This is the Transcendental Experience of the Absolute Self.

Janaka here denies for himself all these four delusions of Consciousness, as he has got fully established in the Self, as the Self.

All 'fears' belong to the ego, due to its desires, so declares the *Bṛhadāraṇyaka Upaniṣad* (I-iv-2):

द्वितीयात् वै भयं भवति ।

Dvitīyat vai bhayaṁ bhavati :

"From the perception of the other fear comes."

The Liberated-in-life, awakened to the Infinite Self, experiences nothing other than Self within and without, and as such, asks *Janaka*, "Where is even fear for me?"

In sheer spiritual audacity there is no text that can stand a parallel to the firm and daring assertions of *Avadhūta-Gītā* (III-20):

स्थानत्रयं यदि च नेति कथं तुरीयं, कालत्रयं यदि च नेति कथं दिशश्च ।
शान्तं पदं हि परमं परमार्थतत्त्वं, ज्ञानामृतं समरसं गगनोपमोऽहम् ॥

Sthāna-trayaṁ yadi ca neti kathaṁ turīyaṁ
kāla-trayaṁ yadi ca neti kathaṁ diśaś-ca,
śāntaṁ padaṁ hi paramaṁ paramārtha-tattvaṁ
jñānāmṛtaṁ sama-rasaṁ gagano-pamo-'ham.

"When the three are not there, how can there be the Fourth-State-of-Consciousness? When the three-fold division of Time is not there, how can there be 'direction' (Space)? The Supreme Truth is a State of

Peace. I am Immortal, Knowledge ever-the-same, like the sky."

क्व दूरं क्व समीपं वा बाह्यं क्वाभ्यन्तरं क्व वा ।
क्व स्थूलं क्व च वा सूक्ष्मं स्वमहिम्नि स्थितस्य मे ॥ ६ ॥

Kva dūraṁ kva samīpaṁ vā
bāhyaṁ kvā-bhyantaraṁ kva vā,
kva sthūlaṁ kva ca vā sūkṣmaṁ
sva-mahimni sthitasya me.

क्व *kva* = where; दूरम् *dūram* = distance; क्व *kva* = where; समीपम् *samīpam* = near; वा *vā* = or; बाह्यम् *bāhyam* = outside; क्व *kva* = where; अभ्यन्तरम् *abhyantaram* = inside; क्व *kva* = where; वा *vā* = or; क्व *kva* = where; स्थूलम् *sthūlam* = the gross; क्व *kva* = where; च *ca* = and; वा *vā* = or; सूक्ष्मम् *sūkṣmam* = the subtle; स्वमहिम्नि स्थितस्य मे *sva-mahimni sthitasya me* = for me who abide in my own grandeur.

6. *Where is distance, where is nearness, where is outside, where is inside, where is the gross and where is the subtle—for me, who abide in my own grandeur.*

All these distinctions are recognised by the ego as it looks out upon the illusory world-of-plurality, when the Truth is misinterpreted by the mind-in-agitation. The *Tamoguṇa* dims the powers of discrimination in the human-intellect, and it comes to 'ignore' the Truth. To ignore 'the Reality' is the condition of "*ignorance.*" When the intellect is thus veiled, the mind projects, in fanciful imaginations, a world-of-multiplicity and it gets itself restless in the play of *Rajas*. Thereafter, it distinguishes "far and near," "outside and inside," "gross and subtle"— and such other endless varieties of delusions.

When the mind was hushed, in the alert moments of intense listening, in *Janaka*, the veiling of his intellect dropped and the Truth revealed Itself. "One who is thus firmly abiding in the experience of the Infinite Self," wonders *Janaka*, "how can he now have the illusions, which the mind then created for his temporary entertainment!"

क्व मृत्युर्जीवितं वा क्व लोकाः क्वास्य क्व लौकिकम् ।
क्व लयः क्व समाधिर्वा स्वमहिम्नि स्थितस्य मे ॥ ७ ॥

Kva mṛtyur-jīvitaṁ vā kva lokāḥ kvāsya kva laukikam,
kva layaḥ kva samādhir-vā svamahimni sthitasya me.

क्व *kva*= where; मृत्युः *mṛtyuḥ* = death; जीवितम् *jīvitam* = life; वा *vā* = or; क्व *kva* = where; लोकाः *lokāḥ* = worlds; क्व *kva* = where; अस्य (मम) *asya (mama)* = my; क्व *kva* = where; लौकिकम् *laukikam* = worldly relation; क्व *kva* = where; लयः *layaḥ* = dissolution-of-Consciousness; क्व *kva* = where; समाधि *samādhi* = *samādhi* (concentration); वा *vā* = or; स्वमहिम्नि स्थितस्य मे *sva-mahimni sthitasya me* = for me who abide in my own grandeur.

7. *Where is life or where is death? Where are the worlds or where are the worldly relations? Where is dissolution-of-Consciousness? Where is Samādhi— for me, who in my own grandeur abide?*

Life and death, the world as fields-of-experiences, the worldly relations—all these are interpretations and concepts of the mind and intellect. As ego, which is living in the awareness of plurality, strives in its spiritual pursuit, to liquidate its 'consciousness-of-objects' by withdrawing its mind entirely from the objects, and by turning it into the contemplation of the Immutable Self—the Witness of All. In this way, the ego tries to reach a *State of Laya* wherein it achieves to a larger extent the "dissolution-of-Consciousness" of the multiple world. This process of *Laya* is often advised as a pre-condition before diving into *Samādhi*, wherein the ego ends in the Infinite flare of Enlightenment. *Janaka*, who has already gained the Goal and has established himself in the Self, must necessarily wonder what has he to do any more with *Laya* or *Samādhi*.

अलं त्रिवर्गकथया योगस्य कथयाऽप्यलम् ।
अलं विज्ञानकथया विश्रान्तस्य ममात्मनि ॥ ८ ॥

Alaṁ trivarga-kathayā yogasya kathayā-'pyalam,
alaṁ vijñāna-kathayā viśrāntasya mamātmani.

अलम् *alam* = needless; त्रिवर्ग-कथया *trivarga-kathayā* = of talking about the three ends of life; योगस्य *yogasya* = of *Yoga*; कथया *kathayā* = of talking; अपि *api* = even; अलम् *alam* = needless; अलम् *alam* = needless; विज्ञान-कथया *vijñāna-kathayā* = talks of direct knowledge; विश्रान्तस्य *viśrāntasya* = reposing; मम *mama* = my; आत्मनि *ātmani* = in Self.

8. *For me, who repose in the Self, talks about the three 'goals-of-life' is useless; talks about Yoga is purposeless. And even talks about direct-knowledge is needless!*

The shoreless-Peace and the boundless-Contentment experienced by the Man-of-Self-realisation in his divine sense of fulfilment is vividly echoed in this brilliant verse, with which, *Janaka* concludes his authobiographical spiritual confession. The three "goals-of-life" (*Dharma*, *Artha*, *Kāma*), *Yoga* and direct-experience in *Samādhi*, are all means for the realisation of the Self. To one who has already realised, the means are no more of any significance. Should one who has crossed river, carry the boat on his head?

The Experience of the Self is self-sufficient unto Itself. It needs nothing else to complete It. It is Absolute in Its perfection. All the means of realisation are to smuggle the ego out of its illusions into the Effulgent Light of the Reality Supreme.

Chapter XX

The Absolute State

Introduction

In communicating to the seekers the unsurpassing beauty and indefinable perfections of the Absolute, the *Upaniṣad*-s stammer; the *Brahma-sūtrā-s* exhaust itself, and the *Bhagavad-Gītā* hesitates with an excusable shyness. A theme, in dealing with which, even these mighty books of *Hindūism* are thus, at best, unsatisfctory; we must, in sheer gratitude, admire *Aṣṭāvakra Saṁhitā* for the brilliant success it has achieved in communicating, through words, perhaps, more clearly the nature and glory of the Supreme Reality, than by the *Prasthāna Traya.* In this concluding chapter, the Absolute State of Transcendence is brought home to us, not so much because of the frenzied eloquence of the teacher, nor by the extra fluidity of the diction chosen, but essentially because of the human-touch that has been imparted to it by putting this chapter into the mouth of King *Janaka.* The student of this *Saṁhitā* is himself giving the autobio-data of the liberated-in-life. We have here in this chapter a revealing autobiography of the Saint, the Liberated-in-life in King *Janaka.*

The Absolute Self with no relationship with anything is the subtle theme of this sacred chapter. The Aloneness of the Self surpasses all empirical terms that generally determine, and often clearly define, any-other phenomenon in the relative-field of experiences. Beyond all assertions and denial, beyond the concepts of bondage and liberation, lies this Realm of the Self, wherein there is neither the individual-ego (*jīva*), nor is there even the Supreme-Reality (*Brahman*)!

Aṣṭāvakra here dexterously uses contradictions and paradoxes as a painter would artistically use his colours, or a surgeon would clinically wield his instruments. Repeatedly the reader is shocked, and often jerked out of his intellectualism—to a point certainly nearer the direct experience of the Pure Self!

There is a geometry in the very construction of this chapter. In every verse, *Janaka*, indicates the Liberated-in-life in him, with a significant and revealing term, which can rocket the mind of a meditative student onto Realms Transcendental. Each of these chosen phrases serve as an ego-to-Self-rocket! The 'Stainless' (*Nirañjana*), 'beyond the sense of duality' (*Gata-dvandva*), 'State of no-attributes' (A-*rūpa*) etc., are examples. Each of these terms must be considered as highly inflammable, when it comes to the bosom of a true meditator! Each one of them can get ignited to burn with the clear Light-of-wisdom, and as a torch it can illumine the dark and lonely path, through which must march every seeker—the alone to the Alone, all-alone.

It has already been said earlier by *Aṣṭāvakra* that the Self is beyond speech, understanding, and even contemplation. It was clearly suggested that *to end meditation, in meditation, with meditation is the highest fulfilment of meditation.*

Throughout the *Saṁhitā*, and particularly in this finale, the Sage with artistic precision and with a surgeon's efficient carefulness has used deliberate-contradictions and chosen-paradoxes to blast up and remove from the intellectual student his inherent fascination for objective logic and reason.

No doubt, sense of logic and alertness of reason distinguish man from the animal-kingdom. They are his glory and his beauty. Yet, on the path of the spiritual rediscovery, having made use of these faculties of logic and reason to their maximum, the student must learn the art of discarding them—even the intellect is to be transcended—after they had fulfilled their functions.

The beauty and fragrance of the petals must fade, dry and curl up to fall down, when the delicate blossom perishes into the emergence of the fruit!

Transcending the intellect, stretches the dimensionless Infinitude of Peace and Beatitude, *Aṣṭāvakra*'s technique stands justified and entirely fulfilled in *Janaka*, the Liberated-in-life.

जनक उवाच ।

क्व भूतानि क्व देहो वा क्वेन्द्रियाणि क्व वा मनः ।
क्व शून्यं क्व च नैराश्यं मत्स्वरूपे निरञ्जने ॥१॥

Janaka Uvāca:

Kva bhūtāni kva deho vā kvendriyāṇi kva vā manaḥ,
kva śūnyaṁ kva ca nairāśyaṁ mat-svarūpe nirañjane.

क्व *kva* = where; भूतानि *bhūtāni* = the five great elements; क्व *kva* = where; देहः *dehaḥ* = body; वा *vā* = or; क्व *kva* = where; इन्द्रियाणि *indriyāṇi* = organs; क्व *kva* = where; वा *vā* = or; मनः *manaḥ* = mind; क्व *kva* = where; शून्यम् *śūnyam* = void; क्व *kva* = where; च *ca* = and; नैराश्यम् *nairāśyam* = despair; मत्-स्वरूपे *mat-svarūpe* = in my Essential Nature; निरञ्जने *nirañjane* = stainless.

Janaka Said:

1. *Where are the five Great-Elements, and where is the body, where are the organs, and where is the mind? Where is the void, and where, too, is despair—for me, who am by nature Stainless?*

All through these fourteen verses of this chapter, *Janaka* is giving us the autobiography of the Liberated-in-life in him. Nobody else can write the story of a Saint; biography of a Sage at best, is the description of the physical beauty of a singer and the grace of her enchanting performance to an inspired audience, described by an enthusiastic writer, who is both dumb and deaf from birth!

From the awakened State of the Self, which transcends all relative-planes, there are neither the five elements nor the physical body formed out of them. Neither are there the organs-of-perception, nor the instruments-of-action—nor the mind, that is built up by our perceptions and our responses. If the elements are the *cause*, the body is their *effect*. If the sense-organs are the *cause*, the mind is their *effect*. By denying them, *Janaka* is denying the "*cause-effect*-relationship," which is so true when we are in the ego-centric state of perceiving our world-of-plurality through our mind.

Transcending "*cause* and *effect*"—which have an existence only in the world that we perceive through our body, mind and intellect equipments—is the Self, which, as Consciousness, is the Illuminator of these two assertions of the Intellect. The illuminator is always different from the illumined. Identified with the Self, *Janaka* could recognise neither the cause nor accept the world-of-effects, in his intense Exeprience Immutable.

When all the "*effects*" are thus eliminated, the intellect can conceive only a 'void,' a state of complete absence-of-things, just as the condition we experience in deep-sleep. This 'void' (*Śūnya*) has been conceived by a certain school of Buddhists as the Highest State. *Janaka*, contradicts this fallacious conclusions, when he asks: "where is despair?". To be in the 'void' is to feel utter *despair*. It is a state of total negation of both the worlds of "*objects*" and the "*subject*" — the meditator himself. It is boundless loneliness. It is a sheer tragedy, and weary despair. *Vedānta* asserts that a Man-of-Realisation rises above both the sense-of-void and its consequent *despairs*, into the serene repose of the Stainless Self. *Janaka* endorses this with his own direct experience.

The Self is the ultimate "*subject*," where there are no *objects* at all. In the realm of the *objects* alone can the *cause-effect* phenomenon function. Here three sets of examples are given to represent all *cause-effect*-relationships comprehended at all levels of our personality. The five elements and body includes all *cause-effect-relationships* experienced at the *body-level*; the sense-organs and mind embraces all such relationships that are at *mental-level*; and the "*consequent despair*' can be considered to represent, in itself, all *cause-effect-perceptions at the intellectual-level.*

क्व शास्त्रं क्वात्मविज्ञानं क्व वा निर्विषयं मनः ।
क्व तृप्तिः क्व वितृष्णत्वं गतद्वन्द्वस्य मे सदा ॥ २ ॥

Kva śāstraṁ kvātma-vijñanaṁ
kva vā nir-viṣayaṁ manaḥ,
kva tṛptiḥ kva vitṛṣṇatvaṁ
gata-dvandvasya me sadā.

क्व *kva* = where; शास्त्रम् *śāstram* = scriptures; क्व *kva* = where; आत्म-विज्ञानम् *ātma-vijñanam* = knowledge of the Self; क्व *kva* = where; वा *vā* = or; निर्विषयम् *nirviṣayam* = detachment from sense-objects; मनः *manaḥ* = mind; क्व *kva* = where; तृप्तिः *tṛptiḥ* = contentment; क्व *kva* = where; वितृष्णत्वम् *vitṛṣṇatvam* = desireless-ness; गत-द्वन्द्वस्य *gata-dvandvasya* = who has transcended the duality of the pairs-of-opposites; मे *me* = for me; सदा *sadā* = ever.

2. *Where are the scriptures? Where is the knowledge of the Self? Where is the mind detached from the sense-objects and where is contentment? Where is desireless-ness for me, who have transcended the duality of the pairs-of-opposites?*

So long as we are functioning at the mental level as an ego, we cannot avoid perceiving the world-of-plurality and experiencing the pairs-of-opposites. One who has transcended the mind, has eliminated his ego, and therefore, in him there is no sense of '*enjoyership*' to experience the pairs-of-opposites.

All the scriptural text-books are addressed to the ego, which is suffering from its sense of *doership* and *enjoyership*. The scriptures try to give the student a clear knowledge of the Blissful and Perfect Nature of the Self. In order to realise this

Seat of Consciousness, the scriptures advise the students to detach their minds from sense-objects, since without arresting the outgoing tendencies of the mind, it cannot be persuaded to have a steady inward gaze.

Even the sense of contentment of the mind and the state of desirelessness of the intellect can have no meaning for the Liberated-in-life as he has transcended both his mind and intellect!

This State, indicated here, is not for our intellectual appreciation; it is to be realised. And it can be realised only when the seeker accomplishes what these verses are screaming: The Knowledge of the Self lies not in the texts of even the *Vedā-s*. It awaits for your direct experience in your own Self.

क्व विद्या क्व च वाऽविद्या क्वाहं क्वेदं मम क्व वा ।
क्व बन्धः क्व च वा मोक्षः स्वरूपस्य क्व रूपिता ॥ ३ ॥

Kva vidyā kva ca vā-'vidyā
kvāhaṁ kvedaṁ mama kva vā,
kva bandhaḥ kva ca vā mokṣaḥ
svarūpsya kva rūpitā.

क्व *kva* = where; विद्या *vidyā* = knowledge; क्व *kva* = where; च *ca* = and; वा *vā* = or; अविद्या *avidyā* = ignorance; क्व *kva* = where; अहम् *aham* = 'I'; क्व *kva* = where; इदम् *idam* = this; मम *mama* = my; क्व *kva* = where; वा *vā* = or; क्व *kva* = where; बन्धः *bandhaḥ* = bondage; क्व *kva* = where; च *ca* = and; वा *vā* = or; मोक्षः *mokṣaḥ* = liberation; स्वरूपस्य *svarūpsya* = of my essential nature; क्व *kva* = where; रूपिता *rūpitā* = attribute.

3. *Where is Knowledge and where is 'ignorance'; where is 'I', where is 'this' and where is 'mine'; where is bondage and where is liberation? Where is an attribute to the Essential Nature of my Infinite Self?*

These terms are all valid only in the relative-field. Where the mind is not, how can the ego perceive an object as 'this'? '*Ignorance*' cannot be in the Infinite Knowledge; and Knowledge itself cannot be an attribute of the Self, when all delusions of '*ignorance*' have ended!!

The ego, as the *subject* that experiences the world-of-objects, is universally known in our bosom, expressing as the 'I'-sense. Where the *subject* is, that subject-ego, through its equipments of body, mind and intellect must perceive, feel, and think its world of perceptions, emotions, and thoughts. The ego-experiences together constitute our concept of the world. Thus, so long as the *subject* exists, there cannot but be the "field-of-objects"—the world. On transcending and experiencing the Self, how can there be the sense of *'I'-ness, and its mis-interpretations* which *together form the world*?

This ego-sense, *I-ness*, when it expresses out in the world-of-objects, and relates itself with the world, becomes the ego-*feeling*, expressed as *my-ness*. Since the ego is itself transcended, the idea of '*my-ness*' has also retired. When the husband of my wife is no more, my wife is also gone—when I awake up from my dream in which I experienced that I was married to my wife!

The *Upaniṣad-Ṛṣī-s* were not only adept in reaching the subtlest states of unique spiritual experiences, but they were dexterous technicians in communicating their Wisdom to us, and improvising a variety of means by which we too can be safely transported onto those divine Realms of Perfection. For this purpose, very often, they had to fabricate terms and phrases, as tools in their sacred profession.

The world of the ego and its behaviour in turn—all are cmprehended together by the term *Ahamtā*. Similarly, all possible fields-of-experiences of the ego are together termed as the *Idam*—*Idam* means "this," and the whole world-of-objects is the field defined by the term "*this-ness*" (*Idamtā*)... If we may use such a term! That is the reason why in the commentary we took the term 'this' *(Idam)* as the "world-of-experiences."

The sense of *bondage* and the sense of *liberation* are both conceived by the mind. Mind turned towards the sense-objects is the mind in "*bondage*," and it is such a sad and miserable mind existing ever in sense-pursuits that conceives and comprehends a state of its own "liberation" from its own present thraldom. To one who has transcended the equipments and has thus blasted the ego, which has now rediscovered its identity with the Essential Self, how can there be all these delusory misconceptions, asks the fully-Liberated *Janaka*?

Avadhūta Gītā (I-58) unhesitatingly thunders:

न जातोऽहं मृतो वाऽपि न मे कर्म शुभाशुभं ।
विशुद्धं निर्गुणं ब्रह्म बन्धो मुक्तिः कथं मम ॥

Na jāto'haṁ mṛto vā'pi na
me karma śubhā-śubhaṁ,
viśuddhaṁ nirguṇaṁ brahma
bandho muktiḥ kathaṁ mama.

"I am never born —neither do I die. In me there is no activity—either good or bad. I am all Pure *Brahman*—without any attributes. How then should there be in Me anything like bondage or liberation?"

क्व प्रारब्धानि कर्माणि जीवन्मुक्तिरपि क्व वा ।
क्व तद्विदेहकैवल्यं निर्विशेषस्य सर्वदा ॥ ४ ॥

Kva prārabdhāni karmāṇi jīvan-muktir-api kva vā,
kva tad-videha-kaivalyaṁ nir-viśeṣasya sarvadā.

क्व *kva* = where; प्रारब्धानि *prārabdhāni* = commenced; कर्माणि *karmāṇi* = actions; जीवन्-मुक्तिः *jīvan-muktiḥ* = liberation-in-life; क्व *kva* = where; वा *or* = or; क्व *kva* = where; तत् *tat* = that; विदेह-कैवल्यम् *videha-kaivalyam* = liberation-at-death; निर्विशेषस्य *nir-viśeṣasya* = undifferentiated (मे *me* = for me); सर्वदा *sarvadā* = ever.

4. *Where are* Prārabdha *karmā-s, where is liberation-in-life, and where is even liberation-at-death for me, the Ever-Undifferentiated!*

The actions always have their reactions. Good-actions leave good *Vāsanā-s* in the personality, which in their turn create good thoughts, and therefore, they will provide mental peace and inner joy. Evil-actions create evil *Vāsanā-s*, which would generate mental restlessness, and the consequent inner sorrows. Already in the *Saṁhitā*, to satisfy the common-man who sees the Man-of-Perfection functioning in the society, it was explained by *Aṣṭāvakra* that the Liberated-in-life functions in the world outside under the impulsion of the *Prārabdha* of his body.

In these activities of his body, he is not at all involved and to drive home this idea, the functions of the Perfect-man were compared with the apparent movements of the dry-leaf fallen from the tree, and moving about in the breeze! Now *Janaka*, the Liberated from his State of Selfhood, is denying even any *Prārabdha* for himself. The "doer" of the activities is the ego, and reactions must come to the ego. The murderer alone can be punished for his murder. The police may apprehend a murderer, but the law-officer cannot serve the warrant of arrest on the criminal, if, on the previous night, he had died!

No doubt, we cannot escape *Karma*; actions will have their reactions. But actions are undertaken by the ego; the reactions are experienced by the same ego. One in whom the ego has been transcended, the law of action-and-reaction must cease for him. The criminal has deceased—the warrant of arrest is returned! The file is closed! *Janaka* is confident that he has no *Prārabdha*. He is now the Universal, the Undifferentiated; the one who is "free from all particularisation" (*Nirviśeṣa*).

As the Pure Infinite Self Immutable and All-pervading, as the very substratum for the delusory universe of names-and-forms, *Janaka* cannot understand either the State of the Liberation-in-life, nor the State of the Liberated-at-death. He recognises no Liberation. He is the Self, the Ever-Perfect—never contaminated.

क्व कर्ता क्व च वा भोक्ता निष्क्रियं स्फुरणं क्व वा ।
क्वापरोक्षं फलं वा क्व निःस्वभावस्य मे सदा ॥ ५ ॥

Kva kartā kva ca vā bhoktā
niṣkriyaṁ sphuraṇaṁ kva vā,
kvā-parokṣaṁ phalaṁ vā kva
niḥ-svabhāvasya me sada.

क्व *kva* = where; कर्ता *kartā* = doer; क्व *kva* = where; च *ca* = and; वा *vā* = or; भोक्ता *bhoktā* = enjoyer; निष्क्रियम् *niṣkriyam* = cessation of activities (thinking); स्फुरणम् *sphuraṇam* = rising up of thoughts; क्व *kva* = where; वा *vā* = or; क्व *kva* = where; अपरोक्षम् *aparokṣam* = direct knowledge; फलम् *phalam* = reflected knowledge; वा *vā* = or; क्व *kva* = where; निःस्वभावस्य *niḥ-svabhāvasya* = devoid of natural attributes (impersonal); मे *me* = for me; सदा *sada* = ever.

5. *Where is the 'doer' or the 'enjoyer'? Where is the cessation-of-thoughts or the rising-of-thoughts? Where is direct-knowledge or reflected-knowledge for me, who am ever devoid of natural attributes?*

"The natural attributes" of a human-being is that he is promted always by his ego and ego-centric desires. He has an irresistible fascination for the sense-gratifications. He always lives a life of duality constantly tossed between his likes and dislikes. The Liberated-in-life is one who has freed himself from his ego and ego-centric desires. Therefore, in his behaviour, in the world outside, we can define him only as one who is "devoid of his natural attributes" (*Niḥ-Svabhāvaḥ* = *Svabhāva-Rahita*).[1]

When the ego is no more functioning in the bosom, there canot be, in that individual, the sense of *doership* or

1. In the *Jīvan-Mukti-Gītā*, Sage *Dattātreya* also, in same context, uses a very expressive phrase: "स्वभावगुणवर्जितम्" (*Svabhāva-guṇa-varjitam*).

enjoyership. Within the mind-intellect the ego exists and functions. Where there is no ego, the equipments are also transcended. Mind is the thought-flow and, therefore, to one who has transcended the mind and is living in the Self, where is the *cessation-of-thought* or the *rising-of-thought*?

In every school of philosophy, it will have an elaborate theory of how man comes to gain knowledge. Of them all, the *Vedāntik* theory of perception and knowledge is most rational. Mind, through sense-organs, flows out to the place where the object is, and there the mind gets itself moulded into the shape of the object. The ripple of disturbance so created in the mind, gets illuminated in the Light-of-Consciousness, and then the individual considers that he has seen and understood the object.

The knowledge-of-the-object reaches our bosom as a disturbance (*Vṛtti*) which glows in the Light-of-Consciousness (*Caitanya*). Hence the knowledge-of-objects is called as "the final result" (*Phala*).[1] The very first impact of the sense-stimuli upon our mind is to create a disturbance therein (*Vṛtti*). This then shines in the Light-of-Consciousness. "The final result" (*Phala*) is the "reflected-knowledge."

As a constrast to this reflected-knowledge, which changes from object to object, there is the "direct-knowledge" (*Aparokṣa-jñāna*) which is the experience of the objectless-Consciousness. One who has realised the Self, and lives in the Self, as the Self,—since in its non-dual Infinitude, there are no objects other than Itself—the Man-of-Realisation will not have any "reflected-knowledge." Those who are struggling in the confusions of the "reflected-knowledge," must strive hard to gain "direct-knowledge" in their personal experience of the *objectless* Pure-Consciousness. The Liberated-in-life has become the Consciousness Infinite, the Self and, therefore, where is "direct-knowledge" for him?

---

1. विषयाकारवृत्त्यवच्छिन्नचैतन्यम् .... फलम् । (*Viṣayākāra-vṛtty-avacchinna-caitanyam—*
—phalam :

In short, the Self-Realised-Master is no more human; he is not a native of this relative world of ours—he is, in himself, the Universal Self, the *Brahman*. There is no other way of defining him.

क्व लोकः क्व मुमुक्षुर्वा क्व योगी ज्ञानवान् क्व वा ।
क्व बद्धः क्व च वा मुक्तः स्वस्वरूपेऽहमद्वये ॥ ६ ॥

Kva lokaḥ kva mumukṣurvā kva yogī jñānavān kva vā,
kva baddhaḥ kva ca vā muktaḥ svasvarūpe'hamadvaye.

क्व *kva* = where; लोकः *lokaḥ* = world; क्व *kva* = where; मुमुक्षुः *mumukṣuḥ* = aspirant for liberation; वा *vā* = or; क्व *kva* = where; योगी *yogī* = Man-of-Contemplation; ज्ञानवान् *jñānavān* = Man-of-realisation; क्व *kva* = where; वा *vā* = or; क्व *kva* = where; बद्धः *baddhaḥ* = the bound-man; क्व *kva* = where; च *ca* = and; वा *vā* = or; मुक्तः *muktaḥ* = the Man-liberated; अहम्-अद्वये स्वस्वरूपे *aham-advaye sva-svarūpe* = for me who am non-dual in nature.

6. *Where is the world, and where is the seeker after liberation? Where is the Man-of-contemplation and where is the Man-of-realisation? Where is the bound-man and where is the Liberated-man for me, who am non-dual by Nature?*

In the unitive-experience of the Universal-Self, wherein the subject-object-perceptions have all merged, the world, the seeker, Man-in-meditation, Man-of-realisation, the bound-man and the Liberated-man, etc.—all have no significance, and all efforts and aspirations are totally nullified in the grand experience of the Universal-Self, the One without-a-second. The Awakened-One realises, "I am non-dual by Nature," and in this Non-duality no other concept of *seeker*, *seeking* and *sought* can ever exist.

क्व सृष्टिः क्व च संहारः क्व साध्यं क्व च साधनम् ।
क्व साधकः क्व सिद्धिर्वा स्वस्वरूपेऽहमद्वये ॥ ७ ॥

Kva sṛṣṭiḥ kva ca saṁhāraḥ
kva sādhyaṁ kva ca sādhanam,
kva sādhakaḥ kva siddhir-vā
sva-svarūpe-'ham-advaye.

क्व *kva* = where; सृष्टिः *sṛṣṭiḥ* = creation; क्व *kva* = where; च *ca* = and; संहारः *saṁhāraḥ* = destruction (withdrawing); क्व *kva* = where; साध्यम् *sādhyam* = end; क्व *kva* = where; च *ca* = and; साधनम् *sādhanam* = means; क्व *kva* = where; साधकः *sādhakaḥ* = the seeker; क्व *kva* = where; सिद्धिः *siddhiḥ* = the accomplishment; वा *vā* = or; अहम्-अद्वये स्वस्वरूपे *aham-advaye-svasvarūpe* = for me who am non-dual by nature.

7. *Where is creation and where is destruction; where is the end and where is the means; where is the seeker and where is the accomplishment for me, abiding in my own Non-dual Nature?*

Creation and destruction are concepts of the mind which projects in its imagination the world-of-objects and withdraws those projections when the perceived world is absorbed. This is what is happening during the sleep of every individual. Macro-cosmically conceived, Lord Creator creates a universe, and Lord of Destruction withdraws or absorbes the world into total dissolution called *Pralaya*. The ego, under the throes of its desires, gets agitated and the agitated-mind projects the world-of-experiences. When the mind is withdrawn from its activities— may it be in sleep or *Samādhi*, the contentious world of conflicts and sorrows gets dissolved.

To one who has already realised the Self, which is One without-a-second, he has transcended his mind, and therefore, to him "where is creation, and where is withdrawal?" In this state it becomes amply clear that there are no "means" of realisation (*Sādhanā*), and there is no "end" for one who has already Realised? The Man-of-Perfection is no more a seeker (*Sādhaka*), nor has he any accomplishment (*Siddhi*); He has become the very Self which is the Substratum for all accomplishments.

These two verses (6 & 7) together negate all pluralistic concepts, which are natural for the human mind—creation-dissolution, means-end, seeking-accomplishment, bound-man and liberated-man—all these are denied in the One Non-dual Self. This reminds us how *Gauḍapāda* has taken up this idea and elaborated it in his *Kārikā* (II-32), while discussing "the Unreality of the Objective World." Says *Gauḍapāda*:

न निरोधो न चोत्पत्तिः न बद्धो न च साधकः ।
न मुमुक्षुर्न वै मुक्त इत्येषा परमार्थता ॥

Na nirodho na cotpattiḥ na baddho na ca sādhakaḥ,
na mumukṣurna vai mukta ityeṣā paramārthatā.

"There is neither dissolution, nor creation; neither anyone in bondage, nor any aspirant-for-wisdom; neither can there be any seeker for liberation, nor any liberated as such. This alone is the Supreme Truth."

क्व प्रमाता प्रमाणं वा क्व प्रमेयं क्व च प्रमा ।
क्व किञ्चित् क्व न किञ्चिद्वा सर्वदा विमलस्य मे ॥८॥

Kva pramātā pramāṇaṁ vā
kva prameyaṁ kva ca pramā,
kva kiñcit kva na kiñcidvā
sarvadā vimalasya me.

क्व *kva* = where; प्रमाता *pramātā* = knower; प्रमाणम् *pramāṇam* = the means-to-knowledge; वा *vā* = or; क्व *kva* = where; प्रमेयम् *prameyam* = the object-of-knowledge; क्व *kva* = where; च *ca* = and; प्रमा *pramā* = objective-knowledge; क्व *kva* = where; किञ्चित् *kiñcit* = something; क्व *kva* = where; न किञ्चित् *na kiñcit* = nothing; वा *vā* = or; सर्वदा *sarvadā* = ever; विमलस्य *vimalasya* = pure; मे *me* = for me.

8. *Where is the 'knower' and where is the 'means-to-knowledge'; where is the 'object-of-knowledge,' and where is the objective-knowledge; where is*

'anything' and where is 'nothing' for me, who am Ever-Pure?

The Self is declared as "Ever Pure," because it is not contaminated by the illusory 'mis-apprehensions' of the equipments-of-experiences, or by their delusory world-of-experiences. As the Self is realised, on transcending the mind, the diseases and tragedies of the mind cannot be there in the Self. Thus the 'mis-apprehensions of the Reality' caused by the play of thoughts in the intellect and the agitations of the mind created by the *Rajas*, are both not in the Self, and therefore, it is considered as Ever-Pure (*Guṇātīta*). As there is neither *Rajas* nor *Tamas*, there is no ignorance of Reality, and naturally, the Pure Consciousness is ever un-conditioned by the equipments-of-experiences (*Upādhi-rahit*).

We have already pointed out the "theory of perception" in *Vedānta.*[1] The technical terms used here are borrowed from our scriptural texts. The knower-ego (*Pramātā*), its means-of-knowledge (*Pramāṇam*), the objects-of-knowledge (*Prameyam*), and the final result, objective-knowledge (*Pramā*)—all these are negated in the Objectless-Consciousness, Ever Non-dual and Immutable.

क्व विक्षेपः क्व चैकाग्र्यं क्व निर्बोधः क्व मूढता ।
क्व हर्षः क्व विषादो वा सर्वदा निष्क्रियस्य मे ॥ ९ ॥

Kva vikṣepaḥ kva caikāgryaṁ
kva nirbodhaḥ kva mūḍatā,
kva harṣaḥ kva viṣādo vā
sarvadā niṣkriyasya me.

क्व *kva* = where; विक्षेपः *vikṣepaḥ* = distraction; क्व *kva* = where; च *ca* = and; एकाग्रयम् *akāgryam* = concentration; क्व *kva* = where; निर्बोधः *nirbodhaḥ* = sure-knowledge; क्व *kva* = where; मूढता *mūḍatā* = delusion; क्व *kva* = where; हर्षः *harṣaḥ* = joy; क्व *kva* = where;

1. Commentary on Verse-V in the same chapter.

विषादः *viṣādaḥ* = sorrow; वा *vā* = or; सर्वदा *sarvadā* = ever; निष्क्रियस्य *niṣkriyasya* = actionless; मे *me* = for me.

9. *Where is distraction and where is concentration; where is sure-knowledge and where is delusion; where is joy and where is sorrow for me, who am ever the Actionless?*

Where the mind is tossed about and is constantly gushing out into the world of sense-objects, seeking a fulfilment of its impetuous desires of sense-gratifications, there certainly, spiritual practice of mental-withdrawal is necessary. To call back the mind from its association and indulgence with the world-of-objects is accomplished by deliberate and wilful concentration of all its thoughts at the altar of an inspiring Lord. Since there is no distraction in his State of Transcendence, to one who has realised the Self, and since he is living ever established in the Self, where is for him the need for concentration?

When the intellect is veiled by *Tamas*, the mind in its restlessness imagines a world-of-plurality, and thereafter. the illusory ego comes to yearn for the fancied possibilities of pleasure, joy and satisfaction in the sense-world. To live thus as a limited, crushed entity, a slave to one's own desires and thoughts, persecuted constantly by the world of happenings around is the self-created tragedy of one who is rotting in his own delusion. A Man-of-Realisation is one who has awakened from the fancies of his mind, conjured up by the delusions of his intellect. Therefore, he has no more any delusions. Since he has no false-knowledge, nor wrong-values, he needs no true-knowledge, firm and certain (*Nir-bodha*). Here the word employed by *Aṣṭāvakra* is an example of poetic-licence.[1]

---

1. '*Nirbodha*' grammatically by its construction should mean "dullness of understanding." It is a poetic-licence of a great philosopher, exploding in inspired eloquence, that we should understand the word to mean "*Niścaya-bodha=Nir-bodha*." The meaning, "Sure-knowledge" alone can here keep the polarisation with "delusion."

When the mind and the intellect are transcended, the sense of ego gets automatically annihilated, and therefore, the vanity of "enjoyership" cannot be in the Man-of-Perfection: "Where is joy or sorrow?" In the experience of the Transcendental Reality of the Self, which is One without-a-second, All-pervading and Immutable, there cannot be any action and as the Self *Janaka* here exclaims, "I am the Actionless and Infinite Self."

क्व चैष व्यवहारो वा क्व च सा परमार्थता ।
क्व सुखं क्व च वा दुःखं निर्विमर्शस्य मे सदा ॥ १० ॥

Kva caiṣa vyavahāro vā kva ca sā parmārthatā,
kva sukhaṁ kva ca vā duḥkhaṁ nirvimarśasya me sadā.

क्व *kva* = where; च *ca* = and; एषः *eṣaḥ* = this; व्यवहारः *vyavahāraḥ* = activities in the state of relativity; वा *vā* = or; क्व *kva* = where; च *ca* = and; सा *sā* = that; परमार्थता *parmārthatā* = the State of the Absolute; क्व *kva* = where; सुखम् *sukham* = happiness; क्व *kya* = where; च *ca* = and; वा *vā* = or; दुःखम् *duḥkham* = misery; निर्विमर्शस्य *nirvimarśasya* = devoid of all discursive thoughts; मे *me* = for me; सदा *sadā* = ever.

10. *Where is activity in the state-of-relativity, and where is the state-of-the-Absolute? Where is happiness and where is misery for me, who am ever beyond any discursive thought.*

The Self, the *Brahman* is beyond all cogent intellectual assessments. All analytical discursive reasonings are possible only within the fields of the world-of-plurality, conceived as objects of experiences of the mind and intellect. Transcending the mind and intellect, none of these activities of emotion and feeling, of analysis and reasoning can reach the true State of the Self.

Established in the Self, the Liberated-in-life, has divorced himself from all the equipments, and therefore, the Man-of-

Realisation in *Janaka* exclaims that He has neither any activity in the relative world-of-plurality, nor has he any sense, any longer, in claiming his identification with the Absolute Self! The concept of the "Absolute" is but the other pole of the "relative."

Beyond "happiness and misery," unaffected by any of delusory storms of the mind, created by its illusions of the world-of-objects, shines the Effulgent Self, which is the very Essence and Substance of the Man-of-Realisation.

क्व माया क्व च संसारः क्व प्रीतिर्विरतिः क्व वा।
क्व जीवः क्व च तद्-ब्रह्म सर्वदा विमलस्य मे ॥११॥

Kva māyā kva ca saṁsāraḥ kva prītir-viratiḥ kva vā,
kva jīvaḥ kva ca tad-brahma sarvadā vimalasya me.

क्व *kva* = where; माया *māyā* = illusion; क्व *kva* = where; च *ca* = and; संसारः *saṁsāraḥ* = the world of change; क्व *kva* = where; प्रीतिः *prītiḥ* = attachments; विरतिः *viratiḥ* = detachment; क्व *kva* = where; वा *vā* = or; क्व *kva* = where; जीवः *jīvaḥ* = *jīva*; क्व *kva* = where; च *ca* = and; तत् *tat* = that; ब्रह्म *brahma* = *Brahman*; सर्वदा *sarvadā* = ever; विमलस्य *vimalasya* = pure (dirtless); मे *me* = for me.

11. *Where is illusion and where is the world of change? Where is attachment and where is detachment? Where is* Jīva *and what is* Brahman *for me, who am ever Pure?*

In '*Vivekacūḍāmaṇi*' (V-171) *Śaṅkarācārya* elaborately proves and asserts, "there is no *Māyā* nor 'ignorance' other than our own mind; the mind is nothing but a grosser, and therefore, a more perceptible expression of *Avidyā* :

न ह्यस्त्यविद्या मनसोऽतिरिक्ता मनो ह्यविद्या भवबन्धहेतुः ।
तस्मिन्विनष्टे सकलं विनष्टं विजृम्भितेऽस्मिन्सकलं विजृम्भते ॥

Na hyasty-avidyā manaso-'tiriktā
mano hy-avidyā bhava-bandha-hetuḥ,
tasmin-vinaṣṭe sakalaṁ vinaṣṭam
vijṛmbhite-'smin-sakalaṁ vijṛmbhate.

"Apart from the mind there is no 'ignorance' (*Avidyā*). The mind itself is the 'ignorance' which is the cause for the bondage of rebirth. When the mind is destroyed, everything else is destroyed. When the mind manifests, everything else manifests.

The macro-cosmic expression of 'ignorance' (*Avidyā*) is the concept of *Māyā*, which maintains the illusion of the entire universe. On transcending the mind, the vision and the experience change, and then viewed from the Self "where is illusion, where is the world-of-change?"

Identified with the mind-intellect equipment, the Light of Consciousness assumes an apparent attitude of limitation, and this limited personality-sense is "ego" (*Jīva*). The reflected-sun-in-the-bucket disappears when the water is thrown out, and the pool-of-light, that was dancing in the bucket, merges back with the universal sun-light. Similarly, when the waters of thoughts are dried up, the mind is ended, and the Light of Consciousness that was 'reflected' in it (*Cidābhāsa*), the "ego," disappears into the Light of the Universal Self.

This fact of Spiritual life is fully endrosed by '*Yoga-Vāsiṣṭha*' when it claims:

व्यपगतकलनाकलंकशुद्धः स्वयममलात्मनि पावने पदेऽसौ ।
सलिलकेण इवांबुधौ महात्मा विगलितवासन एकतां जगाम ॥

Vyapa-gata-kalanā-kalaṁka-śuddhaḥ
svayam-amalātmani pāvane pade'sau,
salila-kaṇa evāṁ-budhau mahātmā
vigalita-vāsana ekatāṁ jagāma.

"When all thought-disturbances have ended, the purified mind enters the State of one's own Pure nature-divine, and there, like a drop that has entered the ocean, with all its desires gone, becomes one with the Self."

To one who has thus realised the Pure Self, thereafter, from his stand-point, "where is *Jīva*?" And since there is no illusory ego-centric personality, to him "what is the concept of *Brahman*?" In short, the verse here confirms the unequivocal assertion in the *Muṇḍakopaniṣad* (III-ii-9): *"the knower of the Self becomes the Self."*

"स यो ह वै तत् परमं ब्रह्म वेद ब्रह्मैव भवति ....।"

Saḥ yo ha vai tat paramaṁ
brahma veda brahmaiva bhavati ....

"He who knows that Supreme *Brahman* becomes *Brahman*."

क्व प्रवृत्तिर्निर्वृत्तिर्वा क्व मुक्तिः क्व च बन्धनम् ।
कूटस्थनिर्विभागस्य स्वस्थस्य मम सर्वदा ॥ १२ ॥

Kva pravṛttir-nivṛttir-vā kva muktiḥ kva ca bandhanam,
kūṭastha-nirvibhāgasya svasthasya mama sarvadā.

क्व *kva* = where; प्रवृत्तिः *pravṛttiḥ* = activity; निवृत्तिः *nivṛttiḥ* = inactivity; वा *vā* = or; क्व *kva* = where; मुक्तिः *muktiḥ* = liberation; क्व *kva* = where; च *ca* = and; बन्धनम् *bandhanam* = bondage; कूटस्थ-निर्विभागस्य *kūṭastha-nirvibhāgasya* = Immutable and Indivisible; स्वस्थस्य *svasthasya* = established in the Self; मम *mama* = for me; सर्वदा *sarvadā.* = ever.

12. *Where is activity, where is inactivity, where is liberation, and where is bondage for me, who am Immutable and Indivisible, and ever-established in the Self?*

The seat of the Essential Consciousness in an individual set of equipments is indicated in the metaphorical term *Kūṭasthaḥ* by the *Upaniṣadik Ṛṣī-s*, and the term idicates "that which remains (*Stha*) as an anvil (*Kūṭam*)." Very often the *Ṛṣī-s* use such pictorial terms to communicate to the students the nature and the function of the Self. An anvil remains unchanged, although in contact with it, other pieces of metal are hammered by the world of happenings around and total personality of the individual gets constantly shaped and re-shaped. In this process, the steady Consciousness in the depth of our bosom remains like an anvil 'without itself changing, but at the same time presiding over all changes.'

In short, the terms *Kūṭasthaḥ* means that which remains Immutable in the midst of all mutations. The Man-of-Realisation is one who has discovered and identified completely with this Immutable (*Kūṭastaḥ*) and Indivisible (*Nir-vibhāga*) Self. Aṣ the illuminating principle behind all activities of the body, mind and intellect, it, in itself, is not involved in any activity; nor can we declare It as inactive. Activity and inactivity are the two states of the mind and body. The Consciousness is neither active, nor inactive—It being merely the Knowing-Principle that illumines these two conditions into our awareness.

The concepts of bondage and liberation are different experiences of the ego, depending upon how far it is involved, and therefore, conditioned, by the illusory vehicles and the delusory world-of-plurality. The Self is merely the Witness of both these conditions of the ego, and therefore, *Janaka* readily declares, "where is liberation or bondage for me, who am ever Immutable and Indivisible?"

Established in the Self, the Royal Sage has no identity other than the Self. He has no impulsion to act as there is no ego or desire in him. In the absence of the ego-centric individuality in him he has no duties from which he must, with exertion and suffering, learn to withdraw!

क्वोपदेशः क्व वा शास्त्रं क्व शिष्यः क्व च वा गुरुः ।
क्व चास्ति पुरुषार्थो वा निरुपाधेः शिवस्य मे ॥ १३ ॥

Kvopadeśaḥ kva vā śāstraṁ
kva śiṣyaḥ kva ca vā guruḥ,
kva cāsti puruṣārtho vā
nirupādheḥ śivasya me.

क्व *kva* = where; उपदेशः *upadeśaḥ* = instruction; क्व *kva* = where; वा *vā* = or; शास्त्रम् *śāstram* = scripture; क्व *kva* = where; शिष्यः *śiṣyaḥ* = disciple; क्व *kva* = where; च *ca* = and; वा *vā* = or; गुरुः *gurūḥ* = preceptor; क्व *kva* = where; च *ca* = and; अस्ति *asti* = is; पुरुषार्थः *puruṣārthaḥ* = goals of life; वा *vā* = or; निरुपाधेः *nirupādheḥ* = free from limitations; शिवस्य *śivasya* = Absolute Good; मे *me* = for me.

13. Where are instructions or where are scriptural injunctions? Where is the disciple and where is the preceptor? Where, indeed, is the 'goals-of-life' for me, who am the Absolute Good (Śiva), free from all limitations?

The term '*Śiva*' means the "Supremely Blissful"—the "Tranquil"—the "Good"—the "Most Auspicious." Lord *Śiva* is considered in the *Paurāṇik* literature as one of the Trinities who is the Lord of Destruction. A spiritual seeker's sole purpose is to destroy the ego, and the "non-apprehension of the Reality" (*Avidyā*) which is the cause for it. Where this destruction is complete, the very Lord of Destruction, *Śiva*, alone remains. Hence, Lord *Śiva* is represented, often, as the Lord of Meditation. Though the term *Śiva* is not found in the early *Vedik*-texts, later on it has been incorporated and accepted as a term to indicate the Pure Infinite Self, which is the Substratum for the entire Universe.

Here identifying with the Self within, *Janaka* declares in his Self-Realisation: "I am the Absolute Good—the Supremely Blissful—the Ever-Auspicious—*Śiva*, free from all limitations."

To such an individual who has re-discovered his perfect identity with the Effulgent Self, which is Pure Knowledge, of what use are "teacher's instructions or scriptures' injunctions?" In the one Immutable Self where are the distinctions of the teacher and the taught? Very often we have ncticed all along the *Saṁhitā* how, describing and singing the joys of the Absolute, Sage *Aṣṭāvakra* assumes an apparently blasphemic, shattering, iconoclastic mood and temper, in his uncompromising experience of the Non-dual Reality. That is the sole reason why this text-book has been carefully kept even in India, as a secret. In the hands of the unprepared society it can blast the very basis of theology and religion, the very *Dharma*, that holds the community together, and provides easy stages therein for the individuals to grow in their evolution. The child in the womb must patiently remain there for a full ten-months, until it has grown sufficiently to live under the atmospheric pressure, and profitably meet the challenges and experiences of the wider-world from the lap of its mother!

क्व चास्ति क्व च वा नास्ति क्वास्ति चैकं क्व च द्वयम् ।
बहुनाऽत्र किमुक्तेन किञ्चिन्नोत्तिष्ठते मम ॥ १४ ॥

Kva cāsti kva ca vā nāsti kvāsti caikaṁ kva ca dvayam,
bahunā-'tra kim-uktena kiñcin-nottiṣṭhate mama.

क्व *kva* = where; च *ca* = indeed; अस्ति *asti* = is; क्व *kva* = where; च *ca* = and; वा *vā* = or; न अस्ति *na asti* = non-existing; क्व *kva* = where; अस्ति *asti* = is; च *ca* = and; एकम् *akam* = the One, unity; क्व *kva* = where; च *ca* = and; द्वयम् *dvayam* = duality; बहुना *bahunā* = much; अत्र *atra* = here; किम् *kim* = what need; उक्तेन *uktena* = by saying; किञ्चित् *kiñcit* = anything; न *na* = not; उत्तिष्ठते *uttiṣṭhate* = emanates; मम *mama* = from me.

14. *Where is 'existence or where is 'non-existence'? Where is the One (unity) and where is duality? What need is there to say more? Nothing indeed emanates from Me.*

In this concluding verse of the *Saṁhitā, Aṣṭāvakra*[1] talks to the world from the Self, as the Self. There is neither Existence nor Non-existence. These two are the interpretations of the intellect. The Self is the Consciousness that illumines our experiences. This Consciousness can neither be called as 'dual' or 'non-dual'—as these concepts are true only in the relative world. These two are again judgements of the intellect.

Having thus indicated, through a double-process of denial and assertion, the State of Selfhood all through the fourteen verses of this chapter, *Janaka* feels exhausted and declares: "What need is there to say anything more?" He is concluding all his frail and ineffectual explanations, so far given in reporting to his teacher his inner experience of the Supreme State. In a crescendo of despair, in an apparent hysterical screaming, *Janaka* roars with a spontaneity of an *Upaniṣadik Ṛṣi*: "Nothing indeed emanates from me."

This statement is, no doubt repeatedly endorsed by many-many solid passsages in the entire *Upaniṣadik* literature, but nowhere is this brutal truth so vividly expressed, and so courageously declared, ever before, as we read it in the *Aṣṭāvakra Saṁhitā*.

Hence the special historical value for this little-known, but very important, *Hindū* mystic text-book.

As a mystic-philosopher, *Aṣṭāvakra* is to be recognised, if not as the father, certainly as the Archangel and the Guardian-spirit of the Supreme *Advaitik*-theory of "Non-origination" (*Ajāta-vāda*). Later on it was left for *Śrī Guadapāda* to elaborate this theory in his *Kārikā* to *Māṇḍūkya Upaniṣad.*

Yoga Vāsiṣṭha also has elaborated upon this Absolute stand-point from wherein nothing has ever emerged in all the three periods of time. The world of names-and-forms is an illusion created by the restless mind. Says *Yoga Vāsiṣṭha*:

1. Though this verse is in the mouth of *Janaka*, let us not forget that the *Saṁhitā* declares *Aṣṭāvakra's* philosophy and mysticism.

देहसंस्थोऽप्यदेहत्वाददेहोऽसि विदेहदृक् ।
व्योमसंस्थोऽप्यसक्तत्वादव्योमेव हि मारुतः ॥

Deha-saṁstho-'py-adeha-tvāda-deho-'si videha-dṛk,
vyọm-saṁstho-'py-asakta-tvāda-vyom-eva hi mārutaḥ.

"Though dwelling in body, since Self has no body, you are the bodiless Pure-*Seer*. Even though wind moves in space, because of its perfect detachment, it is without space!!"

This ultimate Truth is the Transcendental Reality and, certainly, it should be ever beyond all empirical speculations such as *existence* and *non-existence*, or as *non-duality* and *duality*. It is not to be reached through the intellect by its reasoning, but it is a state to be arrived at only through man's intuitive insight. To cultivate this intuitive insight, all other *Sādhanā*-s are necessary. Hence in *Kaivalyopaniṣad* (*mantra*-2) it is said:

....

श्रद्धाभक्तिध्यानयोगादवैहि ।

....

Śraddhā-bhakti-dhyāna-yogād-avaihi.

"Through faith, devotion and meditation alone," you come to know It yourself.

Oṁ Śāntiḥ ! Śāntiḥ ! Śāntiḥ !

Aṣṭāvakra Gītā

Alphabetical Index to Ślokā-s

Note : Where first line is identical in more than one *śloka*, to enable readers to distinguish and locate the right *śloka*, first word of the second line is given within brackets.